The Transformation of Rural Africa

Contemporary discussions of Africa's recent growth have largely interpreted such growth in terms of structural transformation, based mainly on national and sectoral data. However, the micro-level processes driving this transformation are still unclear and remain the subject of debate. This collection of articles provides a micro economic foundation for understanding the particular growth processes at work within the region's rural areas, and in so doing provides important insights for policy action. The book provides valuable household- and farm-level evidence about the drivers of rural labour productivity, improvements in access to markets, investment in food value chains, and indeed the role of rural economic growth in Africa's overall structural transformation processes. Some of the features of Africa's ongoing rural transformation are similar to those of agricultural transformation as experienced in Asia and elsewhere. However, other features of Africa's rural transformation are unique and pose important challenges for development policy and planning. Together, the studies compiled in this volume provide an updated, evidence-based, and policy-relevant understanding of where African countries are in their developmental trajectories and the region's prospects for achieving inclusive forms of development over the next several decades.

This book was originally published as a special issue of the *Journal of Development Studies*.

T. S. Jayne is University Foundation Professor of Agricultural, Food, and Resource Economics at Michigan State University, East Lansing, USA. He is also Co-Director of the Alliance for African Partnership and Distinguished Fellow of the African Association of Agricultural Economists.

Jordan Chamberlin is a Spatial Economist with the International Maize and Wheat Improvement Center, based in Ethiopia.

Rui Benfica is a Lead Economist at the Research and Impact Assessment Division, Strategy and Knowledge Department, International Fund for Agricultural Development (IFAD), Rome, Italy.

The Transformation of Rural Africa

Edited by
T. S. Jayne, Jordan Chamberlin, and
Rui Benfica

Routledge
Taylor & Francis Group

LONDON AND NEW YORK

First published 2019
by Routledge
2 Park Square, Milton Park, Abingdon, Oxon, OX14 4RN, UK

and by Routledge
52 Vanderbilt Avenue, New York, NY 10017

First issued in paperback 2020

Routledge is an imprint of the Taylor & Francis Group, an informa business

British Library Cataloguing-in-Publication Data
A catalogue record for this book is available from the British Library

ISBN 13: 978-0-367-58613-3 (pbk)
ISBN 13: 978-1-138-32549-4 (hbk)

Typeset in Times New Roman
by codeMantra

Publisher's Note
The publisher accepts responsibility for any inconsistencies that may have arisen
during the conversion of this book from journal articles to book chapters, namely the possible
inclusion of journal terminology.

Disclaimer
Every effort has been made to contact copyright holders for their permission to reprint
material in this book. The publishers would be grateful to hear from any copyright
holder who is not here acknowledged and will undertake to rectify any errors or omissions in
future editions of this book.

Contents

Citation Information

The chapters in this book were originally published in the *Journal of Development Studies*, volume 54, issue 5 (May 2018). When citing this material, please use the original page numbering for each article, as follows:

Introduction
Africa's Unfolding Economic Transformation
T. S. Jayne, Jordan Chamberlin and Rui Benfica
Journal of Development Studies, volume 54, issue 5 (May 2018) pp. 777–787

Chapter 1
Agricultural Transformation, Nutrition Transition and Food Policy in Africa: Preston Curves Reveal New Stylised Facts
William A. Masters, Nathaniel Z. Rosenblum and Robel G. Alemu
Journal of Development Studies, volume 54, issue 5 (May 2018) pp. 788–802

Chapter 2
Africa's Evolving Employment Trends
Felix Kwame Yeboah and Thomas S. Jayne
Journal of Development Studies, volume 54, issue 5 (May 2018) pp. 803–832

Chapter 3
Understanding the Role of Rural Non-Farm Enterprises in Africa's Economic Transformation: Evidence from Tanzania
Xinshen Diao, Eduardo Magalhaes and Margaret McMillan
Journal of Development Studies, volume 54, issue 5 (May 2018) pp. 833–855

Chapter 4
Roads and Rural Development in Sub-Saharan Africa
Claudia N. Berg, Brian Blankespoor and Harris Selod
Journal of Development Studies, volume 54, issue 5 (May 2018) pp. 856–874

Chapter 5
Youth Migration and Labour Constraints in African Agrarian Households
Valerie Mueller, Cheryl Doss and Agnes Quisumbing
Journal of Development Studies, volume 54, issue 5 (May 2018) pp. 875–894

Chapter 6
The Quiet Rise of Large-Scale Trading Firms in East and Southern Africa
Nicholas J. Sitko, William J. Burke and T. S. Jayne
Journal of Development Studies, volume 54, issue 5 (May 2018) pp. 895–914

Chapter 7
Micro-Level Welfare Impacts of Agricultural Productivity: Evidence from Rural Malawi
Francis Addeah Darko, Amparo Palacios-Lopez, Talip Kilic and Jacob Ricker-Gilbert
Journal of Development Studies, volume 54, issue 5 (May 2018) pp. 915–932

Chapter 8
Changing Patterns of Wealth Distribution: Evidence from Ghana
Abena D. Oduro and Cheryl R. Doss
Journal of Development Studies, volume 54, issue 5 (May 2018) pp. 933–948

For any permission-related enquiries please visit:
http://www.tandfonline.com/page/help/permissions

Notes on Contributors

Robel G. Alemu is a PhD candidate in the School of Nutrition Science and Policy at Tufts University, Boston, USA.

Rui Benfica is Lead Economist for the International Fund for Agricultural Development, Research and Impact Assessment Division, based in Rome, Italy.

Claudia N. Berg is an Economist at the International Monetary Fund, Research Department, based in Washington, DC, USA.

Brian Blankespoor is an Environmental Specialist in the Development Data Group at the World Bank, based in Washington, DC, USA.

William J. Burke is Assistant Professor of International Development at Michigan State University, East Lansing, USA.

Jordan Chamberlin is a Spatial Economist with the International Maize and Wheat Improvement Center, based in Ethiopia.

Francis Addeah Darko works in Poverty and Equity Global Practice for the World Bank Group in Jakarta, Indonesia.

Xinshen Diao is Deputy Division Director and Senior Research Fellow in the Development Strategy and Governance Division of the International Food Policy Research Institute, based in Washington, DC, USA.

Cheryl R. Doss is Senior Departmental Lecturer in Development Economics and Associate Professor in the Department of International Development at the University of Oxford, UK.

T. S. Jayne is University Foundation Professor of Agricultural, Food, and Resource Economics at Michigan State University, East Lansing, USA. He is also Co-Director of the Alliance for African Partnership.

Talip Kilic is a Senior Economist in the Survey Unit of the World Bank Development Data Group, based in Rome, Italy.

Margaret McMillan is Professor of Economics at Tufts University, Boston, USA.

William A. Masters is Professor in the School of Nutrition Science and Policy, with a secondary appointment in the Department of Economics, at Tufts University, Boston, USA.

Eduardo Magalhaes was an Independent Consultant at the time that his contribution to the book was prepared.

NOTES ON CONTRIBUTORS

Valerie Mueller is Assistant Professor in the School of Politics and Global Studies at Arizona State University, Tempe, USA.

Abena D. Oduro is Director of the Centre for Social Policy Studies and Associate Professor in the Department of Economics at the University of Ghana, Accra, Ghana.

Amparo Palacios-Lopez is an Economist in the Development Data Group of the World Bank, based in Washington, DC, USA.

Agnes Quisumbing is a Senior Research Fellow in Poverty, Health, and Nutrition for the International Food Policy Research Institute, based in Washington, DC, USA.

Jacob Ricker-Gilbert is Associate Professor of Agricultural Economics at Purdue University, West Lafayette, USA.

Nathaniel Z. Rosenblum is a Program Associate for the One Acre Fund, a non-profit social enterprise that supplies financing and training to smallholders.

Harris Selod is a Senior Economist with the Development Research Group of the World Bank based in Washington, DC, USA.

Nicholas J. Sitko is a Programme Coordinator in the Agricultural Development and Economics Division of the Food and Agriculture Organization of the United Nations, based in Rome, Italy.

Felix Kwame Yeboah is Assistant Professor in the Department of Agricultural, Food and Resource Economics at Michigan State University, East Lansing, USA.

Editorial Policy

The *Journal of Development Studies* was the first international journal in development studies and is still one of the best known. Since its foundation in 1964, it has helped to shape the discipline through promoting high quality disciplinary and interdisciplinary social science research.

The *Journal of Development Studies* welcomes research papers on development issues from all social science disciplines, with priority to papers that:

- are relevant to important current issues in development policy and theory;
- make a novel and significant contribution to the field;
- provide critical analysis of theories, perspectives or schools of thought;
- are interdisciplinary or, if in a specific discipline, written to be accessible to readers across the social sciences.

The Managing Editors also welcome Review Articles that survey recent contributions to the literature in important fields of development research or policy. Rather than comprehensive literature surveys, *JDS* is interested in reviews that show where we are on the issue, how we got there (with a focus on recent contributions that reshape research), where the gaps are and hence what questions need further work, and what seem to be the most promising avenues for future research.

All submissions undergo rigorous peer review, based on initial editor screening and double blind peer review. The high level of submissions means the majority are rejected at the screening stage. This is done quickly and with reasons provided.

JDS is proud to be able to award the **Dudley Seers Prize**, valued at £1,500, annually for the best article(s) published in the journal. All articles published in the relevant volume are eligible. Nominations for consideration for the Prize are made by the Managing Editors and a panel of judges is drawn from members of the Editorial Board. The outcome is announced in the Journal.

JDS has a long tradition of commissioning high quality book reviews (but does not accept unsolicited reviews).

Introduction: Africa's Unfolding Economic Transformation

T. S. JAYNE, JORDAN CHAMBERLIN⊙ & RUI BENFICA

ABSTRACT *Despite the continued deep challenges that the region is facing, mounting evidence points to profound economic transformation in sub-Saharan Africa since the early 2000s. The contributions in this special issue highlight three aspects of Africa's unfolding economic transformation since 2000: remarkable progress for the region as a whole, highly uneven progress across countries, and unresolved questions about the sustainability of the transformations. The drivers of the region's economic transformations are diverse, and include improved governance, strong agricultural growth in some countries, employment expansion in informal rural off-farm activities, strong local and foreign investment, a period of high global commodity prices, and policy reforms undertaken in earlier decades. Agricultural growth, by expanding job opportunities in the non-farm sectors through multiplier effects, is likely to remain an important driver of continued transformation, though it will increasingly need to rely on productivity growth rather than area expansion.*

1. Introduction

The past two decades witnessed remarkable progress in understanding the nature and pace of economic transformation in sub-Saharan Africa (SSA). Investments in nationally representative household panel survey data in many African countries has made it possible to detect with greater accuracy and disaggregate the changes over time in various indicators of living standards and the drivers of these changes. While major pieces of the puzzle remain unclear, mounting evidence points to profound economic transformation in SSA since the early 2000s. The contributions in this special issue underscore three aspects of Africa's unfolding economic transformation since 2000: substantial progress for the region as a whole, highly uneven progress across countries, and unresolved questions about the sustainability of the transformations.

Evidence of remarkable progress for the region as a whole is unmistakable. A greater proportion of young Africans are acquiring secondary and university educations (Africa-America Institute, 2015). Africa's labour force is diversifying away from subsistence farming (Yeboah & Jayne, 2018). The share of the labour force in non-farm employment has risen dramatically since 2000 (Diao, Harttgen, & McMillan, 2017; McMillan, Rodrik, & Verduzco, 2014). Governance has improved, albeit unevenly across countries. The days of hyperinflation, black market exchange rates and macro-economic turmoil are largely over, and the region has benefited from massive new local and foreign investment in many economic sectors (African Center for Economic Transformation, 2017). The region's per capita GDP increased between 2000 and 2014 by almost 35 per cent in real terms, doubling in some countries (Barrett, Christiaensen, Sheahan, & Shimeles, 2017). Sub-Saharan Africa has achieved 4.6 per cent inflation-adjusted annual mean increases in agricultural growth between 2000 and 2016 (World Bank, 2017), roughly double that of the prior three decades. Since 2000, the SSA has been the world's second-fastest growing regional economy, exceeded only by Asia (Badiane & Makombe, 2015). Women have become considerably more active in labour markets (Diao, Harttgen, et al., 2017) and may be gaining greater influence over household resources in many areas (Oduro & Doss, 2018). Poverty rates have declined significantly for the region as a whole since 2000.[1] Nutritional indicators also show gradual but clear improvement (Masters, Rosenblum, & Alemu, 2018).

At the same time, the pace of transformation has been highly uneven across the region. About five of the 16 SSA countries shown in Table 1 have made little or no progress in reducing headcount poverty rates since 2000; four of the 16 experienced an increase in poverty rates. Of the 28 African countries with annual GDP growth higher than 4 per cent in 2000–2016, 19 experienced agricultural GDP growth of more than 3 per cent per year in the same period. Ethiopia, Nigeria and Rwanda have been particular stand-outs. At least six SSA countries have experienced negative real GDP growth in per capita terms over this period, and 14 of 45 SSA countries had agricultural growth rates below population growth rates (Badiane, Diao, & Jayne, in press). The diversity in the pace and pathways of economic transformation in Africa warrants caution against over-generalisation.

There remain many unresolved issues about the sustainability of the region's transformations. Valid questions arise as to whether the transformation narrative will falter (Fioramonti, 2017), the extent to which it has been sustained by primary commodity price booms, and the extent to which transformation is occurring without industrialisation or poverty reduction (Gollin, Jedwab, & Vollrath, 2016). Indeed, some countries' performance may validate these concerns, while others do not, highlighting the widely heterogeneous nature of transformation in the region.

This introduction has three objectives. First, to introduce the issues and highlight major trends. Second, to raise critical unresolved questions for research and policy discussion, and third, to indicate

Table 1. Indicators of agricultural growth and poverty reduction for selected African countries

	Agricultural value added, annual % growth (2000–2016)	Agricultural value added per ag worker, annual % growth (2000–2016)	% of population living in poverty (based on $1.25/day 2005 consumption PPP)		
			Initial year	Latest year	(annual percentage point change)
Burkina Faso	3.52	0.07	51.6 (2003)	47.5 (2014)	−0.37
Cameroon	3.94	3.75	52.1 (2001)	56.8 (2014)	+0.36
DR Congo	1.52	0.47	69.3 (2004)	63.9 (2012)	−0.68
Cote d'Ivoire	2.45	−	62.5 (2008)	56.8 (2015)	−0.81
Ethiopia	6.20	3.75	39.3 (2004)	30.4 (2010)	−1.48
Ghana	3.77	1.14[b]	43.7 (2005)	37.9 (2012)	−0.83
Kenya	3.07	1.21	−	−	−
Madagascar	1.37	−1.88	78.2 (2001)	81.5 (2010)	+0.37
Malawi	1.89	0.31	55.9 (2004)	56.6 (2010)	+0.12
Mali	4.55	3.13	64.8 (2001)	50.6 (2009)	−1.78
Mozambique	4.72	2.11	55.3 (2002)	56.9 (2008)	+0.27
Nigeria	5.91[a]	4.89	56.6 (2003)	52.8 (2009)	−0.63
Rwanda	5.47	2.23	61.9 (2005)	48.7 (2010)	−2.64
Senegal	3.23	2.11	58.8 (2005)	57.1 (2010)	−0.34
Sierra Leone	4.82	3.53	78.7 (2003)	66.1 (2011)	−1.58
Tanzania	4.06	0.79	−	−	−
Uganda	2.46	−0.59	42.7 (2002)	22.4 (2012)	−2.03
Zambia	−0.92	−3.27	79.1 (2002)	77.9 (2010)	−0.15
Sub-Saharan Africa	4.62	2.17	54.6 (2000)	41.2 (2013)	−1.01

Notes: [a]2002–2016 period. [b]2006–2016 period. Both columns (a) and (b) are in inflation-adjusted local currency units. Sub-Saharan Africa's 4.62 per cent annual agricultural value added growth rates over the 2000–2016 period compare favourably with rates in Latin America and Caribbean (2.49), East Asia (3.07), South Asia (2.96), and the world (2.75).
Source: World Bank (2017).

how the contributions in this Special Issue shed light on these questions. The eight articles contained in this issue assemble fresh evidence to address these big picture questions, each filling in a bit more of the region's complex and rapidly evolving economic picture.

2. A framework for understanding transformation – agricultural, rural, and structural

Agricultural transformation in most regions of the world has generally been an important component of broader economic transformation processes (Mellor, 1976; Timmer, 1988). *Agricultural transformation* is the process by which an agri-food system[2] transforms over time from being subsistence-oriented and farm-centred into one that is more commercialised, productive, and off-farm centred (Timmer, 1988). The process is embedded in the broader processes of structural and rural transformation that entail a greater diversification of livelihoods (on and off-farm) and stronger interactions between rural and urban spaces, altering the role of agriculture and broadening investment opportunities beyond farming (International Fund for Agricultural Development [IFAD], 2016). Stylised facts about the role of agriculture within the broader economic transformation processes are:

- The process generally starts with growth in agricultural productivity at least where farming has been the primary source of employment for most of the population. Agricultural productivity growth is generally initiated by technical innovation, economies of scale, shifts to higher-return crops and animal products associated with rising rural incomes, urbanisation and improving market access conditions, and later by the exit of less productive labourers from farming.
- Productive farmers generate surplus production and earn cash income from the sale of farm output.
- The money they spend from their rising surplus production stimulates demand for goods, services and jobs in the off-farm sectors of the economy. This induces a gradual transition of the labour force from farm to non-farm activities, rural-urban migration, and a slowing of population growth in rural areas. As a result, agriculture declines in its relative share of total gross domestic product (GDP) over time, even as the absolute value of farm output continues to grow.
- Overall labour productivity rises as people move from less productive agriculture to more productive manufacturing and service sectors (inter-sectoral gains) and through productivity growth within agriculture (intra-sectoral gains) (McMillan et al., 2014).

Agricultural transformation is generally associated with the following trends: (i) gradual movement of labour out of farming to take advantage of better economic opportunities off-farm, while farmers remaining in farm production become more productive and commercialised; (ii) farms transition from producing a diversity of goods motivated by self-sufficiency to becoming more specialised to take advantage of regional comparative advantage in specific crops/products, and in the process they become more dependent on markets; (iii) the ratio of agribusiness value added to farm value added rises over time as more economic activity takes place in upstream input manufacturing and supply and downstream trading, processing, and retailing; (iv) more medium to large farms begin to supply the agricultural sector to capture economies of scale in production and marketing; (v) the technologies of farm production evolve to respond to changes in relative factor prices (land, labour, and capital) as a country develops (in most cases as non-farm wage rates rise with broader economy-wide development, farms become more capital-intensive as the cost of labour and land rise and the cost of sourcing capital declines); (vi) there is a transition from shifting cultivation to a focus on more intensive, sustainable and management-intensive cultivation of specific fields; and (vii) the agri-food system becomes more integrated into the wider economy.

For countries in their early stages of agricultural transformation, dynamism in the non-farm economy rarely arises spontaneously. When most of a country's population starts out primarily in farming, agricultural productivity growth is generally necessary to generate transformative income growth and money circulating in rural areas to stimulate and sustain the growth of non-farm goods and services.[3] In much of Asia, Green Revolution technologies and supportive government policies kickstarted rural economic growth processes, primarily in irrigated lowland areas. As millions of rural farmers had more cash to spend, this stimulated the demand for local non-farm goods and services, and thereby pulled millions of people off the farm into more productive and remunerative rural non-farm jobs (Haggblade, Hazell, & Reardon, 2007). This process of *rural transformation* features reinforcing synergies between farm, downstream food system, and non-farm activities, where rising incomes in each sector provide a growing market for each other.[4]

Over time, the growth in demand for goods and services spreads spatially according to market access conditions, thereby concentrating employment opportunities in cities and towns (Christiaensen & Todo, 2014), fuelling urbanisation, and agglomeration economies associated with improved health and education opportunities (Glaeser, 2011). The structure of the entire economy becomes gradually transformed (hence, *structural transformation*), whereby the workforce continues to move into more productive non-farm sectors, becomes increasingly urbanised, and benefits from improvements in food security, health and educational levels. Higher incomes change dietary patterns toward higher-processed foods, thereby expanding employment opportunities in downstream agri-food value chains (Tschirley et al., 2015).

Agricultural and rural transformation are widely viewed as components of broader structural transformation processes, even though agricultural productivity growth is still regarded as a major catalyst to structural transformation processes among countries in their early stages of development, as with the green revolution in much of Asia. The remainder of this article explores the extent to which Africa's transformations conform to these stylised facts.

3. Unresolved questions about Africa's transformations

While the greater availability of micro-level data in many African countries has made it possible to detect and understand key trends in the region's unfolding transformations, many issues remain unclear. This section explores four unresolved questions and potential clues to their answers.

3.1. What have been the drivers of Africa's transformation?

Several key factors have contributed to Africa's recent transformations and their relative importance varies by country. Diao and colleagues have emphasised endogenous growth of the informal economy, and foreign financial inflows (Diao, Harttgen, et al., 2017; Diao, Kweka, & McMillan, 2017; Diao, Magalhaes, & McMillan, 2018). Tschirley et al. (2015) emphasise urbanisation, rising incomes, and dietary transformations. Reardon (2015) points to the rise of small- and medium-scale trading firms powering employment growth and development of food systems. Certainly, rapid population growth, especially in urban areas, transitioned almost all of Africa to import parity pricing conditions, thereby providing a rapidly growing market for local food production. Local food production and other primary product industries all benefited when global commodity prices rose for a sustained period starting in the mid-2000s. An under-appreciated contributory factor has been the contentious agricultural market and economy-wide policy reforms undertaken over the 1990s. These policy reforms removed major barriers to private trade. The effects of the reforms were mostly dormant until the mid-2000s when world food prices suddenly skyrocketed, enabling thousands of small-, medium- and large-scale private firms to rapidly respond to profitable incentives, thereby rapidly building up the region's agri-food systems during this period (Jayne, Mather, & Mghenyi, 2010).

New methodological approaches are highlighting ways in which transformation plays out at microeconomic levels. For example, Mueller, Doss, and Quisumbing (2018) study the effects of youth outmigration – a major pathway through which structural transformation occurs – on the sending household's internal labour allocations and welfare outcomes. They find that these impacts vary considerably by context, for example, whether or not household labour is replaced through hired labour. This study illustrates the context dependency of household-level impacts of broader structural changes. Yet other work is starting to illuminate intra-household differences in such impacts. For example, Oduro and Doss (2018) use data from Ghana to show how the changing sectoral composition of labour and output in modernising rural economies corresponds to changes in household assets. Rapid economic growth in Ghana has been accompanied by increasing non-farm orientation of rural households, rising incomes and urbanisation. These processes have in turn been associated with a decreasing share of land in household asset portfolios (relative to savings, business assets, housing and consumer durables) and an increase in women's share of assets, particularly for non-land assets, which have fewer institutional barriers constraining women's access. These findings imply that an increasingly diversified rural economy might bode well for reducing gendered asymmetries in access to resources, and may help to partially offset the less-benign rural welfare implications of increasingly constrained access to farmland by rural households.

3.2. How are African countries' transformations different from Asia?

The unfolding economic transformations in many African countries appear to diverge in important respects from the stylised Asian structural transformation process. First, the vast majority of African countries are not successfully developing their manufacturing sectors. In countries such as Bangladesh, China, and South Korea, labour-intensive and export-oriented manufacturing pulled people out of farming into activities that provided much greater labour productivity and returns per capita. While African countries' labour forces are diversifying out of farming, the major forms of off-farm employment growth are in informal goods and services' sectors, some of it providing gainful employment but most of it in activities with low entry barriers and low returns to labour (Diao, Harttgen, et al., 2017, Diao, 2018). Jobs registering the highest employment growth are those driven by rapid population growth such as construction, agricultural wage labour, trading of food, clothing, cooking goods, construction materials, and personal care services. Importantly, in most countries examined, jobs in the informal and formal private sectors are growing more rapidly than public sector jobs (Yeboah & Jayne, 2018). Even within Africa's relatively small manufacturing sectors, which account for less than 10 per cent of total GDP in most countries, non-farm industrialisation is quite limited. Agricultural-related processing and trading constitute over 50 per cent of manufacturing value added for most African countries (IFAD, 2016), which nevertheless represents a relatively small share of total employment.

Acute challenges are being experienced in areas where rapid population growth, a decline in agriculture's share of the labour force, and urbanisation – all signs of transformation – are occurring without broad-based economic dynamism, either in agriculture or any other sector. This 'urbanisation without industrialisation' scenario is playing out in many parts of Africa (for example, Angola, Equatorial Guinea and Zambia) where growth has indeed been driven by primary product exports (for example, oil, minerals and timber) which contribute little in the way of economic synergies with surrounding rural areas. Poverty rates have declined slowly if at all in these countries (Gollin et al., 2016; IFAD, 2016; McMillan et al., 2014).

A third distinction noted in African transformation processes may be the importance of off-farm dynamism in small- and medium-sized towns in driving employment growth. Small towns and cities are experiencing the most rapid growth in employment in parts of Africa and may therefore be a major catalyst for structural transformation (for example, Christiaensen & Todo, 2014). Relatedly, Berg, Blankespoor, and Selod (2018) show that African road infrastructure expansion is associated with GDP gains which suggest the expansion of rural non-farm activities. However, the causal relationships between farm, downstream agri-food system, and non-farm job growth have yet to be clearly disentangled. Using the same data as Christiaensen & Todo (CT), a subsequent study by Imai, Gaiha, and Garbero (2017) differentiates between population growth in secondary towns and the employment shares allocated to rural non-farm activities, and finds that: (i) an increase in population share in agriculture is strongly associated with poverty reduction; (ii) the rural non-farm sectors are also poverty-reducing in some cases; and (iii) increased population in the largest cities is not associated with poverty reduction. The study argues that greater emphasis should be placed on policies that enhance support for rural agricultural and non-agricultural sectors, as opposed to CT's implications emphasising the role of secondary towns and urbanisation as the main driver of poverty reduction in Africa. While agricultural productivity growth is certainly an important component of economic transformation, such growth is not in itself sufficient for poverty reduction and welfare gains (Darko, Palacios-Lopez, Kilic, & Ricker-Gilbert, 2018), and, in some cases, may not even be the primary driver of economic growth (Diao et al., 2018).

A fourth and ominous distinction with Asia is that Sub-Saharan Africa's agricultural growth still relies mainly on expansion of area under cultivation, not yield growth (Fuglie & Rada, 2013). Improvements in road infrastructure appear to have facilitated cropland expansion in the region (Berg et al., 2018). Area expansion has been accompanied by massive land degradation and soil fertility depletion (Barbier & Hochard, 2016), suggesting unsustainable forms of intensification in much of the region (Drechsel, Gyiele, Kunze, & Cofie, 2001; Tittonell & Giller, 2013). Sustainable agricultural growth will need to rely on increasing the value of farm output per unit of land and labour. Continued reliance on area expansion cannot be sustained as rural populations continue to grow and exhaust the land frontier (Masters et al., 2018; also Chamberlin, Jayne, & Headey, 2014). This argues for renewed emphasis on promoting agricultural productivity growth. However, views seem quite divided as to whether commercialised smallholder agriculture can or should be the driver of agricultural growth or whether a new class of entrepreneurial and capitalised African investor farmer, operating at a relatively larger scale, should lead the way, a model that many African governments are now promoting (Jayne et al., 2016).

3.3. What is the evolving role of agriculture?

The economic landscapes in which small farmers have traditionally operated are shifting rapidly. Urbanisation and the rapid rise of secondary towns in Africa is improving market access for many rural farmers by extending the reach of value chains into areas formerly considered remote (Richards et al., 2016). A growing proportion of African farmers are enjoying better access to inputs and markets, and the share of the population living in truly remote locations is declining rapidly (Masters et al., 2013). The scale of demand in these cities, and the sheer volume of food needed to support the growing urban populations are creating new opportunities for not only farmers, but for small-, medium- and large-scale enterprises within food value chains (Reardon, 2015).

Parts of SSA are experiencing major changes in farm size distributions as a new class of relatively capitalised and commercialised African farmers invest in medium- and large-scale farm operations. Farmer participation in agricultural factor markets for land, labour, labour-saving inputs such as fertiliser, pesticides and herbicides, and mechanisation are rising rapidly in areas of favourable market access (Alliance for a Green Revolution [AGRA], 2016; Chamberlin & Ricker-Gilbert, 2016; Deininger, Xia, & Savastano, 2015). New private actors are investing heavily in areas of agricultural commercialisation. Sitko, Burke, and Jayne (2018) document the rapid investment by large-scale traders in regions where medium-scale farms (and hence marketed farm surpluses) are growing rapidly. The sheer volume of food needed to support Africa's rapidly growing cities is creating major new opportunities for not only farmers, but for small- and medium-scale trading and processing enterprises within food value chains (Reardon, 2015). These transformations are clearly leading to new opportunities in rural areas, in farming, off-farm small-scale employment, and in farm and non-farm wage labour. But the shifting economic landscape is also bringing new and intense competition, and changing how farmers farm.

Given the more limited role to date of manufacturing in SSA's structural transformation story, as well as the region's rural population growth projections, one might reasonably ask what role does agriculture (and rural development more generally) play in the region's prospective growth trajectory. Available evidence suggest that countries experiencing sustained agricultural growth have tended to experience more rapid economic transformation (Badiane et al., in press; Badiane & Makombe, 2015). At the same time, there appears to be fairly low correlation between African countries' agricultural growth rates and progress with

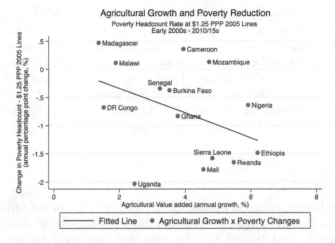

Figure 1. Limited correlation between agricultural growth and poverty reduction.
Source: World Development Indicators (2017).
Notes: Pearson's correlation coefficient is −0.407, but it is not statistically significant (p = 0.1482).

poverty reduction (Figure 1). Diao, Harttgen, et al. (2017) and Diao et al. (2018) point to population-driven demand growth in the informal non-farm economy accounting for a large part of the region's employment growth and poverty reduction along with foreign investment inflows.

Nevertheless, it seems clear that African economies which transform most rapidly are characterised by broad improvements in living standards with strong and inclusive agricultural sector growth. Many of the contributions in this special issue indirectly highlight the strategic importance of maintaining a policy and investment focus on agriculture and rural development even as agriculture diminishes in relative importance in the wider economy. To begin with, the region's expanding rural populations is a background thread running through many of the contributions in this special issue. There are considerable challenges presented by a swelling rural labour force in the African context of increasing competition for farm land, low public investments in agricultural productivity (Masters et al., 2018), and limited scope for the rural non-farm economy to generate quality jobs in the short-run (Diao et al., 2018; Yeboah & Jayne, 2018).

Increasing competition for accessible farmland will almost certainly continue to result in continued holding fragmentation and dwindling median farm sizes. The low marginal welfare returns to productivity gains on very small holdings mean that much larger investments in closing the yield gap will be required to generate welfare improvements (Darko et al., 2018). The importance of agricultural investments is further emphasised by the likely limitations of the rural non-farm sector to absorb all or even most of the 11 million young Africans entering the labour market each year (Yeboah & Jayne, 2018). Despite the rapidly growing employment in the off-farm and downstream agri-food systems, their finite limits on absorbing a rapidly growing labour force would seemingly warrant strong and sustained investment in raising agricultural productivity. Moreover, the growth in non-farm employment appears linked to the pace of agricultural productivity growth through the multiplier effects that it creates (Badiane & Makombe, 2015; Yeboah & Jayne, 2018).

Berg et al.'s study (2018) shows that infrastructure investments which improve physical market access do have the potential to stimulate growth in areas which benefit from such investments. At the same time, African agricultural intensification has largely *not* been characterised by the fertiliser investments required for maintaining soil fertility. Furthermore, the distribution of access improvements may matter greatly: they may effectively unlock the economic potential of under-utilised land resources (Chamberlin et al., 2014) or they may contribute to increased competition for accessible farmland, which may exacerbate land poverty (Jayne et al., 2016).

Some recent institutional aspects of an evolving market access landscape are even more striking: Sitko et al.'s study (2018) shows that important changes are taking place in the structure of market intermediation in some countries, with large-scale traders increasing partly in response to the expansion of large farms and potential economies of scale in transactions. The challenge will be in finding innovative ways to help the smallest farmers take advantage of new marketing opportunities in those contexts. The magnitude of welfare improvements arising through lowered intermediation costs may possibly be greater in magnitude than the limited welfare gains of productivity for very small farmers (Darko et al., 2018).

4. Conclusions

Agricultural, rural and overall economic transformation is underway in much of Africa, though at varying pace and depth across the region. Signs of rapid economic transformation are clearly evident in parts of Ghana, Ethiopia, Tanzania, and Rwanda, featuring a rise in the workforce engaged in non-farm sectors, rising per capita incomes, major self-investments by households in youth education and skills training, and a rapid reduction in poverty rates. Other countries have made less clear progress, for example, Zambia and Malawi, which have experienced stagnant rural poverty rates and slow agricultural growth.

Since 2000, the share of the labour force primarily engaged in small-scale farming has been declining very rapidly. Today, farming accounts for 40–65 per cent of primary employment in sub-Saharan Africa's working-age population, down from 70 to 80 per cent just a decade ago. The share of the workforce engaged in farming has declined most rapidly among countries enjoying the highest rates of agricultural productivity growth. This pattern is consistent with historical economic transformation processes in Asia and elsewhere in previous decades, where agricultural productivity growth was the primary driver of economic transformation and associated employment shifts to non-farm sectors among countries in their early stages of development where a large share of the workforce was still engaged in farming.

Driven by rapid population growth, African agri-food systems in many countries have transformed impressively over the past two decades. This transformation has featured rapid urbanisation, diet transformation, structural change from farm to retail, and impressive farm productivity growth in many countries. This combination of changes has led to an 800 per cent increase in the volumes and value of food marketed through rural-to-urban value chains since 2000 (Reardon, 2015). Rapid rises in food purchases by rural households has also enabled the development of a large food market in rural areas. All of this adds up to major opportunities for African farmers.

Rapid population growth and rising incomes are opening up major new markets for African farmers in areas once considered isolated. Urban-based demand for food is rising exponentially, putting major pressure on African food systems to invest massively in supply chains. Income growth in Africa's cities is also influencing dietary patterns and expanding the demand for food processing and value addition in agri-food systems (Tschirley et al., 2015). As new towns spring up in former hinterland areas and as agricultural value chains develop, smallholder farmers are enjoying more favourable market access conditions than they used to (Chamberlin & Jayne, 2013; Richards et al., 2016). Improved market access conditions combined with relatively high food prices are providing unprecedented opportunities for Africa's farmers and value chain actors. Yet the sustainability of the region's agricultural, rural and overall economic transformation will increasingly depend on the achievement of greater agricultural value per hectare and per person in farming rather than continued reliance on area expansion.

Africa is still facing tremendous challenges. The continent is the world's most food insecure region of the world, with relatively low levels of agricultural productivity, low rural incomes, high rates of malnutrition and a worsening food trade balance. It is a region challenged by climate change, a daunting prevalence of poverty despite progress in recent years, and an urgent need for jobs. In many countries, agriculture remains the predominant sector of the economy, accounting on average for 25 per cent of the GDP in SSA and well above this level for many countries. It appears likely, therefore, that stronger agricultural growth will continue for the next several decades to be an important catalyst for broad economic growth that is sustainable and inclusive.

Acknowledgements

The authors acknowledge support for this study from USAID's Bureau for Food Security, through the Food Security Policy Innovation Lab, and by a grant to Michigan State University's Food Security Group and to CIMMYT from the CGIAR Research Program on Policies, Institutions, and Markets (PIM), which is led by the International Food Policy Research Institute (IFPRI) and funded by CGIAR Fund Donors. The contents are the responsibility of the study authors and do not necessarily reflect the views of any particular organisation.

Disclosure statement

No potential conflict of interest was reported by the authors.

Funding

This work was supported by the CGIAR Fund Donors and by USAID/Bureau for Food Security.

Notes

1. The share of people in SSA living on less than $1.90 a day declined from 54 per cent in 1990 to 41 per cent in 2013 (Barrett et al., 2017).
2. Agri-food systems are the set of activities, processes, people, and institutions involved in supplying a population with food and agricultural products. The agri-food system encompasses the provision of farming inputs and services, production at farm level, post-farm marketing, processing, packaging, distribution, and retail, and the policy, regulatory, environmental, and broader economic environment in which these activities take place.
3. Lipton (2005) notes that, except in the cases of a handful of city-states, there are virtually no examples of mass poverty reduction since 1700 that did not start with sharp rises in employment and self-employment income due to higher productivity in small family farms.
4. The 2016 IFAD Rural Development Report defines rural transformation (RT) as 'involving rising agricultural productivity, increasing commercialisation and marketable surpluses, and diversification of production patterns and livelihoods. It also involves expanded decent off-farm employment and entrepreneurial opportunities, better rural coverage and access to services and infrastructure, and greater access to, and capacity to influence, relevant policy processes. All of this leads to broad-based rural (and wider) growth, and to better managed, more sustainable rural landscapes' (p. 23).

ORCID

Jordan Chamberlin ⓘ http://orcid.org/0000-0001-9522-3001

References

Africa-America Institute. (2015). *State of education in Africa report, 2015: A report card on the progress, opportunities and challenges confronting the African education sector*. New York, NY: Author.

African Center for Economic Transformation. (2017). *African transformation report 2017. Agriculture powering Africa's economic transformation*. Accra: Author.

Alliance for a Green Revolution in Africa (AGRA). (2016). *Africa agriculture status report 2016: Progress towards agricultural transformation in Africa*. Nairobi: Author.

Badiane, O., Diao, X., & Jayne, T. S. (in press). Africa's unfolding agricultural transformation. In K. Otsuka, & S. Fan (Eds.), *Agricultural development: New perspectives in a changing world*. Unpublished book manuscript.

Badiane, O., & Makombe, T. (Eds.). (2015). *Beyond a middle income Africa: Transforming African economies for sustained growth with rising employment and incomes* (ReSAKSS Annual Trends and Outlook Report 2014). Washington, DC: International Food Policy Research Institute.

Barbier, E., & Hochard, J. (2016). *Poverty and the spatial distribution of rural population* (Policy Research Working Paper, WPS 7101). Washington, DC: World Bank Group.

Barrett, C. B., Christiaensen, L., Sheahan, M., & Shimeles, A. (2017). On the structural transformation of rural Africa. *Journal of African Economies, 26*(suppl_1), i11–i35.

Berg, C. N., Blankespoor, B., & Selod, H. (2018). Roads and rural development in sub-Saharan Africa. *Journal of Development Studies, 54*(5), 856–874.

Chamberlin, J., & Jayne, T. S. (2013). Unpacking the meaning of 'market access': Evidence from rural Kenya. *World Development, 41*, 245–264.

Chamberlin, J., Jayne, T. S., & Headey, D. (2014). Scarcity amidst abundance? Reassessing the potential for cropland expansion in Africa. *Food Policy, 48*, 51–65.

Chamberlin, J., & Ricker-Gilbert, J. (2016). Participation in rural land rental markets in sub-Saharan Africa: Who benefits and by how much? Evidence from Malawi and Zambia. *American Journal of Agricultural Economics, 98*, 1507–1528.

Christiaensen, L., & Todo, Y. (2014). Poverty reduction during the rural-urban transformation: The role of the missing middle. *World Development, 63*, 43–58.

Darko, F. A., Palacios-Lopez, A., Kilic, T., & Ricker-Gilbert, J. (2018). Micro-level welfare impacts of agricultural productivity: Evidence from rural Malawi. *Journal of Development Studies, 54*(5), 915–932.

Deininger, K., Xia, F., & Savastano, S. (2015). *Smallholders' land ownership and access in sub-Saharan Africa. A new landscape?* (Policy Research Working Paper 7285). Development Research Group Agriculture and Rural Development Team. Washington, DC: World Bank.

Diao, X., Harttgen, K., & McMillan, M. (2017). The changing structure of Africa's economies. *The World Bank Economic Review, 31*(2), 412–433.

Diao, X., Kweka, J., & McMillan, M. S. (2017). *Economic transformation in Africa from the bottom up: Evidence from Tanzania* (IFPRI Discussion Paper 1603). Washington, DC: International Food Policy Research Institute.

Diao, X., Magalhaes, E., & McMillan, M. (2018). Understanding the role of rural non-farm enterprises in Africa's economic transformation: Evidence from Tanzania. *Journal of Development Studies, 54*(5), 833–855.

Drechsel, P., Gyiele, L., Kunze, D., & Cofie, O. (2001). Population density, soil nutrient depletion, and economic growth in sub-Saharan Africa. *Ecological Economics, 38*, 251–258.

Fioramonti, L. (2017, October 30). The Africa rising story was based on faulty logic – Here's how to fix it. *The Conversation.* Retrieved from https://theconversation.com/the-africa-rising-story-was-based-on-faulty-logic-heres-how-to-fix-it-86327

Fuglie, K., & Rada, N. (2013). *Resources, policies, and agricultural productivity in sub-Saharan Africa* (Economic Research Report 145). Washington, DC: Economic Research Services, United States Department of Agriculture.

Glaeser, E. (2011). *Triumph of the city: How our best invention makes us richer, smarter, greener, healthier, and happier.* New York, NY: Penguin Press.

Gollin, D., Jedwab, R., & Vollrath, D. (2016). Urbanization with and without industrialization. *Journal of Economic Growth, 21*(1), 35–70.

Haggblade, S., Hazell, P., & Reardon, T. (Eds.). (2007). *Transforming the rural nonfarm economy: Opportunities and threats in the developing world.* Baltimore, MD: Johns Hopkins University Press.

Imai, K., Gaiha, R., & Garbero, A. (2017). Poverty reduction during the rural–urban transformation: Rural development is still more important than urbanisation. *Journal of Policy Modeling, 39*, 963–982.

International Fund for Agricultural Development. (2016). *Rural development report: Fostering inclusive rural transformation.* Rome: Author.

Jayne, T. S., Chamberlin, J., Traub, L., Sitko, N., Muyanga, M., Yeboah, F. K., & Kachule, R. (2016). Africa's changing farm size distribution patterns: The rise of medium-scale farms. *Agricultural Economics, 47s*, 197–214.

Jayne, T. S., Mather, D., & Mghenyi, E. (2010). Principal challenges confronting smallholder agriculture in sub-Saharan Africa. *World Development, 38*(10), 1384–1398.

Lipton, M. (2005). *Crop science, poverty, and the family farm in a globalizing world* (2020 Discussion Paper 40). Washington, DC: International Food Policy Research Institute.

Masters, W. A., Rosenblum, N. Z., & Alemu, R. G. (2018). Agricultural transformation, nutrition transition and food policy in Africa: Preston Curves reveal new stylized facts. *Journal of Development Studies, 54*(5), 788–802.

Masters, W. A., Djurfeldt, A. A., De Haan, C., Hazell, P., Jayne, T., Jirström, M., & Reardon, T. (2013). Urbanization and farm size in Asia and Africa: Implications for food security and agricultural research. *Global Food Security, 2*, 156–165.

McMillan, M., Rodrik, D., & Verduzco, Í. (2014). Globalization, structural change and productivity growth, with an update on Africa. *World Development, 63*, 11–32.

Mellor, J. (1976). *The new economics of growth: A strategy for India and the developing world.* Ithaca, NY: Cornell University Press.

Mueller, V., Doss, C., & Quisumbing, A. (2018). Youth migration and labour constraints in African agrarian households. *Journal of Development Studies, 54*(5), 875–894.

Oduro, A. D., & Doss, C. R. (2018). Changing patterns of wealth distribution: Evidence from Ghana. *Journal of Development Studies, 54*(5), 933–948.

Reardon, T. (2015). The hidden middle: The quiet revolution in the midstream of agrifood value chains in developing countries. *Oxford Review of Economic Policy, 31*, 45–63.

Richards, P., Reardon, T., Tschirley, D., Jayne, T., Oehmke, J., & Atwood, D. (2016). Cities and the future of agriculture and food security: A policy and programmatic roundtable. *Food Security, 8*, 871–877.

Sitko, N. J., Burke, W. J., & Jayne, T. S. (2018). The quiet rise of large-scale trading firms in East and Southern Africa. *Journal of Development Studies, 54*(4), 895–914.

Timmer, C. P. (1988). The agricultural transformation. Chapter 8. *Handbook of Development Economics, 1*, 275–331.

Tittonell, P., & Giller, K. (2013). When yield gaps are poverty traps: The paradigm of ecological intensification in African smallholder agriculture. *Field Crops Research, 143*(1), 76–90.

Tschirley, D., Snyder, J., Dolislager, M., Reardon, T., Haggblade, S., Goeb, J., & Meyer, F. (2015). Africa's unfolding diet transformation: Implications for agrifood system employment. *Journal of Agribusiness in Developing and Emerging Economies, 5*, 102–136.

World Bank. (2017). *World development indicators*. Washington, DC: Author.

Yeboah, F. K., & Jayne, T. S. (2018). Africa's evolving employment trends. *Journal of Development Studies, 54*(5), 803–832.

Agricultural Transformation, Nutrition Transition and Food Policy in Africa: Preston Curves Reveal New Stylised Facts

WILLIAM A. MASTERS, NATHANIEL Z. ROSENBLUM & ROBEL G. ALEMU

ABSTRACT   *This paper uses a Preston Curve approach to test for changes over time in agriculture, nutrition and food policy, comparing national averages in Africa and elsewhere at each level of national income per capita from the 1990s to the 2010s. Our statistical tests and data visualisations reveal that, at each level of income, African countries have faster rural population growth, a larger share of workers in agriculture and lower agricultural labour productivity than countries elsewhere, with no significant shift in these patterns from the 1990s to the 2010s. In contrast, there have been structural shifts towards less child stunting everywhere, and towards more adult obesity in high-income countries. The overall pattern of African governments' food policies and government expenditures have not shifted, however, as they continue price interventions and low investment levels characteristic of low-income countries around the world.*

1. Introduction and motivation

In the first 15 years of the twenty-first century many African countries have experienced rapid economic growth and poverty reduction, accompanied by big changes in agri-food systems and human nutrition. This paper places Africa's recent surge in the context of previous transformations in Asia, Latin America, and Africa itself. We use a wide variety of data to test whether and how Africa's recent changes in agriculture, nutrition and food policy differ from experience elsewhere, and from the patterns experienced within Africa in previous decades. To describe these relationships and test for structural shifts we use non-parametric regression of each agricultural, nutritional or policy variable on national per-capita income, adapting the Preston curve approach that has been widely used in public health research (Bloom & Canning, 2007) to test for stylised facts about national averages at each income level.

The changes in agriculture and food systems that we observe so far in twenty-first century Africa have been broadly consistent with the patterns first described in modern economic terms by Clark (1940), Chenery (1960) and others. From the start of economic growth, workers move from food production to services and industry in ways that could be explained by productivity growth in any sector, combined with limited opportunities for agricultural expansion due to relatively fixed supply of land and water, and relatively fixed demand for food or other farm products. These structural constraints on expansion of farming ensure that increases in agricultural productivity serve to fuel the growth of nonfarm sectors, while failure to improve farming leaves rural people struggling to feed themselves until they can find nonfarm work.

Regional differences in agricultural transformation and rural poverty are closely linked to the speed and timing of population growth, following paths first described by Dovring (1959) and then documented in detail by Tomich, Kilby, and Johnston (1995). In tropical Asia during the late 1940s and 1950s, and then in Africa in the 1960s and 1970s, sudden introduction of public health programmes in rural areas sharply improved maternal and child health, leading to a child-survival baby boom that raised population growth rates for several decades until fertility rates could decline enough to overcome demographic momentum. Given the small initial number of urban and rural nonfarm jobs, even the rapid year-to-year annual rates of economic growth observed in Asia during the 1980s and 1990s and then in Africa during the 2000s were not enough to absorb all the children of farmers. The result has been a continued rise in rural populations and decline in land available per farmer, despite urbanisation and income growth among non-farmers.

This paper documents the timing and pattern of changes from the 1990s to the 2010s, comparing the experience of African countries to other regions, starting with the agricultural transformation described above, then turning to nutrition and food policy. Nutrition transition, a term coined in the early 1990s by Popkin (1993, 1994), refers to systematic differences in body size and dietary intake associated with economic development. The term focuses particularly on the transition from stunting and underweight that have been successfully addressed over many decades as documented by Fogel (2004), Deaton (2007) and others, to the relatively sudden rise in obesity observed since the 1980s. Stunting results from deprivation in infancy and is rarely reversed, while obesity results from later weight gain, so the two forms of malnutrition often coexist in the same people. Shifts in overweight and obesity by region are shown in Stevens et al. (2012), and changes in specific dietary risk factors are linked to their overall burden of disease in Lim et al. (2013).

The agricultural transformation and nutrition transition described above are heavily influenced by government interventions, in ways that alter the path and may sometimes accelerate and sometimes slow the pace of change. Most notably, as documented most recently by Anderson and Nelgen (2013), through the twentieth century agricultural transformation was generally accompanied by the apparent paradox that governments in low-income countries typically intervened to reduce food prices, while middle- and high-income country governments typically intervened to raise them. This food policy transition was seen as paradoxical because, within each country, it tended to redistribute income from the poorer majority to a richer minority, delaying the agricultural transformation towards a perma-nently smaller share of resources devoted to food production. Policy-makers may have also distorted prices towards staple foods, delaying any dietary transition towards healthier foods. We conclude this review by examining these food policy trends in Africa relative to other regions.

2. The demographic context

Changes in agricultural life are driven in part by year-to-year variation in the number of people living in rural areas, especially in poor countries where most rural people are farming. Given a fixed total area of accessible land, water, forests and other natural resources, an increase in the number of rural people reduces the amount of those resources per person, with less land area available per rural household. During economic development, demographic transition towards slower growth of the total population combined with outmigration from rural areas gradually reduces the rate of rural population growth to below zero, at which time land area per rural person can increase over time. The year when rural population growth crosses zero has been called a 'structural transformation turning point' (Tomich et al., 1995), after which each remaining rural resident can expand their farm size, contributing to higher rural incomes.

Figure 1 uses UN population projections and urbanisation prospects from 1950 to 2050 to show how the timing of structural transformation and its turning point differs for sub-Saharan Africa relative to the world as a whole. The top line for each panel is the world or region's total population, which grows exponentially at an increasing rate in the initial decades of demographic transition when child mortality falls, and continues growing at a declining rate when fertility falls. The dashed line is urban population, which accounts for a small fraction of the total in the early years of structural transforma-tion, and then rises quickly as cities house and employ a rising share of people over time. The change

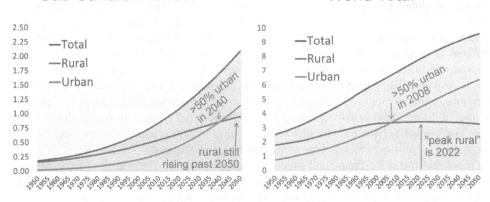

Figure 1. Despite rapid urbanisation, Africa's rural population will keep growing past 2050.
Notes: Vertical axis is population, in billions. All data are calculated from United Nations (2014), UN Population Projections and World Urbanization Prospects, 2014 Revision, released July 2014 at http://esa.un.org/unpd/wup.

in rural population depends on total population growth minus urban growth, with rural people moving to towns and cities as quickly as migration opportunities allow. The right panel shows how the world as a whole reached 50 per cent urban around 2008, while the combination of slowing total population growth with continued urbanisation puts the turning point towards negative rural population growth around 2022; the left panel shows how population dynamics in Africa follow the same pattern but much later in time with different magnitudes, reaching 50 per cent urban around 2040 and the rural population continuing to grow past 2050.

The results shown in Figure 1 set the stage for our specific results presented below, in which we use Preston curves to show how countries in Africa differ from nations elsewhere.

3. Data and methods

To characterise the overall pattern of agricultural change and nutrition transition in Africa and elsewhere from the 1990s into the 2010s, we build on Masters et al. (2016) by constructing Preston Curves that compare the averages observed among countries around each level of national income per capita, measured in real terms controlling for the purchasing power of local currencies obtained from the World Development Indicators dataset of the World Bank. The specific variables we use are described in Table 1, and were chosen to illustrate principal features of three changes: (a) agricultural transformation, described in terms of rural population growth, agriculture's share of total employment, and the productivity of agricultural workers relative to non-agricultural workers; (b) nutrition transition, in terms of child stunting and adult obesity then diet quality with intake of healthy and unhealthy diets, and (b) food policy in terms of consumer prices and public investment levels.

The Preston Curve method allows us to analyse changes over time and differences across countries for all these variables in a consistent manner, testing for statistically significant changes in each region's means at each level of income between data from before and after 2000. This technique was first developed to identify changes in the relationship between life expectancy and per-capita income (Bloom & Canning, 2007; Preston, 1975), and can be generalised from that to any aspect of socio-economic development. In our tests, if the twenty-first century so far is like the 1990s, in the sense that countries with more purchasing power produce and consumer more of the same things, then countries will have moved along each curve. Any shift in the curves' level will be due to innovations in global or regional technology, institutions or other structural conditions. The Preston Curve approach provides a powerful test of whether changes are due to innovations that are new to the region as a

Table 1. Variables used for Preston Curve analyses

Variable	Definition	Source	Years	Countries
National income (independent variable)				
GDP per capita (PPP, Constant 2011)	National income, adjusted for purchasing power	WB World Development Indicators, 2016	1990–2014	214
Agricultural transformation				
Rural population growth (pct/yr)	Year-to-year increase in number of people in rural areas	UN World Urbanisation Prospects, 2014	1950–2050	228
Employment in agriculture (pct of total)	Fraction of all workers who are working in agriculture	ILO World Economic & Social Outlook, 2015	1991–2013	173
Labour productivity in agriculture relative to other sectors (index)	Value added (VA) per worker in agriculture, divided by VA/wkr in all other sectors	World Bank & ILO, 2016	1991–2013	127
Nutrition transition				
Stunting prevalence (pct of children aged <5yrs)	Pct of children, based on height for age z scores (HAZ<2)	UNICEF/WHO/World Bank JMP, 2016	1983–2015	146
Obesity prevalence (pct of adults aged >20yrs)	Fraction of adults with body mass index (BMI>30)	Global Burden of Disease project estimates, 2015	1990–2013	188
Diet quality (score for intake of healthy diets)	Score from 1 to 100, higher = more intake of 10 healthy foods	Average of 10 intake estimates, from Imamura et al., 2015	1990–2010	187
Diet quality (score for less intake of harmful diets)	Score from 1 to 100, higher = less intake of 7 unhealthy foods	Average of 7 intake estimates, from Imamura et al., 2015	1990–2010	187
Food policy				
Price policy (proportional increase in consumer prices)	Consumer tax equivalent (CTE) increase in prices due to interventions	Anderson and Nelgin, 2013	1990–2011	82
Public spending for agriculture and health (pct of gvt budget)	Pct of government spending in health or agriculture	IFPRI SPEED data, 2016	1980–2012	147

Note: Each variable is described with citations to data sources where results are presented.

whole, or can be explained in terms of an established path of socio-economic development associated with per-capita income and purchasing power. Each curve describes the shape and tests for shifts in a bivariate relationship that could then be explained as a function of other variables in other models.

In this paper we test the statistical significance of changes in nine kinds of relationships, each using non-parametric regressions with no assumptions about the shape of development paths. Some variables could be a linear function of national income, but they could also be U-shaped or S-shaped reflecting both consumers' income elasticities of demand and the political economy of government policies at each level of national income. The significance of changes in that function depends not only on the mean but also variance, which we show with a 95 per cent confidence interval around the estimated mean at each income level in each region. The mean and confidence interval for each variable is estimated at each level of income using a local polynomial regression (Henderson & Parmeter, 2015), implemented in Stata version 14.2 using the command lpolyci. These are Epanechnikov kernel regressions, fitting a polynomial of degree zero so that the estimate at each point is a moving average, imposing a uniform bandwidth set at 0.75 log points of national income to ensure that local means are computed over the same range in each curve for ease of comparison. The result provides both a convenient visualisation and a statistical hypothesis test for the difference in local means at each national income level.

Our approach is statistical but is presented graphically, and for visual clarity all charts are formatted in a consistent manner. Preston Curves with non-overlapping confidence intervals reveal a statistically significant shift from one decade to the next, or significant differences in the pattern between Africa and the rest of the world. African countries are shown using solid squares or circles, and non-African countries are shown with hollow squares or circles. Africa is on the left panel with others on the right where splitting the figure is helpful. If both regions can be shown on a single panel, results for Africa are shown with a solid regression line and others with a dashed line. To compare changes over time, where the data are modelled to fill every year we use data for just 1990 and 2010, and where data are from occasional surveys we use an average of available years in the 1990s and 2010s. The earlier observations are always shown using circles in lighter shades (of green, if colour is available) for the 1990s, and squares in darker shades (of blue) for data for the 2010s.

3.1. Agricultural transformation

3.1.1. Rural population growth. We introduce the Preston Curve method using the same rural population data as Figure 1, presented in Figure 2 in terms of year-to-year growth rates. This and other charts also show the number of observations for each region and year, with notes below the figure and country codes for outliers shown on the chart.

Figure 2 reveals no shift over time within each panel in rural population growth rates at each level of income, but looking across panels there are significantly higher rural growth rates in Africa than elsewhere, at all but the highest levels of income. The gap arises because there is a significant downward income gradient in the rest of the world, from above 2 per cent per year in the poorest places towards zero and then negative rural population growth when income passes about $6000 per year, whereas Africa's rural population growth rates remain around 2 per cent per year at all but the highest income levels.

The distinctive fact about African demography revealed in Figures 1 and 2 arises due to rapid total population growth and other aspects of demographic change described in Masters et al. (2013). The increases in rural population shown here ensure that, even with very rapid urbanisation and rising nonfarm incomes, the amounts of rural land and water or other natural resources per rural resident is shrinking much faster in Africa than elsewhere, reducing rural income growth.

3.1.2. Employment shares. Another perspective on economic transformation concerns the allocation of labour between agricultural and non-agricultural activity. Yeboah and Jayne (2018) use the limited available time-use data to show how rural households are often engaged in both farm and non-farm work, some of which involves temporary or permanent migration within rural areas as well as to or from urban settlements. Barrett, Reardon, and Webb (2001) show how reallocation over time is driven

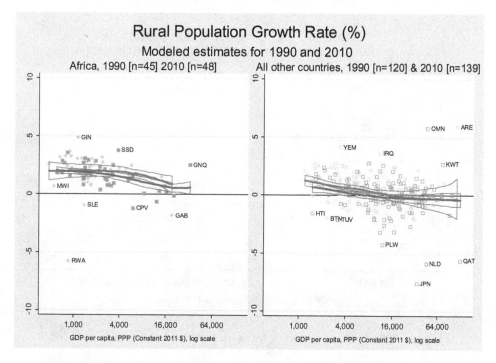

Figure 2. Rural population grew faster in Africa than elsewhere at each income level.

by the rise of new nonfarm opportunities as well as change in available farmland and other agricultural resources per rural worker. Yeboah and Jayne (2018) find only five African countries with repeated surveys on time use by sector, so for a broader comparison, we use International Labour Organization (ILO) estimates of primary employment in agriculture from the most recent ILO (2015) World Employment and Social Outlook database.

The data visualisation in Figure 3 combines both African and other countries in one panel, because the two regions' employment shares are so different. The Preston Curve shows primary employment in agriculture to be consistently above 60 per cent in Africa's poorer countries and around 30 per cent in Africa's richest countries, whereas it ranges from below 50 per cent to under 20 per cent elsewhere at comparable income levels. This difference has not changed from 1991 to 2010, and is associated with the high rates of rural population growth shown in Figures 1 and 2 that reduce land area per household, holding back transformation and leaving more people in agriculture as shown in Figure 3.

3.1.3. Labour productivity. Africa is distinctive not only because so many of its workers are in agriculture as shown above, but also because those agricultural workers have much lower productivity than nonfarm workers as shown below.

Figure 4 plots each country's total agricultural value added per agricultural worker, divided by the country's non-agricultural value added per non-agricultural worker. This uses the same ILO data source as Figure 3, showing the total value of all outputs produced by each sector (where agriculture includes forestry, hunting and fishing) minus the value of intermediate inputs used by each sector, divided by the number of workers in each sector. At each level of national income per capita, agriculture clearly offers much lower value added per worker than non-agriculture. The difference is accounted for partly by smaller quantities of capital and other factors per worker, and partly by lower productivity per unit of each factor, including labour.

A remarkable feature of Figure 4 is the statistically significant rise from 1991 and 2010 in relative productivity for agricultural labour outside of Africa but only at higher income levels. In Africa, there

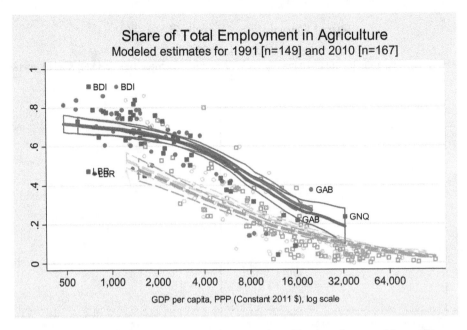

Figure 3. Agricultural employment is far higher in Africa than the rest of the world.

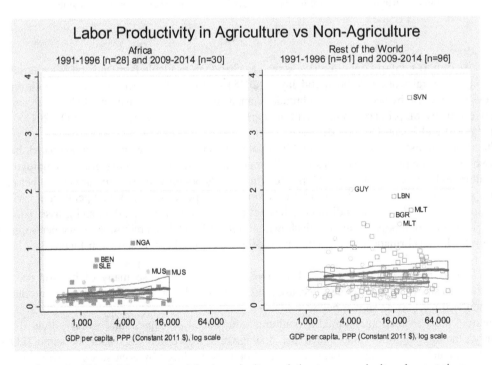

Figure 4. Africa's labour productivity in agriculture relative to non-agriculture has not risen.

is no significant shift from the earlier to the later regression lines, and no significant upward slope associated with higher incomes. In other words, while the richer parts of the rest of the world experienced an upward shift in agricultural labour productivity relative to non-agricultural labour productivity, African farmers did not benefit from this increase in resources and productivity per agricultural worker.

The difference in productivity between agriculture and non-agriculture shown in the ILO data on Figure 4 is not merely an artefact of data collection methods. Gollin, Lagakos, and Waugh (2014) control for various other factors and confirm that Africa's agricultural workers have significantly lower productivity than non-agricultural workers. This is consistent with Timmer (2009) and many other assessments, reflecting Africa's delayed demographic and structural transformations that leaves rising numbers of African workers no choice but to try to feed themselves using limited resources with a declining area of land per worker.

3.2. Nutrition transition

The agricultural transformation described above involves a gradual transition from primarily rural, mainly agricultural employment at relatively low incomes to primarily urban, mainly non-agricultural work at higher incomes. This change involves a corresponding transition in nutritional outcomes, which we analyse here in terms of child stunting, adult obesity, and then intake of healthy as opposed to unhealthy diets.

3.2.1. Stunting.
The most widely used measure of undernutrition in public health research is stunting, defined as the proportion of a population's children with a height-for-age z scores (HAZ) less than two standard deviations below the median of a healthy population. The onset of stunting typically occurs in early childhood and persists thereafter, so that prevalence rates among children under five years of age provides a useful measure of malnutrition experienced in recent years. Here we report national averages from the authoritative UNICEF/WHO/World Bank joint database of anthropometric surveys (WHO, 2010).

Figure 5 reveals that Africa's stunting rates have improved sharply over time at each income level, when comparing the earliest surveys in 1985–1999 to the most recent ones in 2000–2011. Africa differs from the rest of the world primarily in having a less steep income gradient, and correspondingly

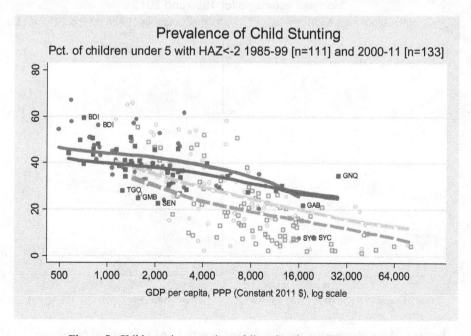

Figure 5. Child stunting rates have fallen sharply at all income levels.

higher stunting rates at middle income levels. The few African countries we observe at those levels of per capita income have not been able to reduce child stunting in the way that countries elsewhere have done, perhaps because of their rapid rural population growth and low agricultural productivity.

3.2.2. Obesity.   Whether or not a person's height was stunted in early childhood, lifelong weight gain through fat deposition is associated with risk for diabetes, cardiovascular disease and other disorders. A common threshold for high risk is obesity, defined in terms of Body Mass Index (BMI, in kg/m2) of 30 or more. For comparability across countries, we use modelled estimates of obesity prevalence in adults aged 20 or older, computed for 162 countries from the Global Burden of Disease 2013 study (Imamura et al., 2015).

Figure 6 reveals that Africa has a steep income gradient in adult obesity rates, but no upward shift from 1990 to 2010 at any income level. In contrast, for the rest of the world, there is a statistically significant upward shift from 1990 to 2010 for countries with per capita income levels exceeding about $16,000. Below that level there is relatively little income gradient in the rest of the world, and poorer African countries have significantly lower obesity rates than other countries at comparable income levels.

A notable aspect of these obesity data is their wide variability, as some African countries such as South Africa and oil-rich Equatorial Guinea had obesity rates of 22 per cent and 26.3 per cent, respectively. Conversely, the majority of low income African countries with per capita income below $4000 had very low adult obesity levels (<10%). A succession of reports such as FAO (2006), Abubakari, Lauder, Charles, and Bhopal (2008), Arojo and Osungbade (2013) and NCD-RiskC (2016) have focused attention on increases in adult obesity in particular regions, which does pose a high risk for chronic disease, calling for sharp increases in detection and treatment of conditions such as diabetes and hypertension which have had low prevalence in the past but are and will continue to account for a rising share of Africa's disease burden.

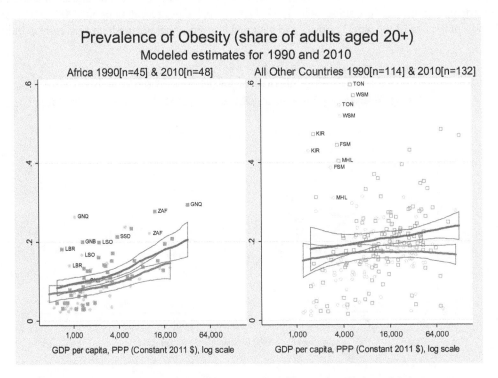

Figure 6. Adult obesity rates rise with income in Africa, and are below global averages.

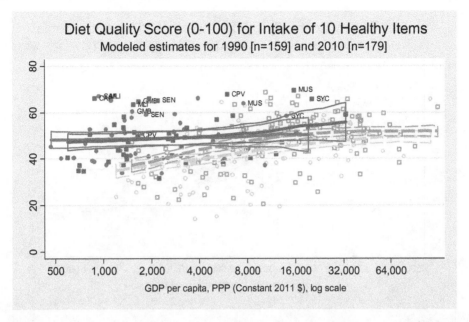

Figure 7. Diet quality over 10 healthy items is relatively good in Africa with no income gradient.

3.2.3. Diet quality. Stunting and obesity are the most visible forms of malnutrition, but food quality can contribute to diet-related disease in people of any height and weight. Here we use the global dietary data assembled by NutriCoDE for the Global Burden of Disease study, producing modelled estimates for all countries in 1990 and 2010 of two distinct diet-quality measures based on mean adult intake of 10 dietary items for which more intake is healthier, and seven items for which less intake is healthier. Both diet quality indexes count all of their food items equally, and are normalised for a 2000 calorie diet in an ordinal scale from one to 100 where higher values mean a healthier diet (Imamura et al., 2015).

Figure 7 shows mean intake of 10 healthy dietary items at each level of income, revealing that African countries with per capita income below $4000 had significantly higher intake of these foods than others at similar income levels. Unlike Africa, the rest of the world has a strong income gradient with poor countries consuming low levels of these foods, converging up to higher levels observed in Africa over the income level of about $4000, with a small upwards shift from 1990 to 2010 in the rest of the world but not in Africa.

Figure 8 shows mean intake of seven unhealthy dietary components, expressed in a diet quality score so that less intake of these foods gives a higher score (closer to 100). Like the healthy-item score this reveals that African countries at most income levels have relatively better diet quality than the rest of the world at similar income levels, while diet qualities converge at higher income levels. Similar to the pattern observed through the healthy diets score, there was hardly any change in diet quality between 1990 and 2010 in African countries across all income levels.

3.2.4. Food policy. To measure cross-country differences in food policy we begin with Consumer Tax Equivalent (CTE) estimates from the World Bank's Distortions to Agricultural Incentives project, using data originally compiled for Africa by Anderson and Masters (2009). The CTE is defined as the percentage change in the wholesale price paid for each food item, relative to the price that would have prevailed if government policy permitted free international trade and a competitive domestic market. CTEs are among the most direct and internationally comparable measure of food policy interventions, representing the tariff-equivalent percentage by which government policies raise or lower food prices. The data shown in Figure 9 are updated values from Anderson and Nelgen (2013), drawing on prices

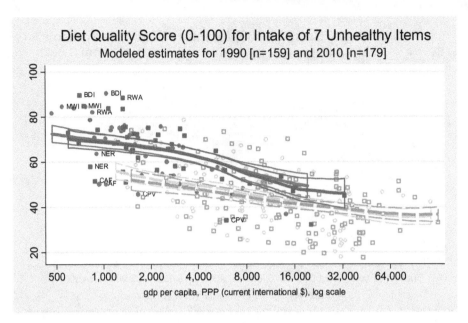

Figure 8. Diet quality over seven unhealthy items is better in Africa than elsewhere, at low incomes.

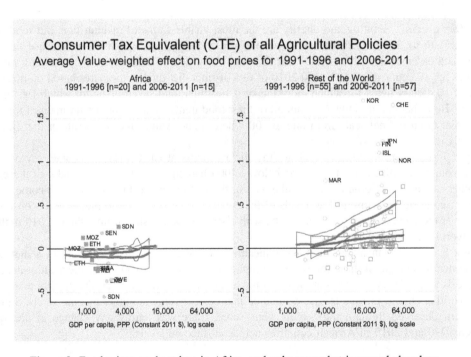

Figure 9. Food prices are kept low in Africa, and only somewhat increased elsewhere.

for major food products across 85 countries from 1950 to 2011. To focus on the cross-country pattern, we show the average CTE for all food items, weighted by their share of food spending, for the time periods 1991–1996 and 2006–2011.

Figure 9 reveals that African countries pursue policies that lower food prices, transferring real income from farmers to consumers, with no significant change in average CTEs over time and no gradient associated with national income. In contrast, observations from the rest of the world where incomes are higher show a steep income gradient in the 1991–1996 data which largely disappears in the 2006–2011 period. In the later period, governments outside Africa continued to raise food prices, although the price increase is smaller than it had been.

The 1991–1996 data across both panels to cover the world as a whole reveals the development paradox observed over much of the twentieth century, in which governments in poor countries reduce food prices while governments in richer countries do the reverse. This was considered paradoxical in that both kinds of policy favour a relatively richer minority at the expense of a poorer majority within each country. As shown in Figure 9, that paradox has largely though not entirely disappeared, with many African governments still taxing their agricultural producers to help food consumers, while other governments do much less taxing of food consumers to help farmers.

Beyond prices, another aspect of government policy is fiscal expenditure by sector. Here we present government spending on health (including nutrition) relative to agriculture (including fisheries), as compiled in the database of Statistics on Public Expenditures for Economic Development (SPEED) from the International Food Policy Research Institute (IFPRI, 2016). Collected from multiple sources, the SPEED dataset offers the best available global data on public expenditures for these two sectors.

Figure 10 shows public expenditures as percentages of total public spending, reflecting each government's commitment to health and agriculture relative to other sectors. Spending levels for health along the top two panels are generally above those for agriculture along the bottom two panels, and spending on health shows an upward income gradient outside Africa while spending on agriculture has a downward income gradient in both Africa and elsewhere.

The SPEED data shown in Figure 10 support other reports that African governments are still investing far less in agriculture than their commitments under the 2003 Maputo and 2014 Malabo

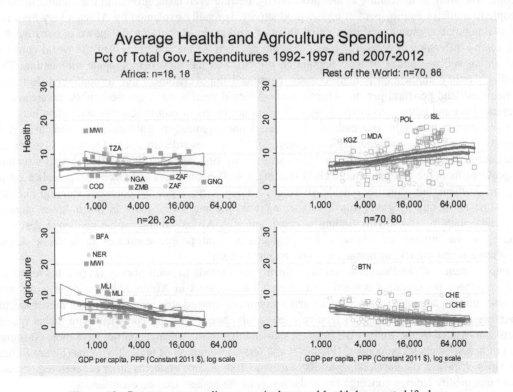

Figure 10. Government spending on agriculture and health have not shifted up.

agreements (Mink, 2016). In these agreements they set targets of 10 per cent of government spending on agriculture, which only a very few countries reached in 2010.

4. Conclusions

This paper documents the timing and pattern of three broad changes associated with economic growth between the 1990s and the 2010s, comparing Africa with the rest of the world in terms of economic transformation from farm to nonfarm activity, nutrition transition from less stunting to rising obesity, and agricultural policy from lowering to raising food prices. Many factors contribute to the patterns we see. In this paper the aim is to describe stylised facts, notably about economic transformation in terms of rural population growth, agriculture's share of total employment, and the productivity of agricultural workers relative to non-agricultural workers; about nutrition transition in terms of child stunting and adult obesity and diet quality with intake of healthy and unhealthy items; and about agricultural policy in terms of food prices and public investment levels.

For economic transformation, the main result we find is that Africa – compared to other regions, at each level of per-capita income – has faster rural population growth (Figures 1 and 2), a larger share of workers in agriculture (Figure 3) and lower labour productivity for them relative to non-agricultural workers (Figure 4). The pattern in rates of change observed across African countries are consistent with those observed elsewhere, but different in magnitude, with the central distinction being Africa's relatively recent and rapid increase in the number of rural people and consequent decline in agricultural land, water and other rural resources per rural person. This pattern was present in the 1990s, remains present in the 2010s and is likely to persist even as African towns and cities grow faster than urban areas elsewhere, and as the share of African workers who are in agriculture declines.

The apparent paradox in economic transformation of year-to-year increases in the number of rural people who work in agriculture at low productivity, despite even faster growth in the number of urban people in nonfarm employment at higher productivity, is readily explained by Africa's very high rate of total population growth and high initial share of workers in agriculture. As shown in our Figure 1, the central difference in economic transformation between Africa and the rest of the world concerns the timing and magnitude of total population growth, and the rural demographic momentum. This finding's policy implication is that, to avoid continued impoverishment due to continued decline in agricultural land per rural person, African farmers would need to see increased public investment to increase land and labour productivity, as well as higher levels of public services and safety nets.

For nutrition transition, our main result is rapid improvement in child stunting at each level of income in both Africa and other regions (Figure 5). The downward shift in child stunting between the late twentieth century (1985–1999) and the early twenty-first century (2000–2011) reveals structural improvements in the determinants of child stunting. Our Preston Curve approach also reveals a strong income gradient, but primarily outside of Africa. Among Africa's poorest countries stunting rates are the same as in other regions, but at higher national income levels there is much lower stunting elsewhere than in Africa. This finding is consistent with Africa's demographic challenge described above, as the number of relatively low-productivity rural people continues to increase despite urbanisation and the rise of non-agricultural employment.

Improvements in child stunting contrasts sharply with trends in adult obesity (Figure 6), for which there has been no structural upward shift at each income level in Africa, although there is a strong income gradient among African countries and a significant upward structural shift among higher income countries in other regions. Africa's relatively low adult obesity rates are consistent with higher quality diets as measured by the NutriCoDE indexes, showing that most African countries have more consumption of healthy dietary components (Figure 7) and less consumption of unhealthy items (Figure 8) than countries elsewhere at corresponding levels of income. But, income gradients differ between regions, and these diet quality indexes converge to similar levels in the highest income countries.

In food policy, our main result is that African governments continue to keep consumer prices of major farm products relatively low, benefiting consumers at the expense of producers (Figure 9). Governments elsewhere in higher-income countries continue to keep consumer prices relatively high, but with a large structural shift downwards in the income gradient as richer countries outside Africa did so to a much smaller degree in the recent 2006–2011 data than they did in the earlier 1991–1996 period. The long-standing development paradox is now much smaller in magnitude than it was during the twentieth century. Policy-makers in both Africa and elsewhere continue to use food price policy to tax their poorer citizens and provide concentrated benefits to more influential groups, who tend to be food consumers in Africa and other low-income countries but food producers in higher-income countries elsewhere.

Public investments in agriculture and health, including nutrition, have contrasting income gradients (Figure 10). The poorest African countries have similar levels of government spending across the two sectors, but there is a negative income gradient for agricultural expenditure so higher-income African countries spend less on agriculture than on health. The rest of the world also has a negative income growth for agricultural expenditure, whereas there is a positive gradient for health spending, so expenditure levels are higher for health, especially in the richest countries.

The Preston Curve results presented here focus on regional averages at each level of national income, using confidence intervals and scatter plots to see variation among countries within Africa and in the rest of the world. Beyond these national averages, further research addresses within-country variation in the kind of data shown here, and also extends these results to other kinds of data. This particular paper summarises only a few of the major challenges ahead for African agriculture, nutrition and food policy. We find that even if economic development proceeds rapidly in urban Africa, rural Africans will face continued impoverishment unless government interventions change to improve the lives of people working in agriculture at low productivity levels. Clear gains in child stunting reveal the potential for success despite these challenges, and could inspire interventions to achieve similar improvements in other aspects of African food systems.

Acknowledgements

We thank Dariush Mozaffarian, Anwar Naseem, Jim Oehmke, Carl Pray and Patrick Webb for support and comments on previous work related to this paper, as well as the editor and two anonymous referees for improvements in this manuscript. All data are from the public domain as noted in cited sources; Stata code to construct the Preston Curves is available via the author's website at https://sites.tufts.edu/willmasters.

Disclosure statement

No potential conflict of interest was reported by the authors.

Funding

This work was supported by the Bill & Melinda Gates Foundation [Global Dietary Database project and Policy Consortium (OPP1176682)]; U.S. Department of Agriculture [Feed the Future Policy Impact Study Consortium (USDA TA-CA-15-008)]; United States Agency for International Development [Feed the Future Innovation Lab for Nutrition (AID-OAA-L-1-00005)].

References

Abubakari, A. R., Lauder, W., Charles, A., & Bhopal, A. (2008). Prevalence and time trends in obesity among adult West African populations: A meta-analysis. *Obesity Reviews*, 9(4), 297–311. doi:10.1111/j.1467-789X.2007.00462.x
Anderson, K., & Masters, W. A. (2009). *Distortions to agricultural incentives in Africa*. Washington, DC: World Bank Publications.
Anderson, K., & Nelgen, S. (2013). *Updated national and global estimates of distortions to agricultural incentives, 1955 to 2011*. Washington, DC: The World Bank. Retrieved from www.worldbank.org/agdistortions

Arojo, O. O., & Osungbade, K. O. (2013). Trends of obesity epidemic and its socio-cultural dimensions in Africa: Implications for health systems and environmental interventions. *iConcept Journal of Emerging Issues in Medical Diagnosis and Treatment, 1*(7), 1–9.

Barrett, C. B., Reardon, T., & Webb, P. (2001). Nonfarm income diversification and household livelihood strategies in rural Africa: Concepts, dynamics, and policy implications. *Food Policy, 26*(4), 315–331. doi:10.1016/S0306-9192(01)00014-8

Bloom, D. E., & Canning, D. (2007). Commentary: The Preston Curve 30 years on: still sparking fires. *International Journal of Epidemiology, 36*(3), 498–499. doi:10.1093/ije/dym079

Chenery, H. B. (1960). Patterns of industrial growth. *American Economic Review, 50*(4), 624–654.

Clark, C. (1940). *The conditions of economic progress.* London: Macmillan Press.

Deaton, A. (2007). Height, health, and development. *Proceedings of the National Academy of Sciences, 104*(33), 13232–13237. doi:10.1073/pnas.0611500104

Dovring, F. (1959). The share of agriculture in growing populations. *FAO Monthly Bulletin of Agricultural Economics and Statistics, 8*(8), 1–11.

FAO. (2006). *The double burden of malnutrition: Case studies from six developing countries* (FAO Food and Nutrition Paper 84). Rome: Food and Agricultural Organization of the United Nations.

Fogel, R. W. (2004). *The escape from hunger and premature death, 1700-2100: Europe, America, and the third world.* Cambridge: Cambridge University Press.

Gollin, D., Lagakos, D., & Waugh, M. E. (2014). The agricultural productivity gap. *The Quarterly Journal of Economics, 129* (2), 939–993. doi:10.1093/qje/qjt056

Henderson, D. J., & Parmeter, C. F. (2015). *Applied nonparametric econometrics.* New York: Cambridge University Press.

IFPRI. (2016). *Statistics on public expenditures for economic development (SPEED).* Washington, DC: Author.

ILO. (2015). *World employment and social outlook (WESO) database.* Geneva: Author. Retrieved from http://www.ilo.org/global/statistics-and-databases/lang–en/index.htm

Imamura, F., Micha, R., Khatibzadeh, S., Fahimi, S., Shi, P., Powles, J., & Mozaffarian, D. (2015). The global burden of diseases nutrition and chronic diseases expert group (NutriCoDE). Dietary quality among men and women in 187 countries in 1990 and 2010: A systematic assessment. *The Lancet Global Health, 3*(3), e132–e142. doi:10.1016/S2214-109X(14)70381-X

Lim, S. S., Vos, T., Flaxman, A. D., Danaei, G., Shibuya, K., Adair-Rohan, H., & Ezzati, M. (2013). A comparative risk assessment of burden of disease and injury attributable to 67 risk factors and risk factor clusters in 21 regions, 1990–2010: A systematic analysis for the Global Burden of Disease Study 2010. *The Lancet, 380,* 2224–2260. doi:10.1016/S0140-6736 (12)61766-8

Masters, W. A., Djurfeldt, A. A., De Haan, C., Hazell, P., Jayne, T., Jirström, M., & Reardon, T. (2013). Urbanization and farm size in Asia and Africa: Implications for food security and agricultural research. *Global Food Security, 2*(3), 156–165. doi:10.1016/j.gfs.2013.07.002

Masters, W. A., Hall, A., Martinez, E. M., Shi, P., Singh, G., Webb, P., & Mozaffarian, D. (2016). The nutrition transition and agricultural transformation: A Preston Curve approach. *Agricultural Economics, 47*(S1), 97–114. doi:10.1111/agec.2016.47. issue-S1

Mink, S. D. (2016). *Findings across agricultural public expenditure reviews in African countries* (IFPRI Discussion Paper 1522). Washington, DC: International Food Policy Research Institute.

NCD-RiskC. (2016). Trends in adult body-mass index in 200 countries from 1975 to 2014: A pooled analysis of 1698 population-based measurement studies with 19·2 million participants. *The Lancet, 387,* 1377–1396. doi:10.1016/s0140-6736(16)30054-x

Popkin, B. (1993). Nutritional patterns and transitions. *Population and Development Review, 19*(1), 138–157. doi:10.2307/2938388

Popkin, B. (1994). The nutrition transition in low income countries: An emerging crisis. *Nutrition Reviews, 52*(9), 285–298. doi:10.1111/j.1753-4887.1994.tb01460.x

Preston, S. H. (1975). The changing relation between mortality and level of economic development. *Population Studies, 29*(2), 231–248. doi:10.1080/00324728.1975.10410201

Stevens, G. A., Singh, G. M., Lu, Y., Danaei, G., Lin, J. K., Finucane, M. M., ... Ezzati, M. (2012). National, regional, and global trends in adult overweight and obesity prevalences. *Population Health Metrics, 10*(1), 22. doi:10.1186/1478-7954-10-22

Timmer, C. P. (2009). *A world without agriculture? The historical paradox of agricultural development.* Washington, DC: American Enterprise Institute for Public Policy Research.

Tomich, T. P., Kilby, P., & Johnston, B. (1995). *Transforming Agrarian economies: Opportunities seized, opportunities missed.* Ithaca: Cornell University Press.

United Nations. (2014). *World urbanization prospects: The 2014 revision, CD-ROM edition.* New York: United Nations.

WHO. (2010). *Global database on child growth and malnutrition.* Geneva: Author. Retrieved from http://www.who.int/nutgrowthdb/estimates/en

Yeboah, F. K., & Jayne, T. S. (2018). Africa's evolving employment trends. *Journal of Development Studies, 54*(5), 803–832. doi: 10.1080/00220388.2018.1430767

Africa's Evolving Employment Trends

FELIX KWAME YEBOAH & THOMAS S. JAYNE

ABSTRACT *Using nationally representative data from nine countries, we document demographic and employment trends in Africa's workforce based on full-time labour equivalents (FTE). The FTE approach takes account of individuals' multiple jobs throughout the year and is therefore likely to give more accurate estimates of the pace of structural transformation. Since 2000, Africa has experienced a sharp decline in the share of its labour force in farming. Because of the seasonal nature of farming, the share of the labour force remaining in farming is substantially lower using the FTE approach than when examined in terms of individuals' primary sources of employment or total numbers of jobs. Using the FTE approach, the share of the labour force in farming ranges across the nine countries from 35 per cent in Ghana to 54 per cent in Rwanda. Employment in off-farm segments of agri-food systems is expanding rapidly in percentage terms, but in terms of absolute numbers, non-farm activities are by far the major source of employment outside of farming. Contrary to widespread perceptions, the mean age of adults engaged primarily in farming is not rising – in fact it is falling slightly in some countries and remains stable in most others. The pace at which the labour force is shifting out of agriculture is strongly and positively tied to the rate of lagged farm productivity growth. Given the unprecedented growth in the number of young Africans entering the labour market, an effective youth employment strategy in most African countries will rely on massive job expansion, which in turn will rely on the multiplier effects of agricultural productivity growth. Strategies that raise the returns to labour in farming therefore remain crucial for achieving rapid economic transformation and may constitute the core of effective youth employment strategies.*

1. Introduction

Sub-Saharan Africa (SSA) has enjoyed nearly two decades of sustained economic growth (AfDB, OECD, and UNDP, 2014; IMF, 2013).[1] At the same time, SSA is experiencing the world's fastest population growth. The sub-continent's share of the world's population is projected to rise rapidly from 12 per cent in 2015 to 23 per cent by 2050 (United Nations, 2016). With over 62 per cent of the population below the age of 25 and a labour force growing at 3 per cent per year, about 17 million young Africans will become of working age each year until 2035 (Losch, 2012).

Africa's growing workforce offers opportunities for economic transformation if their talents can be productively utilised in an expanding economy. Conversely, chronic youth under-employment could lead to economic stagnation, disillusionment, and social unrest. There are worrying signs that African economies, even with impressive economic performance, are not expanding job opportunities quickly enough to absorb the rapidly growing labour force (Filmer & Fox, 2014; Fine et al., 2012; Page & Shimeles, 2015). It is projected that even under the most favourable growth conditions, less than a quarter of young Africans entering the labour force over the next decade will find wage employment (Losch, 2012). Unsurprisingly, the most recent round of nationally representative AfroBarometer data for 34 African countries revealed that Africans feel that addressing unemployment is by far the greatest priority for government action (Dome, 2015).

In response to these challenges, African policymakers and their development partners have begun implementing strategies to expand job opportunities and develop new skills of young people.

However, these strategies are based on limited evidence about labour market trends in SSA. The question of employment transformation and its implications for future economic transformation in SSA has received little attention in the literature, with a few notable exceptions (Filmer & Fox, 2014; Fox & Thomas, 2016; ILO, 2015). The role of agriculture within a rapidly transforming Africa is also particularly poorly understood.

This study therefore documents salient demographic and employment trends in Africa's workforce over the past decade and examines the evolving role of agriculture in Africa's economic transformation process. The study breaks new ground in two ways: First, building on Filmer and Fox (2014), which is based on data prior to 2010, we use more recent nationally representative data to explore the extent to which sectoral employment patterns have shifted and do so in a more disaggregated way that distinguishes between different types of sectors within the non-farm economy and disaggregates 'agriculture' into farm-based activities versus off-farm employment in agri-food value chains, which has been projected to be a major vehicle for economic transformation in the region (Tschirley et al., 2015). Second, we compare sectoral employment trends based on the total number of jobs as stated by survey respondents (given that many people report having multiple jobs), and by computing 'full-time equivalents' (FTE). The FTE approach computes the share of individuals' work time over the survey year that can be allocated to various work activities, many of which are seasonal in nature. Given that different jobs occupy differing amounts of a person's time, the FTE approach therefore provides a more accurate (yet still somewhat crude) estimate of various sectors' employment shares and trends.

The paper is organised as follows: Sections 2 and 3 describe the data and analytical methods used in this study. Section 4 presents the main findings, starting with broad demographic and employment trends among the working-age population in various African countries and then examining youth employment trends specifically. Section 5 examines the linkages between observed patterns of sectoral employment shifts and agricultural productivity growth. Section 6 concludes by summarising key findings and their implications for the nature and pace of economic transformation in Africa.

2. Data

Our analysis draws on four data sets: First, the *Africa Sector Database* is utilised as a starting point for understanding broad employment trends by sector for multiple African countries. The Groningen Growth and Development Center developed this data set. Employment and labour productivity data were derived for particular years from national micro-surveys, and the remaining years were interpolated to arrive at annual data on employment for various sectors between 1960 and 2010.

Our primary empirical analysis utilises micro-level data from three sources: the Living Standards Measurement Study with its Integrated Surveys of Agriculture (LSMS-ISA);[2] Labour Force Surveys; and the Integrated Public Use Microdata Series (IPUMS) that are based on 10 per cent random samples of national population censuses conducted between 1990 and 2010 and managed by the University of Minnesota Population Center (see: https://international.ipums.org/international/). Each of these data sources had multiple waves of nationally representative surveys for numerous African countries. We focus on labour market information on individual household members, by age, gender, and rural/urban location.

Classifications of individuals into the various employment sectors were based on respondents' stated industry of employment, defined as the activity or product of the sector in which the person is employed and based on the International Standard for Industrial Classification (ISIC) categories established by the United Nations Statistics Division. The classification is subdivided into a hierarchical, four-level structure of mutually exclusive categories: section, division, group, and class.

Our primary empirical analysis covered nine countries in sub-Saharan Africa: Ghana, Kenya, Malawi, Mali, Nigeria, Rwanda, Tanzania, Uganda, and Zambia.[3] Country selection was based on availability of comparable data over two or more periods separated by at least five years, and based on regional representation across SSA.

Some limitations to the data should be acknowledged. The IPUMS census data reported only the type of employment in which individuals are primarily engaged. This limited our ability to account for secondary and other seasonal economic activities for the three countries using IPUMS census data (Kenya, Malawi, and Mali). There were also some cross-country variations in the recall period for employment and level of information on reported economic activity; some countries (for example, Zambia) only reported employment in the past seven days instead of the past 12 months. Others did not provide information on the work time allocated to reported job activities. In those cases, FTE-based sectoral employment shares could not be computed. Moreover, country surveys differed in the level of ISIC coding detail. It was therefore possible to clearly categorise individuals into specific employment sectors in some countries but not in others. For instance, sufficient ISIC code detail was available in some countries to enable individuals listed as being engaged in *wholesaling and retailing* to be categorised into the wholesale and retail trade of agricultural commodities versus wholesale and retail trade of non-farm commodities. In other countries, this level of detail was not available. In the latter cases, we apportioned those specifying *wholesale and retail trade*, for instance, into off-farm segments of the agri-food system versus non-farm employment (outside the agri-food system) based on relative consumer expenditure shares within these categories. Details of the classification scheme used to categorise individuals into the various employment categories across the nine countries are available in Yeboah and Jayne (2016).

3. Analytical methods

Our analysis covers the working-age population, defined as those individuals between the ages of 15 and 64 years (OECD, 2015), and focuses in particular on those in the 15 to 34 year age range. The first step involves the classification of the working-age population into three employment categories: (i) farming, (ii) off-farm within agri-food system (upstream and downstream), and (iii) non-farm sector. Jobs in these categories were further disaggregated between self-employment and wage employment jobs, and between public and private sector jobs. The employment category *farming* includes all activities related to growing crops, raising livestock, aquaculture, and hunting. The off-farm segments of the agri-food system included all pre- and post-farm value-addition activities within the agricultural value chains including assembly trading, wholesaling, storage, processing, retailing, preparation of food for selling to others outside the home, beverage manu-facturing, farmer input distribution and irrigation equipment operators. Together, categories (i) and (ii) constitute the 'agri-food system'. The third employment category, *non-farm sector* included all other types of employment not counted above. This employment classification scheme allowed us to estimate the relative size and job growth in the agri-food system, which is envisioned to be a major vehicle for economic transformation in the region given its rapid population growth, rising income growth, urbanisation, and dietary transformations reportedly underway in Africa (Filmer & Fox, 2014; Tschirley et al., 2015; World Bank, 2017).

We also created two additional economic activity categories following the definition of the International Labour Organization (ILO, 1982): (iv) the unemployed and (v) the economically inactive. The unemployed is comprised of individuals not engaged in any economic activity during the reference period, available to work, and either looking for employment or not seeking employment because they thought no work was available.[4] The economically inactive population was made up of individuals who were not engaged in any economic activity during the set period and who are neither looking for work nor available to work for various reasons.

From these five classifications, employment shares and employment changes over time are com-puted. We report employment both in terms of the full range of jobs as stated by survey respondents (many people have multiple jobs), and in terms of 'full-time equivalents' (FTE) by weighting the jobs by the total number of hours worked in that job. A full time equivalent of 40 hours a week, four weeks per month for a 12-month year period was assumed as one FTE. The FTE of any one job is thus computed as the actual number of hours worked as a share of this benchmark 1920-hour work year.

Employment shares for a given sector are also computed in two ways. When including the economically inactive and unemployed, we compute employment shares as a percentage of the entire working-age population. When computing employment shares among the labour force – the subset of the working-age population that was employed – we take the ratio of jobs in a given sector as a percentage of the total number of jobs, taking into account multiple jobs per person.

Given the historical importance of agricultural productivity growth to the economic transformation process, we explore the extent to which observed labour shifts among the working-age population are related to agricultural productivity growth. To do this, we specify and estimate annual multi-country data models of changes in farming's share of the labour force, using pooled OLS and fixed effects models in Section 5. These models estimate the relationship between a country's annual change in the share of the labour force in farming and lagged agricultural productivity growth after controlling for other demographic, economic and political variables hypothesised to potentially influence sectoral employment patterns.

4. Results and discussion

4.1. Urbanisation and demographic shifts among the working-age population

Africa's urban population is growing rapidly, but the rate at which the region is urbanising is in fact slowing down (United Nations, 2016). In the 1960s, 1970s, and 1980s, massive rural-to-urban migration fuelled rapid growth in Africa's urban population and this was accompanied by high rates of urbanisation (the percentage of the total population residing in urban areas). However, since 2000, and despite considerable country-specific variability, a major underappreciated demographic fact is that Africa's urban population growth is mainly due to natural growth of the urban population (birth rates minus death rates of people residing in urban areas) and reclassification of formerly rural towns as urban once a threshold number is reached (Bocquier, 2005; Moriconi-Ebrard, Harre, & Heinrigs, 2016; Potts, 2012).

While rural-to-urban migration continues, it appears to have slowed down considerably in most of sub-Saharan Africa (deBraw, Mueller, & Lee., 2014). Some scholars contend that in some countries, most migration is rural-to-rural, with young people accounting for most of it (Bilsborrow, 2002; Beauchemin, 2011). For example, of all Tanzanians aged 15–64 who migrated away from their rural home between 2008 and 2013, 68 per cent of them migrated to another rural area (Wineman & Jayne, 2016). The multi-regional analysis by Masters, Rosenblum, and Alemu (2018) shows that for any given level of income, African countries have faster rural population growth, a larger share of workers in agriculture, and lower agricultural labour productivity than countries elsewhere, with no structural shifts observed in these patterns between 1990 and 2010. United Nations projections of rural population growth have been revised upward in recent years, from roughly 1.0 per cent per year based on projections around 2000 to 1.7 per cent per year over the next decade based on the United Nations (2016). Revised projections now indicate that rural sub-Saharan Africa will contain 53 per cent more people in 2050 than it did in 2015 (United Nations, 2016).

These demographic trends are all sensitive to changes in relative employment opportunities in rural versus urban areas and, hence, are potentially influenced by government policy and programmes. Early models attributed rural-urban migration to differences in labour market conditions (specifically expected earnings) between rural and urban areas (Harris & Todaro, 1970), and the search for viable job opportunities continues to be regarded as the major determinant of migration patterns. Access to land for farming and access to employment opportunities are the two most important reasons cited by rural Zambian youth having migrated between 2000 and 2012 according to a nationally representative rural survey (Chamberlin & Ricker-Gilbert, 2016). Potts (2009) observed slowing levels of urbanisation in some parts of Africa partly due to circular migration of people between urban and rural areas in response to growing economic hardship in urban centres. Potts (2013) argues that the cost of low-income housing in urban areas will be a major determinant of the future rate of urbanisation in the region. Therefore, to the extent that national conditions and policies differ across countries, with respect to relative expected earnings and costs of living in urban and rural areas, we would expect to see cross-country differences in sectoral employment trends associated with differential rural/urban population growth patterns.

Table 1 presents the number of working-age individuals in the base year and the year of the most recent nationally representative surveys. Specific survey years are listed on the heading row of Table 1. Several surprises emerge from the data. First, while the conventional view of a rising percentage of the working-age population residing in urban areas is borne out in four of the nine countries examined (Ghana, Kenya, Tanzania, and Zambia), this is not the case in the remaining five countries. In Malawi, the share of the working-age population residing in urban areas rose by less than one percentage point over a 10-year period, whereas in four countries (Mali, Nigeria, Rwanda, and Uganda) the urban share of the working-age population actually declined. In Nigeria, the share of the working-age population in urban areas declined by 6.7 per cent over a nine-year period. Analogously, while the working-age population in urban areas is growing at a faster rate than in rural areas in Ghana, Kenya, Tanzania, and Zambia, the rural work force is growing more rapidly in Nigeria, Uganda, Rwanda, and Mali. This pattern of growth in the rural workforce is also replicated among young people (15–34 years) in Rwanda and Nigeria. And the share of youth population (15–24 years) living in rural areas remains high in all countries examined, ranging from about 50 per cent in Ghana to about 83 per cent in Rwanda. Although urbanisation is expected to continue, it appears that the majority of the youth who may be seeking employment may still be residing in rural areas. We must therefore acknowledge highly variable patterns across sub-Saharan Africa in the pace of urbanisation and rates of expansion of the urban and rural labour force. This conclusion is in accord with Potts (2013), who cautions against overgeneralisation about rapid urbanisation and shifts in the locus of job growth in the region.

Another important observation is the rapid growth rates in the workforce. The workforce in the countries examined is growing on average about 3.2 per cent per year, more rapidly than any other region in the world. A recent flagship report of the World Bank indicates that Africa's demographic transition has been slow (Filmer & Fox, 2014). The region has witnessed significant declines in child mortality and morbidity arising from improvements in the quality and access to health care. Fertility rates, however, remain stubbornly high, with an estimated average of 5.4 children per woman between 2005 and 2010, down from 6.5 children per woman in the 1950s. Comparatively, fertility declined from 5.6 to 1.6 over the same period in East Asia (Canning, Raja, & Yazbeck, 2015). Such high fertility rates hinder the region's ability to reap a demographic dividend. Persistently high fertility rates increase youth dependency, depress private and public savings, and reduce the fiscal space for investments in human capital (education, socio-behavioural skills) required for productive employment (Fox, Senbet, & Simbanegavi, 2016). High fertility rates also expand the numbers of new people seeking employment each year in an already overstretched labour market. Therefore, public actions to support Africa's demographic transition remain an essential component of successful economic transformation in SSA. Reviews show that policy actions that promote girls' education, empower women to have greater control over their fertility decisions, and make reproductive health information and contraceptive methods more accessible are effective strategies to reduce fertility rates (Canning et al., 2015; Upadhyay et al., 2014)

4.2. Employment structure among the working-age population

Structural transformation, which can be defined as the reallocation of economic activity away from less productive sectors of the economy to more productive ones, has long been considered a funda-mental driver of economic development (Barrett, Carter, & Timmer, 2010; Duarte & Restuccia, 2010). Both in theory and actual experiences of now developed countries, movement of labour from low-productivity semi-subsistence agriculture to more productive manufacturing and service sectors has been strongly correlated with overall increases in productivity, living standards and poverty reduction. Countries in the early stages of development almost always have a large share of their labour force in agriculture. Productivity growth in agriculture accumulates additional purchasing power among millions of rural families that generates powerful multiplier effects on the rest of the economy,

Table 1. Trends in the share of working-age individuals (15–64 years) residing in rural versus urban areas

	Ghana	Kenya[a]	Malawi[a]	Mali[a]	Nigeria	Rwanda	Tanzania	Uganda	Zambia
	2006–2013	1999–2009	1998–2008	1998–2009	2004–2013	2006–2011	2009–2015	2006–2012	2005–2012
Total # of working age individuals (15–64) in base year	12,531,725	14,979,080	5,195,510	4,957,820	69,681,783	5,075,138	19,017,377	13,779,475	6,236,683
% of working age in urban area	41.7	28.2	16.0	29.4	45.5	18.2	26.8	20.0	39.6
% of working age in rural area	58.3	71.8	84.0	70.6	54.5	81.8	73.2	80.0	60.4
Total # of working age individuals (15–64) in end year	14,679,955	20,543,290	6,802,300	7,021,500	89,075,132	5,795,397	24,502,093	16,027,014	7,478,049
% of working age in urban area	53.4	36.0	16.7	26.0	38.8	16.2	34.1	19.6	44.6
% of working age in rural area	46.6	64.0	82.5	74.0	61.2	83.8	65.9	80.4	55.4
Annual % change in # of working age individuals from base to end year	2.1	3.7	3.1	3.8	3.1	2.8	4.8	2.3	2.8
Urban	6.3	7.5	3.6	2.3	1.0	0.9	10.6	2.0	5.0
Rural	-0.8	2.2	2.9	4.4	4.8	3.6	2.7	2.4	1.4

Sources: Author's estimates from Ghana Living Standard Survey 5 and 6; Nigeria's Living Standard Survey (2004) and General Household Survey (2013); Rwanda Integrated Household Living Survey (EICV 2 and 3); Tanzania National Panel Survey (2009 and 2015); Uganda National Panel Survey (2006 and 2012); Zambia Labor Force Surveys (2005 and 2012).

Notes: [a]Microdata of population and housing census data in IPUMS.

expanding job opportunities in off-farm sectors and thereby releasing labour to non-farm sectors. Consequently, a reduction in the share of the work force in agriculture has generally been associated with success of the agricultural sector in setting in motion the initial stages of economic transformation through expenditure multipliers. In this section, we examine the extent to which these familiar patterns are playing out in the region.

4.2.1. Sectoral employment trends across Africa. Figure 1 reports trends in employment across industrial sectors in select African countries and China using the Groningen Growth and Development Center (GGDC) Africa Sector Dataset. An important observation from the figure is an increasing trend in the number of people engaged in agriculture[5] in most African countries. Compared to China, where the agricultural labour force peaked around 1990 and has since been declining, each of the African countries examined is still experiencing rising numbers of people involved in agriculture over time (Figure 1). While the share of the labour force engaged in farming is generally declining, farming still remains the single largest employment category. For instance, in 2011, agricultural employment accounted for nearly 40 per cent of total employment in Ghana and 47 per cent in Kenya. In the remaining countries, over 60 per cent of the labour force is in agriculture. The declining share of agricultural employment over time in most countries is consistent with the findings from many previous studies using different datasets (De Vries, Timmer, & De Vries, 2015;

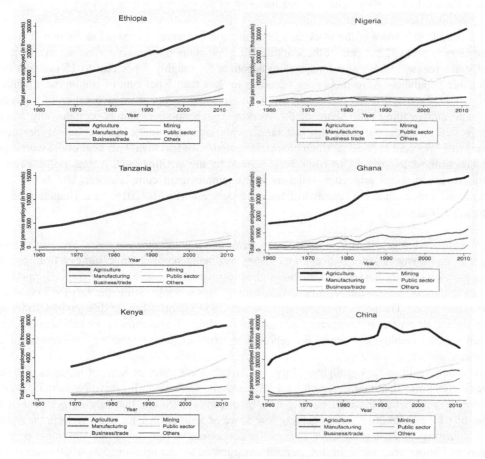

Figure 1. Trends in sectoral employment in various countries.
Source: Authors based on GGDC data.

Proctor & Lucchesi, 2012; Sackey, Liverpool-Tasie, Salau, & Awoyemi, 2012). This decline accelerated post-2000 but with some variations across countries.

For most countries, the declining share of labour in agriculture has been accompanied by higher labour shares in the service-related sectors such as commerce, transport and hospitality, making services the second largest contributor to total employment. The share of jobs in the manufacturing sector has generally either stagnated or declined over time in most countries, with a couple of exceptions such as Kenya and Ethiopia. These results are consistent with Badiane, Ulimwengu, and Badibanga (2012) and McMillan and Harttgen (2014) who found the service sector to be the primary driver of the rapid growth in non-agricultural employment. While growing rapidly in percentage terms, results from the GGDC database shows that growth in employment in each of the non-agricultural sectors has started from a relatively low base with little indication of eclipsing agriculture as the single largest source of employment at least over the next few decades.

4.2.2. Economic activity status of working-age population. The trends observed from the GGDC Africa sector data are broadly consistent with the findings from our micro-level analysis of employment trends. Table 2 presents the share of the working-age population primarily engaged in the various economic activities from the most recent nationally representative household surveys. The results confirm that farming remains the single largest employment activity in all the countries studied. Farming serves as the primary economic activity for over 50 per cent of the workforce in Mali, Rwanda, Tanzania and Uganda. At least a third of the workforce in the remaining countries is also primarily engaged in farming, with the vast majority of people engaged in farming, not surprisingly, residing in rural areas (Table 2).

The second largest share of the working-age population is primarily engaged in the non-farm sector – about 19 per cent to 32 per cent of the working-age population in those countries with available data. The off-farm segment of the agri-food system accounts for roughly 5 per cent to 15 per cent of the working-age population. Agro-processing accounts for less than 5 per cent of employment, while the majority of off-farm agri-food system jobs are in commerce, transport, and preparation of foods away from home and retailing. The share of the working-age population that is economically inactive, primarily due to education, disability and family care activities, range from about 11 per cent in Tanzania to 33 per cent in Nigeria. Unemployment accounts for less than 9 per cent of the working-age population in most countries. This could be explained by the fact that most Africans of working-age have no access to social protection schemes like unemployment compensations and hence cannot afford not to work even if the returns to labour are very low (Fields, 2015; Fox, Haines, Muñoz, & Thomas, 2013).

4.2.3. Sectoral employment shifts among the working-age population over time. We also computed changes in employment patterns over time. Using nationally representative surveys from two time periods for each country (and always including the most recent available survey), Table 3 reports how total jobs in the labour force are apportioned to farming, off-farm jobs within the agri-food system, and the non-farm sector. The off-farm segment of the agri-food sector is further disaggregated into agro-processing and downstream commerce and distribution. Table 3 also shows how different results can be when sectoral employment shares are reported in terms of total number of jobs versus full-time equivalents.

Several new findings are highlighted. First, the employment share of farming in terms of FTEs is almost always lower than that based on total job numbers. In Rwanda for instance, farming accounts for about 67 per cent of the total number of jobs in terms of counts but only 54 per cent of total number of FTE jobs in 2011. The relatively low share of farming in FTE terms reflects the seasonal nature of farming in these economies. Due to the dominance of rain-fed agriculture, most people do not work as farmers year round. In fact, farming is estimated to take up about 500–1000 hours per year whereas most jobs in the off-farm sectors entail more than 2000 hours per year (McCullough, 2015). Hence, in any given year the share of farming jobs declines when weighted by the amount of time allocated to it during the year. Correspondingly, FTE-based employment shares in the off-farm sectors

Table 2. Economic activity status of the working-age population (15–64 years) from most recent nationally representative surveys

		Total working age population (millions)	% of working age population primarily engaged in				
			Farming	Off-farm stages of agri-food system	Non-farm outside agri-food system	Economically inactive	Unemployed
Ghana (2012/13)	Total	**14.3**	**35.6**	**14.3**	**31.8**	**16.0**	**2.3**
	Rural	6.7	62.2	9.6	16.6	10.4	1.1
	Urban	7.6	12.0	18.5	45.2	20.8	3.4
Nigeria (2012/13)	Total	**89.6**	**27.3**	**13.3**	**24.2**	**33.1**	**2.1**
	Rural	54.3	40.9	11.7	14.5	31.9	1.0
	Urban	35.3	6.4	15.8	39.0	35.1	3.7
Rwanda (2010/11)	Total	**5.8**	**55.4**	**5.0**	**21.2**	**17.7**	**0.8**
	Rural	4.8	61.6	4.4	16.7	17.1	0.2
	Urban	1.0	23.0	8.2	44.3	20.7	3.7
Tanzania (2014/15)	Total	**24.5**	**52.4**	**11.1**	**23.3**	**10.9**	**2.3**
	Rural	16.2	70.3	7.7	14.9	6.3	0.7
	Urban	8.4	16.6	17.8	40.1	19.9	5.5
Uganda (2011/12)	Total	**14.2**	**59.7**	**6.3**	**18.5**	**15.5**	**0.0**
	Rural	11.4	67.5	5.2	14.8	12.5	0.0
	Urban	2.8	27.6	10.5	33.9	27.9	0.1
Zambia (2012)	Total	**7.5**	**42.5**	**4.5**	**23.4**	**23.6**	**6.1**
	Rural	4.1	63.4	2.5	11.4	20.1	2.7
	Urban	3.3	16.5	7.1	38.2	28.0	10.2
Kenya (2009)[a]	Total	20.5	31.6	37.7		23.3	7.4
	Rural	13.2	43.0	27.7		23.3	6.1
	Urban	7.4	11.3	55.5		23.4	9.7
Malawi (2008)[a]	Total	3.3	32.4	27.8		24.7	8.6
	Rural	2.7	36.5	21.8		25.0	9.4
	Urban	0.6	14.0	55.1		23.3	5.1
Mali (2009)[a]	Total	**3.4**	**49.7**	**27.8**		**20.0**	**2.4**
	Rural	2.5	64.5	16.0		16.8	1.7
	Urban	0.9	10.7	59.0		27.0	3.3

Notes: [a]Data do not permit disaggregation of off-farm into within and outside the agri-food system. Microdata of population and housing census data in IPUMS.
Reference period of employment for Zambia is previous seven days.
Source: Author's estimates from Ghana Living Standard Survey 6; Nigeria's General Household Survey (2013); Rwanda Integrated Household Living Survey (EICV 3); Tanzania National Panel Survey (2015); Uganda National Panel Survey (2012); Zambia Labor Force Surveys (2012).

are relatively high. Nevertheless, the employment *trends* based on FTEs are remarkably similar to that based on total job numbers (Table 3).

Second, the results reveal a rapid exit of labour from farming to off-farm employment, signifying fundamental economic transformation in the region. The rate of labour exit from farming is more pronounced when job shares are computed in FTE terms. The decline in farming's employment share is at least one percentage point per year more in FTE terms than in terms of total job counts or primary jobs. This leads us to conclude that estimates based on counts could potentially mask the pace of the economic transformation underway in the region.

Moreover, the pace at which labour is transitioning out of farming varies substantially across countries. It might be useful to categorise African countries' structural transformation trajectories into three types: The first category comprises countries where the absolute number of people employed in farming is still increasing but the share of the workforce engaged in farming is declining over time, largely due to more rapid growth in the share of off-farm employment. Most African countries fall in this category including Ghana, Kenya, Rwanda, Mali, Tanzania, and Uganda (Table 3). For instance,

Table 3. Proportion of labour force in farming, off-farm agri-food systems, and non-farm activities among working-age population (15–64 years)

Country	Survey years	Total # of jobs in millions	Farming % of jobs	Farming % of FTE jobs	Agro-processing % of jobs	Agro-processing % of FTE jobs	Downstream commerce and distribution % of jobs	Downstream commerce and distribution % of FTE jobs	Non-farm outside AFS % of jobs	Non-farm outside AFS % of FTE jobs
Ghana	2005/06	10.1	52.1	43.5	7.5	6.3	7.1	8.6	33.3	41.6
	2012/13	13.9	43.6	34.3	3.7	3.7	13.8	15.5	38.9	46.5
Nigeria	2003/04	34.6	25.7	21.8	1.3	1.4	2.9	3.3	70.2	73.5
	2012/13	69.7	42.1	33.7	4.8	4.6	16.2	18.6	36.9	43.1
Rwanda	2005/06	6.1	75.2	65.7	0.4	0.4	6.5	7.4	18.0	26.6
	2010/11	9.1	67.4	54.0	1.1	1.2	5.7	7.7	25.9	37.0
Tanzania	2008/09	18.2	70.4	60.8	1.4	1.7	3.6	4.5	24.7	32.9
	2014/15	21.4	59.8	49.1	0.9	1.2	11.8	14.1	27.5	35.6
Uganda	2005/06	10.8	72.6	57.0	2.1	2.8	5.7	10.2	19.6	30.0
	2011/12	15.9	67.1	48.1	2.8	3.3	6.6	12.3	23.5	36.3
Zambia	2005	4.7	73.8	61.2	1.2	1.6	1.9	3.1	23.1	34.1
	2012	5.3	60.4	46.7	1.6	2.1	4.9	7.1	33.2	44.1
Kenya[a]	1999	11.1	54.4	-			45.6			
	2009	14.2	45.6	-			54.4			
Malawi[a]	1998	1.9	73.3	-			26.7			
	2008	2.0	53.9	-			46.1			
Mali[a]	1998	2.0	79.6	-			20.4			
	2009	2.6	64.2	-			35.8			

Notes: [a]IPUMS data do not have time use information so FTE could not be computed, nor could this data permit disaggregation into off-farm employment within versus outside of the agri-food system (*AFS represents the agri-food system*). Microdata of population and housing census data in IPUMS.
Source: Author's estimates from Ghana Living Standard Survey 5 and 6; Nigeria's Living Standard Survey (2004) and General Household Survey (2013); Rwanda Integrated Household Living Survey (EICV 2 and 3); Tanzania National Panel Survey (2009 and 2015); Uganda National Panel Survey (2006 and 2012); Zambia Labor Force Surveys (2005 and 2012).

Rwanda experienced a decline of about eight percentage points (11 in FTE) in farming's share of total jobs between 2006 and 2011. Ghana and Uganda recorded declines of about nine and six percentage points in the share of the workforce in farming over a seven-year period. See Table A1 in the Appendix for estimates of sectoral employment growth rates. The second category includes countries where both the shares and absolute number of the workforce engaged in farming are declining over time, as in Malawi and Zambia. The third category consists of countries where both the share of jobs and number of the growing workforce engaged in farming is rising, which probably reflects temporary and somewhat unique causes rather than a departure from the historical structural transformation process. In these countries, the workforce appears to be engaging in farming at a faster rate than the rate at which their population is growing and the rate of job creation in the off-farm sectors. An example is Nigeria, which experienced a 12 percentage point increase in farming's employment share between 2004 and 2013. Other studies using different data sets have also observed similar employment trends in Nigeria (McMillan & Harttgen, 2014). A steady growth in the oil sector in the 1960s and subsequent oil boom in the 1970s in Nigeria drew labour away from agriculture primarily into service-related sectors of the economy. Recent declines in world oil prices and Nigeria's specific oil sector problems over the past decade may have driven much of the labour reallocation towards agriculture as observed here. Sackey et al. (2012) also highlights the increased public investment in agriculture, particularly in Nigeria's rural areas in the 2000s, as part of efforts to stem rural-urban migration. The

Federal Government of Nigeria through its Agricultural Transformation Agenda sought to create 3.5 million jobs in agriculture for youth and women through direct investment in farming and agribusiness (Adesugba & Mavrotas, 2016). It is possible that these renewed public investments in the agricultural sector following decades of neglect under an oil-sector-driven economy might have contributed to temporary labour entry into farming in Nigeria.

A third finding highlighted by Table 3 is the rapid percentage growth in employment shares in the off-farm sectors both within the agri-food system and the non-farm sector. In most countries, the number of the working-age population employed in these off-farm sectors grew at least about three times faster than the rate of growth in the working-age population (see Table A1). However, the off-farm segments of the agri-food system, particularly agro-processing, are growing from a low base. For those countries where it was possible to measure employment in the off-farm segment of the agri-food system, these jobs currently account for less than 20 per cent of the total number of jobs and between 9 per cent to 23 per cent in FTE terms. Comparatively, between 24–39 per cent of the total number of jobs and 35–47 per cent of all FTE jobs come from the non-farm sector.

Fourth, the agri-food system dominates employment in the region, contributing about 61–77 per cent (54%–66% in FTE terms) of all jobs. Most of the jobs in the agri-food system are still in farming and not in the other segments of the agri-food value chain. Farming accounts for 67–91 per cent (60%–86% in FTE terms) of all jobs within the agri-food system. In every country, farming accounts for a greater share of the jobs than the off-farm segment of the agri-food system, about four to 10 times more in share of jobs in Rwanda, Uganda, Tanzania and Zambia and about twice as many in Nigeria and Ghana.

A further examination of the composition of the jobs in the off-farm segment of the agri-food system reveals the bulk of the jobs in this sector are concentrated in downstream commerce, food transportation, and distribution. Perhaps surprisingly, less than 5 per cent of the labour force is engaged in agro-processing, in terms of either FTE or total number of jobs, in any of the countries where employment data is sufficiently disaggregated to assess this issue. By contrast, downstream commerce and distribution accounted for 22 per cent of total jobs and 26 per cent of FTE jobs, on average. Moreover, the rate of growth in the share of jobs from agro-processing is highly variable: rising over time in Nigeria, Rwanda and Zambia, but declining somewhat in Ghana and Tanzania. Especially considering economies of scale in agro-processing and the likelihood of consolidation and more capital-intensive forms of processing in the future, it is our view that agro-processing may not employ more than 5 per cent of the work force in most African countries as their economic transformation process unfolds, even with continued growth in the broader agri-food systems.

Fifth, the rate of increase in farm-based self-employment is particularly pronounced in urban areas, where it is generally rising more rapidly than growth in the working-age population (for example, Ghana, Rwanda, Nigeria, Zambia, Tanzania and Kenya). To some extent, this may partly be influenced by reclassification of localities from rural to urban once a threshold number of households is exceeded. It may also reflect an increasing engagement of urban dwellers in farming either as a strategy to cope with rising food insecurity and/or cost of living in African cities or as an investment. Moyo (2015) describes how urban farming is mushrooming in African cities and towns with an associated scramble for unoccupied land in urban and peri-urban areas for food crop and/or livestock production. Jayne et al. (2016) also show that urban households control 15–45 per cent of the land on farms over 20 hectares in size, suggesting a growing proportion of urban-based *investor farmers* in many African countries. In fact, in Kenya, Nigeria, Tanzania and Uganda, the fastest growth in farming employment for urban based individuals is among the oldest age categories (45–54 and 55–64 years of age), who perhaps may be entering farming as a means of earning additional livelihood after retirement. The growing engagement of urban dwellers in farming is also confirmed in other studies using different data sets (McMillan & Harttgen, 2014). Nonetheless, the rate of job growth in farming in urban areas is starting from a very low base relative to rural areas where growth rates in employment in farming is generally slower than the rate at which the working-age population is growing.

Sixth, off-farm employment within the agri-food system and in the non-farm sector is generally growing more rapidly in rural areas than urban areas, albeit from a low base as well (see Table A1 in the Appendix). This may suggest rural dynamism and growth linkages between farming and off-farm activities. It may also indicate that the region has been, at least for the past decade or two, considerably more economically diversified than conventional estimates have suggested.

Seventh, the proportion of the working-age population that is considered economically inactive has risen over the past decade or two, and may continue to do so. Economic inactivity is particularly prevalent among the youth (15–24 years) due to increasing enrolment in school. Globalisation and technology is creating an economy that demands a more educated workforce to be competitive and young Africans appear to be responding to this demand by staying longer in school. While the share of the working-age population who are economically inactive is greater in urban areas than in rural areas, economic inactivity is rising most rapidly in rural areas (see Table A1).

Eighth, unemployment among the working-age population is generally rising, often rapidly. In Zambia, Rwanda, and Malawi, unemployment among the working-age population is growing at about 10 times the growth in the working-age population. Moderate growth rates are recorded in Mali, Kenya, and Nigeria while declines in share of working-age population unemployed are observed in Ghana, Tanzania, and Uganda. The share of the working-age population who are unemployed is generally lower in rural areas than urban settings. The fastest growth in rural unemployment is witnessed in Zambia, Malawi, and Rwanda – countries that also happen to be experiencing the greatest declines in the share of the rural workforce engaged in farming. Comparatively, the rise in farming's share of jobs in Nigeria has been associated with a significant decline in unemployment among the working-age population in rural areas. While no causal interpretation can be inferred, the rise of unemployment amidst rapid declines in the share of the work force in farming may deserve more detailed study.

A major threat to job growth in African agri-food systems is the region's rising dependence on food imports (Rakotoarisoa, Iafrate, & Paschali, 2011). Sub-Saharan Africa's food import bill has risen from US$6 billion in 2001 to US$45 billion in 2014 – a seven-fold increase in 13 years. The value ratio of food imports to agricultural output for the region has also been steadily rising since 2000, from 9.2 per cent in 2001 to 24.1 per cent in 2014 (FAO, 2017; United Nations, 2017). Net trade statistics for the region show that food grain and oilseed imports are driving sub-Saharan Africa's rising food deficits, which fundamentally reflect the region's inability to increase local food production fast enough over the past three decades to keep up with its rapidly growing population and rising income-related growth in food demand (Figure 2). Food imports can still contribute to job growth in food distribution, retailing, restaurants, and some types of processing. However, to the extent that imports crowd out local food production, it is likely that local jobs will be lost in farming, the supply of agro-inputs and equipment, services and finance to farmers, aggregation, wholesaling, transport, storage, insurance, and many other types of jobs created by local agricultural production.

A recent FAO report also identifies bottlenecks underlying the slower transformation in the agro-processing sector in Africa (Hollinger & Staatz, 2015). The report highlights the dualistic nature of the agro-processing sector, which is largely comprised of large industrial processors and small-scale informal processors. Its noted that growth among the more dynamic large-scale industrial processors is usually impeded by a general lack of a reliable supply of local raw materials of consistent quality. As a result, these large industrial operators often rely on imported food inputs. A large part of processing of domestically produced food products (especially those based on domestic staples) is still in the hands of the relatively less efficient, small-scale and largely informal-sector operators, characterised by low capacity utilisation rates and low productivity levels. Their activities are also seasonal, and often generate outputs of variable quality, limiting their entry into emerging urban food distribution systems (Hollinger & Staatz, 2015). Addressing the capacity and productivity constraints to growth in the agro-processing sector is critical to expanding job opportunities in the broader agri-food system. Nonetheless, greater local farm production is required to ensure an adequate supply of

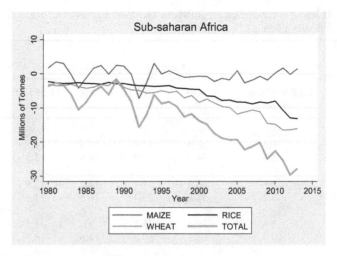

Figure 2. Trends in net grain exports by sub-Saharan Africa.
Source: Authors based on FAO 2015 data.

raw material for local processors, and, more importantly, to generate greater job growth at all stages of the agri-food system that are currently being inhibited by imports. For these reasons, farm productivity growth remains a crucial source of economy-wide multiplier effects (Johnston & Kilby, 1975; Lipton, 2005; Mellor, 1976) and is therefore a central component of an effective employment policy in virtually all African countries.

4.3. Employment structure among the youth

Africa is a youthful continent. Young people within the 15–24 year age bracket comprise between 35 per cent and 40 per cent of the workforce in the various countries examined. An additional one-fourth of the work force is contained in the 25–34 age bracket. Ensuring gainful opportunities for young people has therefore become a major policy priority in the region. This section explores labour force dynamics among Africa's young people.

The United Nations defines youth as individuals between the ages of 15–24 years, while the African Union uses the 15–35 year range. To accommodate these two definitions of youth, we classify our youth population into two categories: individuals aged 15–24 years, whom we refer to as the 'youth' in the traditional sense, and individuals aged 25–34 years, hereafter referred to as 'young adults'. Considering that the majority of individuals within the 15–24 year age bracket still reside with their parents or remain dependent on their parents for their sustenance (Bezu & Holden, 2014), their current employment situation would at least partially reflect their parents' family labour allocation decisions. The 'young adult' category, by contrast, is more likely to reflect the decisions of more independent young adults.

Our analysis indicates that the employment structure among young people generally mirrors that of the entire working-age population (Table 4). This is not surprising because the youth and young adults account for such a large fraction of the total labour force. We find that farming remains the single largest source of employment among young people, despite its declining employment share. The share of youth in farming in the latest available surveys ranges from 39.9 per cent in Ghana to 63.2 per cent in Tanzania. Non-farm jobs also account for a large share of FTE youth jobs, between 26.9 per cent in Tanzania to 56.8 per cent in Ghana. The off-farm segments of the food system accounted for between 7.8 per cent of FTE jobs for youth in Zambia, up to 17.8 per cent in Ghana.

As young Africans leave home or leave school and enter more fully into the work force, they tend to reduce their engagement in farming. A clear pattern in Table 4 is the decline in the per cent of FTE jobs in farming, and an increased engagement in both non-farm and off-farm agri-food system jobs as

Table 4. Proportion of labour force in farming, off-farm agri-food systems, and non-farm activities among the youth (15–24 years) and young adults (25–34 years)

Country	Age category	Total # of jobs in millions	Farming % of jobs	Farming % of FTE jobs	Off-farm within AFS % of jobs	Off-farm within AFS % of FTE jobs	Non-farm outside AFS % of jobs	Non-farm outside AFS % of FTE jobs
Ghana	15–24							
	2005/06	1.8	58.0	47.9	11.8	11.9	30.2	40.2
	2012/13	2.9	54.5	39.9	14.6	15.5	30.9	44.6
	25–34							
	2010/11	2.8	46.2	37.4	14.2	13.8	39.6	48.8
	2012/13	3.2	31.8	25.4	16.5	17.8	51.7	56.8
Nigeria	15–24							
	2003/04	3.6	30.4	25.2	3.0	4.5	66.6	70.2
	2012/13	10.9	61.1	50.8	14.6	16.7	24.4	32.5
	25–34							
	2003/04	8.3	23.1	20.1	4.8	5.2	72.2	74.8
	2012/13	16.0	33.4	26.2	23.6	24.5	43.0	49.3
Rwanda	15–24							
	2005/06	2.0	76.0	65.3	6.0	6.3	17.9	28.4
	2010/11	2.4	65.1	50.0	7.0	8.2	27.9	41.7
	25–34							
	2005/06	1.6	70.7	59.3	8.3	10.3	21.0	30.4
	2010/11	2.9	64.1	49.0	7.8	11.4	28.0	39.6
Tanzania	15–24							
	2008/09	4.1	78.0	70.1	3.8	5.0	18.2	24.9
	2014/15	6.4	72.3	63.2	8.5	10.0	19.2	26.9
	25–34							
	2008/09	5.4	64.0	52.6	6	7.9	30.0	39.5
	2014/15	5.9	50.6	35.7	14.6	20.1	34.8	44.2
Uganda	15–24							
	2005/06	3.6	81.2	65.5	5.7	11.4	13.1	23.1
	2011/12	5.5	75.5	53.5	5.7	13.5	18.8	33.0
	25–34							
	2005/06	3.1	62.9	48.3	10.2	14.8	26.9	36.9
	2011/12	4.1	57.6	40.0	13.1	18.7	29.2	41.3
Zambia	15–24							
	2005	1.6	84.5	75.9	2.4	3.8	13.2	20.3
	2012	1.4	70.3	56.3	4.7	7.8	24.9	35.9
	25–34							
	2005	1.4	64.6	49.7	4.0	6.0	31.4	44.4
	2012	1.7	53.9	41.1	7.0	9.5	39.1	49.4

Source: Author's estimates from Ghana Living Standard Survey 5 and 6; Nigeria's Living Standard Survey (2004) and General Household Survey (2013); Rwanda Integrated Household Living Survey (EICV 2 and 3); Tanzania National Panel Survey (2009 and 2015); Uganda National Panel Survey (2006 and 2012); Zambia Labor Force Surveys (2005 and 2012)

youth move into young adulthood (25–34 years of age). It is also noteworthy that the percentage of FTE jobs in farming among young adults has declined quite rapidly between the initial and most recent survey years. With the exception of Nigeria, the share of farming in FTE jobs declined by eight to 13 percentage points within a five to eight year period.

A major difference between young people and the rest of the working-age population is the extent to which they are economically inactive. Economic inactivity among the youth (15–24 years) ranges from 23 per cent in Tanzania to 63 per cent in Nigeria, primarily due to pursuit in advanced education and training, and secondarily because of child rearing in the case of women. Indeed, 92 per cent of the youth determined as economically inactive in Rwanda in 2011 were full-time students.[6] Similarly, about 79 per cent and 58 per cent of the work force was economically inactive in the latest survey in Ghana and Zambia respectively. This trend is consistent with global labour participation rates among the youth (15–24 years), which declined from 59 per cent to 47.3 per cent between 1991 and 2014 primarily because of increased enrolment in school (ILO, 2015). As Filmer and Fox (2014) note, African youth entering the labour force now have more schooling than previous generations, although they also note a declining quality of education in many countries. Assuming the education these students are receiving is valuable, the increased inactivity among the youth could mean a more educated, competitive, and productive labour force in the next several decades.

4.4. Age distribution of farmers

The farming population around the world is aging, with some reports estimating that average farmer age is roughly 60 years of age (Gorman, 2013; Vos, 2015). Based on these trends, some analysts argue that global food production may be in jeopardy unless more young people can be attracted into farming (Jöhr, 2012). Some recent reports also suggest the farming population in SSA is following these global trends. However, an examination of the age distribution of individuals engaged in farming in some African countries reveals a very different picture.

First, based on the most recent available data for our nine study countries, we find the mean age of individuals aged 15 years or more engaged in farming ranges from 34 years in Uganda to about 42 years in Nigeria (Table 5). Unlike other regions, average farmer age in most of the SSA countries

Table 5. Mean age of individuals engaged in farming

Country	Survey years	Individuals aged 15 years or more engaged in farming			Individuals aged 15 years or more with at least 50 per cent FTE in farming			Individuals aged 25 years or more with at least 50 per cent FTE in farming		
		Total	Males	Females	Total	Males	Females	Total	Males	Females
Ghana	2005/06	**40**	40	40	**40**	40	40	**44**	44	43
	2012/13	**39**	38	39	**42**	42	41	**45**	46	44
Nigeria	2003/04	**43**	44	41	**43**	44	42	**46**	47	45
	2012/13	**42**	42	42	**43**	44	42	**48**	49	46
Rwanda	2005/06	**35**	35	35	**35**	35	35	**42**	42	42
	2010/11	**37**	36	38	**37**	37	38	**42**	42	42
Tanzania	2008/09	**39**	39	38	**39**	39	39	**44**	44	44
	2014/15	**36**	35	36	**36**	36	37	**44**	45	44
Uganda	2005/06	**34**	34	34	**34**	35	34	**41**	41	40
	2011/12	**34**	34	35	**35**	34	36	**41**	41	42
Zambia	2005	**33**	33	34	**34**	34	33	**42**	42	41
	2012	**35**	37	34	**36**	38	35	**42**	42	41
Kenya[a]	1999	**35**	35	35	-	-	-	-	-	-
	2009	**37**	38	37	-	-	-	-	-	-
Malawi[a]	1998	**37**	38	36	-	-	-	-	-	-
	2008	**37**	37	37	-	-	-	-	-	-
Mali[a]	1998	**35**	36	33	-	-	-	-	-	-
	2009	**35**	36	33	-	-	-	-	-	-

Notes: [a]Data do not have time use information so FTE could not be computed. Microdata of population and housing census data in IPUMS.
Sources: Author's estimates from Ghana Living Standard Survey 5 and 6; Nigeria's Living Standard Survey (2004) and General Household Survey (2013); Rwanda Integrated Household Living Survey (EICV 2 and 3); Tanzania National Panel Survey (2009 and 2015); Uganda National Panel Survey (2006 and 2012); Zambia Labor Force Surveys (2005 and 2012).

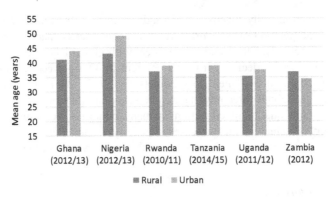

Figure 3. Mean age of individuals aged 15 years or more who are engaged at least 50 per cent of a full-time work equivalent in farming.

examined has either declined slightly or remained stable over time. Only three out of the nine study countries experienced a slight increase in the mean age of farmers over 15 years of age. Even when restricting the sample to individuals over 25 years of age who spend at least half of a full-time equivalence in farming, the picture is mixed, with two countries showing a slight increase over time in mean age and the other four holding steady. Even for this sub-population, the mean age of farmers from the most recently available survey ranges from 41 years in Uganda to 48 years in Nigeria (Table 5). The average age for this sub-population ranges from 36 years to 42 when the lower bound is extended to include the youth (15–24 years) with at least 50 per cent FTE in farming. The upward pressure on the average age of the farmer population is ironically coming from urban areas. In most countries examined, the mean age of farmers is at least several years older in urban areas than in rural areas (Figure 3). This may perhaps reflect the rising number of investor (retiree) farmers based in urban areas (Jayne et al., 2016).

Although a large number of rural youth are leaving farming, a significant proportion of the rapidly growing youth population is still engaged in farming, which is putting downward pressure on the average age of the farming population. SSA may, therefore, not yet be at risk of problems arising from an aging farmer population. However, it is indeed the case that the age distribution of individuals in non-farm jobs is younger than those in farming. The extent to which young people remain in farming will depend on the future return to labour from farming, which will in turn depend on agricultural policies and programmes influencing adoption of new technologies and access to markets. Youth access to finance and land, especially in increasingly densely populated rural areas, may be particularly important future determinants of youth engagement in farming, and hence the age distribution of farmers (Allen et al., 2016).

4.5. Trends in public versus private sector wage employment versus self-employment

While addressing unemployment remains critical, the overriding challenge in many developing countries is how to create more remunerative jobs (Fields, 2015). As countries transform their economies, the importance of self-employment in the labour market is likely to decline over time (La Porta & Shleifer, 2014; Yamada, 1996). A slowing workforce growth rate following demographic transition, and rapid growth in registered firms during the development process, combine to increase the availability of wage/salary employment and eventually make wage jobs a dominant form of livelihood. Here we examine the extent to which the relative share of self-employment is declining as part of the ongoing economic transformation in the region.

Table 6 presents the share of self-employment/unpaid family labour and wage/salary employment over time. The self-employment/unpaid family labour category consist of three types of workers: (i) own account workers (persons operating their own economic enterprises without employees); (ii) employers (persons operating their own economic enterprises with employees); and (iii) unpaid family

Table 6. Types of employment over time

Countries	% of employment		
	Wage/salary		
	Public	Private	Self-employed/unpaid family labour
Ghana			
2005/06	5.7	11.9	82.4
2012/13	5.9	16.6	77.5
Nigeria			
2003/04	6.57	3.28	90.2
2012/13	4.41	6.99	88.6
Rwanda			
2005/06	3.2	20.4	86.6
2010/11	3.6	28.4	77.8
Tanzania			
2008/09	2.5	17.4	80.1
2014/15	3.4	31.8	64.8
Uganda			
2005/06	2.7	17.4	79.9
2011/12	3.9	14.8	81.3
Zambia			
2005/06	3.3	3.5	93.3
2011/12	5.3	6.5	88.2
Malawi[a]			
1998	14.1		85.9
2008	21.6		78.4
Mali[a]			
1998	5.7		84.2
2009	4.5		85.9

Source: Author's estimates from Ghana Living Standard Survey 5 and 6; Nigeria's Living Standard Survey (2004) and General Household Survey (2013); Rwanda Integrated Household Living Survey (EICV 2 and 3); Tanzania National Panel Survey (2009 and 2015); Uganda National Panel Survey (2006 and 2012); Zambia Labor Force Surveys (2005 and 2012).
Notes: [a]Microdata of population and housing census data in IPUMS.

workers (persons working without pay in an economic enterprise operated by a household member). We combine these three groups here as most available data did not permit disaggregation at this level. The share of own account workers and unpaid family workers in total employment is suggestive of the level of *vulnerable* employment in the labour market (ILO, 1993). The wage employment category includes persons working for a public or private employer and receiving remuneration in wages/salary or in kind. Wage employment is further disaggregated between the public and private sector. Note that wage employment includes both formal wage (where employee has a contract and may be entitled to social security) and informal wage employment. The two types of wage employment are grouped together here, as most datasets do not allow consistent disaggregation of wage employment at this level. Fox and Thomas (2016) estimates about half of all wage workers in SSA to be in non-contract jobs often referred to as informal employment. Similarly, in a recent report on Africa's economic transformation, ACET (2014) noted that the share of formal employment in the labour force in most African economies for which data were available, is seldom above 25 per cent.

As shown in Table 6, self-employment, including unpaid family labour, accounts for over 75 per cent of total employment, highlighting the level of informality of the labour market. Farming is the largest source of self-employment, constituting between 46 per cent (Nigeria) and 65 per cent (Rwanda) of all self-employment jobs, followed by the non-farm sectors (30%–35%). More strikingly, further analysis revealed that those engaged in unpaid or family labour constitute about 25–40 per cent of total employment and about 33–47 per cent of all self-employment jobs for those countries with available data. Nearly 90 per cent of all unpaid family labour jobs are in farming. The youth (15–24 years) are more likely than any other age group to engage in unpaid jobs or family labour. From the most recent surveys, about 43 per cent of all unpaid jobs or family labour in Rwanda, 50.8 per cent in Nigeria, and 63 per cent in Tanzania and Ghana were held by the youth (15–24 years). Individuals in the 15–24-year age range who are active in the labour force are typically out-of-school, and often lack significant employable skills, experience, and connections to secure employment, especially in the formal wage sector. Their job prospects are thus often restricted to farming and informal enterprises, which are associated with low skill requirements, low entry barriers, and hence generally low returns to labour. The high proportion of young people in such low-quality work may therefore be reflective of the labour-market entry difficulties young people face.

The data in Table 6 also suggest that self-employment will remain a key feature of African labour markets for at least the next several decades. Most of the observed wage job growth is being accounted for by the private sector. Indeed, in Ghana, Rwanda, Zambia and Malawi, wage employment is growing at nearly three times the rate of growth in self-employment. This is very encouraging, but we must keep in mind that this rapid growth is starting from a very low base and thus translates into a relatively small number of jobs each year. As a result, the share of wage jobs in total employment remains low in most countries, typically less than 30 per cent. The massive importance of self-employment jobs in these economies indicates that the share of self-employment in total employment will not differ greatly from the figures shown in Table 6 for at least the next decade.

In fact, a recent analysis suggests the share of wage/salary employment in total employment in SSA grew only slightly from 25 per cent to 28 per cent between 2000 and 2014 despite the number of wage/salaried jobs increasing by roughly 70 per cent during this period. Vulnerable employment, comprising self-employment and unpaid/family labour constituted the majority of the jobs created during the period (Ulimwengu, Collins, Yeboah, & Traub, 2016). The low share of wage employment is partly explained by the general slow growth in wage employment in the public sector, which has historically been the predominant source of wage/salaried employment. According to Aryeetey, Baah-Boateng, Ackah, Lehrer, and Mbiti (2014), most African countries have witnessed a shedding of public sector wage jobs since the 1990s owing to policies aimed at reducing the government wage bill. Rapid economic growth in some African countries has also contributed to the expansion of private sector jobs. Consequently, the private sector accounts for a growing share of wage jobs. As shown in Table 6, the share of private sector wage jobs in total employment is at least three times that of public sector wage jobs in Ghana, Tanzania, Uganda, and Rwanda. The non-farm sector is the main source of wage employment, contributing over 85 per cent and 60 per cent of the public and private sector wage jobs respectively.

These positive signs notwithstanding, self-employment enterprises including farming will remain an important pathway to employing a large share of the workforce. The persistence of low-productivity and low-quality jobs among the working-age population raises questions about the appropriateness of the widely-used ILO definition of unemployment as a measure of joblessness in sub-Saharan Africa. Poverty and lack of social protection for the unemployed often forces Africans to work in some fashion, even if under poor conditions and at very low returns to labour, in order to support themselves. By virtue of their engagement in these low quality economic activities, such individuals are often excluded from the account of joblessness as per ILO standards. As a result, they may be excluded from policy interventions aimed at combating joblessness. Expanding the definition of joblessness to cover the quality of employment and underemployment would provide a better picture of the extent of the employment challenge facing sub-Saharan Africa.

5. Relationship between employment structure and agricultural productivity growth

Agricultural productivity growth has historically been an important driver of economic transformation, and for this reason it might have something to do with why the labour force has rapidly shifted out of farming in many African countries. In fact, sustained agricultural productivity growth in most currently industrialised countries created the demand for, and enabled labour to be pulled into, better paying non-farm jobs. As this process continued, incomes rose relative to the cost of food, resulting in major improvements in food security and living standards (Johnston & Mellor, 1961; Lipton, 2005; Mellor, 1976).

To examine the extent to which lagged agricultural productivity growth has influenced the employ-ment shifts documented in this study, we estimate a set of descriptive models examining the pace of labour exit from farming. First, we explore the bivariate relationship by computing the change in farming's employment shares between the available survey years for the countries in our analysis and pairing them with average annual agricultural total factor productivity growth over the comparable period.[7] Figure 4 suggests that agricultural productivity growth is correlated with the pace of labour exit from farming over the past decade. In addition, countries achieving the highest rates of agricul-tural productivity growth (over two distinct periods since 2000) also tended to have relatively high labour productivity growth rates in the off-farm sectors of the economy (Figure 5).

We explore these relationships in more depth by conducting a time series multivariate analysis using annual data on 11 African countries over the 1995–2011 period from the *Africa Sector Dataset*.[8] Our model controls for factors that could plausibly influence agricultural employment shares including population density, country-level governance indicators, road density (tarmac roads per 100 km^2 of land) as a proxy for market access conditions, a time trend, and country fixed effects to control for unobserved time-constant heterogeneity. Indicators of governance were obtained from the Worldwide Governance Indicator database, 2015 Update (1996–2014). Labour productivity in agriculture was computed as the ratio of gross value added in constant 2005 prices in US dollars to the number of persons engaged in agriculture, while labour productivity in the non-agriculture sector was the weighted average of productivities from all non-agricultural sectors. To ensure confidence about the direction of causality, the variables for labour productivity in agriculture and non-agriculture sectors as well as governance variables were computed as lagged moving averages over the five years prior to the year of the dependent variable, the share of employment in farming. Varying the time lag period

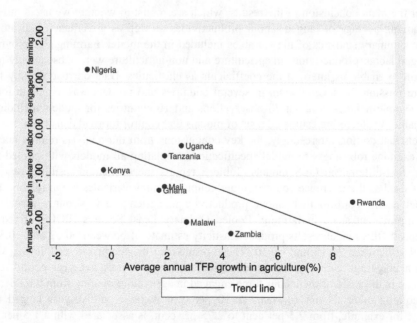

Figure 4. Relationship between total factor productivity growth and change in share of labour force engaged in farming.
Source: Authors. Mean annual agricultural TFP growth rates for 2003–2012 from USDA TFP dataset (Fuglie, 2015); Spearman Correlation coefficient = −0.6862, prob > |t| = 0.0412.

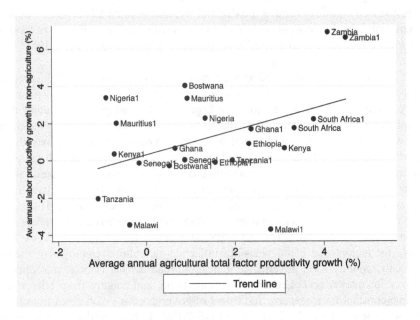

Figure 5. Relationship between total factor productivity growth and labour productivity in non-agricultural sector. *Source*: Authors Agricultural total factor productivity growth rates derived from USDA TFP dataset (Fuglie, 2015) and computed as mean annual rates over 2001–2005 and 2006–2011 periods; labour productivity growth rates (mean annual rates over 2001–2005 and 2006–2011 period) derived from Groningen Global Development Centre employment.*Notes*: Two points are shown for each country; the latter period (2006–2011) for each country is denoted with '1' (for example, Malawi1 represents Malawi 2006–2011).Spearman Correlation coefficient = 0.3721, rob > |t| = 0.0881.

did not alter the main conclusion of the results, which are robust to whether we use a three-, four- or five-year moving average of lagged labour productivities as well as governance indicators. Table 7 presents the summary statistics of the variables included in the model. Farming's employment shares and the lagged labour productivities in agriculture and non-agriculture were subsequently transformed into log form to enable us interpret the coefficients as elasticities. Data on road density for on road density were missing for several years in several countries and no data was available for Tanzania. Hence, the sample reduces to about 78 observations and 10 countries for models including the road density variable. We therefore estimated a set of models that control for road density, and an analogous set of models that do not. Interestingly, the key conclusions from our analysis remain unchanged.

We also examine robustness to model specification, estimating all models with pooled OLS, fixed effects, and first-differenced OLS models. Table 8 reports the estimation results. For each model, Nigeria was used as the reference country (other country dummy variables are in relation to Nigeria).

All model results confirm that labour productivity in agriculture is strongly associated with a declining employment share in farming. Pooled Ordinary Least Squares (POLS), fixed effect and first differenced OLS model results produce elasticity estimate of between −0.02 and −0.30, with the majority being between −0.15 and −0.30. These results can be interpreted as follows: a 1 per cent increase in average agriculture labour productivity over the previous five-year period results in an annual decline in the share of the labour force engaged in agriculture ranging from 0.02 per cent to 0.3 per cent, holding other factors constant. A 10 per cent increase in five-year lagged agricultural productivity, for example, from 2.5 per cent to 2.75 per cent, is associated with a 1.5 per cent to 3.0 per cent reduction in the share of the labour force in farming.

Most other covariates in the model are only occasionally related to the rate of labour exit from agriculture. The coefficient on logged and lagged index of governance is significantly negative in some models, indicating that better governance may be associated with a more rapid transition of the labour force out of farming. Lagged labour productivity in the non-agriculture sector, population

Table 7. Summary statistics of variables in the model

Variable	Unit	Source	Mean	25th	50th	75th
				Percentiles		

Variable	Unit	Source	Mean	25th	50th	75th
Agriculture employment share (year t) (Percentage of total labour force engaged in agriculture)	Percentage of labour force	GGDC's Africa Sector Data	54.5	38.9	58.1	73.7
Lagged ag labour productivity (Total value added in ag/total labour force in ag) (5-year moving average, t-1,..., t-5)	Dollars per worker per year	GGDC's Africa Sector Data	1.4	0.3	0.7	1.3
Lagged non ag labour productivity (Total value added in non-ag/total labour force in non-ag) (5-year moving average, t-1,..., t-5)	Dollars per worker per year	GGDC 's Africa Sector Data	6.5	2.1	3.3	10.0
Time trend (year t)	Years		8.6	5.0	9.0	13.0
Lagged index of governance (5-year moving average, t-1,..., t-5)	Annual governance score on a scale from −2.5 to 2.5	Worldwide Governance Indicator	−0.2	−0.7	−0.4	0.4
Population density (year t)	Number of people per square km of land land area	World Development Indicators	116.2	37.7	62.0	117.1
Road density (year t)	Roads per 100km square of land area	FAOSTAT	26.7	7.4	11.0	27.7

density and road density were all found to be negatively related to changes in farming's employment share, but their effects were generally not statistically significant. We also see important country-level differences in the pace at which the labour force is exiting farming. The rate of decline of agriculture's employment share is significantly slower in Nigeria than in most other countries. For instance, the agriculture's share of employment in Ghana and Ethiopia declined roughly 19 per cent and 51 per cent more over the past 15 years than that experienced in Nigeria, other factors held constant.

The observed strong relationship between agricultural productivity and labour exit from agriculture is consistent with historical structural transformation processes in Asia and elsewhere, where agricultural productivity growth was a major driver of economic transformation and associated shifts in the labour force to non-farm sectors in countries' early stages of development (Mellor, 1976; Timmer, 1988; McArthur & McCord, 2017). The majority of applied studies of early developing countries found that multiplier effects resulting from agricultural productivity growth are considerably higher than multiplier effects resulting from off-farm productivity growth (see Haggblade, Hazell, & Dorosh, 2007 for a useful review; also Christiaensen, Demery, & Kuhl, 2011). Our descriptive multivariate results therefore support the notion that government policies and programmes affecting the rate of farm productivity growth is a powerful means of promoting structural transformation.

6. Conclusions and implications

This paper has documented the major demographic and employment shifts observed within the working-age populations of nine African countries: Ghana, Kenya, Malawi, Mali, Nigeria, Rwanda, Tanzania, Uganda, and Zambia. To our knowledge, this study is the first detailed assessment of

Table 8. Determinants of changes in agriculture's employment shares over time

	(i)	(ii)	(iii)	(iv)	(v)	(vi)
		Model without road density variable			Model with road density variable[a]	
	Pooled OLS	Pooled OLS	Fixed effect	First difference	Pooled OLS	Fixed effect
Log lagged labour productivity in agriculture	-0.443***	-0.311***	-0.133*	-0.0228***	-0.157*	-0.284**
(5-year moving average, t-1,..., t-5)		(-9.82)	(-2.15)	(-3.98)	(-2.39)	(-2.77)
Log lagged labour productivity in non-agriculture	-	-0.0179	-0.0121	0.00271	-0.096*	-0.176
(5-year moving average, t-1,..., t-5)		(-0.65)	(-0.23)	(1.28)	(-2.64)	(-1.89)
Other covariates						
Lagged index of governance	-	-0.456***	-0.0205	-0.00173	-0.321***	0.0698
(5-year moving average, t-1,..., t-5)		(-14.12)	(-0.45)	(-0.22)	(-6.50)	(1.06)
Time trend (year t)	-	-0.00494	-0.00961***	0.000178	-0.00808	-0.00458
		(-1.56)	(-4.62)	(0.54)	(-1.88)	(-0.96)
Population density (year t)	-	-0.00111***	-0.00181	-0.00116	-0.00791	-0.00475
		(-8.38)	(-1.51)	(-0.55)	(-1.15)	(-1.89)
Road density (year t)	-	-	-	-	-0.00627	-0.000260
					(-1.16)	(-0.21)
Countries						
Bostwana	-0.512***	-	-	-0.000929	-	-
	(-15.34)			(-0.10)		
Ethiopia	-0.448***	-	-	-0.0128*	-	-
	(-4.75)			(-2.22)		
Ghana	-0.195***	-	-	-0.0133*	-	-
	(-6.43)			(-2.57)		
Kenya	-0.356***	-	-	-0.00851	-	-
	(-9.40)			(-1.31)		
Mauritius	-1.043***	-	-	0.00425	-	-
	(-8.47)			(0.83)		
Malawi	-0.478***	-	-	-0.0174***	-	-
	(-5.28)			(-4.47)		
Senegal	-0.349***	-	-	-0.00655	-	-
	(-8.54)			(-1.00)		
Tanzania	-0.285***	-	-	-0.0132	-	-
	(-4.12)			(-1.89)		
South Africa	-0.926***	-	-	-0.00594	-	-
	(-14.49)			(-0.69)		

(continued)

Table 8. (*Continued*)

| | Model without road density variable | | | | Model with road density variable[a] | |
	(i)	(ii)	(iii)	(iv)	(v)	(vi)
	Pooled OLS	Pooled OLS	Fixed effect	First difference	Pooled OLS	Fixed effect
Zambia	-0.0807* (-2.07)	-	-	-0.00491 (-0.55)	-	-
Constant	-0.486*** (-17.51)	-0.797*** (-10.70)	-0.519** (-3.07)	0.000667 (0.07)	-0.529*** (-4.99)	0.0690 (0.20)
Number of observations	183	161	161	95	78	78
Number of Countries	11	11	11	11	10	10
Adjusted/Overall R-square	0.98	0.94	0.71	0.398	0.97	0.87
Time period	1995–2011	1995–2011	1995–2011	1995–2011	1995–2011	1995–2011

Notes: t and z statistics in parentheses. * $p < 0.05$; ** $p < 0.01$; *** $p < 0.001$. [a]Not enough data to run a first difference model controlling for road density.

49

employment patterns and trends in sub-Saharan Africa comparing full-time equivalents (FTE) versus total numbers of jobs. Because of the seasonal nature of agriculture in most of the region, employment patterns based on FTEs is likely to provide a more accurate picture of labour force participation in farming, broader agri-food systems, and non-farm activities than analyses based on total numbers of jobs or primary types of employment.

While acknowledging cross-country variations and the study's focus on only nine countries in Africa (which nevertheless account for slightly under half of sub-Saharan Africa's total population), some broad trends are clearly apparent. First, African economies have been unmistakably transforming since 2000 with rapid but highly variable rates of labour exit from farming to off-farm sectors. Generally, the number of working-age individuals (young people) engaged in farming is increasing in absolute terms but the share of farming in total employment is declining over time in most countries. The decline in farming's employment share is particularly pronounced in FTE terms, which reflects both the seasonal nature of farming, the extent to which better paying off-farm employment opportunities are expanding and pulling youth out of farming in zones of economic dynamism, and the extent to which acute land pressures are pushing youth out of farming in other areas. Among the six countries where data permit FTE computations, the shares of the labour force in farming range from 34 per cent in Ghana and Nigeria to a high of 54 per cent in Rwanda. Over the time span separating the first and second nationally representative surveys in the nine countries, which range from five to 10 years, the proportion of the labour force in farming has fallen in eight of them, by over 10 percentage points in five (Malawi, Mali, Tanzania, Rwanda and Zambia). Nigeria is the outlier, where the share of the labour force in farming rose in FTE terms from 21.8 per cent in 2003/04 to 33.7 per cent in 2012/13.

Second, employment in off-farm segments of agri-food systems is expanding rapidly in percentage terms, but in terms of absolute numbers, non-farm activities constitute the major source of new employment. Third, contrary to widespread perceptions, the mean age of individuals engaged primarily in farming is not rising – in fact it has fallen slightly in some countries and remained stable in most others. Even when counting only adults 25 years and over who are engaged in farming for at least half of their total work time, the mean age of farmers in six countries analysed ranged from 41 to 48 years of age. Fourth, the rate of increase in farm-based self-employment is particularly pronounced in urban areas, where it is generally rising more rapidly than the growth in the working-age population. Fifth, self-employment, including unpaid family labour, accounts for over 75 per cent of total employment, highlighting the level of informality of the labour market. Young people 15 to 24 years of age are more likely than any other age group to engage in unpaid jobs or family labour. Their job prospects are thus often restricted to farming and informal enterprises, which are associated with low skill requirements, low entry barriers, and hence generally low returns to labour. Sixth, the proportion of jobs that are wage-based is generally rising, impressively in some countries (for example, Ghana, Rwanda and Tanzania), driven in most cases by non-farm private sector firms. The growth in wage jobs is starting from a very low base and thus translates into a relatively small number of new jobs each year. As a result, the share of wage jobs in total off-farm employment remains low in most countries, typically less than 30 per cent.

Perhaps most importantly, the performance of farming is found to significantly influence the rate of job growth in the rest of the economy. Our cross-country econometric analysis shows that the five-year lagged moving average rate of agricultural productivity growth is positively and significantly associated with the pace at which countries' off-farm labour force shares grow. Over the past decade, countries with the highest rates of agricultural productivity growth generally experienced the most rapid exit of labour out of farming, and the highest growth in labour productivity in non-agriculture sectors. These patterns, also seen in Asia's structural transformation process, suggest that agricultural productivity growth may remain an important policy objective not only for national food security but for employment growth and the diversification of the work force associated with economic transformation. Given the unprecedented growth in the number of young Africans entering the labour market, an effective youth employment strategy in most African countries will rely on massive job expansion, which in turn will rely on agricultural productivity growth. Because of its extensive forward and backward linkages with other sectors of the economy, including agricultural value chains and food systems, strategies that raise the returns to labour in farming constitute an important component of effective youth employment strategies.

Young people between 15–24 year of age constitute between 35 and 40 per cent of the workforce in sub-Saharan Africa. Every year, roughly 17 million young Africans are becoming of working age. Under the most favourable projections, only a quarter of these new workers over the next decade will find wage jobs. If agriculture can be made more profitable and less physically arduous through policies and public goods expenditures that stimulate private investment in agri-food systems, this sector has the power to absorb many rural youth into decent employment. Agriculture is currently perceived by many young Africans as unattractive – an obvious result of decades of neglect. The emerging evidence is that young Africans are fleeing from poverty, not from farming *per se*. By making farming more profitable and less arduous, governments can attract young Africans into a nearly trillion-dollar industry in Africa.

A comprehensive youth livelihoods strategy would have the following key features:

- First, focus on investing in agricultural productivity growth to create new opportunities for youth in farming and generate the multiplier effects that expand the number of job opportunities for youth in the broader economy.
- Develop evidence-based strategies for assisting rural youth to access land and finance, two of the most salient barriers inhibiting youth participation in agriculture.
- Invest in education and skills to enable young people to fully realise their economic potential and maximise their productivity in the opportunities that arise.

All this requires redoubling public investments in primary, secondary and tertiary education, vocational and technical schools, and soft skills. But more research is urgently needed to determine what forms of education and skill training provide the greatest payoffs to young people, recognising that the answers are likely to differ across Africa given the wide differences in economic conditions.

Acknowledgements

The authors acknowledge support for this study from the Gates Foundation-funded Guiding Investments in Sustainable Agricultural Intensification in Africa (GISAIA) Project, from the USAID-funded Feed the Future Innovation Lab for Food Security Policy (FSP), and from the MasterCard-funded Agrifood Youth Employment and Engagement Study (AgYEES) to Michigan State University. The authors also appreciate discussions of earlier versions of this study with David Atwood, Alemayehu Konde, Meredith Lee, Milu Muyanga, and David Tschirley.

Funding

We gratefully acknowledge funding for this study from The MasterCard Foundation through the Agri-food Youth Employment and Engagement Study (AgYees), the Bill and Melinda Gates Foundation through the Guiding Investments in Sustainable Agricultural Intensification in Africa (GISAIA) grant, and the Food Security Policy Innovation Lab to Michigan State University, funded by USAID's Bureau for Food Security.

Disclosure statement

No potential conflict of interest was reported by the authors.

Notes

1. Six of the world's 10 fastest growing economies between 2000 and 2010 were in Africa. The region's average GDP growth was 4.84 per cent during this period, but it has slowed slightly between 2011–2015 to 3.89 per cent (World Development Indicators, 2017).
2. LSMS-ISA surveys are implemented by national statistical offices with technical assistance from the World Bank Economic Research Group. Datasets and survey descriptions for the various countries can be found at http://econ.worldbank.org/WBSITE/EXTERNAL/EXTDEC/EXTRESEARCH/EXTLSMS/0,,
contentMDK:23,617,057~pagePK:64,168,445~piPK:64,168,309~theSitePK:3,358,997,00.html .
3. Specific surveys used are Ghana's Living Standard Survey (GLSS 5 and 6); Nigeria's Living Standard Survey (2004) and General Household Survey (2013); Rwanda's Integrated Household Living Survey (EICV 2 and 3); Tanzania National Panel Survey (2009 and 2015); Uganda's National Panel Survey (2005, 2012); Zambia's Labor Force Surveys (2005, 2012); Data for Kenya's Population and Housing Census (1999 and 2000), Malawi's Household and Population Census (1998 and 2009) and Mali's Quatrieme recensement general de la population et de l'habitat (1998 and 2009) were obtained from IPUMS (https://international.ipums.org/international/).
4. By ILO (1982) definition, an individual cannot be classified as unemployed if he/she has worked for even one hour on any economic activity including household enterprises during the reference period.
5. Agriculture is defined in the traditional sense to include crop and livestock production, hunting and related services, forestry and logging and fishery and aquaculture.
6. In most countries, the 15–24 year age range spans the period during which secondary and tertiary education is obtained.
7. TFP growth rates were obtained from the Economic Research Service Total Factor Productivity Database, courtesy of Keith Fuglie.
8. Africa sector data is compiled by the Groningen Growth and Development Center and is available at http://www.rug.nl/ggdc/productivity/10-sector/.

References

Adesugba, M. A., & Mavrotas, G. (2016). Delving deeper into the agricultural transformation and youth employment nexus: The Nigerian case. NSSP Working Paper 31. Washington, DC: International Food Policy Research Institute http://ebrary.ifpri.org/cdm/ref/collection/p15738coll2/id/130281

AfDB, OECD, and UNDP (2014). *African economic outlook 2014: Global value chains and Africa's industrialisation*. Paris: Organisation for Economic Co-operation and Development. Retrieved from http://www.oecd-ilibrary.org/content/book/aeo-2014-en

African Center for Economic Transformation (ACET). (2014). *Growth with depth: 2014 African transformation report*. Accra, Ghana: African Center for Economic Transformation. Retrieved from http://africantransformation.org/wp-content/uploads/2014/02/2014-african-transformation-report.pdf

Allen, A., Howard, J., Kondo, M., Jamison, A., Jayne, T., Snyder, J., … Yeboah, F. K. (2016), Agrifood Youth Employment and Engagement Study (AgYees), Michigan State University, International Studies and Programs, East Lansing.

Aryeetey, E., Baah-Boateng, W., Ackah, C. G., Lehrer, K., & Mbiti, I. (2014). Country studies, Chapter 5, Ghana. In H. Hino & G. Ranis (ed.), *Youth and Employment in Sub-Saharan Africa: Working but poor*. New York, NY: Taylor & Francis Group.

Badiane, O., Ulimwengu, J., & Badibanga, T. (2012). Structural transformation among African economies: Patterns and performance. *Development*, 55(4), 463–476.

Barrett, C. B., Carter, M. R., & Timmer, C. P. (2010). A century-long perspective on agricultural development. *American Journal of Agricultural Economics*, 92(2), 447–468.

Beauchemin, C. (2011). Rural-urban migration in West Africa: Towards a reversal? Migration trends and economic situation in Burkina Faso and Côte d'Ivoire. *Population, Space and Place*, 17(1), 47–72. doi:10.1002/psp.573

Bezu, S., & Holden, S. (2014). Are rural youth in Ethiopia abandoning agriculture? *World Development*, 64, 259–272.

Bilsborrow, R. E. (2002). Migration, population change, and the rural environment. In G. D. Dabelko (ed.), *Environmental Change and Security Project Report, Issue 8*. Washington, DC: Environmental Change and Security Project, The Woodrow Wilson Center.

Bocquier, P. (2005). World urbanization prospects: An alternative to the UN model of projection compatible with urban transition theory. *Demographic Research*, 12, 197–236.

Canning, D., Raja, S., & Yazbeck, A. S. (2015). Africa's demographic transition: Dividend or Disaster? Africa development forum; Washington, DC: World Bank; and Agence Française de Développement. World Bank. Retrieved from https://openknowledge.worldbank.org/handle/10986/22036

Chamberlin, J., & Ricker-Gilbert, J. (2016). Participation in rural land rental markets in sub-Saharan Africa: Who benefits and by how much? Evidence from Malawi and Zambia. *American Journal of Agricultural Economics*, 98(5), 1507–1528.

Christiaensen, L., Demery, L., & Kuhl, J. (2011). The (evolving) role of agriculture in poverty reduction: An empirical perspective. *Journal of Development Economics*, 96(2), 239–254.

De Vries, G., Timmer, M., & De Vries, K. (2015). Structural transformation in Africa: Static gains, dynamic losses. *The Journal of Development Studies, 51*(6), 674–688.

deBraw, A., Mueller, V., & Lee., H. (2014). The role of rural–urban migration in the structural transformation of sub-Saharan Africa. *World Development, 63*, 33–42.

Dome, M. Z. (2015). *A Window of Policy Priorities: Evidence from Citizens of 34 African Countries*. Afrobarometer policy paper no. 18. Accra, Ghana: Afrobarometer. Retrieved from http://afrobarometer.org/publications/pp18-window-policy-priorities-evidence-citizens-34-african-countries

Duarte, M., & Restuccia, D. (2010). The role of the structural transformation in aggregate productivity. *The Quarterly Journal of Economics, 125*(1), 129–173.

FAO. (2017). *FAOSTAT database collections*. Rome: Food and Agriculture Organization of the United Nations. Retrieved from http://faostat.fao.org

Fields, G. (2015). Aid, growth and jobs. *African Development Review, 27*(S1), 5–16.

Filmer, D., & Fox, L. (2014). *Youth employment in sub-Saharan Africa. Africa development series*. Washington, DC: World Bank. Retrieved from https://openknowledge.worldbank.org/bitstream/handle/10986/16608/9781464801075.pdf

Fine, D., Van Wamelen, A., Lund, S., Cabral, A., Taoufiki, M., Dörr, N., ... Cook, P. (2012). *Africa at work: Job creation and inclusive growth*. Boston: McKinsey Global Institute.

Fox, L., Haines, C., Muñoz, J. H., & Thomas, A. (2013). *Africa's got work to Do: Employment prospects in the new century*. IMF Working Paper No. 13/201. Washington, DC: IMF. Retrieved from http://dx.doi.org/10.5089/9781484389195.001

Fox, L., Senbet, S. L. W., & Simbanegavi, W. (2016). Youth employment in sub-Saharan Africa: Challenges, constraints and opportunities. *Journal of African Economies, 25*(1), 3–15

Fox, L., & Thomas, A. (2016). Africa's got work to do: A diagnostic of youth employment challenges in sub–Saharan Africa. *Journal of African Economies, 25*(1), i16–i36.

Fuglie, K. O. (2015). Agricultural Total Factor Productivity Growth Indices for Individual Countries 1961–2012. Washington, DC: USDA Economic Research Services. Retrieved from http://www.ers.usda.gov/data-products/international-agricultural-productivity.aspx

Gorman, M. (2013). Older women, older farmers—the hidden face of agriculture. Briefing, London: HelpAge. Retrieved from http://www.helpage.org/silo/files/older-women-older-farmers-the-hidden-face-of-agriculture.pdf

Haggblade, S., Hazell, P. B .R., & Dorosh, P. A. (2007). Sectoral growth linkages between agriculture and the rural nonfarm economy. In S. Haggblade, P. B.R. Hazell, & T. Reardon (Eds.), *Transforming the rural nonfarm economy: Opportunities and threats in the developing world*. Baltimore, MD: Johns Hopkins University Press.

Harris, J. R., & Todaro, M. P. (1970). Migration, unemployment and development: A two-sector analysis. *American Economic Review, 60*, 126–142.

Hollinger, F., & Staatz, J. M. (2015). Agricultural Growth in West Africa: Market and Policy Drivers. Rome: Food and Agriculture Organization of the United Nations and African Development Bank. Retrieved from http://www.fao.org/3/a-i4337e.pdf

International Labour Organization (1982). Resolutions concerning economically active population, employment, unemployment and underemployment. Adopted by the 13th International Conference of Labour Statisticians, October 1982, para. 10. Geneva: ILO.

International Labour Organization (1993): Fifteenth international conference of labour statisticians, report of the conference. ICLS/15/D.6 (Rev. 1). International Labour Office, Geneva.

International Labour Organization (2015). Global employment trends for youth 2015: Scaling up investments in decent jobs for youth. Geneva: ILO.

International Monetary Fund. (2013). *Regional economic outlook - sub-Saharan Africa: Building momentum in a multi-speed world*. Washington DC: IMF.

Jayne, T. S., Chamberlin, J. B., Sitko, N., Traub, L. N., Yeboah, F., Muyanga, M., ... Kachule, R. (2016). Africa's changing farm size distribution patterns: The rise of medium-scale farms. *Agricultural Economics, 47*(S1), 197–214.

Johnston, B. F., & Kilby, P. (1975). *Agriculture and structural transformation: Economic strategies in late developing countries*. New York: Oxford University Press.

Johnston, B. F., & Mellor, J. W. (1961). The role of agriculture in economic development. *American Economic Review, 51*(4), 566–593.

Jöhr, H. (2012). Where are the future farmers to grow our food? *International Food and Agribusiness Management Review, 15* (Special Issue A), 1–3.

La Porta, R., & Shleifer, A. (2014). Informality and Development. *Journal of Economic Perspectives, 28*(3), 109–126.

Lipton, M. (2005). *Crop science, poverty, and the family farm in a globalizing world*. 2020 IFPRI Discussion Paper No. 40. Washington, DC: International Food Policy Research Institute.

Losch, B. (2012). *Agriculture: The Key to the Employment Challenge*. Perspective No. 19. Montpellier: CIRAD.

Masters, W., Rosenblum, N., & Alemu, R. (2018). Agricultural transformation, nutrition transition and food policy in Africa: Preston curves reveal new stylised facts. *Journal of Development Studies, 54*(5), 788–802. doi: 10.1080/00220388.2018.1430768

McArthur, J. W., & McCord, G. C. (2017). Fertilizing growth: Agricultural inputs and their effects in economic development. *Journal of Development Economics, 127*, 133–152.

McCullough, E. B. (2015) 'Labor productivity and employment gaps in sub-Saharan Africa', World Bank Policy Research Working Paper No. WPS 7234.

McMillan, M., & Harttgen, K. (2014). *The changing structure of Africa's economies*. National Bureau of Economic Research Working Paper No. 20077. Cambridge, MA: National Bureau of Economic Research. Retrieved from http://legacy.wlu.ca/documents/57803/McMillian_ChangingAfrica_140317.pdf.

Mellor, J. W. (1976). *The new economics of growth*. Ithaca, NY: Cornell University Press.

Moriconi-Ebrard, F., Harre, D., & Heinrigs, P. (2016). *Urbanisation dynamics in West Africa 1950-2010: Africapolis I, 2015 update*. Paris: West African Studies, OECD Publishing. 10.1787/9789264252233-en

Moyo, J. (2015). Urban farming mushrooms in africa amid food deficits. *Inter Press Service News Agency*. September 2, 2015. Retrieved from http://www.ipsnews.net/2015/09/urban-farming-mushrooms-in-africa-amid-food-deficits/

Organisation for Economic Cooperation and Development (2015). Working-age Population (Indicator). Paris: OECD. Retrieved from 10.1787/d339918b-en

Page, J., & Shimeles, A. (2015). Aid, employment and poverty reduction in Africa. *African Development Review, 27*(S1), 17–30.

Potts, D. (2009). The slowing of sub-Saharan Africa's urbanization: Evidence and implications for urban livelihoods. *Environment and Urbanization, 21*(1), 253–259.

Potts, D. (2012). Whatever happened to Africa's rapid urbanisation? *World Economics, 13*(2), 1729.

Potts, D. (2013). *Urban Livelihoods and Urbanization Trends in Africa: Winners and Losers?* Environment, politics and development working paper series paper no. 57. London: Department of Geography, King's College London. Retrieved from http://urban-africa-china.angonet.org/sites/default/files/resource_files/african_migration_urban_development_-_potts_-_kings_college_2013_0.pdf

Proctor, F. J., & Lucchesi, V. (2012). *Small-scale farming and youth in an era of rapid rural change*. London: International Institute for Environment and Development.

Rakotoarisoa, M., Iafrate, M., & Paschali, M. (2011). *Why has Africa become a net food importer? Explaining Africa agricultural and food trade deficits*. Rome: Trade and Markets Division, FAO.

Sackey, J., Liverpool-Tasie, S., Salau, S., & Awoyemi, T. (2012). Rural-urban transformation in Nigeria. *Journal of African Development, 14.2*, 131–168.

Timmer, P. (1988). The agricultural transformation. In H. Cheneo' & T. N. Srinivasan (Eds.), *Handbook of development economics* (Vol. I, pp. 275–330, 882). North Holland: Elsevier Science Publishers.

Tschirley, D., Snyder, J., Dolislager, D., Reardon, T., Haggblade, S., Goeb, J., ... Meyer, F. (2015). Africa's unfolding diet transformation: implications for agri-food system employment. *Journal Agribusiness in Developing and Emerging Economies, 5*(2), 102–136.

Ulimwengu, J., Collins, J., Yeboah, F. K., & Traub, L. N. (2016). Driving economic transformation. In Alliance for a Green Revolution in Africa (AGRA). 2016. *Africa Agriculture Status Report: Progress towards an Agriculture Transformation in Sub-Saharan*, Nairobi, Kenya.

United Nations (2016) World Urbanization Prospects, the 2014 Revision. New York: Author. Retrieved from https://esa.un.org/unpd/wup/DataQuery/

United Nations (2017) *UN commodity trade statistics database*. New York: United Nations Statistics Division. Retrieved from https://comtrade.un.org/

Upadhyay, U. D., Gipson, J. D., Withers, M., Lewis, S., Ciaraldi, E. J., Fraser, A., ... Prata, N. (2014, 2014 Aug). Women's empowerment and fertility: A review of the literature. *Social Science & Medicine, 115*, 111–120.

Vos, R. (2015). Thought for Food: Strengthening global governance of food security. committee for development policy background paper no. 29. UN Department of Economic and Social Affairs, New York, NY. Retrieved from http://www.un.org/en/development/desa/policy/cdp/cdp_background_papers/bp2015_29.pdf

Wineman, A., & Jayne, T. S. (2016). *Intra-rural migration and pathways to greater well-being: Evidence from Tanzania*. MSU Staff Paper, Michigan State University, East Lansing.

World Bank. (2017). *World Development Indicators 2017*. Washington, DC: Author. Retrieved from https://openknowledge.worldbank.org/handle/10986/26447

Yamada, G. (1996). Urban informal employment and self-employment in developing countries: Theory and evidence. *Economic Development and Cultural Change, 44.2*, 291–314.

Yeboah, K., & Jayne, T. S. (2016). *Africa's evolving employment structure*. International Development Working Paper 148, Michigan State University, East Lansing.

Appendix
Table A1. Changes in economic activity status among working-age population, by sector

	Ghana 2005–2013	Nigeria 2004–2013	Rwanda 2006–2011	Tanzania 2009–2015	Uganda 2005–2012	Zambia 2005–2012	Kenya[a] 1999–2009	Malawi[a] 1998–2008	Mali[a] 1998–2009
Farming									
# of working age people in end year	6,105,975	29,299,579	6,101,014	12,521,538	10,696,861	3,175,578	6,490,390	2,190,530	2,614,640
Urban	1,223,515	3,509,024	459,981	1,323,741	1,084,535	550,461	837,790	83,180	99,080
Rural	4,882,461	25,790,554	5,641,032	11,197,797	9,612,326	2,625,117	5,652,600	2,107,350	2,515,560
Annual % change in # of working age people from base to end year	3.2	25.5	6.8	-0.3	18.5	-4.3	0.7	-3.2	0.9
Urban	68.3	13.6	7.2	9.9	27.3	15.7	6.9	0.7	-5.2
Rural	7.4	28.1	6.8	-1.1	5.0	-2.6	0.2	-3.3	1.6
Off-farm within the agri-food system									
# of working age people in end year	2,633,020	14,651,519	612,524	2,639,193	1,501,476	337,823	–	–	–
Urban	1,575,947	6,025,676	105,966	1,412,386	387,207	236,282	–	–	–
Rural	1,057,073	8,625,843	506,558	1,226,807	1,114,270	101,542	–	–	–
Annual % change in # of working age people from base to end year	15.8	104.0	9.6	32.9	39.1	66.3	–	–	–
Urban	146.4	76.4	1.5	46.8	1.5	16.2	–	–	–
Rural	27.0	136.5	12.2	22.9	21.4	27.9	–	–	–
Non-farm outside agri-food system									
# of working age people in end year	5,173,690	25,723,248	2,342,336	5,567,200	3,742,274	1,746,941	7,738,710	1,352,300	1,355,590
Urban	3,669,932	14,992,524	558,051	3,193,239	1,110,327	1,274,439	4,098,730	477,390	793,500
Rural	1,503,758	10,730,724	1,784,285	2,373,961	2,631,947	472,501	3,639,980	874,910	562,090
Annual % change in # of working age people from base to end year	10.7	0.6	23.0	4.1	38.7	30.3	5.2	9.5	11.1
Urban	70.2	4.3	7.6	8.5	3.2	5.5	7.7	3.3	7.4
Rural	24.1	-2.3	32.2	0.1	20.6	26.4	3.2	16.0	20.2
Unemployed									
# of working age people in end year	341,632	1,865,493	46,177	557,352	4,896	452,607	1,521,100	865,860	69,500
Urban	265,133	1,307,103	34,867	440,521	4,053	339,992	720,160	127,340	45,980
Rural	76,499	558,390	11,310	116,831	843	112,615	800,940	738,520	23,520
Annual % change in # of working age people from base to end year	-6.9	9.9	31.1	7.8	-49.0	133.4	2.5	54.8	17.3

(continued)

Appendix
Table A1. (Continued)

	Ghana	Nigeria	Rwanda	Tanzania	Uganda	Zambia	Kenya[a]	Malawi[a]	Mali[a]
	2005–2013	2004–2013	2006–2011	2009–2015	2005–2012	2005–2012	1999–2009	1998–2008	1998–2009
Urban	−36.1	20.8	28.5	8.7	−16.2	29.9	3.4	10.9	17.1
Rural	−28.1	0.6	40.9	4.9	−16.5	106.1	1.7	91.8	17.6
Economically inactive									
# of working age people in end year	2,565,943	29,716,963	1,019,472	2,594,516	2,189,430	1,763,629	4,793,090	1,854,950	2,849,850
Urban	1,784,988	12,389,755	192,960	1,586,289	772,207	932,314	1,730,510	353,130	851,360
Rural	780,955	17,327,208	826,512	1,008,227	1,417,223	831,315	3,062,580	1,501,820	1,998,490
Annual % change in # of working age people from base to end year	−5.0	15.6	4.2	−7.2	−2.2	13.8	8.3	6.3	4.4
Urban	7.2	11.4	−2.4	−2.0	−1.1	−1.5	9.9	0.5	1.1
Rural	−55.7	19.8	6.5	−10.6	−0.6	20.6	7.5	8.8	6.6

Notes: [a]Data do not permit disaggregation of off-farm into within and outside the agri-food system. AFS represents the agri-food system. Microdata of population and housing census data in IPUMS.

Sources: Author's estimates from Ghana Living Standard Survey 5 and 6; Nigeria's Living Standard Survey (2004) and General Household Survey (2013); Rwanda Integrated Household Living Survey (EICV 2 and 3); Tanzania National Panel Survey (2009 and 2015); Uganda National Panel Survey (2006 and 2012); Zambia Labor Force Surveys (2005 and 2012).

Understanding the Role of Rural Non-Farm Enterprises in Africa's Economic Transformation: Evidence from Tanzania

XINSHEN DIAO, EDUARDO MAGALHAES & MARGARET MCMILLAN

ABSTRACT *Tanzania's recent growth boom has been accompanied by a threefold increase in the share of the rural labour force working in nonfarm employment. Although households with nonfarm enterprises are less likely to be poor, a substantial fraction of these households fall below the poverty line. Heterogeneity in the labour productivity of rural nonfarm businesses calls for a two-pronged strategy for rural transformation. Relatively unproductive enterprises may be part of a poverty reduction strategy but should not be expected to contribute to employment and labour productivity growth. Failure to account for this heterogeneity is likely to lead to disappointing outcomes.*

1. Introduction

Since the beginning of the twenty-first century, Tanzania's economy has grown more rapidly than at any other point in recent history. Between 2000 and 2015, the average annual GDP growth rate was 6.8 per cent and the average annual labour productivity growth rate was more than 4 per cent. Between 2002 and 2012, more than three quarters of this labour productivity growth was accounted for by structural change; the remainder of the growth is largely attributable to within sector productivity growth in agriculture. The growth attributable to structural change is almost entirely explained by a rapid decline in the agricultural employment share and an increase in the non-agricultural private sector employment share (Diao, Kweka, McMillan, & Qureshi, 2017).

Despite these changes, Tanzania remains heavily rural; between 2002 and 2012, the share of the population living in rural areas declined by only 6.5 percentage points: from 76.9 per cent to 70.4 per cent (Table 1). Living in rural areas is traditionally associated with farming. However, the census and household survey data also shows that between 2002 and 2012, the share of the rural population engaged in agricultural activities decreased by almost 14 percentage points (Table 1). The data also show that growth in rural nonfarm employment has been very rapid at between 11.1 per cent and 13.5 per cent per annum depending on the data source (Table 1). Thus, while the agricultural sector still employs the majority of the rural population in Tanzania, the rural nonfarm economy is becoming increasingly important.

The purpose of this paper is threefold. The first is to describe the characteristics of the households that make up the rural nonfarm sector in Tanzania. The second is to describe the businesses run by households in the rural nonfarm sector; we also describe characteristics of the owners of these businesses and their self-reported motivations for running a business. The final purpose of this paper is to assess the productivity of rural nonfarm businesses. This last exercise is meant to inform the following question: does the rural nonfarm sector have the potential to contribute to long-run

Table 1. Rural population and agricultural employment shares and annual growth rates

	Rural areas	National total
Share of rural population (percentage)		
2002	76.9	
2012	70.4	
Share of agricultural employment in total employment (percentage)		
2000/01 (HBS)	91.8	82.6
2002 (Census)	93.2	81.1
2006 (ILFS)		76.5
2011/2012 (HBS)	77.4	63.8
2012 (Census)	79.5	65.8
2014 (ILFS)		66.9
Annualised growth rate in population, total employment and employment in agriculture and non-agriculture (percentage)		
Population (2002–2012, Census)	1.8	2.7
Total employment		
2000–2011 (HBS)	1.3	2.4
2002–2012 (Census)	1.6	2.5
2006–2014 (ILFS)	0.3	2.4
Employment in agriculture		
2000–2011 (HBS)	−0.3	0.1
2002–2012 (Census)	0.1	0.4
2006–2014 (ILFS)		0.7
Employment in non-agriculture		
2000–2011 (HBS)	11.1	9.4
2002–2012 (Census)	13.5	8.8
2006–2014 (ILFS)		6.8

Notes: For the Census employment, data for current employees aged 10 years old and above is used. Agricultural employment is based on the industry classification. For the Household Budget Survey (HBS), employees are for aged 10 years old and above. The definition of employment differs between the two rounds of HBS. In HBS 2000/2001, 'unpaid family helper' counts for 7.8 per cent of total employment and is all considered as non-agricultural employment. This causes two problems: (1) total employment of HBS 2000/2001 is more than that of Census 2002, which was conducted two years later; and (2) share of non-agricultural employment in HBS 2000/2001 is too high. Moreover, given that population calculated from HBS 2000/2001 is lower than that in Census 2002, the ratio of employment to population in HBS 2000/2001 becomes too high compared with that of Census 2002. For these reasons, we decided to exclude 'unpaid family helpers' from total employment in HBS 2000/2001. After this adjustment, the ratio of total employment to population is similar between HBS 2000/2001 and Census 2002, as well as the shares of agricultural and non-agricultural employment. Employees in the Integrated Labor Force Survey (ILFS) are for age 15 years old and above, and the data for rural employment is not available in the survey report published by Tanzania National Bureau of Statistics (NBS) (2015).

Source: Most numbers in the table are calculated by authors using the micro data downloaded from the NBS website as well as from official government documents. For Census 2012 and ILFS 2006 and 2014, the micro data is not available, and the calculation for these surveys is solely based on official government documents published by NBS (NBS, 2006, 2011a, b, 2014a, b, 2015). The micro data for Census 2002 is downloaded from IPUMS (https://usa.ipums.org/usa/).

productivity growth in Tanzania. The importance of this question is highlighted in recent work by Diao, McMillan, and Rodrik (2017) who show that: (i) the pattern of growth in Tanzania is common across Africa and; (ii) without labour productivity growth in nonfarm enterprises, labour productivity growth in Africa is likely to stall.

Using Tanzania's 2012 Household Budget Survey (HBS) – we classify rural households into three groups: (i) households uniquely engaged in farming; (ii) households uniquely engaged in the nonfarm sector and; (iii) mixed households. Our analysis shows that more than 10 per cent of Tanzanian rural households engage only in the nonfarm economy. The heads of these households tend to be younger and better educated than the heads of households in the two comparison groups. Gender of the household head does not seem to affect the likelihood of being a nonfarm household. Households in communities with access to daily public transportation are found to have a higher probability of participating in rural nonfarm activities.

In order to analyse business in the rural nonfarm sector, the Tanzania National Baseline Survey of Micro, Small and Medium Enterprise (MSME) has been employed. The survey has been conducted by the Tanzania government, and it was the first nationally representative survey of MSME. It is also one of the only comprehensive nationally representative surveys of MSME types in sub-Saharan Africa.[1] It covers roughly three million businesses and five million people; around 75 per cent of these businesses are in rural areas. 20 per cent of rural nonfarm businesses operate in the manufacturing sector while the remainder operate in various service sectors.

Our firm level analysis begins with a description of the characteristics of the owners of these businesses; roughly half say they would not quit their business for a full-time salaried position. We then document the enormous degree of productive heterogeneity in both rural and urban enterprises. Using the information about the productive heterogeneity of the rural nonfarm enterprises, we identify a group of small firms which appear to have the potential to contribute significantly to rural transformation. A probit analysis is conducted to better understand which readily observable characteristics of these firms and their owners are correlated with labour productivity. The analysis is an attempt to search for firm and/or owner attributes that might be used by policy-makers for targeting services to a select group of firms.

This research contributes to a large and growing literature on the rural nonfarm economy in Africa. One strand of this literature focuses on farm/nonfarm linkages and the estimation of multipliers (see for example Haggblade, Hazell, & Brown, 1989). A second strand of this literature focuses on rural-urban linkages and stresses the importance of reducing barriers to the movement of labour and products from rural to urban areas (see for example, De Brauw, Mueller, & Lee, 2014 on migration; and Gollin & Rogerson, 2009 on transportation costs). A third strand of this literature studies the effects of farm/nonfarm linkages and rural/urban linkages simultaneously; (see for example, Hagglade, Hazell, & Reardon, 2010). Unlike these papers, our work focuses on the productivity of rural nonfarm businesses and their potential to contribute to economy-wide labour productivity growth.

This research also contributes to a large body of work on SMEs in developing countries. Numerous studies in this field focus on documenting and analysing the heterogeneity of SMEs in both rural and urban areas (Banerjee, Breza, Duflo, & Kinnan, 2015; Bezu & Barrett, 2012; Fafchamps, McKenzie, Quinn, & Woodruff, 2014; Grimm, Krüger, & Lay, 2011; La Porta & Shleifer, 2011, 2014; McKenzie, 2015; McKenzie & Woodruff, 2008; Nagler & Naudé, 2017; Nordman, Rakotomanana, & Roubaud, 2016; Rijkers & Costa, 2012; Rijkers, Soderbom, & Loening, 2010). Some other studies in the SME literature focus on assessing employment growth in SMEs (McPherson, 1996; Mead, 1994; Mead & Liedholm, 1998), while others focus on the factors that constrain SME development (Beck, 2007; Gibson & Olivia, 2010; Jin & Deininger, 2009; Raj & Sen, 2013).

Most of this previous work relies on small samples and where samples are nationally representative, labour productivity is not examined since the nationally representative surveys do not include operating data.[2] This point was made recently by Li and Rama (2015) in an article published in the World Bank Research Observer. According to Li and Rama (2015), in most African countries enterprise censuses or surveys generally cover formally registered firms, therefore excluding the vast majority of micro- and small-enterprises, which are typically informal (Li & Rama, 2015). The surveys that do cover SMEs are often small in sample size.[3] It follows that the role of small, largely informal firms in the growth and development of poor economies is likely not well known using data from such small sized surveys, given the large heterogeneity among SMEs in developing countries. In addition, analyses of the rural nonfarm economy typically do not compare the productivity of rural enterprises to the productivity of urban enterprises.[4]

The remainder of this paper is organised as follows. Section 2 demonstrates the growing importance of the rural nonfarm economy in the context of the broader Tanzanian economy. Section 3 describes the data and methods used in the analyses. Section 4 focuses on the household level analysis and examines the characteristics of households with and without rural nonfarm activities. Section 5 turns to the firm data and describes the characteristics of rural entrepreneurs and their businesses. This section also identifies a group of firms – the 'in-between' firms – with the potential to contribute to rural transformation. Section 6 studies the characteristics of the 'in-between' firms to better understand how policy-makers might target these firms. Section 7 concludes with a summary of the main points and a brief discussion of policy implications.

2. The role of rural nonfarm enterprises in Tanzania's economy

Three nationally representative surveys are used to describe the changes in shares of rural population and rural employment. These are the 2000/2001 and 2011/2012 rounds of the Household Budget Surveys (HBS), the 2002 and 2012 Population Censuses, and the 2006 and 2014 Integrated Labor Force Surveys (ILFS). According to the two rounds of the census, which capture the change in population structure, the share of Tanzania's population living in rural areas declined from 76.9 per cent in 2002 to 70.4 per cent in 2012 (Table 1, first panel). Thus, Tanzania is urbanising but still heavily rural.

The second panel of Table 1 contains agricultural employment shares from the three different surveys in their different rounds. While different surveys cannot be directly compared because of differences in the definition for agricultural employment, there is a clear trend in which the share of agricultural employment declines much more rapidly than the share of rural population. Between the two rounds of the Census (2002–2012), the agricultural share of employment declined by 15.3 percentage points nationally and 13.7 percentage points in rural areas. The two rounds of HBS conducted in 2000/2001 and 2011/2012 and the two rounds of ILFS conducted in 2006 and 2014 all show a similar trend (Table 1). Comparing these large declines with the modest changes in the share of rural population discussed above indicates that growth in rural nonfarm employment outpaced growth in agricultural employment over this period.

Indeed, the annualised employment growth rates in the recent 15 years presented in the third panel of Table 1 clearly indicate this pattern. These employment growth rates are computed from each of the three surveys' two most recent rounds. In general, employment in agriculture has been growing at a slower pace than total employment nationwide and in rural areas. According to the census data, the growth rate of agricultural employment is almost zero between 2002 and 2012 in rural areas. By contrast, growth in rural non-agricultural employment has been in the double-digit range growth rate over this period (the bottom of Table 1).

To help better understand the changing structure of Tanzania's employment, Table 2 displays the structure of net increases in employment across different economic sectors between 2002 and 2012 for total employment and formal and informal employment. While the agricultural sector still accounts for two-thirds of total employment in Tanzania, as shown in Table 1, it has played a relatively minor role in the net job increase as shown in Table 2. In fact, almost 90 per cent of the net increase in jobs occurred in the non-agricultural sector over the period of 2002–2012. Considering that agricultural employment made up more than 80 per cent of total employment nationwide in 2002 (Table 1), this rapid non-agricultural employment growth is remarkable.

As is evident from Table 2, about 73 per cent of the net increase in total employment has taken place in the informal non-agricultural sector, accounting for 88 per cent of the increase in private non-agricultural employment. We do not have access to detailed employment data disaggregated by rural and urban among different sectors. However, we know from Table 1 that nonfarm employment increased significantly in rural areas. If one assumes that formal non-agricultural employment is more likely to take place in urban than in rural areas, which is a realistic assumption, then the 88 per cent of increased private sector's non-agricultural employment created by the informal sector nationwide can be taken as the lower bound for informal employment growth in rural areas. Section 4 of this paper will use the MSME data to further investigate the nature of this rural nonfarm employment.

Table 2. Contribution to new increases in employment by sector, total, formal and informal in 2002–2012

	Total		Formal		Informal	
	Net increase in employment	Share in total net increase	Net increase in employment	Share in total net increase	Net increase in employment	Share in total net increase
Agriculture	446,677	11.2	−3,865	−0.1	450,542	11.3
Mining	404,212	10.1	9,021	0.2	395,192	9.9
Manufacturing	313,882	7.8	103,049	2.6	210,833	5.3
Utilities	194,960	4.9	194,960	4.9	–	0.0
Construction	281,864	7.0	21,185	0.5	260,679	6.5
Trade services	966,807	24.2	1,304	0.0	965,503	24.1
Transport services	182,383	4.6	18,497	0.5	163,886	4.1
Business services	105,635	2.6	56,924	1.4	48,711	1.2
Public sector	224,579	5.6	224,579	5.6		0.0
Personal services	881,289	22.0	0	0.0	881,289	22.0
Total private non-agriculture	**3,331,032**	**83.2**	**404,940**	**10.1**	**2,926,093**	**73.1**
Total private economy	3,375,978	84.4	845,077	21.1	2,530,901	63.2
Total non-agriculture	3,555,611	88.8	629,519	15.7	2,926,093	73.1

Notes: Employment is defined by the current employment status with age 10 or more years old.
Source: Authors' calculation based on data from the Formal Employment and Earnings Survey and the Census 2002 and 2012 (NBS, 2006; 2007, 2014b, c, d, e).

3. Data and methods

The two datasets used for the analyses are briefly discussed in this section, followed by a description of the methodologies employed to analyse two distinct research questions. We provide a more detailed description of the HBS data in the Appendix since the data are fairly standard and have been used frequently. We devote more space here to the description of the MSME data which is unlikely to be familiar to readers both because of its' limited use and because these kinds of nationally representative firm level surveys of mostly informal firms are much rarer. First, what are the characteristics of households which participate in the rural nonfarm economy compared to other types of households? And second, can the firm level data be used to assess the characteristics and potential of rural enterprises in comparison with those in urban areas?

3.1. The HBS data

The 2011/2012 Household Budget Survey (HBS) is a nationally representative survey, which is designed to provide estimates of household income and expenditures for poverty assessments, similar to how the Living Standard Measurement Surveys (LSMSs) are conducted routinely in many other countries. The 2011/2012 HBS surveyed 4130 rural households and 6056 rural households, and is also representative at three geographic locations – rural, Dar es Salaam and other urban. Similar to a standard LSMS, the HBS has an occupational module that provides information for all household members' primary employment by industries (including farming). This is the module used for the rural employment analysis in this paper. The survey also asked whether the households have their home enterprises, a question also used in the discussion in Section 3. However, the HBS only covers mainland Tanzania and excludes Zanzibar. Like the MSME survey to be discussed later, the sampling framework used to conduct the HBS survey is based on the 2002 Census, which could possibly oversample rural households given that, as discussed in Section 1, the 2012 Census has shown a decline of 6.5 percentage points in the share of rural population from the 2002 Census. A set of summary statistics based on the 2011/2012 HBS for the variables used in our analysis is presented in Appendix Table A1.

3.2. The MSME data

As mentioned in Section 1, the Micro, Small, and Medium Sized Enterprise (MSME) survey is Tanzania's first nationally representative survey of small businesses. The data was collected during interviews with 6134 small business owners identified in a three-step sampling process. In the first step, a sample of 640 representative enumeration areas were selected. A complete listing of all households was carried out to identify households that currently owned and ran small businesses or had recently closed businesses. In the second step, about nine to 12 households with currently operating businesses (and two to three households with closed businesses) were selected. Finally, if more than one member in a selected household owned and ran a small business, a Kish Grid was applied to select the interviewee. There are three questionnaires for the survey. The main questionnaire, which is used for this study, includes 192 questions on 20 topics that are asked to owners of currently operating enterprises. Based on the enterprise's main activities, main products and services, all enterprises in the survey were assigned to an industry according to the International Standard for Industrial Classification (ISIC). There are 80 unique ISIC industries, of which many have few sampled firms. Thus, in this study, the 80 industries are aggregated into 24 subsectors, six of which are in the manufacturing sector and the rest in service sectors.

A set of summary statistics of the MSME survey data is reported in Table 3 for the three areas separately: rural, other urban area and Dar es Salaam. Among the 6134 sampled firms, a total of 5609 firms have all the information required for the analysis. Based on the information that is available, there is no reason to believe that the firms with missing information are significantly different from the rest of the sample; for example, they are dispersed across regions and firm size.

As shown in the first row of Table 3, most MSMEs are extremely small: mean employment is 1.5 in rural areas, 1.65 in urban areas outside Dar es Salaam and 1.7 in Dar es Salaam. The very small size of MSMEs is at least in part possibly due to a sample selection bias. The sampling framework is household based rather than enterprise based, and is based on the 2002 Population and Housing Census. This could possibly lead to oversampling rural households given that, as discussed in Section 1, the 2012 Census has shown a decline of 6.5 percentage points in the share of rural population from the 2002 Census. The household-based sampling means that the survey probably under-sampled businesses outside households, which in practice translates into under-sampling relatively larger sized firms. The fact that more than 40 per cent of firms with five or more employees in the survey are sampled in rural areas might support this concern, as it is known that most larger sized firms are often in urban areas instead of rural areas. Among the 6134 enterprises sampled in the survey, there are only 96 firms with five or more employees. While for the largest firm in the sample there are 80 employees, the second and third largest ones have employees of 34 and 33 respectively. In fact, there are only four firms in the survey with employees more than 20. While the larger sized firms are usually assigned larger weights than the smaller ones in the data, this potential issue of possibly under-sampling larger urban firms is unlikely to be fully corrected by the assigned sample weights given that the sampling weights are derived from the relationship between listed households and households currently operating with businesses in selected representative enumeration areas.

As expected, few small firms are registered with Tanzania's Business Registration and Licensing Agency (BRELA) and there is little difference between rural and urban firms in this regard.[5] In contrast, more urban enterprises (8%) have tax identification numbers than rural enterprises (3%). While the MSME survey is a household based survey, 49 per cent of rural firms report that their businesses actually operate out of their homes and the number in urban areas is almost identical at 47 per cent. Therefore, the shares of nonfarm enterprises reported in Table 4 calculated from HBS 2011/2012 data could significantly underestimate the importance of MSMEs in rural areas, given that HBS captures only businesses run out of the home.

Table 3 also reports average monthly value-added and average monthly sales per firm. Firms in the MSME database report sales on a monthly basis and also provide their own judgement on whether a particular month is a good, bad or normal month. By taking the possible seasonality into account, value added is then computed as the firm's average monthly sales minus the firms' average monthly

Table 3. Rural and urban MSME summary statistics

Names of variables Business characteristics	Value unit or range	Rural Observations	Mean	S.D.	Other urban Observations	Mean	S.D.	Dar es Salaam Observations	Mean	S.D.
Number of employees per firm	Person	4,160	1.40	1.01	1,093	1.64	1.94	353	1.74	1.52
Number of full-time employees per firm	Person	4,160	1.23	0.69	1,093	1.38	1.30	353	1.52	1.07
Annual employment growth	[-.09,.25]	4,150	0.02	0.18	1,090	0.02	0.21	352	0.01	0.18
% of firms registered with BRELA	[0,1]	4,160	0.03	0.16	1,093	0.03	0.18	353	0.05	0.22
% of firms with tax ID	[0,1]	4,160	0.03	0.18	1,093	0.11	0.31	353	0.10	0.31
% of firms with business run out of home	[0,1]	4,160	0.08	0.27	1,093	0.09	0.28	353	0.05	0.21
Average monthly value added per firm	1,000 TZS	4,160	199	429	1,093	252	496	353	256	661
Average monthly sales per firm	1,000 TZS	4,160	383	979	1,093	463	1,4 21	353	466	797
Firm's age	Year	4,121	6.46	6.08	1,079	6.24	5.98	348	5.43	5.35
% of firms with business as full-time	[0,1]	4,160	0.80	0.40	1,093	0.80	0.40	353	0.83	0.38
Keeps accounts in ledger	[0,1]	4,160	0.39	0.49	1,093	0.51	0.50	353	0.46	0.50
Hires paid workers	[0,1]	4,160	0.07	0.26	1,093	0.16	0.37	353	0.23	0.42
>20 customers per day	[0,1]	4,160	0.28	0.45	1,093	0.29	0.46	353	0.32	0.47
Firms powers business with electricity	[0,1]	4,160	0.09	0.28	1,093	0.35	0.48	353	0.42	0.50
Owner saves in formal bank account	[0,1]	4160	0.05	0.22	1093	0.15	0.36	353	0.16	0.37
Owner/household characteristics										
Age of owner	Year	4,160	36.92	10.53	1,093	37.07	11.01	353	36.97	10.62
Whether owner is female	[0,1]	4,160	0.47	0.50	1,093	0.67	0.47	353	0.68	0.47
% of firms with business as main source of income	[0,1]	4,160	0.43	0.49	1,093	0.35	0.48	353	0.26	0.44
% of firms with farming as main source of income	[0,1]	4,160	0.24	0.43	1,093	0.06	0.25	353	0.00	0.00
% of firms with business as only source of income	[0,1]	4,160	0.28	0.45	1,093	0.46	0.50	353	0.55	0.50
% of firms' households that are not poor	[0,1]	4,160	0.41	0.49	1,093	0.53	0.50	353	0.61	0.49
% of firms' households that are moderately poor	[0,1]	4,160	0.37	0.48	1,093	0.32	0.47	353	0.27	0.45
% of firms' households that are very poor	[0,1]	4,160	0.22	0.41	1,093	0.15	0.36	353	0.12	0.32

Notes: Full-time employees include business owners and their family members if they work full-time in the firms. BRELA is Tanzania's Business Registration and Licensing Agency opened in 1999. Household poverty was reported in the survey by an indicator variable equal to zero if the household is not poor, one if the household is moderately poor and two if the household is very poor. The measure of poverty was computed using monthly household income as reported by survey respondents, and the poverty measured in the HBS is considered. TZS denote Tanzanian Shillings and 1000 TZS equivalent to $0.7 US dollars in 2010.

Source: Authors' calculations using the MSME Survey 2010

Table 4. Distribution of rural households with and without nonfarm activities (2011/2012)

| | | With nonfarm | | | |
| | | Farm/nonfarm mixed | | Nonfarm only | |
	Without nonfarm	With nonfarm enterprises	Without nonfarm enterprises	With nonfarm enterprises	Without nonfarm enterprises
Share by household numbers	61.4	22.1	5.4	5.8	5.4
Share by youth-headed households	56.9	20.5	4.7	8.7	9.2
Share by population	58.4	25.8	6.3	5.1	4.4
Share by employment	59.4	26.6	6.6	3.9	3.5
Share by youth employment	58.1	24.1	5.3	6.1	6.4
Headcount poverty rate (%)	39.3	27.3	31.8	14.2	15.3

Notes: The HBS asked individual households whether they have a home business and an ISIC rev4 code is used for assigning sectors to the business. We consider ISIC non-agricultural sectors only as nonfarm enterprises. The employment of non-agriculture is defined by the current primary employment that is not in agriculture.
Source: Authors' calculations based on the data of HBS 2011/2012 (NBS, 2014a).

costs of production. The mean value-added of rural firms reported in Table 3 is about 20 per cent lower than the mean value-added of urban firms in both Dar es Salaam and other urban areas. However, there is significant variation among surveyed firms in monthly value-added in both rural and urban areas, indicated by the high value of the standard deviation (s.d.) in Table 3. We will return to this point in detail later in this paper.

Most MSME firms are young, with a mean age of 6.9 years for rural firms, 6.1 years for urban firms outside Dar es Salaam, and 5.5 years for firms in Dar es Salaam. This is consistent with the findings in Section 1 that most nonfarm jobs created in Tanzania between 2002 and 2012 were created by the informal sector. Table 3 also indicates that 76 per cent of rural businesses operate full time, compared to 82 per cent in urban areas outside Dar es Salaam and 87 per cent in Dar es Salaam. More than 40 per cent of rural business owners report that the business is the owners' main source of income with a significantly lower share of rural business owners (28%) reporting that the business is the owners' only source of income. By contrast, 44 per cent and 51 per cent of business owners in other urban and Dar es Salaam report that the enterprise is their only source of income. Only about a quarter of rural business owners report that farming is their main source of income, a fact that supports the finding from the 2011/2012 HBS, that many households (about 10%) in rural areas only participate in the nonfarm economy as their primary employment.

Like their businesses, the owners of these small businesses are also relatively young. For the full sample, the mean age of business owners is roughly 37 years in rural and 36 years in urban areas. In contrast, according to the HBS data, the average age of a rural household's head is 47 years old and 42 years old for an average urban household's head.

Finally, the last three rows of Table 3 report the distribution of business owners by the three categories of their household's income. The measure of these three income categories (very poor, modestly poor and not poor)[6] was computed using monthly household income reported by survey respondents. Poverty appears to be higher among households with MSME owners than among overall rural and urban households. Based on the poverty assessment profile reported by the government (NBS [National Bureau of Statistics], 2013), there are 66.7 per cent of the rural population, 78.3 per cent of the urban population outside of Dar es Salaam and 95.8 per cent of Dar es Salaam's population lives in nonpoor households. In contrast, in the MSME survey, only 45 per cent of rural MSME owners, 54 per cent of urban MSME owners outside of Dar es Salaam and 62 per cent of MSME owners in Dar es Salaam live in nonpoor households. This seems to confirm that in both urban and rural areas, small businesses are often part of a coping strategy for many poor households, while rich households are less likely to choose such small businesses as their main livelihoods.

3.3. Methodologies

The empirical strategy employed in this paper aims to answer to two questions: (1) What determines whether households participate in the nonfarm economy? And (2) what determines whether nonfarm enterprises have the potential to contribute to employment and labour productivity growth? To answer these questions econometric analyses are used.

Descriptive statistics for the HBS and MSME data provide a glimpse of the heterogeneity that is observed across households and firms. The means and standard errors presented in all the descriptive tables of this paper were generated using the sampling design of the two surveys (HBS and MSME).

To address the first question, the rural households in the HBS data are classified into three types based on their family members' primary employment in the econometric analysis, while more subgroups of households are further classified in the descriptive analysis. The three types of rural households are: (1) farm, in which all family members' primary employment is agriculture; (2) mixed, indicating that in the same household some family members work in agriculture and others in rural nonfarm economy; and (3) nonfarm, in which all family members work in the rural nonfarm economy as their primary employment. A multinomial probit model is used in the analysis. The choice of a multinomial probit over a multinomial logit arose from the fact that the multinomial probit is better suited to handle correlations and is not bound by the independence of irrelevant alternatives like the multinomial logit. The farm household group is chosen as the comparison category in the regression.

For the MSME dataset, the left-hand side variable is binary which under normal circumstances could be addressed with a simple probit model. However, we must modify our approach due to possible endogeneity issues in some of the right-hand side variables. Dealing with endogeneity in non-linear models (particularly in a probit model) is a straightforward exercise if the endogenous variable is continuous. In such cases, endogeneity is dealt using a control function approach as explained in Wooldridge (2010) and StataCorp (2015).[7] The endogenous variables in our dataset are binary in nature, however. This eliminates the possibility of using a control function approach but raises the possibility of using a bivariate probit model. However, this last approach is also ruled out because it only allows for one endogenous variable while our dataset contains multiple endogenous variables. To address this issue, we have therefore resorted to estimating the probit model using a generalised method of moments (GMM) approach which allows for the endogeneity of multiple variables.

Estimating probit models using GMM is straight-forward if only exogeneous variables are present in the right-hand side, as is shown in StataCorp (2015). However, in the presence of endogeneity the estimation becomes considerably more complicated, as instruments cannot simply be added to the moment conditions of a GMM instrumental variable approach (as one would do for linear models). Doing so for probit or logit models is not possible since neither the conditional expectations nor the linear projections assumed for the linear model apply in the case of probit models. We have therefore followed Wilde (2008) to estimate a two-stage generalised methods of moments (GMM) model which accounts for both the non-linearity of the model and the binary nature of the endogenous variables.

The GMM estimation as proposed by Wilde takes the following form. In the first stage, a reduced form probit model is estimated for each endogenous variable and the residuals are calculated. Having estimated stage 1, a two-step GMM approach is used to estimate the parameters using the correct moment conditions and the necessary adjustments to the standard errors. We refer the reader to Wilde (2008) for details on the specification of the moment conditions. The method proposed by Wilde and as applied in this paper leads to an exactly identified estimation, meaning that the number of instruments equal the number of parameters. Thus, no tests for overidentification of instruments could be conducted for the final estimation. The left-hand side variable for the structural model was defined as follows. It took the value of one if the firm's value-added per worker (which is used to measure the firm level labour productivity) is greater than the economy-wide labour productivity in the trade sector at the national level and zero otherwise. The small firms with high potential are defined as the 'in-between' firms following Lewis (1979).

The specifications of the models described above are provided in Sections 3.2 for the HBS survey and Section 4.4 for the MSME survey. Average marginal effects, which can be interpreted as the change in the predicted probability given a one unit change in the right-hand side in the case of continuous variables or a discrete change in the case of categorical variables, are reported. With the exceptions of two variables (firm age and number of employees), all our right-hand side variables are binary in nature. Thus, the marginal effects should be interpreted as discrete changes and, as such, we report average marginal effects. All estimations are done using robust standard errors in accordance to the sampling design. Since the survey was not in any way stratified and subnational units are not representative, we have not clustered the standard errors to any specific subnational location.

4. Characteristics of households with rural nonfarm activities

We begin this section using the 2011/2012 HBS to assess the size of the rural nonfarm economy by the number (or share) of rural households that participate in the nonfarm economy and the differences between households with and without rural nonfarm participation. We then analyse the characteristics of the three categories of households using a multinomial probit model.

4.1. How large is the rural nonfarm economy?

As a starting point, we first classify rural households using the HBS data into with and without nonfarm activities. The classification is based on household members' primary employment. Like other low-income countries in Africa, most states in Tanzania are predominantly rural (Davis, Di Giuseppe, & Zezza, 2014). Farm activity dominates rural Tanzania – 61.4 per cent of rural households' members engage only in agricultural activities in 2012 (Table 4), and less than 40 per cent engage in nonfarm activities. Households engaging in rural nonfarm activities can further be classified as farm/nonfarm mixed and nonfarm only households. As shown in Table 4, about 27.5 per cent of total rural households are farm/nonfarm mixed households and about 11 per cent are nonfarm only households.

We also further categorise rural households with nonfarm activities according to whether they have their own nonfarm businesses. This helps us to establish a link between the HBS survey and the MSME survey to be analysed later. According to the HBS, fewer mixed households have their own nonfarm businesses, while almost half of the nonfarm only households own nonfarm businesses. These numbers are comparable to the statistics drawn from the firm data of the MSME survey in Table 3, which shows that 43 per cent of rural nonfarm enterprises are the household's main income source, but only 28 per cent with businesses report that the business is the only source of income. Finally, we also show in Table 4 that rural households with nonfarm businesses are less likely to be in poverty.

4.2. Characteristics of households in the rural nonfarm economy

Characteristics of the different types of households are explored using a multinomial probit model as discussed in Section 2.3. Equation (1) below describes the specification used in the estimation

$$y_i^* = a + \beta_1(H_i) + \beta_2(C_j) + \beta_3(D_r) + \varepsilon_i \tag{1}$$

where y_i is the choice of a given household and takes three values (1 = farm, 2 = mixed, 3 = nonfarm), H_i is a vector of household characteristics, C_j is a vector of infrastructure or other community level factors, D_r is a set of regional dummies. The variables in the vector H_i include a dummy equal to one if the household is headed by a young person (age 15–34); a dummy equal to one if the household head is female; dummies for the levels of education of the household heads (less than primary as the comparable variable) and; dummies for farm size defined by cultivated area categorised into four groups: no-land, farms with less than two ha, farms with two to five ha, and farms with more than five ha (no land is the comparison group). Vector C_j contains a set of variables related to access to infrastructure at the community level and other community level variables including daily public transportation to the regional capital, electricity, mobile phone signal, internet, banks, informal finance, cooperatives, a large employer (for example, a factory), and a weekly market. ε_i is the iid error term.

Table 5 reports the average marginal effects for the three types of households. We begin with the household variables. Being a young household head has a significant and positive effect on being a nonfarm household, with the predicted probability increasing by 3.1 per cent, and has a negative effect at a similar scale on being a mixed household. The level of the household's head education shows a

Table 5. The average marginal effects (predicted probabilities) calculated from the multinomial probit regression using 2012 HBS data

Variable	Farm	Mixed	Nonfarm
Youth (age 15–34) as head of a household	0.00622	−0.0370***	0.0308***
	(0.0153)	(0.0127)	(0.00913)
Female headed household	0.0149	−0.0217	0.00679
	(0.0197)	(0.0145)	(0.0109)
(Compared to less than primary)			
Primary education	−0.0639***	0.00566	0.0583***
	(0.0156)	(0.0103)	(0.0127)
Secondary & higher	−0.299***	0.103***	0.196***
	(0.0259)	(0.0177)	(0.0196)
(Compared to no land)			
Less than 2 ha	0.249***	−0.0283	−0.221***
	(0.0296)	(0.0254)	(0.0162)
2–5 ha	0.273***	−0.0264	−0.247***
	(0.0318)	(0.0259)	(0.0185)
More than 5 ha	0.206***	0.0309	−0.237***
	(0.0377)	(0.0273)	(0.0235)
Community variables			
Daily public transport to the regional capital	−0.0298	−0.00986	0.0397**
	(0.0290)	(0.0179)	(0.0201)
Electricity access	−0.0285	0.0258	0.00277
	(0.0289)	(0.0200)	(0.0171)
Mobile phone signal	0.0678**	−0.0682***	0.000398
	(0.0288)	(0.0188)	(0.0187)
Internet access	−0.0511	0.0365*	0.0145
	(0.0337)	(0.0211)	(0.0198)
Formal banks	−0.0261	0.0236	0.00249
	(0.0492)	(0.0321)	(0.0401)
Informal financial services	0.0667***	−0.0282	−0.0385***
	(0.0248)	(0.0170)	(0.0139)
Cooperatives	−0.0253	0.0331**	−0.00781
	(0.0255)	(0.0145)	(0.0175)
A major state employer (business or factory)	−0.0517	0.00614	0.0455**
	(0.0353)	(0.0220)	(0.0223)
Weekly market	−0.0756***	0.0409**	0.0346**
	(0.0246)	(0.0144)	(0.0154)
Observations	4,053	4,053	4,053

Notes: Standard errors in parentheses. *p < 0.05; **p < 0.01; ***p < 0.001. The average marginal effects (predicted probabilities) based on the multinomial probit regression are reported. In the multinomial probit regression, the farm household group is chosen as the comparison category. See Table 5 in Sosa-Rubi, Galárraga, and Harris (2009) for a similar way to report the result.
Source: Authors' calculation from their estimation results of multinomial probit regression using 2012 Tanzania HBS data.

distinct and contrasting effect on being a farm or a nonfarm household. While both primary and secondary/higher education matter for being a nonfarm household, the more educated the household's head, the larger the effect. Only the higher level of education affects the probability of being a mixed household, as the effect of primary education is insignificant. These results seem to indicate that higher levels of education may be required to obtain nonfarm jobs in rural areas.

Next, we look at farm size. As expected, having a larger farm size decreases the probability of being a nonfarm household by 22–24 per cent. Likewise, a larger farm size is associated with a higher predicted probability of being a farm household by 20.6–27.3 per cent.

Differences among the three types of households are less pronounced for community level variables, perhaps due to the decreased variability that is inherent in these variables. Indeed, public transportation to the regional capital, a proxy for road access, only positively affects the probability of being a nonfarm household. Having a mobile phone signal has the opposite effect on being a farm and a mixed household, positive for the former and negative for the latter, while the effect on being a nonfarm household is insignificant. While the use of electricity for doing business, especially in the manufacturing sector, is important, the variable is not significant for any type of household; this is also true for internet access. This may be because access to electricity or internet at the community level does not necessarily imply access at the household level. Access to informal financial services is associated with a higher probability of being a farm household and a lower probability of being a nonfarm household, suggesting that informal financing is the main channel to borrow money for farm households. The presence of cooperatives is only significant for the effect on being a mixed household with a 3.3 per cent greater predicted probability. As expected, the presence of a large employer is associated with a higher predicted probability of being a nonfarm household by 4.5 per cent, but does not influence being a mixed household. Finally, having access to weekly markets is the only variable that is significant across all types of households. Access to markets reduces the predicted probability of being a farm household by 7.5 per cent and increases the predicted probability of being mixed and nonfarm households by 4 per cent and 3.4 per cent respectively. The mixed results regarding the role of infrastructure are puzzling. As noted, this may be because the community level variables are too 'rough' a proxy for access at the household level. However, the lack of significance of these variables may also be associated with the small scale of rural nonfarm enterprises. According to Tybout (2000), low levels of economic density and interaction may lead to small, diffuse pockets of demand, which in turn result in small, localised production and services. We revisit this issue in the next section using the MSME data.

5. Characteristics of rural nonfarm enterprises and their owners – an analysis at the firm level using MSME survey data

A vibrant rural nonfarm sector can play an important role in rural transformation. To understand the extent to which the rural nonfarm sector can play a role in labour productivity growth and poverty reduction in rural areas, the MSME survey data is used to examine the motivations of business owners in the rural nonfarm sector as well as the characteristics of their businesses. In a previous paper, Diao, Kweka, McMillan and Qureshi (2017) identify a group of MSMEs that can be considered members of what Arthur Lewis (1979) referred to as the in-between sector. According to Lewis (1979), these firms play an important role in the transformation process. Lewis (1979) uses the term in-between to signal that these firms are not just petty traders, rather, they often look more like formal firms and provide important goods and services. Diao, Kweka, et al. (2017) show that rural enterprises are on average slightly less productive than their urban counter-parts (this is confirmed in Table 3 of Section 2 in this paper) but they do not explore in detail the characteristics of rural enterprises or rural entrepreneurs.

This section begins with a description of the location and industrial composition of MSMEs. It follows with an exploration of the extent to which rural entrepreneurs appear to be subsistence or growth-oriented. To analyse this issue, we use the following data from the MSME survey: (i) self-reported motivations for business ownership; (ii) the productive heterogeneity of MSMEs and (iii) employment growth in MSMEs.

5.1. Industrial and geographic composition of MSMEs

Table 6 reports the distribution of employment and the number of MSMEs by rural, other urban and Dar es Salaam, compared with the distribution of population in the three locations. While more than 67 per cent of the population lives in rural areas, rural MSMEs account for 52 per cent of total MSME employment. In urban areas, the distribution of MSME employment/firms and distribution of population seem to be similar in Dar es Salaam and other urban areas. 15.8 per cent of MSME employment and 17.3 per cent of MSME firms are in Dar es Salaam, where 12.2 per cent of the national population resides. Likewise, 32.6 per cent of MSME employment and 30.7 per cent of MSME firms are in other urban areas, which contain 20.4 per cent of the population (Table 6).

Table 7 reports the industrial distribution of MSMEs by rural, other urban and Dar es Salaam. Although the MSMEs operate in a wide range of activities, the bulk of these activities can be classified as trade services (80%) and manufacturing (15%). However, more rural firms (19.8%) engage in manufacturing than urban firms (10.1% in other urban and 7.2% in Dar es Salaam). Seventy-two per cent of manufacturing MSMEs are in rural areas while 52 per cent of trade service MSMEs are in rural areas. This is an expected pattern, as small manufacturing firms operate mainly in food processing, which has strong links to agriculture. Without further information, however, it is not possible to identify exactly what these linkages are and how they work. This is an important area for future research. More firms are in the trade services in Dar es Salaam (87.6%) than in other urban (83.0%), which is clearly driven by demand for tradable goods.

5.2. Self-reported motivations of small business owners

The MSME survey includes three questions designed to elicit the reasons for opening a business. Responses to such self-reported motivations for a business could help us assess the extent to which rural entrepreneurs are in business solely for the purposes of survival or aiming to grow. The responses to these questions are tabulated using sample weights in Tables 8–10.

Table 6. Distribution of population and MSMEs (weighted, percentage)

	Population	MSME employment	Number of business
	All	All MSMEs	
Rural	67.4	51.6	52.1
Other urban	20.4	32.6	30.7
Dar Es Salaam	12.2	15.8	17.3
Total	100	100	100

Source: Population is from HBS (2012) and MSME employment and number are from MSME survey (2010).

Table 7. Sectoral distribution of rural and urban MSME firms in the survey (weighted, percentage)

	Percentage of total in each location				Percentage in each sector (National total by sector = 100)		
	Rural	Other urban	Dar es Salaam	National	Rural	Other urban	Dar es Salaam
Total	100	100	100	100	54.2	31.2	14.6
Manufacturing	19.8	10.1	7.2	14.9	71.9	21.1	7.1
Trade services	76.5	83.0	87.6	80.2	51.7	32.3	16.0
Others	3.8	6.9	5.2	4.9	41.1	43.5	15.4

Source: Authors' calculations using the MSME Survey 2010.

Table 8. Occupation prior to starting business of MSMEs (weighted, percentage)

All MSMEs	Rural	Other urban	Dar es Salaam	Total
Unemployed	4.8	11.3	9.7	7.6
Housewife (home maker)	12.3	26.6	34.1	20.0
In education, at various levels	3.2	5.5	5.4	4.2
Employed in large private enterprise in similar business	0.4	1.7	2.9	1.2
Employed in large private enterprise in a different business	1.7	4.7	6.9	3.4
Employed in a similar sized private business in the same line of business	0.6	1.5	1.9	1.0
Employed in a similar sized private business in another line of business	0.6	0.8	3.0	1.0
Ran a similar sized business in the same line of business	0.9	2.0	1.9	1.4
Ran a similar sized enterprise in another line of business	9.5	16.4	20.0	13.2
Civil servant/employed by the government	1.8	2.1	6.0	2.5
I was employed by some individual	0.6	2.2	1.9	1.3
Rearing of cattle	0.5	0.4	0.2	0.4
Farming	56.5	19.3	0.7	36.7
I was selling food	0.6	1.4	1.1	0.9
Others	4.8	3.5	2.4	4.0
None	1.2	0.6	2.0	1.1

Notes: This table is prepared based on the question 'what was your main occupation before you started this business?' in the MSME survey, and a unique answer is provided by individual MSME owners. The sum of each column in the table is 100.
Source: Authors' calculations using the MSME Survey 2010.

The first question is: 'What was your main occupation before you started this business?' As shown in Table 8, the biggest difference between rural and urban entrepreneurs is that 56.5 per cent of rural entrepreneurs report that their main occupation prior to starting the business was farming compared to 19.3 per cent in urban areas outside Dar es Salaam. Very few respondents (4.8%) in rural areas report that they were unemployed prior to starting the business; this is not true in urban areas where 11.3 per cent and 9.7 per cent of MSME owners in other urban and Dar es Salaam report that they were unemployed before starting their business. Unlike in rural areas, urban business owners are much more likely to report that they were previously employed in a private company or running a similar sized business in another line of business. It is also much more common for urban business owners to report that they were previously a housewife or homemaker (26.6% in other urban and 34.1% in Dar es Salaam) than for rural respondents (12.3%).

The second question is: 'For what reasons did you choose your line of business?' In Table 9, the firms responding to this question are grouped into three broad sectors: manufacturing, trade services and other services, by rural, other urban and Dar es Salaam. In rural areas, half of all business owners say that the reason they chose their line of business is because they saw a market opportunity. This response is similar for firms in manufacturing and trade services. However, this response is less common in Dar es Salaam and other urban areas. The second most common reason for operating in a line of business in rural areas is that the owners' capital could only finance that line of business; this response is more common in urban than rural areas possibly indicating that capital constraints are more severe in urban areas. The third most common reason for choosing a line of business in rural areas was prior experience in that line of business, although shares for this reason are much lower than the two previous reasons.

The third question is: 'If you were offered a full-time salary paying job, would you take it? 'Responses to this question are reported in Table 10 and indicate that only 46.6 per cent of all small business owners would leave their current business for a full time salaried position, but the share is higher in rural areas (47.8%) and other urban areas (48.6%) than in Dar es Salaam (37.7%). Approximately 64 per cent of all respondents who would prefer a full time salaried job say they

Table 9. Reasons for business choice by broad sector in MSME survey (weighted, percentage)

	Rural enterprise			Other urban enterprises			Enterprise in Dar es Salaam		
	Manufacturing	Trade services	Rural total	Manufacturing	Trade Services	Other urban total	Manufacturing	Trade services	Dar Es Salaam total
All MSMEs									
I had previous experience in this line	25.0	15.2	18.3	39.6	15.5	19.5	37.0	9.7	18.5
Friends/relatives are in this line	20.6	13.4	14.8	21.0	19.4	17.8	13.2	16.4	12.8
I saw a market opportunity	48.2	51.6	50.0	36.3	43.1	41.6	14.6	46.4	39.2
My capital could only finance this business	36.1	42.1	41.8	26.2	47.4	43.3	46.8	46.8	47.7
No apparent reason	2.9	6.0	4.5	4.3	2.9	4.2	3.2	5.2	4.7
I could start business gradually	0.0	0.1	0.1	0.0	0.1	0.5	0.0	1.0	0.6
Goods are easy to manufacture and sell	1.4	2.0	2.0	0.2	1.5	1.6	0.0	0.9	1.0
I just wanted to be near my house	0.8	1.0	0.9	0.0	1.8	1.2	0.0	0.0	0.4
I have been trained in it, I am an expert	1.6	0.4	0.6	6.2	0.1	1.1	9.4	0.4	0.9
Goods are available	0.3	0.4	0.5	0.0	0.4	0.2	0.0	2.7	1.4
I perceived it to be profitable	1.3	1.6	1.7	0.0	2.6	1.8	0.0	0.2	0.1
I liked it	0.7	1.0	1.3	3.5	1.5	1.6	1.8	1.1	1.1
Business does not have many problems	1.4	0.6	0.7	0.0	0.3	0.3	0.0	1.6	1.2
Other	1.0	2.5	2.2	5.7	2.4	3.1	1.3	3.2	2.4
None	0.3	1.3	0.8	2.0	0.9	1.2	1.3	0.0	1.1

Notes: Multiple answers are allowed for individual MSME owners.
Source: Authors' calculations using the MSME Survey 2010.

Table 10. Job satisfaction in MSME survey (weighted, percentage)

All MSMEs	Rural	Other urban	Dar es Salaam	Total
If you were offered a full-time salary paying job, would you take it?	47.8	48.6	37.7	46.6
Who would you rather work for?				
A large private company	17.9	27.4	43.1	24.0
Government	68.6	62.9	44.6	63.9
Someone else's business	10.5	6.2	10.8	9.1
Anywhere	3.0	3.4	1.5	3.0
And why do you say that?				
Better security of income	81.7	83.8	81.4	82.3
Shorter hours	5.1	5.7	3.5	5.1
Less risk	1.8	1.8	3.0	1.9
To get pension	1.5	1.6	.	1.4
I am less educated	2.2	0.9	1.9	1.8
They listen to the opinions of the employees	1.1	1.0	.	1.0
As long as I get a living	0.6	0.4	.	0.5
Job security	2.1	0.6	.	1.4
Others	2.2	2.3	9.9	3.1
None/Nothing	1.7	2.1	0.2	1.6

Notes: This table is prepared based on three questions: (1) 'If you were offered a full-time salary paying job, would you take it?' (2) 'Who would you rather work for?' and (3) 'Why do you say that?' A unique answer is provided by individual MSME owners to each of the last two questions. Rural, urban and national total MSMEs, MSMEs owned by youth and MSMEs owned by other adults for the sum of these two questions are 100 respectively.
Source: Authors' calculations using the MSME Survey 2010.

would like to work for the government, with 68.6 per cent and 62.9 per cent in rural areas and other urban areas respectively but only 44.6 per cent in Dar es Salaam, where more government jobs are concentrated. The responses from rural and other urban MSME owners are consistent with results reported in Banerjee and Duflo's analysis of the economic lives of the poor (Banerjee & Duflo, 2007). Large private companies are more attractive to small business owners in Dar es Salaam than in other places. The predominant reason for preferring a full time salaried position is better security of income.

5.3. The productive heterogeneity of rural enterprises

The kernel densities of the log of value added per worker, which is defined as firms' labour productivity, is used to examine the productive heterogeneity of MSMEs. Value added is computed as the firm's average monthly sales minus the firms' average monthly costs of production, and seasonality is taken into consideration in the calculation. Only full-time employees (including owners of the firms) are considered in calculating value-added per worker or labour productivity for individual firms. The kernel densities of labour productivity reveal two important features of the MSME firms.

First, there is a significant degree of productive heterogeneity among both rural, urban and Dar es Salaam enterprises. This can be seen by examining the density of the log of value added per worker in Figure 1. Surprisingly, the distribution of the log of value added per worker or labour productivity for rural firms is almost identical to the distribution for urban firms. In fact, stochastic dominance test rejects the hypothesis that the rural and urban distributions are not identical.[8] One reason for this may be the fact that medium sized enterprises that are mainly in urban areas appear to be under-sampled in the MSME survey discussed in Section 2.

In Figure 1 the vertical lines represent average labour productivity in Tanzania's economy in 2010 in the agricultural sector (the far-left line), the trade services sector (the middle-line) and the manufacturing sector (the far-right line). Economy-wide labour productivity is calculated using national accounts data and census data; since 1997 national accounts data make every attempt to include the informal

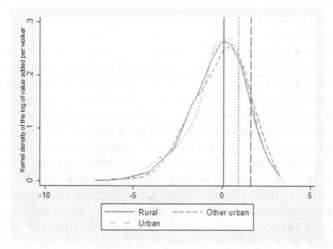

Figure 1. The distribution of the log of value added per worker among MSMES in 2010 by location.

sector (GGDC, Africa Sector Database, 2015). However, in practice it is difficult to accurately measure informal sector activity and so it is likely that economy-wide estimates of labour productivity are biased toward the formal sector.

Figure 1 reveals that a little over half of the firms in the MSME sector have labour productivity levels higher than the average labour productivity in the agricultural sector and this is true in all three locations. This is not surprising and is consistent with evidence presented by Diao, Kweka, et al. (2017), who show that labour productivity for many MSMEs is consistently higher than average labour productivity in the agricultural sector. It is also true that around 25 per cent of rural and urban MSMEs have labour productivity higher than average labour productivity in the services sector – a sector most MSMEs belong to. In fact, as shown in Diao, Kweka, et al. (2017), this group of 25 per cent of small firms accounts for 77 per cent of total value-added produced by the whole MSME sector. In other words, the remaining 75 per cent of MSMEs account for less than 25 per cent of the value added generated by the MSME sector. These results underscore the productive heterogeneity of MSMEs in both rural and urban areas. They also raise the possibility of a growth strategy focused on these most productive firms. This is not to say that the remaining firms should not be part of a strategy for alleviating poverty, perhaps they should. Our point is that the productive heterogeneity most likely calls for different strategies for different types of firms.

6. Using the MSME survey to identify 'high potential' rural enterprises

If we accept that some rural MSMEs have more potential to contribute to rural transformation in Tanzania than others, we are left with the question of how to identify those with potential. This is a complicated problem not least because a properly designed mechanism should be immune from manipulation. We do not pretend to solve it. Instead, what follows is meant to be illustrative of the way in which we are thinking about the problem. We use a productivity cutoff to distinguish in-between MSMEs from the rest of the MSMEs and then we look for readily observable characteristics of these highly productive MSMEs that might be used for targeting. In practice, it would be important to use readily observable characteristics that cannot be manipulated or are too costly to be manipulated by firms.

For the purposes of this exercise, we define the in-between firms as those with labour productivity greater than economy-wide labour productivity in trade services. Using this criterion, we identify 1334 rural firms in the MSME sample that can be classified as belonging to the in-between sector. Having selected our in-between firms, we use the GMM probit analysis previously described to identify characteristics of in-between firms. We use a host of business and owner characteristics that have been used and tested in the literature.

Prior to discussing the results of the GMM probit regressions, we must first identify the endogenous variables and present the instruments used for the reduced form probit estimations. Three endogenous variables were identified: the owner views the business as growing, the firm has regional customers, and the number of daily customers is more than 20. The first two variables were instrumented using the following variables: whether the business was located at home, whether the firm advertised, whether the firm had a business plan, and whether the firm regularly sends or receives money. The model was run using a two-stage GMM with robust standard errors. Results of the first-stage estimations are available upon request.

Table 11 presents the GMM probit results of the increases in predicted probability (the average marginal effect) of being an in-between sector firm in rural and urban areas. Results for the owners' personal characteristics suggest that a female-headed business is associated with a decrease in the probability of being in-between in both rural and urban areas; probabilities decrease by 6.4 and 9.5 per cent, respectively. Owners that perceive their businesses to be growing observe gains in the predicted probability of being in-between by 4.8 per cent and 6.4 per cent nationally and in rural areas, respectively. These results are intuitive; business owners who are optimistic about their firm's future and potential are more likely to be driven to achieve success and to use resources productively. Being a member of a business association increases the probability of being an in-between firm nationally and in urban areas, but not in rural areas, possibly due to the low participation rate of rural firms in such associations. Education was not found to be significant anywhere, likely due to lack of variation in education among business owners.

The second panel of Table 11 shows varying levels of significance between locations, which is expected. A one-year increase in a firm's age has a small effect on the probability of being an in-between firm in the country as a whole and in rural areas, but not in urban areas. A one-unit increase in the number of employees reduces the probability of being an in-between firm by around 5 per cent consistently in both rural and urban areas. On the other hand, operating full time is associated with an increase in the probability of being in-between by 6.2 per cent nationally and 6.7 per cent in rural areas, but is not significant in urban areas possibly for two reasons. First, the survey is designed to capture small businesses, of which many in urban areas may be part-time. Second, unless the businesses are large enough, running a full-time small business in an urban area probably carries a higher opportunity cost if it means not finding a job. Keeping written accounts is significant with an increase in the predicted probability of being in between of around 6.5 per cent in all locations. There are increases in the predicted probability of being in-between for firms which have licenses, with a larger marginal effect in urban areas (6%) than in rural areas (3.4%). The increases in the predicted probability of being in the in-between sector from having regional customers is significant only in rural areas. However, firms that have a daily number of customers greater than 20 are between 7.4 per cent (rural areas) and 6.2 per cent (urban areas) more likely to be in the in-between sector.

The variables associated with the external conditions of doing business, infrastructure and technology, are presented in the third panel of Table 11. Using a mobile phone increases the predicted probability of being in-between by 4.3 per cent in rural areas and 6.2 per cent in urban areas. Whether the business uses electricity to light their businesses is important in rural areas, increasing the predicted probability by 5.6 per cent, but not in urban areas, possibly again due to the lack of variability in electricity access in urban areas. We also include three financing variables in the regression (the last panel of Table 11), and all three variables are related to the ways business owners allocated their profits. It turns out all three variables are insignificant, possibly due to lack of variability in these variables, or they fail to accurately capture firms' investment behaviour.

7. Summary and policy implications

Although Tanzania remains heavily rural, the composition of economic activity in rural areas has changed significantly over the past decade and a half. Between 2002 and 2012, the share of the rural

Table 11. GMM probit results for probability of being in-between rural and urban enterprises – average marginal effects

Variable	National	Urban	Rural
Owner's characteristics			
Education (completed secondary or higher)	0.00852	−0.00511	0.0261
	(0.0220)	(0.0302)	(0.0307)
Female	−0.0740***	−0.0954***	−0.0649***
	(0.0148)	(0.0276)	(0.0161)
Owner would leave for salaried job	−0.0330**	−0.0484**	−0.0206
	(0.0139)	(0.0241)	(0.0145)
Owner is a Member of a Business Association	0.0777***	0.120***	0.00183
	(0.0280)	(0.0382)	(0.0340)
Saw Business as a Market Opportunity	0.0198	0.0374	0.00821
	(0.0137)	(0.0239)	(0.0144)
Views business as growing	0.0485***	0.0326	0.0645***
	(0.0149)	(0.0270)	(0.0154)
Business characteristics			
Firm's age	0.00244**	0.00132	0.00309***
	(0.00100)	(0.00185)	(0.00106)
Firm Size (number of employees)	−0.0508***	−0.0550***	−0.0494***
	(0.00990)	(0.0124)	(0.0172)
Business runs as Full time	0.0622***	0.0438	0.0673***
	(0.0187)	(0.0332)	(0.0211)
Firm keeps Written accounts	0.0643***	0.0627**	0.0678***
	(0.0154)	(0.0271)	(0.0160)
Firm has a License	0.0467***	0.0600**	0.0337*
	(0.0169)	(0.0287)	(0.0197)
Firm has Regional Customers	0.0188	−0.00993	0.0421**
	(0.0176)	(0.0285)	(0.0197)
Number of daily customers is more than 20	0.0686***	0.0622***	0.0742***
	(0.0138)	(0.0241)	(0.0146)
Firm's suppliers are small traders	0.0151	0.0269	0.00865
	(0.0139)	(0.0245)	(0.0150)
Firm's Suppliers are Nationwide	0.0223	0.0523	−0.0514
	(0.0302)	(0.0390)	(0.0496)
Infrastructure and technology			
Owner using Mobile to Conduct Business	0.0529***	0.0617**	0.0427***
	(0.0157)	(0.0282)	(0.0156)
Fir Owner has a Calculator	0.0235	0.0370	0.00891
	(0.0182)	(0.0312)	(0.0201)
Business uses Electricity to Light Business	0.0493***	0.0433	0.0560**
	(0.0187)	(0.0275)	(0.0233)
Financing			
Owner uses profit to Expand Business	0.0204	0.0287	0.0194
	(0.0178)	(0.0329)	(0.0173)
Owner uses profits to Buy Stocks in Advance	0.00483	−0.0100	0.0150
	(0.0145)	(0.0256)	(0.0145)
Owners uses Profits to Invest in Buildings and Land	0.0291	0.0148	0.0360
	(0.0262)	(0.0498)	(0.0289)
Observations	5,548	1,427	4,121

Notes: Standard errors in parentheses; ***$p < 0.01$, **$p < 0.05$, *$p < 0.1$. Dependent variable is a binary variable which takes the value of one if the firm is in-between and zero otherwise. Firms in the 'in-between' category satisfy the following conditions: labour productivity is higher than economy-wide labour productivity in trade. *Source*: Authors' estimation using MSME data.

labour force working in nonfarm employment tripled going from 6.8 per cent to 20.5 per cent, Moreover, in 2011/2012, more than one-third of rural households participated in the rural nonfarm economy and 11.2 per cent of rural households reported that working members of the household had primary employment only in the nonfarm economy.

The heads of 'nonfarm only' rural households tend to be younger and more educated, while the heads' gender does not appear to influence the likelihood of being a nonfarm household. Education of the household head is also a determinant of the likelihood that a household participates in the nonfarm sector; a primary education increases the probability of engaging in nonfarm activities by 5.8 per cent and a secondary education increases the likelihood of engaging in the nonfarm sector by 16.9 per cent. Among a set of selected community level variables, households in communities with access to daily public transportation or a weekly market are more likely to participate in rural nonfarm activities. Consistent with these results, we find that rural households with nonfarm activities are less likely to be poor. However, it is still true that around 15 per cent of rural households whose primary source of income is the nonfarm economy have incomes that place them below the poverty line. The implication is that some nonfarm activities must be very unproductive. By extension, although these activities help families to survive, it would be unrealistic to expect them to contribute significantly to rural transformation.

To explore the nature of the nonfarm businesses owned by rural households in Tanzania, we use Tanzania's first nationally representative survey of micro, small and medium sized enterprises. Roughly 20 per cent of these businesses operate in the manufacturing sector – more than double the share in urban areas – the rest of the businesses operate in the services sector. Labour productivity among these businesses is extremely heterogeneous with roughly half having labour productivity lower than average labour productivity in agriculture. Using a probit specification we show that operating full time, keeping written accounts and using electricity to run the business are all positively correlated with labour productivity.

We conclude that policies designed to stimulate rural transformation must take into account the heterogeneity of the rural nonfarm sector. Unless this heterogeneity is understood, policies designed to stimulate rural transformation are likely to disappoint. Of course, rural nonfarm activities help to generate income and reduce the risks associated with agricultural production for many rural households. These activities should be supported as part of a poverty reduction strategy. But we should not expect the large majority of these activities to transform rural livelihoods. For this to happen, it will be important to target the firms with the potential for employment and labour productivity growth.

Acknowledgements

This work was undertaken as part of the CGIAR Research Program on Policies, Institutions, and Markets (PIM) led by IFPRI. Funding for the study was provided by PIM. We are grateful to two anonymous reviewers for useful comments on previous versions of the paper, and to Peixun Fang and Jed Silver for excellent research assistance. Finally, Xinshen and Margaret would like to dedicate this article to the memory of Eduardo Magalhaes who sadly and prematurely passed away in August 2017.

Funding

This paper has benefited from funding from the CGIAR Research Program on Policies, Institutions, and Markets (PIM) led by IFPRI.

Disclosure statement

No potential conflict of interest was reported by the authors.

Notes

1. Although other nationally representative surveys of MSMEs exist, the data collected in these surveys is minimal and do not allow for the calculation of labour productivity.
2. For example, the nationally representative GEMINI surveys conducted in the early 1990s and funded by the United States Agency for International Development in a handful of African countries only collected location and employment data for the nationally representative sample. For a much smaller group of around 250 firms per country, more detailed information was collected but still not enough information to calculate value added and thus labour productivity.
3. For example, the World Bank Enterprise Survey conducted in Tanzania in January 2013–August 2014 interviewed 813 firms' owners and top managers including 514 small firms.
4. The survey used in Jin and Deininger (2009) covers only rural enterprises (1239) and rural households (1610) in Tanzania and cannot be used for a comparison to urban enterprises.
5. BRELA is Tanzania's Business Registrations and Licensing Agency. It is a Government Executive Agency and was established on the 28 October 1999. The aim of the agency is to ensure that businesses operate in accordance with regulations and to ensure that businesses follow 'sound principles'.
6. See the definition in the notes of Table 3.
7. Stata estimates these models using the ivprobit.
8. A stochastic dominance test compares the cumulative density function of the log of the valued added in rural and urban areas. To establish whether the two curves originate from the same distribution, we have used the Komolgorov-Smirnov test of equality of distribution. We were not able to reject the null hypothesis that the distributions of urban and rural value added were the same (p-value = 0.9).

References

Banerjee, A. V., Breza, E., Duflo, E., & Kinnan, C. (2015). *Do Credit Constraints Limit Entrepreneurship? Heterogeneity in the Returns to Microfinance*. NBER Conference Paper. Cambridge, MA: National Bureau of Economic Research. http://conference.nber.org/confer/2015/SI2015/PRPD/Kinnan.pdf.

Banerjee, A. V., & Duflo, E. (2007). The economic lives of the poor. *The Journal of Economic Perspectives: A Journal of the American Economic Association, 21*(1), 141–168.

Beck, T. H. L. (2007). Financing constraints of SMEs in developing countries: Evidence, determinants and solutions. In *Financing innovation-oriented businesses to promote entrepreneurship*. Unknown Publisher.

Bezu, S., & Barrett, C. (2012). Employment dynamics in the rural nonfarm sector in Ethiopia: Do the poor have time on their side? *Journal of Development Studies, 48*(9), 1223–1240.

Davis, B., Di Giuseppe, S., & Zezza, A. (2014). *Income diversification patterns in rural Sub-Saharan Africa: Reassessing the evidence* (Policy Research Working Paper 7108). Washington, DC: World Bank.

De Brauw, A., Mueller, V., & Lee, H. L. (2014). The role of rural–Urban migration in the structural transformation of Sub-Saharan Africa. *World Development, 63*(2014), 33–42.

Diao, X., Kweka, J., McMillan, M., & Qureshi, Z. (2017). *Economic transformation from the bottom up: Evidence from Tanzania* (IFPRI Discussion Paper 1603). Washington, DC: International Food Policy Research Institute.

Diao, X., McMillan, M., & Rodrik, D. (2017). *The recent growth boom in developing economies: A structural-change perspective* (NBER Working Paper 23132). Cambridge, MA: National Bureau of Economic Research.

Fafchamps, M., McKenzie, D., Quinn, S., & Woodruff, C. (2014). When is capital enough to get female enterprises growing? Evidence from a randomized experiment in Ghana. *Journal of Development Economics, 106*(January), 211–226.

Gibson, J., & Olivia, S. (2010). The effect of infrastructure access and quality on nonfarm enterprises in rural Indonesia. *World Development, 38*(5), 717–726.

Gollin, D., & Rogerson, R. (2009). *The greatest of all improvements: Roads, agriculture, and economic development in Africa*. Williamstown, MA: Department of Economics, a mimeo, Williams College.

Grimm, M., Krüger, J., & Lay, J. (2011). Barriers to entry and returns to capital in informal activities: Evidence from Sub-Saharan Africa. *Review of Income and Wealth, 57*(1), 27–53.

Haggblade, S., Hazell, P. B. R., & Brown, J. (1989). Farm-nonfarm linkages in rural sub-saharan africa. *World Development, 17* (August), 1173–1202.

Hagglade, S., Hazell, P., & Reardon, T. (2010). The rural nonfarm economy: Prospects for growth and poverty reduction. *World Development, 38*(1), 1429–1441.

Jin, S., & Deininger, K. (2009). Key constraints for rural nonfarm activity in Tanzania: Combining investment climate and household surveys. *Journal of African Economies, 18*(2), 319–361.

La Porta, R., & Shleifer, A. (2011). *The unofficial economy in Africa* (NBER Working Paper 16821). Cambridge, MA: National Bureau of Economic Research.

La Porta, R., & Shleifer, A. (2014). *Informality and development* (NBER Working Paper 20205). Cambridge, MA: National Bureau of Economic Research.

Lewis, W. A. (1979). The dual economy revisited. *The Manchester School, 47*(3), 211–229.

Li, Y., & Rama, M. (2015). Firm dynamics, productivity growth, and job creation in developing countries: The role of micro- and small enterprises. *The World Bank Research Observer, 30*(1), 3–38.

McKenzie, D., & Woodruff, C. (2008). Experimental evidence on returns to capital and access to finance in Mexico. *World Bank Economic Review, 22*(3), 457–482.

McKenzie, D. J. (2015). *Identifying and spurring high-growth entrepreneurship: Experimental evidence from a business plan competition* (World Bank Policy Research Working Paper 7391). Washington, DC: World Bank Group.

McPherson, M. (1996). Growth of micro and small enterprises in Southern Africa. *Journal of Development Economics, 48*, 253–277.

Mead, D. C. (1994). The contribution of small enterprises to employment growth in Southern and Eastern Africa. *World Development, 22*(12), 1881–1894.

Mead, D. C., & Liedholm, C. (1998). The dynamics of micro and small enterprises in developing countries. *World Development, 26*(1), 61–74.

Nagler, P., & Naudé, W. (2017). Nonfarm enterprises in rural Africa: New empirical evidence. *Food Policy, 67*(C), 175–191.

National Bureau of Statistics. (2006). *Tanzania 2002 census: Analytic report, Volume X*. Dar es Salaam: National Bureau of Statistics, Ministry of Planning, Economy, and Empowerment, Tanzania.

National Bureau of Statistics. (2007). *Analytic Report for Employment and Earnings Survey 2002*. Dar es Salaam: National Bureau of Statistics, Ministry of Planning, Economy, and Empowerment, Tanzania.

National Bureau of Statistics. (2011a). *National household budget survey 2000-2001*. Dar es Salaam: National Bureau of Statistics, Ministry of Finance, Tanzania.

National Bureau of Statistics. (2011b). *Integrated labor force survey 2014, analytical report*. Dar es Salaam: National Bureau of Statistics, Ministry of Finance, Tanzania.

National Bureau of Statistics. (2013). *Key findings of 2011/12 household budget survey Tanzania Mainland*. Dar es Salaam: National Bureau of Statistics, Ministry of Finance, Tanzania.

National Bureau of Statistics. (2014a). *Household budget survey: Main report, 2011/12*. Dar es Salaam: National Bureau of Statistics, Ministry of Finance, Tanzania.

National Bureau of Statistics. (2014b). *Tanzania 2012 census: basic demographic and socio-economic profile*. Dar es Salaam and Zanzibar: National Bureau of Statistics, Ministry of Finance, Office of Chief Government Statistician, Ministry of State, President's Office, State House and Good Governance, Tanzania.

National Bureau of Statistics. (2014c). *National accounts of Tanzania Mainland 2001–2013*. Dar es Salaam: National Bureau of Statistics, Ministry of Finance, Tanzania.

National Bureau of Statistics. (2014d). *Revised national accounts estimates for Tanzania Mainland, Base Year, 2007*. Dar es Salaam: National Bureau of Statistics, Ministry of Finance, Tanzania.

National Bureau of Statistics. (2014e). *Formal Sector Employment and Earnings Survey: Analytical Report 2013*. Dar es Salaam National Bureau of Statistics, Ministry of Finance, Tanzania.

National Bureau of Statistics. (2015). *Integrated labor force survey 2014, analytical report*. Dar es Salaam: National Bureau of Statistics, Ministry of Finance, Tanzania.

Nordman, C., Rakotomanana, F., & Roubaud, F. (2016). Informal versus formal: A panel data analysis of earnings gaps in Madagascar. *World Development, 86*, 1–17.

Raj, R., & Sen, K. (2013). *How important are credit constraints for small firm growth? Evidence from the Indian informal manufacturing sector* (IGC Working Paper). London: International Growth Center.

Rijkers, B., & Costa, R. (2012). Gender and rural nonfarm entrepreneurship. *World Development, 40*(12), 2411–2426.

Rijkers, B., Soderbom, M., & Loening, J. L. (2010). A rural–Urban comparison of manufacturing enterprise performance in Ethiopia. *World Development, 38*(9), 1278–1296.

Sosa-Rubi, S. G., Galárraga, O., & Harris, J. E. (2009). Heterogeneous impact of the "Seguro Popular" Program on the utilization of obstetrical services in Mexico, 2001–2006: A multinomial probit model with a discrete endogenous variable. *Journal of Health Economics, 28*(1), 20–34.

StataCorp. (2015). *Stata 14 base reference manual*. College Station, TX: Stata Press.

Tybout, J. R. (2000). Manufacturing firms in developing countries: How well do they do, and why? *Journal of Economic Literature, 38*(1), 11–44.

Wilde, J. (2008). A note on GMM estimation of probit models with endogenous regressors. *Statistical Papers, 49*, 471–484.

Wooldridge, J. M. (2010). *Econometric analysis of cross section and panel data* (2nd ed.). Cambridge, MA: MIT Press.

Appendix

Table A1. Summary statistics of main variables of 2012 HBS used in the regression – rural

Variable	Number of HHs or EAs	Means	SE	LL	UL
Youth headed (between ages 15–34)	4,130	0.268	0.010	0.249	0.287
Female headed	4,130	0.241	0.009	0.222	0.259
No Primary Education	4,130	0.270	0.013	0.243	0.296
Completed Primary Education	4,130	0.673	0.012	0.649	0.697
Completed Secondary Education or more	4,130	0.058	0.008	0.043	0.073
Number of Youth (15–34)	4,130	1.577	0.051	1.477	1.677
No Cultivated Land	4,130	0.053	0.009	0.034	0.072
0-2ha of cultivated land	4,130	0.565	0.019	0.528	0.602
2–5 ha of cultivated land	4,130	0.296	0.015	0.267	0.326
>5 ha of cultivated land	4,130	0.086	0.010	0.066	0.105
Household paid loans to bank or family friends in past year	4,130	0.023	0.005	0.013	0.032
Public Transportation to Regional HQ in EA	157	0.756	0.038	0.682	0.830
Electricity in the EA	157	0.238	0.037	0.165	0.311
Mobile Signal in the EA	157	0.821	0.034	0.753	0.889
Internet in the EA	157	0.086	0.024	0.039	0.133
Bank in the EA	157	0.024	0.012	0.000	0.047
Cooperative Primary Society in the EA	157	0.381	0.042	0.298	0.464
Informal Financial Service in the EA	157	0.450	0.043	0.366	0.535
Major Employer (that is business, factory) in the EA	157	0.161	0.032	0.098	0.225
Weekly Market in the EA	157	0.295	0.040	0.217	0.373

Notes: The estimates account for survey sampling design.
Source: Authors' calculation using data of 2012 HBS.

Table A2. Summary statistics of main variables of 2012 HBS used in the regression – urban

Variable	Number of HHs or EAs	Means	SE	LL	UL
Youth headed (between ages 15–34)	6,056	0.343	0.010	0.324	0.362
Female headed	6,056	0.249	0.009	0.231	0.267
No Primary Education	6,056	0.084	0.007	0.071	0.098
Completed Primary Education	6,056	0.632	0.014	0.605	0.659
Completed Secondary Education or more	6,056	0.283	0.017	0.251	0.316
Number of Youth (15–34)	6,056	1.747	0.042	1.663	1.831
No Cultivated Land	6,056	0.702	0.034	0.635	0.769
0-2ha of cultivated land	6,056	0.217	0.024	0.170	0.265
2–5 ha of cultivated land	6,056	0.054	0.010	0.034	0.074
>5 ha of cultivated land	6,056	0.026	0.011	0.004	0.049
Household paid loans to bank or family friends in past year	6,056	0.039	0.006	0.027	0.052
Public Transportation to Regional HQ in EA	223	0.943	0.025	0.894	0.992
Electricity in the EA	223	0.852	0.044	0.764	0.939
Mobile Signal in the EA	223	0.846	0.031	0.786	0.907
Internet in the EA	223	0.292	0.037	0.219	0.366
Bank in the EA	223	0.155	0.024	0.108	0.203
Cooperative Primary Society in the EA	223	0.188	0.033	0.124	0.252
Informal Financial Service in the EA	223	0.650	0.040	0.572	0.729
Major Employer (i.e. business, factory) in the EA	223	0.416	0.044	0.329	0.503
Weekly Market in the EA	223	0.207	0.039	0.129	0.284

Notes: The estimates account for survey sampling design.
Source: Authors' calculation using data of 2012 HBS.

Roads and Rural Development in Sub-Saharan Africa

CLAUDIA N. BERG ⓘ, BRIAN BLANKESPOOR ⓘ & HARRIS SELOD ⓘ

ABSTRACT   *This paper assesses the relationship between access to markets and land cultivation in sub-Saharan Africa. Using a geo-referenced panel over four decades (1970–2010) during which the road network was significantly improved, we find a modest impact of improved market accessibility on local cropland expansion – especially in places that are exposed to better agricultural production conditions – as well as suggestive evidence of an increase in the local intensity of cultivation. Suggestive evidence of a positive association between improved market accessibility and local GDP growth beyond the impact of cropland expansion could reflect the stimulation of non-agricultural activities.*

1. Introduction

Due to climatic and soil conditions, sub-Saharan Africa has enormous potential for agriculture but is not making an efficient use of these endowments. Instead, the continent is exposed to soil fertility decline, threatening food security (Heerink, 2005), and highly suitable land is left uncultivated. Over the past four decades, although the region's total cropped land is estimated to have increased by 44 per cent, reaching almost 230 million hectares (see Table A1 in the Appendix), this vast increase falls short of the available land suitable for cultivation in the region with estimates between approximately 70 and 200 million hectares depending on the definition (Deininger et al., 2011).[1] Despite sub-Saharan African countries being mostly agrarian, agriculture in the region compares poorly to other regions of the world given the low yields, widespread subsistence farming, and the heavy reliance on food imports. Many explanations have been put forward to explain Africa's backlog in agriculture, including the low adoption of modern technologies, poor access to credit, insecure property rights and lack of access to markets due to poor transport infrastructure. Lack of transport infrastructure, in particular, is hindering the development of agriculture in sub-Saharan Africa (see Ali et al., 2015; Berg, Deichmann, Liu, & Selod, 2017). Deininger et al. (2011) report that more than half of the untapped potential for cultivation in the region is located more than six hours away from a major market and Chamberlin, Jayne, and Headey (2014) argue that much of the potential cropland remains unused because of limited transport access.

The objective of this study is to shed light on the relation between road investments and rural development in sub-Saharan Africa. Over the past four decades, there has been a very significant expansion of the paved road network in Africa, which, in our data, increased from 77,800 km in 1970 to over 186,000 km in 2010 (see Appendix Table A2). The network, however, remains of poor quality and of insufficient extent and density. Foster and Briceño-Garmendia (2010) report an average road density of 137 km/100 km^2 in sub-Saharan Africa, which is far below the 211 km/

Supplementary Materials are available for this article which can be accessed via the online version of this journal available at https://doi.org/10.1080/00220388.2018.1430772.

100 km^2 in other comparable low-income countries. Transport in sub-Saharan Africa is also very costly to use, not only because of slow travel times due to the poor state of roads, but because of 'non-physical' transport costs related to delays, poor competition in the transport industry leading to higher prices, and corruption (Raballand, Macchi, & Petracco, 2010). The literature on transport and development shows that roads can have a very important impact on agriculture and rural development more generally, facilitating the transition from subsistence to commercial agriculture (Gollin & Rogerson, 2014). By improving access to markets for agricultural produce and facilitating access to input and service markets, better roads can boost commercial agriculture, participation in markets, and the adoption of modern techniques (see Kyeyamwa, Speelman, Huylenbroeck, Opuda-Asibo, & Verbeke, 2008, on Uganda; Minten, Koru, & Stifel, 2013, on Ethiopia; Damania et al., 2017, on Nigeria). It can also result in the growth of the non-agricultural sector (see Ali et al., 2015, on Nigeria). In Mali, however, although better road connections seem to increase local employment in the agricultural and service sectors in rural areas, it does not seem to have a positive impact on employment in the manufacturing sector (Blankespoor, Mesplé-Somps, Selod, & Spielvogel, 2017).

The evidence above suggests that the development of one sector may occur at the expense of another; some activities may relocate following transport investments, or road investments may be necessary but not sufficient to generate structural transformation. The impact on poverty reduction from rural roads, however, is unambiguously positive in the existing empirical literature. Roads in Tanzania have been found to reduce incentives to migrate out from rural areas (Castaing Gachassin, 2013). The channel can be through higher incomes as in Nepal and Madagascar (Jacoby, 2000; Jacoby & Minten, 2009). All of the above suggest a potentially high return from road investments in the rural areas of sub-Saharan Africa. Unfortunately, road investments have been insufficient in the region, even in places with high agricultural potential (Blimpo, Harding, & Wantchekon, 2013; Wantchekon & Stanig, 2016). This lack of investment can be explained by funding difficulties amplified by corruption (Collier, Kirchberger, & Söderbom, 2015).

In this paper, we mainly study one specific channel whereby roads can facilitate rural development by empirically testing Chamberlin et al.'s (2014) argument that increased market access stemming from road network improvement is necessary to increase the amount of cultivated land in sub-Saharan Africa. We focus on a long period (1970–2010) when significant improvements in the nascent road network were made and when important demographic spatial changes associated with population increases and urbanisation took place. Although agricultural impacts can occur at both the extensive and the intensive margins, due to data constraints, we mainly focus on the extensive margin (cropland area) and only indirectly estimate effects on the intensive margin (as measured by changes in plant biomass). We investigate heterogeneous impacts by interacting our accessibility measure with a local measure of yields which proxies both for land suitability and local efficiency in agricultural production. To explore these relationships, we bring together six geo-referenced panel datasets on roads, cropland, 'local GDP', urban population, yields, and biomass, all defined at the same small geographic level ($10 \text{ km} \times 10 \text{ km}$ grid cell).

The closest papers in the literature are working papers by Baum-Snow et al. (2016), Jedwab and Storeygard (2017) and Blankespoor et al. (2017). Whereas Baum-Snow et al. (2016) study the impact of market access on urban growth in China, Jedwab and Storeygard (2017) and Blankespoor et al. (2017) focus on sub-Saharan Africa using the same panel road data. Jedwab and Storeygard (2017) estimate the impact of a change in market access on urbanisation in 39 sub-Saharan African countries. Blankespoor et al. (2017) focus on the specific case of Mali to investigate the impact of changes in market access on the dynamics of population and sectors of employment. In the present paper, our focus is on the impact on agricultural land use for 43 countries in sub-Saharan Africa.[2]

The remainder of this paper is organised as follows. In Section 2, we present our empirical approach, introducing our measure of market access and presenting our identification strategy.

This is then followed by a section in which we describe our data sources and construction of variables and provide the relevant descriptive statistics for the analysis. Section 4 presents the results. Section 5 concludes.

2. Empirical framework

2.1. Measuring access to markets

Following Jedwab and Storeygard (2017), we calculate the local market access for a given location as a function of the weighted sum of the populations of all other locations, with a weight that decreases with transport time.[3] Formally, we define market access in a location i at time t $(MA_{i,t})$[4]:

$$MA_{i,t} = 1 + \sum_{j \neq i} P_{j,t} \tau_{ij,t}^{-\theta} \tag{1}$$

where $P_{j,t}$ is the population in location j at time t, $\tau_{ij,t}$ is the travel time between locations i and j at time t, and θ is a trade elasticity parameter.[5] Observe that market access depends on the existence and road types between locations i and j at time t through the values $\tau_{ij,t}$.

As our statistical analysis will also focus on changes in market access (see below), we calculate the change in the logarithm of the market access index between dates t and $t - 10$:

$$\Delta \ln MA_{i,t} = \ln(1 + \sum_{j \neq i} P_{j,t} \tau_{ij,t}^{-\theta}) - \ln(1 + \sum_{j \neq i} P_{j,t-10} \tau_{ij,t-10}^{-\theta}) \tag{2}$$

Following Blankespoor et al. (2017), this change can be decomposed to account for changes in the extension and type of road in the network as well as for changes in the spatial distribution of the population. For the decomposition, we use the following formula:

$$
\begin{aligned}
\Delta \ln MA_{i,t} &= \left(\ln(1 + \sum_{j \neq i} P_{j,t} \tau_{ij,t}^{-\theta}) - \ln(1 + \sum_{j \neq i} P_{j,t} \tau_{ij,t-10}^{-\theta}) \right) \\
&+ \left(\ln(1 + \sum_{j \neq i} P_{j,t} \tau_{ij,t-10}^{-\theta}) - \ln\left(1 + \sum_{j \neq i} P_{j,t-10} \tau_{ij,t-10}^{-\theta}\right) \right) \\
&= \Delta_{road} \ln MA_{i,t} + \Delta_{pop.} \ln MA_{i,t}
\end{aligned}
\tag{3}
$$

where $\Delta_{road} \ln MA_{i,t}$ represents the change in travel time between time $t - 10$ and time t, holding population constant for the population distribution at time t, and $\Delta_{pop.} \ln MA_{i,t}$ represents the change in population between time $t - 10$ and t holding travel time constant for the state of the network at time $t - 10$. $\Delta_{road} \ln MA_{i,t}$ thus represents the change in market access due to road changes, whereas $\Delta_{road.} \ln MA_{i,t}$ represents the change in market access due to population changes.

We borrow the value for the elasticity of trade, θ, from Donaldson (in press) who derived it in the case of India by inferring trade costs from interregional price differentials of agricultural goods produced in a single region. In the absence of studies replicating this approach for sub-Saharan African countries we use the same value, equal to 3.8, but as with Jedwab and Storeygard (2017) and Blankespoor et al. (2017), we also use alternative values of the trade elasticity as robustness checks.

2.2. Econometric approach

In the analysis, we explore the links between roads and rural development by assessing the impact of accessibility on cropland area, a proxy for cultivation intensity and on a local measure of economic activity. As explained in the data section below, our geographical units of observation are grid cells at the five arc-minute resolution, or approximately 10 km by 10 km, throughout sub-Saharan Africa.

We first present the regressions of cropland area. For this, we estimate alternative regressions, starting with one of cropland area on the market access index, in levels:

$$\ln C_{i,t} = \alpha \ln MA_{i,t-10} + \alpha_{my} \ln MA_{i,t-10} \times Y_i + \alpha_{ms} \ln MA_{i,t-10} \times S_{i,t-10} + X'_{i,t}\rho + Z'_{i,t-10}\zeta + D'_i\xi + \varepsilon_{i,t} \tag{4}$$

where $C_{i,t}$ is cropland area in the grid cell i at time t, $MA_{i,t-10}$ is the lagged natural logarithm of the market access indicator calculated with Equation (1), Y_i is a measure of cash crop yields, $S_{i,t-10}$ is a dummy variable indicating that the cropland area in the cell shrank in the previous period between dates $t - 20$ and $t - 10$ ('shrinking cropland dummy'), $X_{i,t}$ is a vector of control variables at time t, $Z_{i,t-10}$ is a vector of control variables at time $t - 10$, D_i is a vector of time-invariant dummies, and $\varepsilon_{i,t}$ is the error term. The coefficient of interest is α, the elasticity of cropland with respect to our lagged market access index. We lag the market access index by one period (that is, 10 years) to address concerns of reverse causality whereby areas put into cultivation may influence the measure of market access by attracting population or road investments. To account for heterogeneous effects, we interact the natural logarithm of the market access index with a measure of rain-fed cash crop yields, which accounts for local conditions to do agriculture (proxying for both land suitability and local efficiency in agricultural production).[6] We also interact the natural logarithm of the market access with the shrinking cropland dummy to account for potentially different effects of market access improvements in places where the trend is towards a reduction in cropland. Controls include the shrinking-cropland dummy over the previous decade, the average annual rainfall over the current decade and its square, the lagged population density, and lagged time to the nearest major port. The decreasing cropland dummy locally accounts for trends of reduction in cultivated land, either because of desertification (a serious problem in sub-Saharan Africa) or a trend of land conversion to other uses. The annual rainfall accounts for time-variant climatic conditions influencing agriculture. It is a key determinant of cultivation in sub-Saharan Africa where irrigation is scarce. The lagged population density is included to control for the local level of urbanisation. Time to the nearest major port provides a measure of external market access.[7] To control for any remaining unobserved heterogeneity, we also include country fixed effects, time dummies, and the interaction between the two. This specification is estimated under Ordinary Least Squares (OLS) as well as under a Fixed Effect (FE) regression (for which the invariant controls are removed). The FE regression better addresses time-invariant endogeneity issues through the inclusion of fixed effects accounting for unobserved heterogeneity at the grid cell level.

A second approach consists in regressing the change in the natural logarithm of cropland area on the change in the natural logarithm of the market access index. We have:

$$\Delta \ln C_{i,t} = \beta \Delta \ln MA_{i,t} + \beta_{my} \Delta \ln MA_{i,t} \times Y_i + \beta_{ms} \Delta \ln MA_{i,t} \times S_{i,t-10} + X'_{i,t}\rho + Z'_{i,t-10}\zeta + D'_i\xi + \eta_{i,t} \tag{5}$$

where $\Delta \ln C_{i,t} = \ln C_{i,t} - \ln C_{i,t-10}$ is the change in the natural logarithm of cropland area between $t - 10$ and t, $\Delta \ln MA_{i,t}$ is the change in the natural logarithm of the market access index defined in Equation (2), Y_i is the same measure of cash crop yields, $S_{i,t-10}$ is the dummy variable indicating that the cropland area in the cell shrank between dates $t - 20$ and $t - 10$ ('shrinking cropland dummy'), and

$\Delta \ln MA_{i,t} \times S_{i,t-10}$ is the interaction term between the two. The other controls are the same as before, except for the inclusion of the logarithm of the cropland area at time $t - 10$ to account for the initial level of cultivation. $\eta_{i,t}$ is the error term.

A third approach is to run the same regression as Equation (5) but substituting the change in the logarithm of the market access index with its decomposition provided by Equation (3) and introducing the corresponding interaction terms. We now have:

$$
\begin{aligned}
\Delta \ln C_{i,t} = {} & \beta_r \Delta_r \ln MA_{i,t} + \beta_p \Delta_p \ln MA_{i,t} \\
& + \beta_{rs} \Delta_{road} \ln MA_{i,t} \times S_{i,t-10} + \beta_{ps} \Delta_{pop.} \ln MA_{i,t} \times S_{i,t-10} \\
& + X'_{i,t} \boldsymbol{\rho} + Z'_{i,t-1} \zeta + D'_i \xi + \varphi_{i,t}
\end{aligned}
\tag{6}
$$

where $\Delta_{road} \ln MA_{i,t}$ and $\Delta_{pop.} \ln MA_{i,t}$ are the respective roads and population components in the decomposition of the natural logarithm of the market access index defined in Equation (3), $\Delta_{road} \ln MA_{i,t} \, S_{i,t-1}$ and $\Delta_{pop.} \ln MA_{i,t} \, S_{i,t-1}$ are the respective interaction terms between these components and the shrinking cropland dummy, and $\varphi_{i,t}$ is the error term. All other controls are the same as in Equation (5).

As we are also interested in assessing the intensive margin effect of improved market accessibility on cultivation, controlling for cropland, we also run the additional following regression:

$$
\ln NPP_{it} = \gamma_c \ln C_{i,t-10} + \gamma_m \ln MA_{i,t-10} + \gamma_{my} \ln MA_{i,t-10} \times Y_i + X'_{i,t} \, \boldsymbol{\rho} + Z'_{i,t-10} \zeta + D'_i \xi + \omega_{i,t}
\tag{7}
$$

where NPP_{it} is net primary production for grid-cell i, which measures the rate at which carbon is captured and stored as plant biomass around time t and sheds some light on the intensity of cultivation (see the data section below). All other right hand side variables are the same as in Equation (4) and $\omega_{i,t}$ is the error term.

Finally, we also tentatively explore the association between cropland area and a measure of local activity (local GDP) at the grid cell level with the following regression estimated in levels:

$$
\ln G_{it} = \delta_c \ln C_{i,t-10} + \delta_m \ln MA_{i,t-10} + X'_{i,t} \, \boldsymbol{\rho} + Z'_{i,t-10} \zeta + D'_i \xi + \omega_{i,t}
\tag{8}
$$

where $\ln G_{it}$ is the natural logarithm of the local GDP estimate for cell i at time t, $\ln C_{i,t-10}$ is natural logarithm of cropland area at date $t - 10$, $\ln MA_{i,t-10}$ is the natural logarithm of the market access index at date $t - 10$, and ω_{it} is the error term. The other controls are the same as in Equation (4) except that population has been added to control for size effects. As we investigate whether cropland expansion is associated with local economic development, our parameter of interest is $_c$. However, because the local GDP variable is constructed with a spatial allocation model that takes local population into account (see the data section below), our market access – which also depends on population – could exhibit some degree of endogeneity in Equation (8).[8] The problem, however, is attenuated by the exclusion of 'own population' in the market access index and our lagging of the market access index. We also substitute in Equation (8) an alternate measure of market access to by modifying Equation (1) where, in addition to excluding the cell's own population, we also exclude all other population within a 25 km radius. In the absence of a satisfying instrumentation, we nevertheless interpret the results only as indicative of the association in the data between local GDP and cropland and market access but not in a causal way.[9]

3. Data

The above regressions require the use of geo-referenced panel datasets at a common spatial unit and all the data we use are available or reconstructed at the exact same five arc minute resolution (approximately 10 by 10 km, or 10,000 hectares) for the 43 countries of our sample. We start by presenting the datasets from which we extract our left hand side variables for Equation (4)–(8), before presenting the other datasets used for the right hand side variables.

For cropland area, the explained variable in our main Equations (3)–(6), we use the HYDE 3.2 panel dataset (Goldewijk, 2016), which provides a spatial estimation of cultivated land (excluding urban areas and pasture land) for each of our grid cells. The HYDE 3.2 cropland data is allocated based on satellite imagery of land use and does not make use of roads or population data (that serve to calculate the market access variables in Equations (4)–(6) to estimate cropland extent, relieving us from endogeneity concerns.[10] Although the use of an estimated variable as a dependent variable usually entails lower t-statistics (see Hausman, 2001), the problem is counterbalanced by our use of a very large sample as we use these data for the subset of 290,416 cells in sub-Saharan Africa and for repeated observations for the dates 1970, 1980, 1990, 2000 and 2010 for which we have historic road data available. According to this dataset, cropland area in the 43 countries of our sample increased by 57 million hectares, reaching a total of about 229.7 million hectares in 2010 (see Table A1 in the Appendix). The annual growth rate of cropland area steadily increased over the period from 0.53 per cent in the 1970–1980 decade to 1.67 per cent in the 2000–2010 period. Figure A1 in the Appendix shows the actual spatial distribution of cropland for 1970 and 2010. As can be seen from this map, the increase in cropland area over the period occurred mostly throughout the Guinea Savannah zone that covers a large part of sub-Saharan Africa (World Bank, 2009). The increase is particularly noticeable in west Africa (in particular for Nigeria, Niger, Ghana, Senegal and Burkina Faso), central/east Africa (the countries surrounding Lake Victoria, as well as Sudan, Ethiopia and Kenya) and the southern part of the continent (especially South Africa).

In Equation (7), the explained variable is net primary production (NPP), which measures the rate at which carbon is captured and stored as plant biomass. Technically, it is the difference between the amount of chemical energy as biomass that primary producers create in a given length of time and plant respiration. It is expressed as a mass of carbon per unit and per year. We use it in Equation (7) to assess the possible intensification of cultivation for a given level of cropland. NPP is measured from space for the years 2000 and 2010 and is available for download along with documentation of the methodology from the University of Montana (http://www.ntsg.umt.edu/project/mod17).

Finally, the regressand in Equation (8) is a local measure of economic activity. For this, we use the local GDP measure constructed by UNEP (United Nations Environment Program) and the World Bank and aggregate it to our spatial unit for the above-mentioned dates. The spatial model to allocate national or subnational GDP across space uses subnational population data estimated by UNEP-GRID Geneva and The World Bank. The spatial allocation uses imagery analysis techniques to disaggregate census counts within administrative boundaries at the 30 arc second (approximately 1 by 1 km). National or subnational GDP is then allocated by giving more weight to urban than to rural areas with an urban/rural dichotomy based on a density threshold. The construction did not make any use of road or cropland information however, so the only endogeneity issue for Equation (8), which we already mentioned in the econometrics section, is related to the use of population information.

Now, turning to the data for our right-hand side variables, our main variable of interest is the natural logarithm of the market access index defined in Equation (1). It makes uses of the road panel dataset that Jedwab and Storeygard (2017) constructed by importing information on road types from paper maps published by the same editor throughout the period into the road geometry of Buys, Deichmann, and Wheeler (2010). In the absence of road quality information, uniform speeds are then assumed for each road category (see Supplementary Materials for more details). Table A2 in the Appendix presents the evolution of the road categories over time for the period

1970–2010 in the dataset. It clearly provides evidence that the period has had significant increases in paved and improved roads, but the majority of roads remain of poor quality (dirt roads/other). Figure A2 in the Appendix represents the same changes on a map of sub-Saharan Africa for 1970 and 2010. The construction of the market access index also makes use of a regional panel database of urban populations in sub-Saharan Africa that we assembled using the City Population data (see Brinkhoff, 2017) for the same dates and spatial unit as in the HYDE 3.2 data (see the Supplementary Materials). Figure A3 in the Appendix illustrates the increase in urban population in the region between 1970 and 2010.

We also use an estimation of cash crop yields that we interact with our market access variables in all our regressions. This variable, 'Yield of rain-fed cash crops 1 (2000)' is for bananas and coconuts and expressed in tons per hectare. It is produced by Food and Agriculture Organization of the United Nations (FAO) for the same grid cell as HYDE 3.2 under its Global Agro-Ecological Zones (GAEZ) data portal (see http://www.fao.org/nr/gaez/en/) for the year 2000 only.

The other control variables that we include in our regressions – average annual rainfall, population density, and time to nearest major port – are from several sources. We processed monthly rainfall data from PREC/L (Chen, Xie, Janowiak, & Arkin, 2002), which we aggregated to the annual level, averaged over each decade, and aligned with the HYDE spatial unit. The population density was calculated dividing the number of people in a grid cell (available from HYDE) by the land area in that cell. Finally, we also use the travel time from each grid cell to the nearest major port.

Table A4 in the Appendix presents summary statistics of the variables that we use in the regressions. All values are at the cell level. Cropland area varies significantly across cells (from uncultivated to almost fully cultivated areas) and its mean over our 10 km × 10 km cells increases over the period from 559 to 793 hectares. There are, however, a significant number of cells in which cropland decreased, possibly due to the conversion to other land uses or desertification. Table A4 also shows a steady increase in the market access index over the 40-year span of the study. This is due to both improvements in roads and changes in urban population (see Figures A2 and A3 in the Appendix). On average, changes in the population, in particular, contribute two to five times more than road improvements to variations in the logarithm of the market access index (also see Appendix Table A3).

4. Analysis and results

We start with the estimation of baseline panel Equation (4), which assesses the link (in levels), between market access and cropland area. The impact of market access on cropland is consistently estimated to be positive and significant under all OLS estimation (columns 1–3) and under the FE approach (columns 4–6). In column (5), under the FE specification with all controls (our preferred specification), we see that a doubling of the lagged market access index – something which would occur after 20 years at the current rate[11] – is associated, on average, with a 0.6 per cent increase in the cropland area. This seems a very modest effect in comparison with the increase in cropland of 1.7 per cent occurring on average every year over the recent period (see Table A1 in the Appendix). To put this into context, given the total cropland of 230 million hectares in sub-Saharan Africa, a doubling of the market access index would only result in an overall expansion of less than two million hectares. This modest figure, however, is an average that aggregates spatially heterogeneous impacts. We investigate how this heterogeneity plays by interacting our market access variable with two variables that account for important aspects of the feasibility and profitability of agriculture in each grid cell: cash crop yields under rain-fed cultivation as locally estimated by FAO, and our shrinking cropland dummy (equal to one for cells where cropland had been decreasing in the previous period). When introducing these interactions terms in the regression (column 6), the marginal effect of market access improvement remains significant and is slightly increased, and the coefficients on both interaction terms are significant and of opposite signs. Interestingly, in places where cropland has been shrinking in the previous decade, the effect of market access improvement on cropland expansion is more than offset, resulting in a further decrease in cropland area. In theory, this result could be explained by the facilitation of out-migration of farming households outside the area or by the development of non-agricultural activities at the expense of local cropland. On the contrary, looking at locations which are advantaged for agricultural activities, we see that places where cash crop yields are higher will put even more land into cultivation. In the grid cell with the best yield for cash crops, a doubling of market access will result in an increase in cropland by 3.7 per cent, which is almost five times the average effect.[12] Finally, also note that reduction in the time to the nearest port would also increase cropland area, which is indicative of a response to external markets as well. A 10 per cent decrease in this time is associated with a 0.5 per cent increase in cropland.

We now turn to the estimation of the impact of the change in market access on the change in cropland area (Equation (5)). Under this specification in changes, in the FE regression with controls and interaction terms (column 6), doubling of the market access index is associated with an increase in cropland area by 0.8 per cent.[13] The negative impact of the shrinking cropland interaction with market access is confirmed and largely outweighs the positive average effect. The interaction term between the change in market access and the rain-fed cash crop yield, however, is not significant anymore.

Apart from being an alternative specification that confirms our previous findings in levels, the specification in change has the advantage of allowing for a decomposition of the market access effect. To that end, we present in Table 3 the results from Equation (6), where we assess the impact of a change in market access on the change in cropland area, distinguishing between what is due to changes in roads and what is the due to changes in the population distribution according to the decomposition in Equation (3). The impact on cropland is positive for both components, but most of the effect appears to be due to the change in population, not to the change in roads.[14] For instance, in the last period, between 2000 and 2010, we see from Table A1 (see Appendix) that the contribution of population changes to the change in market access over the period was almost six times greater than the contribution of road changes. With a coefficient from Equation (6) much greater for the population component of the change in market access, it is clear that the impact on cropland expansion was mostly driven by population increases in surrounding accessible places. Interestingly, when we interact the local yield for cash crops with the two components of the change in market access, we see that the coefficient is positive only for changes in market access due to population changes. These findings suggest that the extensive margin in agricultural production could respond mostly to local population demand, with an increased response of more productive places to the nearby demand of agricultural goods. This is consistent with possible barriers to trade beyond the local vicinity, for instance because of farmers' possible lack of knowledge of how to sell goods in more distant markets even when connectivity is improved.

With our data, it is difficult to say if improved market accessibility also has an impact on the intensive margin. We indirectly explore this issue by regressing the net primary production of each grid cell on our market accessibility indicator, controlling for cropland (Equation (7)). The positive association presented in Table 4 (see columns 5 and 6) suggests that an increase in market access is associated with more biomass production, which is indicative of somewhat more intense cultivation.

Our results presented in Tables 1–4 point toward a modest but significant relationship between improved market access in sub-Saharan Africa and land under-cultivation. This, however, does not tell us the extent to which this association may actually involve structural transformation (through the shift towards commercial agriculture and non-agricultural jobs) and higher local incomes. In contrast to Blankespoor et al. (2017), who examine the issue of structural transformation induced by improved accessibility by looking at changes in the local structure of employment in a single

Table 1. Estimates of the impact of market access on cropland

	(1) OLS	(2) OLS	(3) OLS	(4) FE	(5) FE	(6) FE
Ln MA$_{t-10}$	0.224***	0.023***	0.039***	0.054***	0.006***	0.007***
	(0.00)	(0.00)	(0.00)	(0.00)	(0.00)	(0.00)
Ln MA$_{t-10}$ × Yield			0.015***			0.009***
			(0.00)			(0.00)
Shrinking cropland$_{t-10}$		−0.755***	−0.735***		−0.073***	−0.076***
		(0.00)	(0.00)		(0.00)	(0.00)
Ln MA$_t$ × Shrinking cropland$_{t-10}$			−0.071***			−0.012***
			(0.00)			(0.00)
Ln time to major port$_{t-10}$		−0.083***	−0.082***		−0.053***	−0.054***
		(0.00)	(0.00)		(0.00)	(0.00)
Avg. rainfall$_t$		0.312***	0.310***		−0.010***	−0.013***
		(0.00)	(0.00)		(0.00)	(0.00)
(Avg. rainfall$_t$)^2		−0.033***	−0.032***		−0.000	0.000
		(0.00)	(0.00)		(0.00)	(0.00)
Ln pop. density$_{t-10}$		0.576***	0.580***		0.110***	0.112***
		(0.00)	(0.00)		(0.00)	(0.00)
Country × Year dummies	No	Yes	Yes	No	Yes	Yes
Observations	1,159,288	1,159,288	1,159,288	1,159,288	1,159,288	1,159,288
R-squared	0.098	0.634	0.637	0.024	0.484	0.488

Notes: This table presents estimates from OLS (columns 1–3) and fixed effect (columns 4–6) regressions of the natural logarithm of cropland area at time *t* on the natural logarithm of the lagged market access index (*Ln MA$_{t-10}$*). The controls included in the OLS regression (column 2) include a dummy variable indicating a decrease in cropland during the previous period (*shrinking cropland$_{t-10}$*), the lagged natural logarithm of time to nearest major port (*Ln time to major port$_{t-10}$*), the average rainfall over the period (*Avg. rainfall$_t$*) and its square, the natural logarithm of lagged population density (*Ln pop. density$_{t-10}$*), and country × year dummies. Column 3 is the same as 2, but introduces the interaction between market access and rain-fed yield for cash crops (*Ln MA$_{t-10}$ × Y*) and between market access and the shrinking cropland dummy (*Ln MA$_t$ × Shrinking cropland$_{t-10}$*). The controls included in the FE regressions (columns 5 and 6) are the time-varying controls of the OLS regressions, and country × year dummies. Column 6 is the same as column 5, but introduces the same interaction terms as column (3). Constants not shown. Robust standard errors are in parenthesis, where ***is significance at the 1 per cent level, **significance at the 5 per cent level, and *significance at the 10 per cent level.

country, this is not possible in our case because such local data do not exist at the regional scale. Instead, we make use of a reconstructed local GDP measure (see the data section) to investigate the links between cropland expansion and local economic activity. Because of the potential endogeneity concern presented earlier, we only interpret this relation as a descriptive association and do not infer causality. The results from Equation (8) are reported in Table 5 for OLS and FE. Our preferred specifications, the FE regressions with controls (column 5 and 6), provide comparable estimates of the association between cropland expansion and local GDP irrespective of the inclusion or the exclusion of the market access variable. According to these estimates, a doubling of cropland area is associated with a 17 per cent increase in local GDP. The market access indicator has a positive coefficient and significant coefficient while controlling for cropland area, suggesting that increases in market access are associated with local GDP growth beyond the effect through cropland expansion. This could reflect the stimulation of non-agricultural activities when access to markets is improved. To further address endogeneity, we also estimated Equation (8) with the modified measure of market access excluding neighbouring population and obtained nearly identical results (omitted for brevity).

As a robustness check, we re-ran all the above regressions with an alternative market access index calculated with a trade elasticity of $\theta = 8.2$ (as in Eaton & Kortum, 2002) instead of 3.8 (as in Donaldson, in press). Under this more rapid decay function, the market access index becomes more dependent on the existence of roads and population in the local vicinity of the grid cell.

Table 2. Estimates of the impact of the change in market access on the change in cropland area

	(1) OLS	(2) OLS	(3) OLS	(4) FE	(5) FE	(6) FE
Δ Ln MA$_t$	0.020***	0.000*	0.014***	0.002***	0.001***	0.011***
	(0.00)	(0.00)	(0.00)	(0.00)	(0.00)	(0.00)
Δ Ln MA$_t$ × Y			0.003***			−0.000
			(0.00)			(0.00)
Shrinking cropland$_{t-10}$		−0.041***	−0.039***		−0.006***	−0.007***
		(0.00)	(0.00)		(0.00)	(0.00)
Δ Ln MA$_t$ × Shrinking cropland$_{t-10}$			−0.055***			−0.035***
			(0.00)			(0.00)
Δ Ln time to major port$_t$		−0.010***	−0.009***		0.005***	0.005***
		(0.00)	(0.00)		(0.00)	(0.00)
Ln Cropland$_{t-10}$		0.035***	0.035***		−0.206***	−0.204***
		(0.00)	(0.00)		(0.01)	(0.01)
Avg. rainfall$_t$		0.024***	0.024***		0.011***	0.011***
		(0.00)	(0.00)		(0.00)	(0.00)
(Avg. rainfall$_t$)^2		−0.002***	−0.002***		−0.001***	−0.001***
		(0.00)	(0.00)		(0.00)	(0.00)
Ln pop. density$_{t-10}$		−0.017***	−0.016***		0.036***	0.036***
		(0.00)	(0.00)		(0.00)	(0.00)
Country × Year dummies	No	Yes	Yes	No	Yes	Yes
Observations	1,159,288	1,159,288	1,159,288	1,159,288	1,159,288	1,159,288
R-squared	0.003	0.520	0.525	0.000	0.483	0.485

Notes: This table presents estimates from OLS (columns 1–3) and fixed effect (columns 4–6) regressions of the change in the natural logarithm of the cropland area between years $t − 10$ and t on the change in the natural logarithm of market access between year $t − 10$ and t (Δ Ln MA$_t$). Controls included in the OLS regression (column 2): dummy variable indicating a decrease in cropland during the previous period (*shrinking cropland$_{t-10}$*), lagged change in the natural logarithm of time to nearest major port (Δ Ln time to major port$_t$), natural logarithm of lagged cropland area (*Ln Cropland$_{t-10}$*), average precipitation over the period (*Avg. rainfall$_t$*) and its square, natural logarithm of lagged population density *(Ln pop. density$_{t-10}$)*, and country × dummies. Column 3 is the same as 2, but introduces the interaction between the change in market access and rain-fed yield (ΔLn MA$_t$ $_{-10}$ × Y) and the interaction term between the change in the natural logarithm of market access and the dummy variable (Δ Ln MA$_t$ × *shrinking cropland* $_{t-10}$). The controls included in the FE regressions (columns 5 and 6) are the time-varying controls of the OLS regressions, and country × year dummies. Column 6 is the same as column 5, but introduces the same interaction terms as column (3). Constants not shown. Robust standard errors are in parenthesis, where ***is significance at the 1 per cent level, **significance at the 5 per cent level, and *significance at the 10 per cent level.

Table A5 in the Appendix reports the estimated coefficients for the variable of interest in each one of the FE regressions previously reported in Tables 1–4. It appears that all our results are robust to this check, except for the impact of the population component of market access on cropland which becomes non-significant when the distance decay function is steeper.

Finally, we also ran each of the above regressions on a country basis. It appears that our average estimates occult interesting heterogeneity, with countries where improved accessibility has stimulated cropland expansion (for example, Guinea-Bissau, Malawi and Mozambique).

5. Conclusion

This paper is an initial attempt to assess the effect of accessibility on rural development in sub-Saharan Africa. Our paper investigates the relation between access to markets from road improvements and the spatial expansion of cultivated land using geo-referenced panel data. Our analysis carried out over 40 years when roads were improved and cropland area expanded quantifies the link between the two. In accordance with theory, we find suggestive evidence that improved

Table 3. Estimates of the impact of the change in market access on the change in cropland area (decomposition the impact due to roads and due to population changes)

	(1) OLS	(2) OLS	(3) OLS	(4) FE	(5) FE	(6) FE
Δ_{road} Ln MA_t	0.002***	0.001**	0.003***	0.001**	0.001***	0.002***
	(0.00)	(0.00)	(0.00)	(0.00)	(0.00)	(0.00)
$\Delta_{pop.}$ Ln MA_t	0.065***	−0.001	0.043***	0.014***	0.005***	0.061***
	(0.00)	(0.00)	(0.00)	(0.00)	(0.00)	(0.00)
Δ_{road} Ln $MA_t \times Y$			−0.003***			−0.002**
			(0.00)			(0.00)
$\Delta_{pop.}$ Ln $MA_t \times Y$			0.014***			0.017**
			(0.00)			(0.01)
Shrinking cropland$_{t-10}$		−0.041***	−0.038***		−0.006***	−0.009***
		(0.00)	(0.00)		(0.00)	(0.00)
Δ_{road} Ln $MA_t \times$ shrinking cropland$_{t-10}$			−0.011***			−0.006***
			(0.00)			(0.00)
$\Delta_{pop.}$ Ln $MA_t \times$ shrinking cropland$_{t-10}$			−0.161***			−0.136***
			(0.00)			(0.00)
Δ Ln time to major port$_{t-10}$		−0.010***	−0.008***		0.005***	0.006***
		(0.00)	(0.00)		(0.00)	(0.00)
Ln Cropland$_{t-10}$		0.035***	0.034***		−0.206***	−0.200***
		(0.00)	(0.00)		(0.01)	(0.01)
Avg. rainfall$_t$		0.024***	0.024***		0.011***	0.009***
		(0.00)	(0.00)		(0.00)	(0.00)
(Avg. rainfall$_t$)^2		−0.002***	−0.002***		−0.001***	−0.001***
		(0.00)	(0.00)		(0.00)	(0.00)
Ln pop. density$_{t-10}$		−0.017***	−0.015***		0.036***	0.037***
		(0.00)	(0.00)		(0.00)	(0.00)
Country × Year dummies	No	Yes	Yes	No	Yes	Yes
Observations	1,159,288	1,159,288	1,159,288	1,159,288	1,159,288	1,159,288
R-squared	0.008	0.520	0.531	0.000	0.483	0.490

Notes: This table presents estimates from OLS (columns 1–3) and fixed effect (columns 4–6) regressions of the change in the natural logarithm of cropland area between year $t-10$ and t on the change in the natural logarithm of market access due to roads between year $t-10$ and t (Δ_{road} Ln MA_t) and the change due to population between year $t-10$ and t ($\Delta_{pop.}$ Ln MA_t). Controls included in the first OLS regression (column 2): dummy variable indicating a decrease in cropland during the previous period (Shrinking cropland$_{t-10}$), lagged change in the natural logarithm of time to nearest major port (Δ Ln time to major port$_{t-10}$), natural logarithm of lagged cropland area (Ln Cropland$_{t-10}$), average precipitation over the period (Avg. rainfall$_t$) and its square, natural logarithm of lagged population density (Ln pop. density$_{t-10}$), and country × year dummies. Column 3 is the same as column 2 but introduces the interaction between rain-fed yield and the change in market access due to roads and population respectively (Δ_{road} Ln $MA_t \times Y$ and $\Delta_{pop.}$ Ln $MA_t \times Y$) and the interaction terms between the change in market access due to roads or population and the shrinking cropland variable (Δ_{road} Ln $MA_t \times$ Shrinking cropland$_t$ and $\Delta_{pop.}$ Ln $MA_t \times$ Shrinking cropland$_t$. The controls included in the FE regressions (columns 5 and 6) are the time-varying controls of the OLS regressions, and country × year dummies. Column 6 is the same as column 5, but introduces the interaction between rain-fed yield and the change in market access due to roads and population, respectively. Constants not shown. Robust standard errors are in parenthesis, where ***is significance at the 1 per cent level, **significance at the 5 per cent level, and *significance at the 10 per cent level.

market access leads to more land put into cultivation. We find the effect on cropland expansion to be quite modest as a doubling of our measure of market access leads to an increase in cropland by approximately 0.6 per cent on average and by no more than 3.7 per cent in the most productive places. Interestingly, this positive effect on land put into cultivation seems driven by increases in local population more than by improved accessibility from better roads, which is suggestive of much of sub-Saharan agriculture mainly responding to local demand. The effect of increased market access is also not homogeneous: an increase in market access will accelerate the reduction

Table 4. Regression of NPP on cropland and market access

	(1) OLS	(2) OLS	(3) OLS	(4) FE	(5) FE	(6) FE
$Ln\ Cropland_{t-10}$	0.448***	0.135***	0.135***	0.349***	0.227***	0.165***
	(0.00)	(0.00)	(0.00)	(0.00)	(0.00)	(0.00)
$Ln\ MA_{t-10}$	0.014***	−0.000	−0.000	0.016***	0.015***	0.001***
	(0.00)	(0.00)	(0.00)	(0.00)	(0.00)	(0.00)
$Ln\ MA_{t-10} \times Yield$			−0.001			−0.006***
			(0.00)			(0.00)
$Ln\ time\ to\ major\ port_{t-10}$		−0.022***	−0.022***		0.166***	−0.026***
		(0.00)	(0.00)		(0.01)	(0.00)
$Avg.\ rainfall_t$		1.072***	1.072***		−0.358***	0.888***
		(0.00)	(0.00)		(0.01)	(0.00)
$(Avg.\ rainfall_t)^2$		−0.088***	−0.088***		0.022***	−0.070***
		(0.00)	(0.00)		(0.00)	(0.00)
$Ln\ pop.\ density_{t-1}$		−0.000***	−0.000***		−0.000***	−0.000***
		(0.00)	(0.00)		(0.00)	(0.00)
Constant	2.448***	1.894***	1.894***	2.552***	2.171***	2.284***
	(0.00)	(0.01)	(0.01)	(0.00)	(0.05)	(0.02)
Country × Year dummies	No	Yes	Yes	No	Yes	Yes
Observations	579,644	579,644	579,644	579,644	579,644	579,644
R-squared	0.121	0.917	0.917	0.022	0.557	

Notes: This table presents estimates from OLS (columns 1–3) and fixed effect (columns 4–6) regressions of the natural logarithm of net primary production (NPP) at time t on the natural logarithm of lagged cropland area ($Ln\ Cropland_{t-10}$) and the natural logarithm of the lagged market access index ($Ln\ MA_{t-10}$). Controls included in the OLS regression (column 2): lagged natural logarithm of time to nearest major port ($Ln\ time\ to\ major\ port_{t-10}$), average rainfall over the period ($Avg.\ rainfall_t$) and its square, natural logarithm of lagged population density ($Ln\ pop.\ density_{t-10}$), and country × year dummies. Column 3 is the same as 2, but introduces the interaction between market access and rain-fed yield ($Ln\ MA_{t-10} \times Yield$). The controls included in the FE regressions (columns 5 and 6) are the time-varying controls of the OLS regressions, and country × year dummies. Column 6 is the same as column 5, but introduces the interaction between market access and rain-fed yield ($Ln\ MA_{t-10} \times Y$). Robust standard errors are in parenthesis, where ***is significance at the 1 per cent level, **significance at the 5 per cent level, and *significance at the 10 per cent level.

in cropland in places were cropland is already shrinking. Although our data do not allow us to test any of the mechanisms involved, this could either reflect outmigration of farming households outside the area or the development of non-agricultural activities at the expense of local cropland.

We also find suggestive evidence of a positive association between increases in cropland and local GDP growth, and between increases in market access and local GDP growth beyond the effect through cropland expansion. Although endogeneity concerns may be biasing the latter results and prevents us from inferring any causality, the latter association could reflect the stimulation of non-agricultural activities when access to markets is improved.

Further research will be needed to analyse in more details the suggestive evidence we found of a link between improved access to markets and the intensity of cultivation. This is an important topic for a region which remains predominantly rural and where agricultural yields are known to have been stagnating or even declining. In particular, is agriculture excessively growing at the extensive margin instead of the intensive margin? Our finding of heterogeneous results across countries will also require further investigation, in particular to identify national and local enabling environments that could allow transport investment to better support rural development in the region.

Table 5. Regression of local GDP on cropland and market access

	(1) OLS	(2) OLS	(3) OLS	(5) FE	(6) FE	(7) FE
Ln Cropland$_{t-10}$	1.727***	0.189***	0.187***	0.834***	0.167***	0.166***
	(0.00)	(0.00)	(0.00)	(0.01)	(0.00)	(0.00)
Ln MA$_{t-10}$			0.020***			0.016***
			(0.00)			(0.00)
Ln time to major port$_{t-10}$		−0.420***	−0.407***		−0.140***	−0.134***
		(0.00)	(0.00)		(0.01)	(0.01)
Avg. rainfall$_t$		0.466***	0.466***		−0.146***	−0.147***
		(0.00)	(0.00)		(0.01)	(0.01)
(Avg. rainfall$_t$)^2		−0.045***	−0.045***		0.013***	0.013***
		(0.00)	(0.00)		(0.00)	(0.00)
Ln density$_{t-10}$		−1.002***	−1.013***		−0.804***	−0.815***
		(0.00)	(0.00)		(0.02)	(0.02)
Ln pop$_{t-10}$		1.556***	1.559***		0.755***	0.760***
		(0.00)	(0.00)		(0.02)	(0.02)
Constant	6.413***	4.575***	4.475***	7.346***	6.973***	6.841***
	(0.00)	(0.03)	(0.03)	(0.01)	(0.10)	(0.10)
Country ×Year dummies		Yes	Yes		Yes	Yes
Observations	1,159,252	1,159,252	1,159,252	1,159,252	1,159,252	1,159,252
R-squared	0.338	0.844	0.844	0.018	0.468	0.468

Notes: This table presents estimates from OLS (columns 1–3) and fixed effect (columns 4–6) regressions of the logarithm of GDP at time t on the natural logarithm of cropland area at time $t-10$ (Ln Cropland$_{t-10}$) and the natural logarithm of lagged market access (Ln MA$_{t-10}$). Controls included in the OLS regression (columns 2–3): lagged natural logarithm of time to nearest major port (Ln time to major port$_{t-10}$), natural average precipitation (Avg. rainfall$_t$) and its square, natural logarithm of lagged population (Ln pop.$_{t-10}$), natural logarithm of lagged population density (Ln density$_t$ $_{-10}$), and country × year dummies. The controls included in the FE regressions (columns 5 and 6) are the time-varying controls of the OLS regressions, and country × year dummies. Constants not shown. Robust standard errors are in parenthesis, where ***is significance at the 1 per cent level, **significance at the 5 per cent level, and *significance at the 10 per cent level.

Acknowledgements

The authors thank Rabah Arezki, Richard Damania, Siobhan Murray, Sandrine Mesplé-Somps and Gilles Spielvogel for earlier discussions related to this paper, as well as Rémi Jedwab and Adam Storeygard for making the roads data they have constructed available for calculation of accessibility indexes and Rose Choi for research assistance. Funding from DFID under the World Bank's Strategic Research Program 'Transport Policies for Sustainable and Inclusive Growth' is gratefully acknowledged. Data links and code are available upon request.

Disclosure statement

No potential conflict of interest was reported by the authors.

Funding

This work was supported by the Department for International Development (DFID) under the World Bank's Strategic Research Program 'Transport Policies for Sustainable Growth and Poverty Reduction'.

Notes

1. Based on calculations from Fischer and Shah (2010), Deininger et al. (2011) report figures for suitable land in non-forest areas under different population density criteria: 68 million hectares (respectively 201 million hectares) for areas of less than five people (respectively 25 people) per km^2 (see Table A2.6, p. 165).
2. Our sample pools all countries from sub-Saharan Africa at the exception of Cape Verde, the Comoros, Djibouti, Lesotho and Mauritius.
3. Ideally, the measure should account for the income of potential consumers, but this information is usually not available, hence the use of population numbers. Examples of papers using a similar market access measure include Harris (1954), Hanson (2005), Emran and Shilpi (2012), Dorosh, Wang, You, and Schmidt (2012), Jedwab and Storeygard (2017), and Blankespoor et al. (2017).
4. We use $1 + \sum_{j\neq i} P_{j,t}\tau_{ij,t}^{-\theta}$ instead of $\sum_{j\neq i} P_{j,t}\tau_{ij,t}^{-\theta}$ even when the weighted sum of the populations is equal to zero, which can occur as we restrict the calculation of the market access index to travel times of six hours or less.
5. We use time indexes t and $t-10$ to refer to the years in our data (1970, 1980, 1990, 2000 or 2010; see Section 3). Note that in Equation (1), we exclude the population of the locality itself and use travel times based on roads prior to $t-10$ (see Appendix), which addresses endogeneity concerns in the regressions (see Section 4).
6. The cash crop yield variable is only available for the year 2000 (see the data section) and we use this constant value for the interaction.
7. Major ports are defined as ports that include direct or trans-shipment capacity as measured in the AICD report (Foster & Briceño-Garmendia, 2010).
8. We face a reflection problem a la Manski (1993) where $\ln G_{it}$ and $\ln MA_{i,t-10}$ may reflect one another. See Baum-Snow et al. (2016) for a discussion of endogeneity issues in the use of market access variables.
9. Another less serious issue in Equation (8) is the use of an estimated variable as the dependent variable. It results in less precision in estimated coefficients from lower t-statistics (see Hausman, 2001).
10. If cropland data were estimated using roads or population, regressing it on our market access variable which is calculated from roads and population data would artificially create a correlation (see the reflection problem described in Manski, 1993).
11. The average market access index has grown at 3.55 per cent annually over the 2000–2010 decade.
12. In the data, the cell with the maximum rain-fed yield for cash crops has a yield of 3.856 tons per hectare (see Table A4). For this cell, doubling of the market access results in a 0.7 + 07 * 3.586 = 3.2 per cent increase in cropland.
13. We have $2^{0.011}-1 \approx 0.008$.
14. The estimates show that a marginal increase in $\Delta_{road}\ln MA_{i,t}$ has an impact three times smaller than a comparable increase in $\Delta_{pop.}\ln MA_{i,t}$. In our sample, the standard deviation in $\Delta_{road}\ln MA_{i,t}$ is also smaller than the standard deviation in $\Delta_{pop.}\ln MA_{i,t}$ (see Tables A3 and A4), from which we conclude that changes in population had more impact on cropland expansion than road improvements.

ORCID

Claudia N. Berg http://orcid.org/0000-0001-8191-6173

Brian Blankespoor http://orcid.org/0000-0003-1806-8129

Harris Selod http://orcid.org/0000-0002-0886-1265

References

Ali, R., Barra, A. F., Berg, C. N., Damania, R., Nash, J., & Russ, J. (2015). *Highway to success or byways to waste* (189 p.). Washington, DC: The World Bank.
Baum-Snow, B., Henderson, V., Turner, M., Zhang, Q., & Brandt, L. (2016). *Highways, market access, and urban growth in China*. IGC Working Paper C-89114-CHN-1.
Berg, C. N., Deichmann, U., Liu, Y., & Selod, H. (2017). Transport policies and development. *The Journal of Development Studies, 53*(4), 465–480.
Blankespoor, B., Mesplé-Somps, S., Selod, H., & Spielvogel, G. (2017). *Roads and structural transformation in Mali*. Unpublished manuscript.
Blimpo, M., Harding, R., & Wantchekon, L. (2013). Public investment in rural infrastructure: Some political economy considerations. *Journal of African Economies, 22*(2), ii57–83.
Brinkhoff, T. (2017). City population. Retrieved from http://www.citypopulation.de/
Buys, P., Deichmann, U., & Wheeler, D. (2010). Road network upgrading and overland trade expansion in sub-Saharan Africa. *Journal of African Economies, 19*(3), 399–432.
Castaing Gachassin, M. (2013). Should I stay or should I go: The role of roads in migration decisions. *Economic Development and Cultural Change, 22*(5), 796–826.

Chamberlin, J., Jayne, T. S., & Headey, D. (2014). Scarcity amidst abundance? Reassessing the potential for cropland expansion in Africa. *Food Policy, 48,* 51–65.

Chen, M., Xie, P., Janowiak, J. E., & Arkin, P. A. (2002). Global land precipitation: A 50-yr monthly analysis based on gauge observations. *Journal of Hydrometeorology, 3*(3), 249–266.

Collier, P., Kirchberger, M., & Söderbom, M. (2015). The cost of road infrastructure in and low middle income countries. *World Bank Economic Review.* doi:10.1093/wber/lhv037

Damania, R., Barra, A. F., Berg, C. N., Russ, J., Nash, J., & Ali, R. (2017). Agricultural technology choice and transport. *American Journal of Agricultural Economics, 99*(1), 265–284.

Deininger, K., Byerlee, D., Lindsay, J., Norton, A., Selod, H., & Stickler, M. (2011). *Rising global interest in farmland: Can it yield sustainable and equitable benefits?* Washington, DC: The World Bank.

Donaldson, D. (in press). Railroads and the Raj: Estimating the impact of transportation infrastructure. *American Economic Review.* Retrieved from https://assets.aeaweb.org/assets/production/files/6389.pdf

Dorosh, P., Wang, H. G., You, L., & Schmidt, E. (2012). Road connectivity, population, and crop production in sub-Saharan Africa. *Agricultural Economics, 43,* 89–103.

Eaton, J., & Kortum, S. (2002). Technology, geography and trade. *Econometrica, 70*(5), 1741–1779.

Emran, M. S., & Shilpi, F. (2012). The extent of the market and stages of agricultural specialization. *Canadian Journal of Economics, 45*(3), 1125–1153.

Fischer, G., & Shah, M. (2010). *Farmland investments and food security: A statistical annex.* Report prepared under a World Bank and International Institute for Applied Systems Analysis, Vienna.

Foster, V., & Briceño-Garmendia, C. (2010). *Africa's infrastructure: A time for transportation.* Washington, DC: The World Bank Africa Development Forum.

Goldewijk, K. (2016). A historical land use data set for the holocene; HYDE 3.2 (replaced). DANS. doi:10.17026/dans-znk-cfy3

Gollin, D., & Rogerson, R. (2014). Productivity, transport costs, and subsistence agriculture. *Journal of Development Economics, 107,* 38–48.

Hanson, G. (2005). Market potential, increasing returns, and geographic concentration. *Journal of International Economics, 67,* 1–24.

Harris, C. D. (1954). The market as a factor in the localization of industry in the United States. *Annals of the Association of American Geographers, 44,* 315–348.

Hausman, J. (2001). Mismeasured variables in econometric analysis: Problems from the right and problems from the left. *Journal of Economic Perspectives, 15*(4), 57–67.

Heerink, N. (2005). Soil fertility decline and economic policy reform in sub-Saharan Africa. *Land Use Policy, 22*(1), 67–74.

Jacoby, H. (2000). Access to markets and the benefits of rural roads. *The Economic Journal, 110*(465), 713–737.

Jacoby, H., & Minten, B. (2009). On measuring the benefits of lower transport costs. *Journal of Development Economics, 89*(1), 28–38.

Jedwab, R., & Storeygard, A. (2017). The average and heterogeneous effects of transportation investments: Evidence from sub-Saharan Africa 1960–2010. Unpublished manuscript. Retrieved from https://docs.wixstatic.com/ugd/ea9b22_2215467cd57448adb93a501709844fbc.pdf

Kyeyamwa, H., Speelman, S., Huylenbroeck, G. V., Opuda-Asibo, J., & Verbeke, W. (2008). Raising offtake from cattle grazed on natural rangelands in sub-Saharan Africa: A transaction cost economics approach. *Agricultural Economics, 39,* 63–72.

Manski, C. (1993). Identification of endogenous social effects: The reflection problem. *The Review of Economic Studies, 60*(3), 531–542.

Minten, B., Koru, B., & Stifel, D. (2013). The last mile(s) in modern input distribution: Pricing, profitability, and adoption. *Agricultural Economics, 44,* 629–646.

Nelson, A., & Deichmann, U. (2004). *The African population database.* New York, NY: United Nations Environment Program (UNEP) and the Center for International Earth Science Information Network (CIESIN), Columbia University.

Raballand, G., Macchi, P., & Petracco, C. (2010). *Rural road investment efficiency: Lessons from Burkina Faso, Cameroon, and Uganda.* Washington, DC: World Bank.

Wantchekon, L., & Stanig, P. (2016). The curse of good soil? Land fertility, roads, and rural poverty in Africa. Unpublished manuscript. Retrieved from https://q-aps.princeton.edu/sites/default/files/q-aps/files/wantstan_sept2016.pdf.

World Bank. (2009). *Awakening Africa's sleeping giant: Prospects for commercial agriculture in the Guinea Savannah zone and beyond* (218 p.). Directions in Development, Agriculture and Development. Washington, DC: The World Bank.

World Bank and UNEP. (2010). *Distributed global GDP dataset sub-national GRP.* Washington, DC: The World Bank.

Appendix

Table A1. Total cropland area in sub-Saharan Africa (million ha), 1970–2010

	Total cropland area (in '000 hectares)	Annual growth rate (in %)
2010	229,692	1.67
2000	194,715	0.79
1990	179,949	0.67
1980	168,371	0.53
1970	159,745	

Source: HYDE 3.2 (Goldewijk, 2016); calculations by authors.

Table A2. Road network in sub-Saharan Africa (1000 kilometres), 1970–2010

	1970	1980	1990	2000	2010
Highways	0.0	1.3	2.6	3.2	3.1
Paved	77.8	120.4	168.7	180.1	186.7
Improved	142.0	153.7	152.0	154.8	154.1
Other	899.0	843.3	795.6	780.7	774.9

Notes: These figures use the cross-sectional road network geometry of Nelson and Deichmann (2004) updated by Jedwab and Storeygard (2017). A highway is a paved road with at least three lanes on each side. An improved road is laterite or gravel. The category 'other' include dirt roads and any segment not identified as a highway, a paved road, or an improved road.
Source: Jedwab and Storeygard (2017); calculations by authors.

Table A3. Average change in the natural logarithm of the market access index

	Average change in the natural logarithm of the market access index		
	Due to roads	Due to population	Overall
2000–2010	0.010	0.058	0.068
1990–2000	0.005	0.057	0.062
1980–1990	0.028	0.066	0.094
1970–1980	0.027	0.072	0.099

Note: Values in this table are averages of values at the cell level (approximately 10 km × 10 km).
Source: Jedwab and Storeygard (2017); Brinkhoff, City Population (2017); calculation by authors.

Table A4. Summary statistics (approx. 10 km × 10 km cell level)

Variable	1970	1980	1990	2000	2005
Cropland (hectares)					
Mean	551	581	621	672	793
Min	0	0	0	0	0
Max	5950	6835	7043	7378	7791
Net Primary Productivity (ton carbon/m^2)					
Mean				42.43	42.41
Min				−0.01	−0.01
Max				202.64	192.81
Local GDP (thousands of constant 2000 USD)					
Mean	54.69	75.32	90.33	112.03	166.35
Min	0	0	0	0	0
Max	231,000	322,000	368,000	436,000	594,000
Ln MA					
Mean	0.52	0.61	0.71	0.77	0.84
Min	0.00	0.00	0.00	0.00	0.00
Max	11.77	12.28	12.88	13.30	13.69
Δ Ln MA					
Mean		0.10	0.09	0.06	0.07
Min		−6.64	−4.99	−4.17	−3.57
Max		5.98	6.74	6.03	7.63
Δ_{road} Ln MA					
Mean		0.03	0.03	0.01	0.01
Min		−6.08	−5.30	−4.49	−3.96
Max		5.60	6.71	5.91	7.42
$\Delta_{pop.}$ Ln MA					
Mean		0.07	0.06	0.06	0.06
Min		−6.65	−0.39	−0.64	−0.54
Max		2.41	2.22	1.88	
Shrinking cropland dummy					
Mean		0.20	0.19	0.31	0.18
Min		0	0	0	0
Max		1	1	1	1
Avg. rainfall (mm)					
Mean	281	267	258	260	260
Min	1	0	0	1	0
Max	1271	1115	1143	1118	1165
Population density (people/km^2)					
Mean	12.19	16.06	21.27	27.56	35.47
Min	0.00	0.00	0.00	0.00	0.00
Max	7966	10,693	14,655	26,110	35,446
Rain-fed Yield (tons/ha)					
Mean	0.100	0.100	0.100	0.100	0.100
Min	0	0	0	0	0
Max	3.856	3.856	3.856	3.856	3.856
Time to major port (minutes)					
Mean	3256	3112	2944	2924	2902
Min	19.58	19.58	19.58	19.58	19.58
Max	16,406	16,410	15,939	15,990	15,969

Notes: All values in this table are averages at the cell level (approximately 10 km × 10 km). *Cropland* stands for cropland area of the cell. *Ln MA* (respectively Δ *Ln MA*) is the natural logarithm of the market access index (respectively the change in the natural logarithm of the market access index over the period). Δ_{road} *Ln MA* (respectively $\Delta_{pop.}$ *Ln MA*) is the change in the logarithm of the market access index due to changes in roads (respectively changes in population) over the period, holding the population distribution constant at the initial date (respectively holding the road network constant at the final date). *Shrinking cropland dummy* takes value one if the cropland area in the cell decreased over the period. *Avg. rainfall* is the yearly average precipitation in the cell during the period. *Population density* is the ratio of population to the cell area. *Time to major port* is the time to the nearest major port listed in the Africa Infrastructure Country Diagnostic (see Foster & Briceño-Garmendia, 2010). *Source*: HYDE 3.2 (Goldewijk, 2016), World Bank and UNEP (2010), Chen et al. (2002), Jedwab and Storeygard (2017), and Nelson and Deichmann (2004). Calculations by authors.

Table A5. Estimates of the effect of market access on cropland and on local GDP under different trade elasticity scenarios

Corresponding table	Variable of interest	(1) $\theta = 3.8$	(2) $\theta = 8.2$
Table 1 (column 5)	$Ln\ MA_{t-1}$	0.006***	0.004***
		(0.00)	(0.00)
Table 2 (column 5)	$\Delta Ln\ MA_t$	0.001***	0.001***
		(0.00)	(0.00)
Table 3 (column 5)	$\Delta_{road}\ Ln\ MA_t$	0.001***	0.001***
		(0.00)	(0.00)
	$\Delta_{pop.}\ Ln\ MA_t$	0.005***	0.002
		(0.00)	(0.00)
Table 4 (column 5)	$Ln\ MA_{t-1}$	0.015***	0.012***
		(0.00)	(0.00)
Table 5 (column 7)	$Ln\ C_{t-1}$	0.166***	0.166***
		(0.00)	(0.00)

Notes: Column (1) reports the coefficients of interest from the FE regressions with controls in Tables 1–4 under our assumption of $\theta = 3.8$. Column (2) presents the coefficients from the same regression when the market access index is calculated with an alternative trade elasticity $\theta = 8.2$. Robust standard errors in parenthesis, where ***is significance at the 1 per cent level, **significance at the 5 per cent level, and *significance at the 10 per cent level.

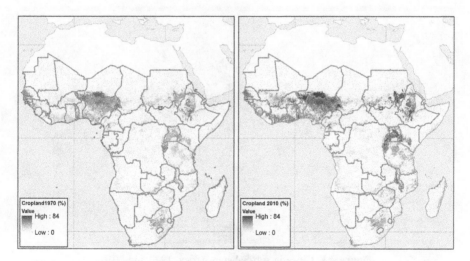

Figure A1. Cropland in sub-Saharan Africa, 1970 and 2010.
Source: HYDE 3.2 (Goldewijk, 2016) and World Bank.
Note: Maps by authors. These maps represent the percentage of a grid cell under cropland.

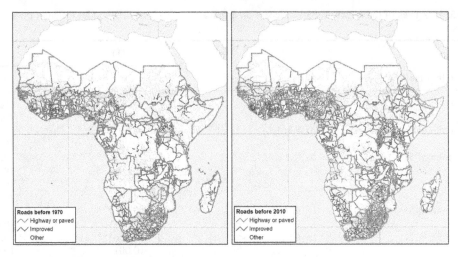

Figure A2. The road network in sub-Saharan Africa, 1970 and 2010.
Source: Nelson and Deichmann (2004) and Jedwab and Storeygard (2017).
Notes: Maps by authors. These maps represent a cross-sectional road geometry derived from Nelson and Deichmann (2004) and updated by Jedwab and Storeygard (2017). A highway is a paved road with at least three lanes on each side. An improved road is laterite or gravel. The category 'other' include any segment not identified as a highway, a paved road, or an improved road, especially dirt roads.

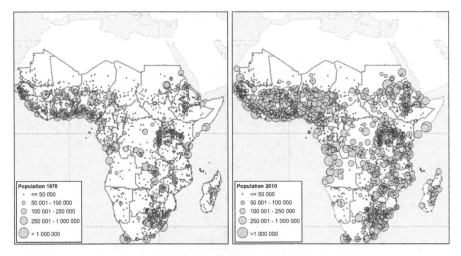

Figure A3. Cities in sub-Saharan Africa, 1970 and 2010.
Source: Maps by authors. Data derived from Thomas Brinkhoff, City Population, http://www.citypopulation.de (see Supplementary Materials for details).

Supplementary Materials

1. Construction of the urban population panel, 1969–2016

We constructed a panel of major urban population places for cities in Africa, using population data available on the website www.citypopulation.de and geo-referenced each of the cities using coordinate information from DeLorme (http://www.delorme.com) and the Global Rural-Urban Mapping Project (http://sedac.ciesin.columbia.edu/data/collection/grump-v1). For the cities which did not appear on either DeLorme or GRUMP, we used coordinates from www.Wikipedia.com or www.latlong.net. Eighteen cities, for which the coordinates could not be found, were dropped.[1] Since population figures were only available for dates when a census was carried out, populations for intermediary dates were estimated using the following exponential growth function:

$$P_t = P_0 \exp(gt)$$

where P_t is the population at time t, P_0 is the initial population at, g is the population growth rate, and t is the number of years elapsed. In the case of two points or more points in time for a given city, g was calculated from that data. For cases where only one observation was available, we used country-level urban population growth rates published in the World Urbanization Prospect (United Nations, 2012). We used these growth rates to fill in the population values for the years before the first available census and after the last available census.

2. Construction of the market access variable

The market access index combines road and population data for the years for which the HYDE 3.2 data is available (1970, 1980, 1990, 2000 and 2010). In order to compute the market access index, we combined the population data that we constructed for the same dates (see Appendix 3) with the roads panel from Jedwab and Storeygard (2017), who provide geo-referenced information on road categories.[2] We sequentially explain below the modifications that were made to the roads and to the urban population data in order to compute the MA index.

We began by modifying the geometry of the Jedwab-Storeygard data to enable network analysis by connecting small gaps in road segments. We then constructed a continent-wide road network for each HYDE year (for example, 1970, 1980, etc.) by considering the road segments and associated functional classes available for the most recent date *prior* to that year (for example, we used road information from 1969 in West Africa to build the 1970 continent-wide road network). For each HYDE year t, we then calculated travel times τ_{ijt} between any two pairs of nodes (i and j) on the reconstructed continent-wide road network using the same speed assumptions as Jedwab and Storeygard.[3]

We also modified the geometry of the urban population data (see Appendix 3 above) by ensuring that each populated place was associated with the nearest node on the reconstructed continent-wide road network, yielding the population measure P_{jt} for each node j. It then became possible to calculate the market access index for all nodes according to Formula (1). We further created a smooth surface for the market access index originating from these nodes using Radial Basis Functions and recovered values for every cell. Finally, we discounted these value by the Euclidian distance of the corresponding cell to the nearest road.

Reference list

Dobson, J. E., Bright, E.A., Coleman, P.R., Durfee, R.C., & Worley, B.A. (2000). LandScan: A Global Population Database for Estimating Populations at Risk. *Photogrammetric Engineering & Remote Sensing*, 66(7): 849–857.

United Nations, Department of Economic and Social Affairs, Population Division (2012) World Urbanization Prospects: The 2011 Revision, CD-ROM Edition.

Notes

1. The 18 cities which are not geo-referenced are: Tchiamba Nzassi in Congo; Massiogo and Mbera in Mali; Canicado and Nhamayabue in Mozambique; Bouhidide, Diogountourou, Hassi Chegar, Lexeibe, Nbeikett Lehouach in Mauritania; Kamuhanda in Rwanda; Al Husayhisa, Al Huwattah, and Umm Shukah in Sudan; Torgbonbu in Sierra Leone; Mondi Forest in Swaziland; Chiwezi and Kibaigwa in Tanzania.
2. Jedwab and Storeygard (2017) built their panel road database by digitizing historical maps from the same publisher to identify the road category in order to update the attribute data linked to the geometry from Buys, Deichmann and Wheeler (2010).
3. We have about 90,000 nodes. We used ESRI 10.1 Network Analyst to construct a Network dataset with the impedance of travel time by road segment. Along with Jedwab and Storeygard (2017). We assume the following speeds by road category: 80 km/h for a highway, 60 km/h for a paved road, 40 km/h for an improved road, 12 km/h for a dirt road, 6 km/h for the unknown category and 5 km/h in the absence of a road.

Youth Migration and Labour Constraints in African Agrarian Households

VALERIE MUELLER, CHERYL DOSS & AGNES QUISUMBING ⓘ

ABSTRACT *Using panel data from Ethiopia and Malawi, we investigate how youth migration affects household labour, hired labour demand, and income, and whether these effects vary by migrant sex and destination. Labour shortages arise from the migration of a head's child. However, the migration of the head's sons produces a greater burden, particularly on female heads/spouses (in Ethiopia) and brothers (in Malawi). Gains from migration in the form of increased total net income justify the increased labour efforts in Ethiopia. Weaker evidence suggests households in Malawi substitute hired for migrant family labour at the expense of total household net income.*

1. Introduction

As economic transformations occur across the African continent, migrants are drawn toward employment opportunities in alternative rural and urban locations within country (De Brauw, Mueller, & Lee, 2014) and abroad (Lucas, 2015). A knowledge gap remains regarding whether these employment shifts constrain the allocation of labour among family members who are left behind and if such adjustments jeopardise agricultural productivity. Multiple factors will determine the direction of the migration impacts. The sex and position of the migrant in the household might influence the migration effects, if the division of agricultural labour is oriented along these dimensions and is not substitutable across them (Croppenstedt, Goldstein, & Rosas, 2013; Doss, 2002; Holden, Shiferaw, & Pender, 2001). In households that become labour-constrained, access to affordable hired labour will determine whether households can overcome the labour constraints arising from the absence of a household member. Finally, the ability of the household to offset the monetary costs of migration and the costs of replacing missing farm labour will additionally depend on the migrant's earning potential at the destination (McKenzie, Stillman, & Gibson, 2010; Beegle, De Weerdt, & Dercon, 2011; de Brauw, Mueller, & Woldehanna, 2017) and the remittances received by the household.

Thus far, the literature has primarily focused on the impact of the migration of the self-identified head and his or her spouse on the labour supply outcomes of those left behind in Asian households (De Brauw, Huang, Zhang, & Rozelle, 2013; De Brauw, Li, Chengfang, Rozelle, & Zhang, 2008; Lokshin & Glinskaya, 2009). However, in Africa, migration rates for youth exceed those of adults (Lee & Mueller, 2016). Despite these growing trends in youth migration, there has been little investigation of the effects on sending family nor whether these effects differ depending on the migrant's sex. We therefore explore how the migration of young men and women affects the intrahousehold allocation of labour, hired labour use, and household income using publicly available panel datasets in Ethiopia and Malawi.

Supplementary Materials are available for this article which can be accessed via the online version of this journal at https://doi.org/10.1080/00220388.2018.1430770

Ethiopia and Malawi provide interesting contexts to study the implications of youth migration on rural households. First, gender roles in agriculture are markedly different in Ethiopia and Malawi, with a much higher participation rate of adult women in farm agriculture in Malawi. Thus, we hypothesise that migration would have different consequences on farm labour in the two countries, depending on the sex of the migrant. Second, both countries have strong yet distinct historical antecedents of internal migration.[1] Urbanisation and strong investments in infrastructure by the Ethiopian government has attracted migrants into Addis Ababa (Moller, 2012; Pankhurst, Dessalegn, Mueller, & Hailemariam, 2013), while internal migrants in Malawi, in contrast, are drawn predominantly to other rural areas with available land or agricultural wage employment (Potts, 2006). Third, policy reforms specific to each country may underlie diverse patterns of migration. For example, households may favour the spatial reallocation of youth family members in Ethiopia due to the Federal Land Use Law which precludes household heads from migrating out of fear that their land will be expropriated (Bezu & Holden, 2014).

We employ a difference-in-difference matching approach to identify the impact of having at least one child of the household head migrate on changes in the labour supply of youth and adult household members left behind, the use of hired labour, and household net income (Abadie & Imbens, 2008; Busso, DiNardo, & McCrary, 2014). Our identification strategy relies on comparing the outcomes of similar individuals residing in two types of households: those in which at least one child of the household head migrated between the baseline and endline survey rounds and those in which no child migrated. We confirm the robustness of our matching estimates by reporting effects using various restrictions on the matching estimator (for example, number of matches and trimming the sample). We additionally examine the sensitivity of our results to the sex of the migrant child and to whether the destination of the migrant is rural or urban. We find evidence of labour shortages in both contexts, where the migration of a head's child increases the supply of existing family labour onto the farm. However, the migration of heads' sons produce a greater burden, particularly on female heads/spouses (in Ethiopia) and the migrants' brothers (in Malawi). The migration gains in the form of increased household net income justify the increased labour efforts in Ethiopia. Households in Malawi compensate for the shortfall in family labour by utilising hired labour at the expense of household net income.

2. Background

Ethiopia and Malawi are landlocked, low-income countries in eastern and southern Africa that are heavily dependent on agriculture. The sector accounts for 30 and 49 per cent of GDP in Ethiopia and Malawi, respectively. As Africa's second most populous country, Ethiopia has a much larger population, at 91.7 million persons on about one million square kilometres of area, whereas Malawi has 14.5 million inhabitants on 94,080 square kilometres of land (Aguilar, Carranza, Goldstein, Kilic, & Oseni, 2015; Kilic, Palacios-Lopez, & Goldstein, 2015). Although both countries are characterised by smallholder agriculture, gender roles in agriculture are quite different, not only because of underlying cultural differences, but also because of their respective histories of policy reform.

Ethiopia has extensive agro-ecological and ethnic diversity, with over 85 ethnic groups and the presence of many of the world's major religions (for example Bevan & Pankhurst, 1996; Fafchamps & Quisumbing, 2002; Webb, Von Braun, & Yohannes, 1992). Social norms regarding the status of women vary widely across the country, depending on ethnicity, religion, and type of agriculture. There are examples of 'women's crops' such as *enset* (false banana), which are the primary responsibility of women and are grown in the south. Additionally, women typically care for livestock and control the proceeds from dairying and other livestock by-products. Although women and men have the same legal rights regarding land ownership and inheritance, particularly after the passage of the Family Law in 2000 (Kumar & Quisumbing, 2015), agricultural cultivation is typically centralised under the control of the household head, whether male or female

(Fafchamps & Quisumbing, 2002). Cultivation practices, however, can affect the division of labour. For example, in parts of Ethiopia that practice plow cultivation, plowing is almost exclusively performed by men, while women are much more involved in weeding, reaping, and winnowing (Pankhurst, 1990). In places with hoe-based shifting cultivation, men and women share agricultural labour more equally (Rahmato, 1991).

In contrast to Ethiopia, Malawi is smaller in terms of population and land area and also diverse with respect to inheritance and marital residence regimes. In particular, southern Malawi follows matrilineal customs, and, traditionally, women own the land and their spouses use the land of their wives' families. Daughters of these marriages inherit the land. Even within matrilineal groups, there is variation. Some matrilineal groups of Chewa in the Central Region practice virilocal residence after marriage and more men (whether as sons or nephews) gain primary rights to land than is possible among the matrilineal-matrilocal groups. Agriculture in Malawi is hoe-based, and men and women farm their own plots, as well as jointly owned and managed plots. In contrast to Ethiopia, on average, female family labour dominates farming in Malawi (Aguilar et al., 2015; Kilic et al., 2015).

Migration for employment is historically more important in Malawi, in part due to the pull effects of labour shortages in rural Mozambique (Thomas & Inkpen, 2013) and in the South African mines (Dinkelman, Kumchulesi, & Mariotti, 2015), whereas the Government of Ethiopia historically limited interregional migration (Pankhurst et al., 2013). In their recent analysis of migration patterns in four African countries, Mueller, Schmidt, Lozano-Gracia, and Murray (2016) find the per cent of individuals (ages 15–65) who out-migrate from rural areas annually is much higher in Malawi than in Ethiopia. In both countries, young men and women ages 15–24 migrate at a higher rate than older men and women ages 25–34, but the rate of rural-rural migration is much greater for young women than young men (Lee & Mueller, 2016), owing to early age at marriage within these countries.

As young adults leave their homes to marry, to further their education and employment prospects, or to search for their own land, their departure can influence labour allocation within the household, consequentially affecting agricultural production. The absence of a household member can create a labour supply gap, which could force the household to reallocate activities to other household members (who might otherwise attend school) or to reduce production. Remittances from the migrant could generate additional sources of income to offset potential losses in production or to hire additional labour. To understand these potential tradeoffs, we focus on how youth migration affects the allocation of labour in rural households and their agricultural and net income in the short-term.[2]

3. Data

We exploit two publicly available panel datasets, the Living Standards Measurement Study-Integrated Surveys on Agriculture in Ethiopia (2011–2012, 2013–2014) and Malawi (2010–2011, 2012–2013) (World Bank, 2016a, 2016b). Approximately 3200 and 2000 panel households in Ethiopia and Malawi, respectively, were surveyed in rural areas.[3] We use these surveys to create three sets of variables: profile of individuals and households at baseline, mobility status at endline, and the changes in the intrahousehold allocation of labour and household net income. We describe the demographics and households of individuals (ages 15 through 65) by their relationship to the household head, sex, and mobility status in Section 3.1 to motivate the discussion of predominant migration patterns. Since exogenous pull and push factors are a crucial component of the matching analysis, we describe how the relevant variables are constructed from separate datasets in Section 3.2. Hired labour and income at the household level are described later in Section 5.2.

3.1. Individual profile and labour allocations

We include variables that reflect an individual's earning potential and origin household wealth. An individual's worker profile is described using his or her baseline sex, age, marital status, and education (binary variables for whether the person completed primary school, secondary school, or is missing the education variable; omitted category reflects not having completed either primary or secondary school). Capital endowments are proxied by the change in household's inherited land in acreage[4] and household size, as well as other baseline housing characteristics less prone to temporal change (that is, the number of rooms in the house, indicators for housing with durable roofs, durable walls, piped water, and a flush toilet at baseline).

An individual is considered a migrant if he or she was present in the household at baseline, but left the household permanently (that is, is no longer considered a household member) by endline.[5] This definition includes both short- and long-distance movers; we have broad categories of the migrant's location. We therefore exploit the information pertaining to whether the migrant relocated to a rural or urban location to analyse how our results may be sensitive to the distance of the migrant from the baseline household.[6]

Our main outcomes of interest are the allocation of labour into agricultural and non-agricultural employment at the extensive and intensive margins. We create a suite of binary variables that indicate the employment status of the individual at baseline and endline over the 12 months preceding the interview: works on farm, works in the nonfarm enterprise,[7] and works in wage labour. These variables are not mutually exclusive; persons can engage in multiple activities at a given time. Additionally, we create labour supply variables to quantify migration effects on the intensive margin of outcomes among those who remain in the original household: the total number of hours spent planting, the total number of hours spent harvesting, and the total hours spent working on wage labour.[8] For all of these outcomes, the frame of reference for the agricultural labour cycle is the main season in Ethiopia (September through March) and both the rainy (November through May) and dimba (May to October) seasons in Malawi.[9] Table 1 displays the baseline averages of the demographic, wealth, and labour supply variables for various subsamples determined by the individual's relationship to the household head and whether or not they will migrate before the next survey round.

Focusing on the nonmigrant samples, we observe substantive differences between men and women. The largest gender differences are in the time spent planting and harvesting in Ethiopia. For example, 10 per cent fewer female heads/spouses work on the farm than male heads/spouses. Female heads/spouses also spend 290 and 74 fewer hours planting and harvesting, respectively, than male heads/spouses. These differences persist when comparing daughters and sons. In contrast, there are no differences in the proportion of women and men working on the farm and the total hours spent planting in Malawi. Only one subtle difference exists between the time men and women spend harvesting, which disappears when comparing daughters and sons. Rather, in Malawi, gendered employment distinctions exist on the extensive and intensive margin of the non-farm supply of adult labour.

We next review whether the employment profile of members within the household at baseline differed by whether they stayed or moved before endline.[10] Distinctions between future movers and nonmovers are more prominent for sons (than daughters) in both countries. Migrant sons have a higher prevalence of completing secondary education. However, despite higher levels of human capital, sons who move by endline in Ethiopia supplied a greater amount of labour in the agricultural sector at baseline than their nonmigrant counterparts, whereas migrant sons in Malawi tended to diversify into non-agricultural employment. Ethiopian migrant sons spend 83 more hours planting at baseline than nonmigrant sons, while in Malawi 9 per cent fewer migrant sons are likely to work on the farm. Furthermore, 7 per cent more of migrant sons are engaged in the wage labour market at baseline in Malawi, spending 82 more hours working on wage labour.

These preliminary findings suggest two alternative channels through which the migration of sons would influence agricultural production and investments. In both contexts, the labour of sons comprises a significant share of total household labour designated to farming. Therefore, sons' absences may cause agricultural production to contract if access to affordable hired labour is limited. Clearly, we would expect the loss of productive labour to entail greater readjustments in Ethiopian households given their heightened reliance on the agricultural sector.

The second channel through which the migration of sons may influence agricultural production is through their access to additional sources of income that could be reinvested in agriculture. Although

Table 1. Baseline characteristics and labour outcomes of household members (means)

	(1) M son	(2) NM son	(3) M daughter	(4) NM daughter	(5) M male head/spouse	(6) NM male head/spouse	(7) M female head/spouse	(8) NM female head/spouse	(1)–(2)	(3)–(4)	(2)–(4)	(8)–(6)
ETHIOPIA												
Age	20.85	19.40	18.97	19.28	42.34	39.78	32.94	36.26	−1.45***	0.31	0.12	−3.52***
Primary education	0.49	0.36	0.46	0.38	0.32	0.14	0.02	0.06	−0.13***	−0.08	−0.02	−0.09***
Secondary education	0.07	0.01	0.02	0.01	0.02	0.01	0.00	0.01	−0.06***	−0.01	0.00	−0.00
Missing education	0.03	0.00	0.00	0.01	0.00	0.01	0.00	0.00	−0.03**	0.01	−0.01	−0.00
Married	0.12	0.06	0.07	0.03	0.93	0.95	0.93	0.86	−0.06**	−0.04*	0.03*	−0.09***
Works on farm	0.77	0.79	0.70	0.68	0.76	0.90	0.77	0.80	0.02	−0.02	0.11***	−0.10***
Total hours spent planting	330.04	247.33	165.55	105.72	603.50	432.41	159.14	142.70	−82.71*	−59.83**	141.61***	−289.71***
Total hours spent harvesting	127.78	103.56	64.92	63.76	101.54	169.90	95.52	95.95	−24.22	−1.15	39.80***	−73.95***
Works in nonfarm enterprise	0.05	0.07	0.12	0.11	0.15	0.14	0.15	0.12	0.01	−0.01	−0.04*	−0.01
Works in wage labour	0.03	0.03	0.03	0.02	0.02	0.07	0.01	0.01	−0.00	−0.01	0.01	−0.06***
Total hours spent working on wage labour	21.49	33.53	31.30	18.14	19.64	70.99	6.75	8.94	12.05	−13.16	15.40	−62.05***
N	301	916	289	480	31	2,068	66	2,752	1,217	769	1,396	4,820
MALAWI												
Age	20.80	19.12	19.89	21.36	37.84	38.70	33.91	36.20	−1.68***	1.46*	−2.24***	−2.51***
Primary education	0.13	0.12	0.13	0.16	0.10	0.11	0.06	0.06	−0.01	0.04	−0.04	−0.05***
Secondary education	0.21	0.11	0.12	0.09	0.21	0.13	0.06	0.04	−0.10**	−0.03	0.02	−0.08***
Missing education	0.05	0.01	0.04	0.01	0.01	0.00	0.01	0.00	−0.04***	−0.03	−0.01	0.00
Married	0.10	0.03	0.17	0.10	0.93	0.97	0.84	0.80	−0.06***	−0.07*	−0.07**	−0.16***
Works on farm	0.66	0.74	0.68	0.72	0.92	0.96	0.98	0.97	0.09**	0.04	0.02	0.01
Total hours spent planting	70.15	65.15	48.40	60.59	86.47	121.83	103.18	124.09	−5.00	12.19	4.56	2.26
Total hours spent harvesting	15.30	17.94	17.64	22.51	50.65	60.43	43.98	49.79	2.64	4.86	−4.57	−10.64***
Works in nonfarm enterprise	0.04	0.02	0.04	0.06	0.14	0.17	0.09	0.11	−0.02	0.02	−0.04**	−0.06***
Works in wage labour	0.08	0.01	0.00	0.00	0.30	0.18	0.04	0.04	−0.07***	0.00	0.01	−0.14***
Total hours spent working on wage labour	97.08	14.75	0.22	1.04	455.40	212.65	46.33	44.16	−82.33***	0.83	13.71	−168.48***
N	203	549	234	394	170	1,164	236	1,536	752	628	943	2,700

Notes: M = migrant; NM = nonmigrant. Standard errors in parentheses. ***p < 0.01; **p < 0.05; *p < 0.1.

migrant sons were less involved in key aspects of agricultural production in Malawi at baseline, their diversification into the non-agricultural sector potentially increased the household's access to auxiliary income to support agricultural production (for example agricultural inputs, hired labour). While migration may raise the earning potential of migrant sons, it remains unclear whether the family would immediately benefit from the migration decision through the receipt of remittances. To further understand which of these two channels play a more significant role in each country, it will be crucial to inspect whether households with migrant sons tend to hire more labour to compensate for the loss of a productive family member and the implications on household net income.

3.2. Migrant selection and exogenous migration push and pull factors

Whether a household participates in migration and who is selected within the household to migrate is often based on the expected household benefits of the person's earnings net the opportunity cost of his/her absence. Thus, the migration decision itself, and who is selected to migrate from the household, is likely a non-random process. Both components of the benefit-cost analysis will likely depend on the traits of the individual (for example, skill transferability) and demographics of the household (for example, number of working age men and women, whether the household is asset poor or landless). This raises concerns over treating a migration explanatory variable as exogenous in a standard regression framework.

To demonstrate how migrant sons and daughters may differ by individual traits, we compare the statistical differences in the average age, education, and marital status of migrants and nonmigrants in the son and daughter subsamples in Table 1. The differences appear more pronounced among migrant sons (rather than the daughters) of heads who move out of the household. For example, 6 and 10 per cent more of the sons of heads who migrate in Ethiopia and Malawi, respectively, completed a secondary education at baseline. In contrast, the educational attainment of daughters at baseline does not appear associated with migration status. Instead, the primary differences between migrant and nonmigrant daughters are their propensities to be married. Because selection into migration within a household is not random, we use a nearest neighbour matching approach to account for the endogeneity of having at least one child of the head migrate from the household.

We use variables that capture baseline wealth and reflect labour market pull and push factors to match each (nonmigrant) individual living in a migrant household with similar (nonmigrant) individuals living in nonmigrant households from the sample. Baseline household size and inherited land are used to match individuals from households facing similar demographic compositions and wealth. Wage growth in the nearest town (city) in Ethiopia (Malawi) is used as a measure of outside employment opportunities driving migration.[11] Household georeferenced location points in conjunction with shapefiles from each country allow for the identification of the nearest town (city) for each individual in our sample. The second and third rounds of the Integrated Household Survey (2004–2005, 2010–2011), collected by Malawi's National Statistical Office, are utilised to compute the mean wage growth of *ganyu* (casual) labour for all cities in Malawi. In Ethiopia, we construct the wage growth variables based on the Country and Regional Level Consumer Price Indices database (CSA, 2013a).[12] The data allow us to measure the percentage increase in wages from the casual labour wage market in 2009 and 2011.

We integrate two additional variables reflecting push factors. First, we use the share of households that left the community before the baseline survey, as extrapolated from the baseline Living Standards and Measurement Study-Integrated Surveys on Agriculture (LSMS-ISA) community questionnaires, to proxy mobility costs. We add an interaction between the migrant networks and wage growth variables to capture the benefits of migration, net of mobility costs. Second, we include the coefficient of variation of rainfall to detect evidence of ex ante risk management in the form of the migration (Dillon, Mueller, & Salau, 2011) or off-farm employment (Rose, 2001) of household members. The historical mean and standard deviation of rainfall parameters were computed using a secondary resource for climate data online (Funk et al., 2015).

4. Empirical strategy

We estimate the effect of having a child of the household head migrate on changes in the labour of individual non-migrant member i in household h in village j using the following difference-in-difference regression:

$$\Delta Y_{ihj} = \alpha + \beta_H H_i + \beta_D W_h + \beta_M M_h + \beta_X \Delta X_h + v_j + t_j + \Delta \varepsilon_{ihj}, \qquad (1)$$

where ΔY refers to the change in the individual's outcome; H is a vector of baseline characteristics that reflect an individual's productivity and human capital (age and indicators for completed primary school, completed secondary school, missing education, married, sex, and relationship to the household head); W includes variables that represent initial household wealth (the number of rooms in the house, indicators for housing with durable roofs, durable walls, piped water, and a flush toilet at baseline); M is a binary variable which indicates whether the household has a migrant child; and ΔX captures changes in household human and physical capital (change in household size and inherited land). District fixed effects v_j control for time invariant cultural, economic and geographic characteristics, such as social norms dictating gender-differentiation in labour activities and labour market structure, which can influence the allocation of labour in the household. Separate regressions are estimated for the pooled sample, male heads/spouses, female heads/spouses, daughters, and sons. Summary statistics of the explanatory variables, outcomes, and matching variables by sample are presented in Table A1 of the Supplementary Materials. Standard errors are clustered by enumeration area, accounting for the correlation of outcomes within a geographic area.

While the difference-in-difference model reduces bias arising from time invariant characteristics, a remaining threat to the identification of migration impacts is the non-random selection of family members to migrate for marriage, employment, or other reasons. We therefore employ a difference-in-difference nearest neighbour matching approach to account for the endogeneity of the migration outcome (Abadie & Imbens, 2008). The procedure enables comparisons of the outcomes of individuals in migrant households with otherwise similar individuals residing in households without migrants. The metric used to characterise individuals from migrant and nonmigrant households as similar is based on the Euclidean distance of the vector of covariates applied in the matching exercise. Individuals residing in migrant households are compared to individuals in households without migrants that have the lowest difference in the distance-metric value. We use the nearest neighbour algorithm rather than other metrics, such as the propensity score, because it is nonparametric (and not limited by smaller sample sizes), the analytical standard errors have been derived (Abadie & Imbens, 2008), and it is easy to implement with more complicated sampling frames.[13] Balancing tests indicate the matching approach performs reasonably well in assigning individuals in households without youth migrants to individuals in households with youth migrants to estimate the migration impacts (Tables A2 and A3 in Supplementary Materials). To reduce any bias caused from inexact matching, we adjust the results using an additional regression-based procedure (Abadie, Drukker, Herr, & Imbens, 2004).

The quality of the matching approach relies on the strength of the variables as migration determinants, in addition to their value in producing quality matches. To validate the use of the matching instruments, we report estimates of the marginal effects and standard errors in a probit regression quantifying the relationships between the individuals in a household having at least one child migrant and the variables used in the matching exercise in Tables A4 and A5 (see Supplementary Materials). For simplicity, we pool the nonmigrant sons, daughters, and female and male heads/spouses and use separate specifications for Ethiopia and Malawi. The regression results indicate that household wealth (with the exception of having a flush toilet) discourages child migration in Ethiopia. In contrast, risk and employment opportunities net of mobility costs encourage the migration of the head's children in Malawi. In both countries, household size increases the migration of the head's children, which is not surprising given the growing land scarcity in these areas.

We verify that the main results are not affected by various parameters in the matching exercise. First, we compare our main results, based on matching individuals from migrant households each with two individuals from nonmigrant households, with estimates using one and four numbers of matches. While increasing the number of matches increases the sample size and therefore the ability to detect significance, it could bias the estimate if the additional matches are more dissimilar. We further show that the results are insensitive to trimming the sample by 1 per cent at the top and bottom of the distribution. When graphing predicted propensities to migrate using the covariates of interest, we find overlap in the distributions varies at the tail ends (Figures A1 and A2 in Supplementary Materials). Thus, trimming the sample can improve the quality of the matches by ensuring the pool of nonmigrants is more comparable to the pool of migrants to be matched.

Our main results report the impact of having at least one migrant child on the outcomes of members left behind using OLS and difference-in-difference nearest neighbour matching. However, accounting for the sex of the migrant child and the destination of the migrant might enhance the interpretation of the results, particularly if divisions of labour are gendered and the barriers to substitute labour differ by the earning potential of the migrant. We therefore also provide OLS and difference-in-difference nearest neighbour matching, replacing M with a binary variable which indicates whether the household has a migrant son, migrant daughter, and rural-urban child migrant.[14]

5. Results

5.1. Impacts of youth migration on labour

Tables 2 and 3 display the OLS and matching estimates of the impacts of having at least one migrant child of the household head on the intrahousehold allocation of nonmigrant labour. The R-squared values indicate that the OLS models provide a reasonable goodness of fit for the pooled sample in Ethiopia, where they explain 10 to 39 per cent of the variation in the outcomes compared to 2 to 9 per cent of the variation in outcomes in Malawi. While both OLS and matching approaches provide similar impact magnitudes (with a few exceptions), the precision in the estimate varies by approach. We can provide robust estimates only for one outcome in Malawi. When a head's child migrates, a son's likelihood of working on the farm increases by 17 to 19 percentage points. The F statistic value of 4.19 from a pooled OLS regression that tests for the equality of migration impacts across daughters, sons, male heads/spouses, and female heads/spouses indicates we can reject that the effects are equal across family members.

One explanation for the lack of precision in our estimates is the existence of various motives for migration. The employment migration dominated by males in Africa (Mueller et al., 2016) can result in remittance receipts for the household, which may relax liquidity constraints and allow them to hire labour, expand, or diversify investments. Moreover, the dominant pattern of migration in many African countries is rural to rural, often with short-distance travel (Mueller et al., 2016), which may allow absent household members to continue to work on the farm with minimal disruption. To understand better these nuances and how they might influence our interpretation of results, we first provide figures that distinguish the migration effects by the sex of the household head's child, and by whether the destination of the migrant is urban.[15]

By focusing on the migration of the head's sons, we can state more conclusively how the allocation of labour is affected.[16] In Ethiopia, the absence of a head's son induces an overall seven percentage point increase in the likelihood that family members work on the farm. Adult women (heads/spouses) compensate for the shortfall in labour (Table 4); 7 to 9 per cent of female heads/spouses are more likely to work on the farm. However, on the intensive margin,

Table 2. Impacts of the migration of a head's child, OLS and matching estimates for Ethiopia

	(1) Works on farm	(2) Hours planting	(3) Hours harvesting	(4) Works in enterprise	(5) Works wage labour	(6) Hours on wage labour
Pooled (N = 6,216)						
OLS	0.03	−12.04	21.03	0.00	−0.01	17.70
	(0.02)	(21.07)	(11.16)*	(0.01)	(0.01)	(15.42)
R^2	0.31	0.39	0.37	0.10	0.11	0.07
Matching	−0.03	−29.26	1.56	−0.01	−0.00	8.88
	(0.02)	(15.99)*	(8.19)	(0.02)	(0.01)	(8.53)
Sons (N = 916)						
OLS	0.02	−1.38	31.07	−0.02	−0.00	−7.77
	(0.06)	(72.18)	(24.91)	(0.04)	(0.03)	(30.17)
R^2	0.37	0.55	0.47	0.30	0.39	0.32
Matching	0.02	−19.58	41.11	−0.08	0.00	3.43
	(0.04)	(31.36)	(16.42)**	(0.03)**	(0.02)	(22.47)
Daughters (N = 480)						
OLS	0.04	−61.02	10.69	0.07	0.00	41.17
	(0.10)	(60.49)	(31.50)	(0.06)	(0.03)	(62.26)
R^2	0.49	0.67	0.59	0.50	0.44	0.46
Matching	0.10	12.36	26.31	0.23	−0.00	−13.39
	(0.09)	(27.64)	(24.02)	(0.07)***	(0.01)	(10.55)
Male Heads/Spouses (N = 2,068)						
OLS	−0.01	−57.58	14.19	−0.04	−0.01	41.77
	(0.02)	(41.90)	(17.13)	(0.03)	(0.03)	(45.52)
R^2	0.57	0.60	0.54	0.24	0.21	0.15
Matching	−0.08	−113.92	−23.07	−0.06	0.00	41.49
	(0.02)***	(33.25)***	(14.92)	(0.02)***	(0.02)	(18.30)**
Female Heads/Spouses (N = 2,752)						
OLS	0.04	−4.10	21.32	0.02	−0.00	−2.38
	(0.03)	(20.65)	(13.32)	(0.02)	(0.01)	(9.70)
R^2	0.40	0.50	0.48	0.13	0.18	0.20
Matching	−0.01	14.46	18.68*	−0.02	−0.00	−1.43
	(0.02)	(19.06)	(11.14)	(0.02)	(0.00)	(9.97)
F test: Equality of coefficients	1.63	0.35	0.66	1.36	0.47	0.59

Notes: NA = not applicable. Standard errors account for sampling weights, enumeration area clustering (OLS), and heteroskedasticity (in matching approach, using two other treatment observations). Matching uses two matches and performs a bias adjustment. Regressions include the following baseline variables: age, the number of rooms in the house, and indicators for primary school completion, secondary school completion, missing education, being married, having a durable roof, having durable walls, having piped water, and having a flush toilet. The change in household size and land, and district fixed effects are also included. Pooled sample regressions include indicators for gender and the relationship to the household head. The F statistic tests whether the differences in migration impacts across subsamples are statistically significant, from a pooled regression which excludes the gender dummy and includes variables that interact the youth migrant dummy variable with dummy variables for being a daughter, female head/spouse, male head/spouse, or son. ***p < 0.01; **p < 0.05; *p < 0.1.

sons devote a greater number of hours to harvesting (61 to 87 hours). While we can conclusively assert that all family members, especially adult women, are spending more time on the farm due to the departure of a son, the F tests suggest we cannot reject that the increased efforts of sons on the intensive margin are equal to the other members in the family (F statistic = 0.80). As in Ethiopia, sons in Malawi are picking up the slack for the departure of their brothers, however, they do so by spending more hours planting rather than harvesting (40 to 49 hours) (Table 5).[17]

Table 3. Impacts of the migration of a head's child, OLS and matching estimates for Malawi

	(1) Works on farm	(2) Hours planting	(3) Hours harvesting	(4) Works in enterprise	(5) Works wage labour	(6) Hours on wage labour
Pooled (N = 3,643)						
OLS	0.05	28.75	13.21	0.03	0.01	4.23
	(0.03)	(11.18)**	(9.86)	(0.03)	(0.01)	(19.73)
R^2	0.06	0.09	0.05	0.03	0.03	0.02
Matching	0.09	−13.19	11.18	0.00	−0.00	−21.66
	(0.02)	(5.37)**	(3.44)**	(0.02)	(0.01)	(20.34)
Sons (N = 549)						
OLS	0.17	38.56	9.86	0.09	0.01	16.74
	(0.07)**	(16.70)**	(14.48)	(0.03)***	(0.03)	(36.06)
R^2	0.14	0.19	0.14	0.11	0.18	0.24
Matching	0.19	7.14	1.06	0.01	0.07	−2.56
	(0.06)***	(12.24)	(8.70)	(0.04)	(0.03)**	(52.93)
Daughters (N = 394)						
OLS	0.20	25.35	−4.94	−0.06	0.02	17.91
	(0.10)**	(14.87)*	(16.53)	(0.07)	(0.01)	(14.43)
R^2	0.14	0.25	0.15	0.17	0.25	0.43
Matching	0.14	18.28	3.41	−0.06	0.02	0.59
	(0.10)	(13.77)	(12.92)	(0.04)	(0.01)	(0.42)
Male Heads/Spouses N = 1,164)						
OLS	−0.04	35.91	17.04	0.08	0.00	−49.41
	(0.04)	(18.16)**	(14.15)	(0.05)*	(0.04)	(67.89)
R^2	0.11	0.11	0.05	0.06	0.04	0.05
Matching	−0.02	−11.87	14.66	0.06	−0.02	−55.16
	(0.03)	(14.76)	(11.63)	(0.04)	(0.03)	(42.75)
Female Heads/Spouses (N = 1,536)						
OLS	−0.00	13.67	16.65	0.01	−0.00	45.07
	(0.03)	(15.02)	(10.64)	(0.04)	(0.01)	(19.49)**
R^2	0.08	0.09	0.06	0.04	0.05	0.05
Matching	−0.00	−35.92	9.36	0.02	−0.02	0.81
	(0.02)	(10.94)***	(7.93)	(0.03)	(0.01)*	(17.23)
F test: Equality of coefficients	4.19***	3.03**	0.42	2.31*	1.23	1.28

Notes: ***p < 0.01; **p < 0.05; *p < 0.1. See Table 2 notes for details on specifications.

In contrast, the departure of young women in the household appears to affect labour allocations only for the households in Malawi, as the estimates in Tables 6 and 7 suggest. A greater percentage of household members are required to work on the farm, especially sons and daughters. Specifically, we witness a 15 to 18 percentage point increase in sons working on the farm and a 27 to 32 percentage point increase in daughters working on the farm. An F statistic value of 5.43 allows us to reject that the effects are equal. In a context where women at all ages play a more unequivocal role in agriculture, other family members are, thus, equally substitutable for the loss of family farm labour.

Lastly, we compare the effects of having a rural-urban migrant child on the allocation of labour among the remaining household members (Tables 8 and 9). Having a child of the household move to an urban location may impose greater demands on sons' time during the harvesting period in Ethiopia (Table 9), but we cannot reject that those effects are statistically different than the effects on others in the family (F statistic = 0.25). Having a rural-urban youth migrant in a household in rural Malawi

Table 4. Impacts of the migration of a head's son, OLS and matching estimates for Ethiopia

	(1) Works on farm	(2) Hours planting	(3) Hours harvesting	(4) Works in enterprise	(5) Works wage labour	(6) Hours on wage labour
Pooled (N = 6,216)						
OLS	0.07	7.95	24.35	0.01	0.01	18.85
	(0.03)***	(23.72)	(12.75)*	(0.03)	(0.01)	(13.99)
R^2	0.31	0.39	0.37	0.10	0.11	0.07
Matching	0.07	16.26	8.93	−0.02	0.02	4.63
	(0.03)***	(19.88)	(10.26)	(0.02)	(0.01)*	(9.28)
Sons (N = 916)						
OLS	0.07	53.19	86.57	−0.00	0.01	−6.62
	(0.08)	(96.13)	(31.36)***	(0.04)	(0.03)	(36.06)
R^2	0.37	0.55	0.47	0.30	0.39	0.32
Matching	0.10	−37.60	60.52	−0.08	−0.01	−7.26
	(0.06)	(47.85)	(19.95)***	(0.04)*	(0.02)	(26.99)
Daughters (N = 480)						
OLS	0.11	−25.89	1.43	0.19	−0.00	89.86
	(0.13)	(76.78)	(33.55)	(0.10)*	(0.06)	(100.50)
R^2	0.49	0.67	0.59	0.50	0.44	0.46
Matching	0.24*	3.86	33.32	0.30	0.12	14.43
	(0.13)	(35.52)	(31.61)	(0.10)***	(0.01)**	(7.45)*
Male Heads/Spouses (N = 2,068)						
OLS	0.01	−23.63	41.98	−0.00	0.04	47.15
	(0.03)	(44.23)	(21.50)*	(0.04)	(0.03)	(41.49)
R^2	0.57	0.60	0.54	0.24	0.21	0.15
Matching	0.01	−19.06	−27.10	−0.07	0.06	68.11
	(0.03)	(47.40)	(20.83)	(0.04)*	(0.03)**	(22.32)***
Female Heads/Spouses (N = 2,752)						
OLS	0.09	3.05	1.46	−0.00	−0.00	−4.91
	(0.04)**	(25.10)	(16.38)	(0.04)	(0.01)	(10.03)
R^2	0.40	0.50	0.48	0.13	0.18	0.20
Matching	0.07	14.87	14.06	−0.02	0.00	4.12
	(0.04)*	(26.02)	(13.73)	(0.03)	(0.00)*	(15.24)
F test: Equality of coefficients	2.83**	0.29	0.80	0.64	0.55	0.69

Notes: ***p < 0.01; **p < 0.05; *p < 0.1. See Table 2 notes for details on specifications.

continues to increase the demand on all household members to work on the farm (Table 9). It, also, increases the demand for daughters to spend time planting, and decreases overall engagement in enterprise activities.

5.2. Mechanisms

We have largely demonstrated that the loss of a family member imposes additional burdens on family members, and the nature of who is affected depends on the gender and destination of the migrant. However, our interpretations have, thus far, ignored the potential for households to use hired labour, which offers the opportunity to overcome labour constraints but at an additional cost to production. In fact, the summary statistics in Table 10 allude to the importance of hired labour in these countries, where 19 and 37 per cent of households in Ethiopia and Malawi, respectively, contracted at least one person to assist on the farm at baseline. We therefore use the previous OLS and matching

Table 5. Impacts of the migration of a head's son, OLS and matching estimates for Malawi

	(1) Works on farm	(2) Hours planting	(3) Hours harvesting	(4) Works in enterprise	(5) Works wage labour	(6) Hours on wage labour
Pooled (N = 3,643)						
OLS	0.03	36.47	17.28	−0.00	0.02	34.81
	(0.04)	(14.73)**	(17.30)	(0.04)	(0.02)	(27.37)
R^2	0.06	0.09	0.05	0.03	0.03	0.02
Matching	0.07	30.79	15.83	0.01	0.03	46.16
	(0.04)*	(7.55)***	(5.14)***	(0.04)	(0.01)**	(20.75)**
Sons (N = 549)						
OLS	0.16	40.07	33.46	0.09	−0.00	23.18
	(0.13)	(21.66)*	(24.62)	(0.04)**	(0.03)	(36.63)
R^2	0.13	0.19	0.15	0.10	0.18	0.24
Matching	0.38	48.84	13.08	0.09	0.02	11.69
	(0.10)***	(17.81)***	(16.23)	(0.06)	(0.05)	(42.39)
Daughters (N = 394)						
OLS	0.15	23.98	17.42	−0.13	0.05	29.62
	(0.15)	(18.59)	(20.48)	(0.09)	(0.02)**	(21.15)
R^2	0.13	0.24	0.15	0.17	0.25	0.43
Matching	−0.00	6.69	26.63	−0.15	0.03	1.08
	(0.16)	(18.86)	(17.35)	(0.06)***	(0.02)	(0.77)
Male Heads/Spouses N = 1,164)						
OLS	−0.12	55.46	17.30	0.02	0.06	33.09
	(0.06)*	(21.53)**	(23.97)	(0.06)	(0.04)	(81.96)
R^2	0.12	0.11	0.05	0.06	0.04	0.05
Matching	−0.14	8.99	13.85	0.04	0.07	60.30
	(0.04)***	(16.29)	(16.11)	(0.07)	(0.05)	(56.88)
Female Heads/Spouses (N = 1,536)						
OLS	0.02	21.14	13.52	−0.00	0.01	54.69
	(0.02)	(19.31)	(16.74)	(0.06)	(0.01)	(29.85)*
R^2	0.08	0.09	0.06	0.04	0.05	0.05
Matching	0.02	−13.86	3.77	0.07	−0.02	21.94
	(0.03)	(17.06)	(12.01)	(0.04)*	(0.01)**	(8.93)**
F test: Equality of coefficients	2.00	2.61*	0.63	1.55	0.84	0.53

Notes: ***$p < 0.01$; **$p < 0.05$; *$p < 0.1$. See Table 2 notes for details on specifications.

specifications to observe whether having a migrant child, migrant son, migrant daughter, and rural-urban migrant child changes the use of hired labour over time at the household level. This specifically involves re-estimating Equation (1) using the change in the use of hired labour as an outcome defined at the household level and dropping individual level covariates. The results in column (1) of Table 10 indicate that there are no changes in the use of hired labour in Ethiopia in response to having at least one migrant child in the household. In contrast, when the household has a migrant child in Malawi, whether it be a migrant son or daughter, the percentage of households that hire at least one employee on the farm increases on the order of 0.17 to 0.30 percentage points (matching estimates, column 4).

We finally explore whether the migration-induced labour constraints in Ethiopia or additional hired labour costs to production in Malawi cause an overall contraction in agricultural and total net household income.[18] From the results in Table 10, there is no strong indication that the migration of heads' children compromises agricultural or overall household income. In Ethiopia, there are clear positive benefits of having a migrant son or rural-urban migrant on overall household income, which potentially justifies the increased efforts of others on the farm. In Malawi, weaker evidence suggests the

Table 6. Impacts of the migration of a head's daughter, OLS and matching estimates for Ethiopia

	(1) Works on farm	(2) Hours planting	(3) Hours harvesting	(4) Works in enterprise	(5) Works wage labour	(6) Hours on wage labour
Pooled (N = 6,216)						
OLS	0.01	−18.62	19.95	−0.02	−0.02	13.77
	(0.02)	(23.35)	(12.58)	(0.02)	(0.01)*	(19.00)
R^2	0.31	0.39	0.37	0.10	0.11	0.06
Matching	−0.06	−16.51	−22.39	−0.04	−0.01	17.26
	(0.02)***	(19.91)	(10.01)**	(0.02)**	(0.01)	(12.92)
Sons (N = 916)						
OLS	−0.00	−62.57	−1.31	0.01	−0.03	−16.44
	(0.05)	(64.80)	(30.34)	(0.06)	(0.04)	(27.77)
R^2	0.37	0.55	0.46	0.30	0.39	0.32
Matching	0.03	29.37	50.98	−0.13	0.01	38.71
	(0.06)	(42.41)	(21.48)**	(0.05)***	(0.02)	(17.03)**
Daughters (N = 480)						
OLS	−0.08	−68.57	4.98	−0.07	0.01	48.74
	(0.11)	(76.28)	(36.95)	(0.08)	(0.04)	(84.92)
R^2	0.49	0.67	0.59	0.50	0.44	0.46
Matching	0.01	10.09	13.99	0.13	−0.03	−38.46
	(0.09)	(38.87)	(28.44)	(0.05)***	(0.01)***	(17.18)**
Male Heads/Spouses (N = 2,068)						
OLS	−0.01	−52.19	1.86	−0.06	−0.04	27.93
	(0.02)	(49.44)	(20.58)	(0.03)**	(0.03)	(58.01)
R^2	0.57	0.60	0.54	0.24	0.21	0.15
Matching	−0.07	−147.47	−21.38	−0.11	−0.04	39.30
	(0.03)**	(43.87)***	(18.28)	(0.03)***	(0.02)	(27.94)
Female Heads/Spouses (N = 2,752)						
OLS	0.02	5.31	33.57	−0.00	−0.01	−1.54
	(0.03)	(23.68)	(13.23)**	(0.02)	(0.00)	(11.62)
R^2	0.40	0.50	0.48	0.13	0.18	0.20
Matching	−0.04	36.47	−8.05	−0.04	−0.01	−6.87
	(0.03)	(23.76)	(16.40)	(0.03)	(0.00)	(9.66)
F test: Equality of coefficients	0.27	0.99	0.82	0.50	0.50	0.33

Notes: ***p < 0.01; **p < 0.05; *p < 0.1. See Table 2 notes for details on specifications.

departure of a migrant son can harm agricultural (matching p-value = 0.01) and total (OLS p-value = 0.11 and matching p-value = 0.14) net income at the household level.

6. Conclusion

Policy-makers in Africa are increasingly expressing concern about the future of agriculture. While the processes of structural transformation typically involve people moving out of agriculture, the specifics of this process may determine who gains and who loses. In some areas, when men migrate out of rural areas, women remain on the farms and we observe what is often called the feminisation of agriculture. In other areas, including Malawi and Ethiopia, youth leave their agricultural households and migrate either to other rural areas or to urban centres. While migration may have long-term effects on the agricultural sector, in this paper, we have considered the short-term impacts on rural households when a child of the head migrates. Since

Table 7. Impacts of the migration of a head's daughter, OLS and matching estimates for Malawi

	(1) Works on farm	(2) Hours planting	(3) Hours harvesting	(4) Works in enterprise	(5) Works wage labour	(6) Hours on wage labour
Pooled (N = 3,643)						
OLS	0.08	23.59	14.86	0.01	−0.01	−11.48
	(0.03)**	(13.08)*	(10.99)	(0.03)	(0.01)	(20.15)
R^2	0.06	0.09	0.05	0.03	0.03	0.02
Matching	0.11***	−8.86	13.43	−0.01	−0.03	−47.92
	(0.02)	(6.98)	(4.28)***	(0.03)	(0.02)	(26.52)*
Sons (N = 549)						
OLS	0.18	37.23	0.62	0.06	0.01	8.78
	(0.08)**	(21.09)*	(18.20)	(0.04)*	(0.03)	(39.71)
R^2	0.14	0.19	0.14	0.10	0.18	0.24
Matching	0.15	−6.63	−1.75	−0.02	0.08	−12.27
	(0.07)**	(15.20)	(10.23)	(0.04)	(0.04)*	(52.16)
Daughters (N = 394)						
OLS	0.32	16.54	−17.08	−0.11	−0.02	8.85
	(0.10)***	(19.18)	(15.74)	(0.10)	(0.02)	(14.46)
R^2	0.15	0.24	0.15	0.17	0.25	0.43
Matching	0.27	27.03	−26.09	−0.11	NA	NA
	(0.10)***	(17.14)	(14.82)*	(0.06)*		
Male Heads/Spouses **N = 1,164)**						
OLS	0.04	21.13	23.51	0.07	−0.03	−96.36
	(0.03)	(19.25)	(16.49)	(0.06)	(0.04)	(69.19)
R^2	0.11	0.11	0.05	0.06	0.04	0.05
Matching	0.07	−3.38	24.82	0.09	−0.08	−109.71
	(0.03)***	(18.36)	(15.96)	(0.05)*	(0.04)*	(45.48)**
Female Heads/Spouses **(N = 1,536)**						
OLS	−0.02	13.26	20.91	−0.02	−0.00	44.14
	(0.04)	(18.17)	(12.15)*	(0.05)	(0.02)	(24.72)*
R^2	0.08	0.09	0.06	0.04	0.05	0.05
Matching	−0.02	−28.68	17.94	−0.02	−0.02	−0.45
	(0.02)	(13.98)**	(9.95)*	(0.04)	(0.02)	(25.85)
F test: Equality of coefficients	5.43***	0.93	1.17	1.50	0.85	1.55

Notes: ***p < 0.01; **p < 0.05; *p < 0.1. See Table 2 notes for details on specifications.

most of the literature focuses on the impact on the youth migrant him or herself, this paper contributes by analysing the impacts on their origin household, particularly the labour allocations, hired labour, and income (which consequentially affects agricultural investments in the long-term).

It is often assumed that there is excess labour in low productivity smallholder agriculture. Yet, we observe sons contribute to both agricultural and nonagricultural activities and when they migrate, some of their labour is replaced by other members of the household. In Ethiopia, the women who are heads/spouses may begin working on the farm when a son leaves. Similarly, in Malawi, when a son of the head migrates, his brothers work more on the farm. When daughters migrate, the demand for farm labour of sons and daughters increases at the extensive margin but only for the case of Malawi. Adjustments in hired labour in response to the migration of sons in Malawi (alone) illustrate a shortfall in on-farm labour. Only in Malawi is labour hired to compensate for the loss in labour of the migrating youth.

Table 8. Impacts of the migration of a head's child to urban areas, OLS and matching estimates for Ethiopia

	(1) Works on farm	(2) Hours planting	(3) Hours harvesting	(4) Works in enterprise	(5) Works wage labour	(6) Hours on wage labour
Pooled (N = 6,216)						
OLS	0.03	15.36	22.60	0.01	0.01	24.05
	(0.03)	(25.29)	(14.77)	(0.03)	(0.01)	(16.56)
R^2	0.31	0.39	0.37	0.10	0.11	0.07
Matching	0.05*	8.55	8.49	−0.02	0.02	10.39
	(0.03)	(22.96)	(10.02)	(0.03)	(0.01)*	(10.93)
Sons (N = 916)						
OLS	0.01	24.42	62.83	0.01	0.04	32.86
	(0.08)	(144.40)	(37.48)*	(0.06)	(0.04)	(34.66)
R^2	0.37	0.55	0.47	0.30	0.39	0.32
Matching	0.12	11.15	85.93	−0.00	0.08	86.81
	(0.05)**	(55.15)	(22.17)***	(0.04)	(0.04)**	(39.75)**
Daughters (N = 480)						
OLS	−0.05	−117.52	−41.08	0.19	0.05	129.37
	(0.19)	(111.65)	(53.55)	(0.12)	(0.06)	(122.47)
R^2	0.49	0.67	0.59	0.50	0.44	0.47
Matching	0.06	−34.15	28.89	0.29	0.02	20.01
	(0.15)	(53.62)	(43/04)	(0.12)	(0.02)	(10.33)*
Male Heads/Spouses (N = 2,068)						
OLS	0.03	−10.33	40.34	−0.04	0.04	37.90
	(0.03)	(38.37)	(21.93)*	(0.04)	(0.03)	(41.02)
R^2	0.57	0.60	0.54	0.24	0.21	0.15
Matching	0.00	−68.48	−19.78	−0.09	0.02	44.58
	(0.04)	(51.10)	(22.96)	(0.03)***	(0.03)	(29.96)
Female Heads/Spouses (N = 2,752)						
OLS	0.05	11.05	10.01	0.01	−0.01	−2.60
	(0.03)	(28.11)	(16.73)	(0.04)	(0.01)	(13.63)
R^2	0.40	0.50	0.48	0.13	0.18	0.20
Matching	0.03	10.23	6.74	−0.03	0.00	12.41
	(0.03)	(28.36)	(15.80)	(0.03)	(0.00)	(7.00)*
F test: Equality of coefficients	0.34	0.04	0.25	1.19	0.86	0.46

Notes: ***p < 0.01; **p < 0.05; *p < 0.1. See Table 2 notes for details on specifications.

Two potential mechanisms could explain the observed impacts of youth migration on household labour constraints and welfare. One hypothesis is that the increased efforts of female heads/ spouses in Ethiopian households and the costs of hired labour in Malawian households may serve as imperfect substitutes for the labour of migrant sons, jeopardising overall agricultural income. A second hypothesis is that the additional income available to the household from the migrant may be used to adopt new technologies or practices that mediate the losses attributable to the loss of migrant labour, such as the use of animal traction. Our findings support the former hypothesis in Malawi but not in Ethiopia. Specifically, our nearest neighbour matching estimate indicates losses in agricultural net income on the order of 30 per cent among households having at least one migrant son in Malawi. In contrast, gains from migration in the form of increased total net income justify the increased labour efforts in Ethiopia.

This analysis considers only the short-run effects of youth migration. Although the survey rounds are two years apart, the child may have migrated in the second year, with relatively little

Table 9. Impacts of the migration of a head's child to urban areas, OLS and matching estimates for Malawi

	(1) Works on farm	(2) Hours planting	(3) Hours harvesting	(4) Works in enterprise	(5) Works wage labour	(6) Hours on wage labour
Pooled (N = 3,643)						
OLS	0.14	7.36	10.37	−0.11	−0.01	54.28
	(0.05)**	(18.39)	(16.46)	(0.05)**	(0.03)	(39.44)
R^2	0.06	0.08	0.05	0.04	0.03	0.02
Matching	0.16	26.61	20.37	−0.11	−0.04	63.87
	(0.05)***	(11.93)**	(5.43)***	(0.05)**	(0.02)*	(22.63)***
Sons (N = 549)						
OLS	0.20	10.15	−13.36	0.02	−0.02	30.63
	(0.13)	(30.25)	(17.62)	(0.06)	(0.03)	(49.43)
R^2	0.13	0.18	0.14	0.09	0.18	0.24
Matching	0.23	−39.25	−17.05	−0.05	−0.12	−27.64
	(0.12)*	(24.35)	(17.56)	(0.07)	(0.06)**	(12.68)**
Daughters (N = 394)						
OLS	0.44	51.24	16.31	−0.16	0.00	8.60
	(0.14)***	(19.67)**	(24.78)	(0.11)	(0.02)	(12.24)
R^2	0.16	0.25	0.15	0.18	0.25	0.43
Matching	−0.11	31.71	−15.40	−0.13	NA	NA
	(0.19)	(17.24)*	(17.63)	(0.07)*		
Male Heads/Spouses N = 1,164)						
OLS	−0.03	2.23	23.36	−0.07	0.08	102.51
	(0.06)	(18.61)	(25.17)	(0.07)	(0.07)	(116.58)
R^2	0.11	0.11	0.05	0.06	0.04	0.05
Matching	0.06	6.34	3.18	−0.07	−0.01	126.69
	(0.06)	(27.61)	(22.90)	(0.11)	(0.07)	(74.66)*
Female Heads/Spouses (N = 1,536)						
OLS	0.03	−14.40	10.34	−0.15	−0.06	100.35
	(0.03)	(30.44)	(17.74)	(0.07)**	(0.05)	(58.53)*
R^2	0.08	0.09	0.06	0.05	0.05	0.05
Matching	0.03	−20.27	−4.09	−0.10	−0.10	80.57
	(0.02)	(25.45)	(16.89)	(0.06)*	(0.04)**	(37.60)**
F test: Equality of coefficients	5.65***	3.27**	0.71	1.31	2.25*	0.71

Notes: ***p < 0.01; **p < 0.05; *p < 0.1. See Table 2 notes for details on specifications.

time for the household to adjust other than the immediate change in labour allocations. In Malawi, there is already marginally significant evidence that a failure to compensate for the loss of a migrant son to the household may lead to losses in agricultural and total household profit. Thus, youth migration may have a broader impact on household outcomes than is captured within this short-term interval; after another round or two of data collection, after further readjustments have occurred, clearer patterns are more likely to emerge.

Acknowledgements

We thank Xiaoya Dou and Mekamu Jedir Jamal for excellent research assistance. Our manuscript has benefitted from helpful discussions with Paul Christian and Emily Schmidt. We thank Fantu Bachewe and Bart Minten for sharing the Ethiopian wage data presented in this paper. Finally, this paper has benefitted from the support provided by the CGIAR Research Program on Policies, Institutions, and

Table 10. Impacts of migration on change in household hired labour and profit, OLS and matching estimates

	Ethiopia (N = 3,032)			Malawi (N = 1,702)		
	(1) Hired labour	(2) Agricultural profit	(3) Total profit	(4) Hired labour	(5) Agricultural profit	(6) Total profit
Has a migrant child						
OLS	−0.03	524.38	987.45	0.17	−17.16	−133.70
	(0.04)	(189.61)***	(389.14)**	(0.05)***	(48.98)	(188.62)
R^2	0.26	0.51	0.48	0.06	0.15	0.08
Matching	−0.01	159.82	314.82	0.17	5.51	5.84
	(0.03)	(185.55)	(289.15)	(0.05)***	(42.51)	(225.78)
Has a migrant son						
OLS	−0.05	662.30	1,310.76	0.20	−96.13	−491.53
	(0.05)	(252.03)***	(523.46)**	(0.07)***	(76.65)	(308.47)
R^2	0.26	0.51	0.48	0.06	0.15	0.08
Matching	−0.04	331.54	935.61	0.23	−149.69	−354.79
	(0.04)	(256.08)	(390.20)**	(0.07)***	(105.30)**	(240.12)
Has a migrant daughter						
OLS	−0.02	306.68	468.04	0.17	23.89	88.63
	(0.05)	(208.71)	(362.23)	(0.06)***	(48.06)	(199.12)
R^2	0.26	0.51	0.47	0.06	0.15	0.08
Matching	0.01	168.97	7.17	0.18	64.47	132.67
	(0.03)	(234.11)	(377.26)	(0.06)***	(47.22)	(306.85)
Has a rural-urban migrant child						
OLS	−0.04	593.90	1,083.58	0.20	88.04	43.72
	(0.05)	(233.10)**	(496.67)**	(0.12)	(72.02)	(460.34)
R^2	0.26	0.51	0.47	0.06	0.15	0.08
Matching	−0.02	278.24	738.03	0.30	162.30	−382.53
	(0.04)	(285.27)	(404.61)*	(0.12)**	(76.38)*	(501.47)
Mean of outcome at baseline	0.19	364.73	593.19	0.37	333.42	1,201.52
Mean change of outcome	0.07	2,302.68	3,059.48	−0.09	−143.16	−519.36

Notes: ***p < 0.01; **p < 0.05; *p < 0.1. Outcomes are the change in the hired labour dummy and total net income (USD 2012) at the household level. Specifications are similar to Table 2 with the exception that individual covariates are dropped given the unit of analysis is the household.

Markets (PIM) led by the International Food Policy Research Institute (IFPRI). Data and dofiles for the analysis are available upon request from the corresponding author.

Disclosure statement

No potential conflict of interest was reported by the authors.

Notes

1. The focus in this paper is the role of youth internal migration, but there are strong differences in the international migration patterns across contexts as well. For example, Ethiopians travel to the Middle East (de Brauw et al., 2017) and Malawians tend to gravitate toward South Africa and Zimbabwe (Lewin, Fisher, & Weber, 2012).
2. It should be noted that the evolution of migration patterns may ultimately have more dynamic impacts on structural transformation in developing countries which are left unexplored here due to data constraints. First, if educated sons move because of land scarcity or concerns over underemployment and if children who are left behind compensate for the shortfall in labour, a lack of human capital in rural areas may stymie advancements in agriculture. Second, remittance income may change who controls income within the household. While remittances have the potential to increase investment in agriculture, depending on the profile of the decision maker, they may also be spent on alternative physical or human capital

investments. If women favour human capital investments (Mueller, Kovarik, Sproule, & Quisumbing, 2015), we might observe a disinvestment in agriculture rather than farm expansions and increased investments in modern technologies. Data covering a longer timeframe would be more fruitful to explore these long-term impacts of migration on human and physical capital investments and future farming systems.

3. Household attrition of the overall (rural and urban) sample is rather low (5% in Ethiopia, and 4% in Malawi) over the two year period (CSA and World Bank, 2015; NSO, 2014).

4. Table 1 shows that there are noticeable positive changes on average in the inherited land variable in both countries, driven by the death of a family member.

5. This information was collected using different protocols in each country. In Ethiopia, the information is constructed based on self-reported information by the proxy respondent (often the head of household). Despite the careful documentation of each household member in the baseline household roster, revealing or recalling the nature of the member's absence is at the discretion of the household head, making the household member's mobility status subject to measurement error. In Malawi, the migration definition is verified by the migrant at their destination at endline. While the tracking protocol offers precision in Malawi, a minority of migrants were unsuccessfully tracked (6%) and therefore are omitted from the analysis (National Statistical Office (NSO), 2014). These limitations in the measurement of migration are not unique to this study.

6. Migration distance is only available in Malawi, where migrants were tracked and georeferenced. Lee and Mueller (2016) find young (ages 15 to 24) rural-rural migrants tend to travel over one kilometre relative to rural-urban migrants who travel approximately 60 kilometres.

7. We may underreport the number of family members employed in the household's nonfarm enterprise in both countries. The Ethiopia survey documents at most five people hired in the enterprise, while the Malawi survey asks for the identification of at most two household members who manage and two household members who own the enterprise. A total of four or less household members may be included in the Malawi data.

8. Values are winsorized at 1 per cent to reduce the influence of outliers.

9. The discrepancy in time frames is due to differences in the survey instrument. In Ethiopia, the labour questions are asked over the current season, while in Malawi, the labour questions are asked over the two seasons.

10. The migration of family members is dominated by the children of the heads in both Ethiopia and Malawi. Twenty-five (27) per cent of sons and 38 (37) per cent of daughters in Ethiopia (Malawi) moved by the follow up round. While the mobility of heads and their spouses in Malawi exceeds that of Ethiopia (13% compared to 2%), the younger generation is much more mobile.

11. Our final list of towns/cities is 25 in Ethiopia and four in Malawi.

12. Wage growth is converted into 2011 real terms in both Ethiopia and Malawi using consumer price indices (CSA, 2013b; NSO, 2016).

13. Busso, di Nardo, and McCary (2014) recommend the use of the nearest neighbour matching approach with bias-correction in lieu of other reweighting or matching estimators particularly when the overlap is poor. We estimate the distribution of the propensity scores based on our covariates of interest to find overlap may be imperfect (Figures A.1–A.2 in Supplementary Materials).

14. Tables A4 and A5 (see Supplementary Materials) model these migration decisions using probit regressions. The covariates are sufficiently strong determinants of the migration of sons in Malawi. Inherited land becomes a significant explanatory variable when evaluating the probability of someone in the pooled sample having a child of the household move to an urban area. This finding supports conventional wisdom regarding migration driven by land scarcity in Ethiopia (De Brauw & Mueller, 2012).

15. Few observations in our sample live in households that either have a head or spouse that migrates or an additional member that moves internationally. To assuage concerns that our estimates are driven by the inclusion of these few occurrences, we present the matching results for the employed on the farm outcomes dropping observations in households with head/spouse migrants and international migrants in Table A6 (Supplementary Materials).

16. Bias-corrected matching estimates are the same irrespective of the number of matches used (not shown here). Trimmed sample matching estimates are qualitatively similar as to those using the entire sample (Tables A7 and A8 in Supplementary Materials).

17. Interestingly, there is weaker evidence to suggest a greater percentage of daughters are tasked with working in the nonfarm enterprise when a head's son migrates in Ethiopia. The order of magnitude far exceeds the percentage point increase in female adults called to work on the farm. Because our F tests do not support that these effects statistically differ from those observed among other family members, the figures are merely suggestive that daughters may also substitute for sons who spend more time on the farm during the harvesting period.

18. Agricultural and total profit are reported in 2012 US dollars and winsorized at 5 per cent. Total income includes agricultural revenue net input expenditures, non-farm enterprise revenue net input costs, wage income, and transfers.

ORCID

Agnes Quisumbing ⓘ http://orcid.org/0000-0002-5429-1857

References

Abadie, A., Drukker, D., Herr, J., & Imbens, G. (2004). Implementing matching estimators for average treatment effects in stata. *The Stata Journal 4*, 290–311.

Abadie, A., & Imbens, G. (2008). On the failure of the bootstrap for matching estimators. *Econometrica, 76*, 1537–1557.

Aguilar, A., Carranza, E., Goldstein, M., Kilic, T., & Oseni, G. (2015). Decomposition of gender differentials in agricultural productivity in ethiopia. *Agricultural Economics, 46*, 311–334.

Beegle, K., De Weerdt, J., & Dercon, S. (2011). Migration and economic mobility in tanzania. *The Review of Economics and Statistics, 93*, 1010–1033.

Bevan, P., & Pankhurst, A. (Eds.). (1996). *Fifteen ethiopian village studies*. Oxford: Oxford University and Addis Ababa University.

Bezu, S., & Holden, S. (2014). Are rural youth in Ethiopia abandoning agriculture? *World Development, 64*, 259–272.

Busso, M., DiNardo, J., & McCrary, J. (2014). New evidence on the finite sample properties of propensity score reweighting and matching estimators. *Review of Economics and Statistics, 96*, 885–897.

Central Statistical Agency (CSA). (2013a). *Country and regional level consumer price indices*. Addis Ababa: Federal Democratic Republic of Ethiopia.

Central Statistical Agency (CSA). (2013b). *Consumer Price Survey*. Addis Ababa: Federal Democratic Republic of Ethiopia.

Central Statistical Authority (CSA) and World Bank. (2015). Ethiopia socioeconomic survey (ESS) wave two (2013/2014): Basic information document. Retrieved April 25, 2016, from http://siteresources.worldbank.org/INTLSMS/Resources/3358986-1233781970982/5800988-1367841456879/9170025-1427144247562/Basic_Information_Document_Wave_2.pdf.

Croppenstedt, A., Goldstein, M., & Rosas, N. (2013). Gender and agriculture: Inefficiencies, segregation, and low productivity traps. *The World Bank Research Observer, 28*, 79–109.

De Brauw, A., Huang, J., Zhang, L., & Rozelle, S. (2013). The feminization of agriculture with chinese characteristics. *Journal of Development Studies 49*, 689–704. doi:10.1080/00220388.2012.724168

De Brauw, A., Li, Q., Chengfang, L., Rozelle, S., & Zhang, L. (2008). Feminization of agriculture in China? Myths surrounding women's participation in farming. *China Quarterly, 194*, 327–348.

De Brauw, A., & Mueller, V. (2012). Do limitations in land rights transferability influence low mobility rates in ethiopia? *Journal of African Economies, 21*, 548–579.

De Brauw, A., Mueller, V., & Lee, H. L. (2014). The role of rural-urban migration in the structural transformation of sub-Saharan Africa. *World Development, 63*, 33–42.

De Brauw, A., Mueller, V., & Woldehanna, T. (2017). Does internal migration improve overall well-being in Ethiopia? *Journal of African Economies*, 1–19. doi:10.1093/jae/ejx039

Dillon, A., Mueller, V., & Salau, S. (2011). Migratory responses to agricultural risk in northern nigeria. *American Journal of Agricultural Economics, 93*, 1048–1061.

Dinkelman, T., Kumchulesi, G., & Mariotti, M. (2015). *Labor migration and the Structure of Rural Labor Markets*. (Unpublished manuscript). Department of Economics, Dartmouth College, Hanover, NH.

Doss, C. (2002). Men's crops? Women's crops? The gender patterns of cropping in Ghana. *World Development, 30*, 1987–2000.

Fafchamps, M., & Quisumbing, A. (2002). Control and ownership of assets within rural ethiopian households. *Journal of Development Studies, 38*, 47–82.

Funk, C., Peterson, P., Landsfeld, M., Pederos, D., Verdin, J., Shukla, S., ... Michaelson, J. (2015). The climate hazards infrared precipitation with stations–a new environmental record for monitoring extremes. *Scientific Data, 2* doi:10.1038/sdata.2015.66

Holden, S., Shiferaw, B., & Pender, J. (2001). Market imperfections and land productivity in the ethiopian highlands. *Journal of Agricultural Economics, 52*, 53–70.

Kilic, T., Palacios-Lopez, A., & Goldstein, M. (2015). Caught in a productivity trap: A distributional perspective on gender differences in malawian agriculture. *World Development, 70*, 416–463.

Kumar, N., & Quisumbing, A. (2015). Policy reform toward gender equality in ethiopia: Little by little the egg begins to walk. *World Development, 67*, 406–423.

Lee, H. L., & Mueller, V. (2016). *Can migration be a conduit for transformative youth employment? Evidence from the LSMS-ISA countries?* (Unpublished manuscript). Development Strategy and Governance Division, International Food Policy Research Institute, Washington, DC.

Lewin, P., Fisher, M., & Weber, B. (2012). Do rainfall conditions push or pull rural migrants: Evidence from Malawi. *Agricultural Economics, 43*, 191–204.

Lokshin, M., & Glinskaya, E. (2009). The effect of male migration on employment patterns of women in Nepal. *The World Bank Economic Review, 23*, 481–507.

Lucas, R. E. B. (2015). African migration. In B. Chiswick & P. Miller (Eds.), *The handbook of the economics of international migration* (Vol. ume 1B). Amsterdam, Holland: Elsevier.

McKenzie, D., Stillman, S., & Gibson, J. (2010). How important is selection? Experimental vs. non-experimental measures of the income gains from migration. *Journal of the European Economic Association, 8*, 913–945.

Moller, L. C. (2012). *The ethiopian urban migration study 2008: The characteristics, motives and outcomes to immigrants to addis ababa*. Washington, DC: World Bank Group.

Mueller, V., Kovarik, C., Sproule, K., & Quisumbing, A. (2015). *Migration, gender, and farming systems in asia: Evidence, data, and knowledge gaps*. International Food Policy Research Institute Discussion Paper No. 1458. Washington, DC: IFPRI.

Mueller, V., Schmidt, E., Lozano-Gracia, N., & Murray, S. (2016). *Household and spatial drivers of migration patterns in Africa: Evidence from four countries*. Paper prepared for the Structural Transformation of African Agriculture and Rural Spaces (STAARS) conference 2015, Addis Ababa, Ethiopia.

National Statistical Office (NSO) (2014). Malawi Integrated Household Panel Survey 2013: Basic Information Document. Retrieved April 25, 2016, from http://siteresources.worldbank.org/INTLSMS/Resources/3358986-1233781970982/5800988-1271185595871/6964312-1404828635943/IHPS_BID_FINAL.pdf.

National Statistical Office (NSO) (2016). Consumer price index rural. Retrieved April 26, 2016, from, http://www.nsomalawi.mw/latest-publications/consumer-price-indices/69-consumer-price-index-rural.html.

Pankhurst, A., Dessalegn, M., Mueller, V., & Hailemariam, N. (2013). Migration and resettlement in ethiopia: Reflections on trends and implications for food security. In A. Pankhurst, D. Rahmato, & G. Van Uffelen (Eds.), *Food security, safety nets and social protection: The ethiopian experience*. Addis Ababa, Ethiopia: Forum for Social Studies.

Pankhurst, R. (1990). *A social history of ethiopia*. Addis Ababa: Institute of Ethiopian Studies, Addis Ababa University.

Peters, P. (1990). Our daughters inherit our land, but our sons use their wives' fields: Matrilineal-matrilocal land tenure and the new land policy in malawi. *Journal of Eastern African Studies*, 4, 179–199.

Potts, D. (2006). Rural mobility as a response to land shortages: The case of malawi. *Population, Space and Place*, 12, 291–311.

Rahmato, D. (1991). Rural women in ethiopia: Problems and prospects. In T. Berhane-Selassie (Ed.), *Gender issues in ethiopia*. Addis Ababa, Ethiopia: Institute of Ethiopian Studies, Addis Ababa University.

Rose, E. (2001). Ex ante and Ex post labor supply responses to risk in a low income area. *Journal of Development Economics*, 64, 371–388.

Thomas, K., & Inkpen, C. (2013). Migration dynamics, entrepreneurship, and african development: Lessons from malawi. *International Migration Review*, 47, 844–873.

Webb, P., Von Braun, J., & Yohannes, Y. (1992). *Famine in ethiopia: Policy implications of coping failure at national and household levels*. International Food Policy Research Institute Research Report 92. Washington, DC: International Food Policy Research Institute.

World Bank. (2016a). Living Standards Measurement Study—Integrated Surveys on Agriculture, Ethiopia. Retrieved from http://go.worldbank.org/HWKE6FXHJ0.

World Bank (2016b). Living Standards Measurement Study—Integrated Surveys on Agriculture, Malawi. Retrieved from http://go.worldbank.org/ZIWEL8UHQ0.

Figure A.1: Propensity Score Distributions, Ethiopia

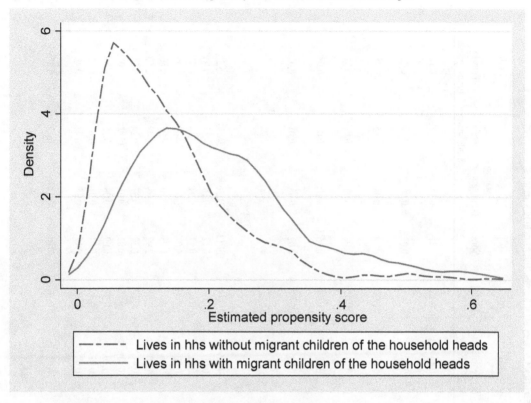

Figure A.2: Propensity Score Distributions, Malawi

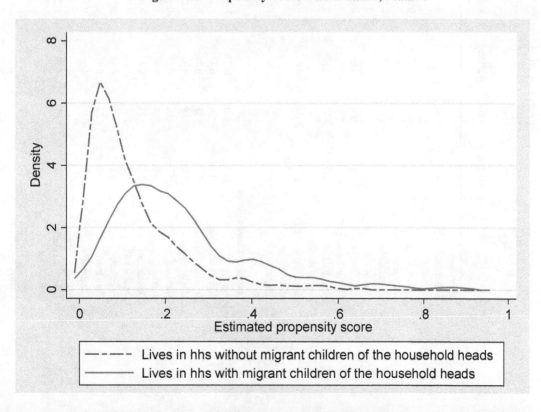

Table A.1: Migration, Member Characteristics, Changes in Outcomes, and Matching Variables

	(1)	(2)	(3) Ethiopia	(4)	(5)	(6)	(7)	(8) Malawi	(9)	(10)
	Pooled	Sons	Daughters	Male heads/spouses	Female heads/spouses	Pooled	Sons	Daughters	Male heads/spouses	Female heads/spouses
Migration										
Household has child migrant	0.15	0.20	0.17	0.14	0.15	0.13	0.21	0.15	0.11	0.12
Household has rural-urban child migrant	0.07	0.08	0.07	0.06	0.07	0.03	0.03	0.06	0.02	0.02
Household has migrant son	0.08	0.11	0.10	0.07	0.08	0.06	0.09	0.08	0.05	0.05
Household has rural-urban migrant son	0.04	0.04	0.06	0.04	0.04	0.02	0.02	0.04	0.01	0.01
Household has migrant daughter	0.09	0.12	0.10	0.09	0.08	0.09	0.15	0.10	0.07	0.08
Household has rural-urban migrant daughter	0.03	0.04	0.03	0.03	0.03	0.01	0.02	0.03	0.01	0.01
Individual Characteristics										
Age	33.51	19.40	19.28	39.78	36.26	33.00	19.12	21.36	38.70	36.20
Primary education	0.16	0.36	0.38	0.14	0.06	0.09	0.12	0.16	0.11	0.06
Secondary education	0.01	0.01	0.01	0.01	0.01	0.08	0.11	0.09	0.13	0.04
Missing education	0.00	0.00	0.01	0.01	0.00	0.00	0.01	0.01	0.00	0.00
Married	0.71	0.06	0.03	0.95	0.86	0.67	0.03	0.10	0.97	0.80
Rooms	1.74	1.81	1.90	1.71	1.70	2.61	2.97	2.98	2.49	2.50
Durable roof	0.42	0.44	0.47	0.41	0.41	0.27	0.32	0.37	0.24	0.25
Durable wall	(0.00)	(0.01)	(0.01)	(0.00)	(0.00)	(0.01)	(0.02)	(0.03)	(0.02)	(0.01)
Piped water	0.10	0.13	0.09	0.10	0.10	0.09	0.09	0.08	0.08	0.09
Flush toilet	0.01	0.02	0.01	0.01	0.01	0.01	0.01	0.01	0.01	0.01
Change in household size	0.08	-0.02	-0.04	0.15	0.08	0.35	0.17	0.15	0.43	0.40
Change in inherited land acreage	6.48	7.67	5.55	6.75	6.02	0.26	-0.01	-0.14	0.42	0.32
Change in Outcomes										
Works on farm	0.07	0.07	0.07	0.06	0.09	0.02	0.10	0.09	-0.01	-0.01
Hours spent planting	-31.70	-21.49	-5.49	-57.28	-20.35	-8.78	-0.52	-4.21	-8.74	-12.69

	(1) Pooled	(2) Sons	Ethiopia (3) Daughters	(4) Male heads/spouses	(5) Female heads/spouses	(6) Pooled	(7) Sons	Malawi (8) Daughters	(9) Male heads/spouses	(10) Female heads/spouses
Hours spent harvesting	32.54	44.23	22.49	46.44	19.52	12.58	19.04	21.95	7.09	12.26
Works in nonfarm enterprise	0.01	0.01	0.03	0.01	0.02	0.05	0.04	0.01	0.05	0.07
Works in wage labor	0.00	0.01	0.00	-0.00	0.00	-0.01	0.03	0.01	-0.04	0.00
Hours spent in wage labor	4.03	-7.60	-4.92	9.67	5.41	13.26	22.20	14.10	27.67	-0.65
Matching Variables										
Household size	5.85	6.81	7.03	5.65	5.45	5.56	6.47	6.88	5.32	5.13
Land inherited (acre)	1.18	1.24	1.20	1.20	1.15	1.57	1.69	1.92	1.55	1.46
Coefficient of variation	0.12	0.12	0.12	0.12	0.12	0.16	0.15	0.15	0.16	0.16
Wage growth in nearest town/10	0.00	0.00	0.00	0.00	0.00	0.77	0.81	0.77	0.75	0.78
Share of households who migrated for employment/10	1.01	1.08	1.19	0.94	1.00	1.29	1.33	1.30	1.24	1.32
Wage growth times share of households who migrated/100	0.01	0.01	0.01	0.00	0.01	1.08	1.17	1.04	1.00	1.11
N	6,216	916	480	2,068	2,752	3,643	549	394	1,164	1,536

Table A.2: Balance Check for Ethiopia Pooled Sample, Difference in Treatment and Control Values [t test, p-values]

	(1) Has migrant child	(2) Has migrant son	(3) Has migrant daughter	(4) Has rural-urban migrant
Household size	-0.15	-0.20	-0.04	-0.18
	[0.01]	[0.01]	[0.57]	[0.04]
Inherited land	-0.05	-0.05	-0.07	-0.01
	[0.52]	[0.59]	[0.48]	[0.94]
Coefficient of variation	0.00	0.00	0.00	-0.00
	[0.51]	[0.45]	[0.86]	[0.94]
Daily wage growth	-0.00	0.00	0.00	0.00
	[0.99]	[0.95]	[0.98]	[0.84]
Community network	-0.05	-0.06	-0.03	-0.05
	[0.18]	[0.19]	[0.48]	[0.33]
Daily wage growth times community network	-0.00	-0.00	-0.00	-0.00
	[0.40]	[0.26]	[0.84]	[0.45]

Notes: P values in brackets for t tests of difference in means.

Table A.3: Balance Check for Malawi Pooled Sample, Difference in Treatment and Control Values [t test, p-values]

	(1) Has migrant child	(2) Has migrant son	(3) Has migrant daughter	(4) Has rural-urban migrant
Household size	-0.14	0.06	-0.13	0.14
	[0.12]	[0.72]	[0.26]	[0.53]
Inherited land	0.05	0.04	0.07	-0.05
	[0.47]	[0.63]	[0.42]	[0.63]
Coefficient of variation	-0.00	0.00	0.00	0.00
	[0.85]	[0.80]	[0.35]	[0.30]
Daily wage growth	-0.02	0.00	-0.02	0.00
	[0.37]	[1.00]	[0.27]	[1.00]
Community network	0.00	0.00	0.00	0.00
	[1.00]	[1.00]	[1.00]	[1.00]
Daily wage growth times community network	0.00	0.00	0.01	0.00
	[0.93]	[1.00]	[0.92]	[1.00]

Notes: P values in brackets for t tests of difference in means.

Table A.4: Probit Regressions of Having at least one Child Migrant in the Household (Marginal Effects)

	(1) Ethiopia	(2) Malawi
Rooms	0.02	-0.00
	(0.01)	(0.01)
Durable roof	0.02	0.04
	(0.02)	(0.03)
Durable wall	-0.12	-0.02
	(0.02)***	(0.02)
Piped water	-0.06	-0.00
	(0.03)**	(0.04)
Flush toilet	0.24	-0.01
	(0.09)**	(0.06)
Household size	0.04	0.04
	(0.00)***	(0.00)***
Land inherited (acre)	-0.00	0.01
	(0.00)	(0.01)
Coefficient of variation of rainfall	-0.23	0.87
	(0.26)	(0.42)**
Wage growth divided by 10	-0.08	-0.02
	(0.66)	(0.03)
Share of households who migrated for employment divided by 10	-0.01	-0.03
	(0.01)	(0.02)
Wage growth times share of households who migrated for employment divided by 100	0.42	0.03
	(0.29)	(0.02)*
N	6,216	3,643

Notes: Baseline household sampling weights applied. Enumeration area clustered standard errors in parentheses. *** $p<0.01$, ** $p<0.05$, * $p<0.1$.

Table A.5: Probit Regressions of Having at least one Migrant in the Household (Marginal Effects)

	(1) Ethiopia, Migrant Son	(2) Malawi, Migrant Son	(3) Ethiopia, Migrant Daughter	(4) Malawi, Migrant Daughter	(5) Ethiopia, RU Migrant	(6) Malawi, RU Migrant
Rooms	0.01	-0.01	0.02	0.00	0.01	0.00
	(0.01)	(0.01)	(0.01)**	(0.01)	(0.01)	(0.00)
Durable roof	0.02	0.04	-0.00	-0.00	0.02	0.02
	(0.02)	(0.02)*	(0.02)	(0.02)	(0.02)	(0.01)*
Durable wall	-0.07	-0.03	-0.06	0.02	-0.06	-0.01
	(0.01)***	(0.01)**	(0.02)**	(0.02)	(0.01)***	(0.01)
Piped water	-0.03	-0.03	-0.03	0.03	-0.02	-0.00
	(0.01)**	(0.01)***	(0.02)*	(0.03)	(0.02)	(0.01)
Flush toilet	0.09	0.06	0.15	-0.04	0.10	0.02
	(0.08)	(0.10)	(0.12)	(0.03)	(0.09)	(0.03)
Household size	0.02	0.02	0.02	0.02	0.01	0.01
	(0.00)***	(0.00)***	(0.00)***	(0.00)***	(0.00)***	(0.00)***
Land inherited (acre)	-0.00	0.00	-0.00	0.00	-0.01	-0.00
	(0.00)	(0.00)	(0.00)	(0.01)	(0.00)**	(0.00)
Coefficient of variation of rainfall	-0.01	0.49	-0.03	0.37	-0.27	0.34
	(0.17)	(0.24)**	(0.19)	(0.26)	(0.22)	(0.10)***
Wage growth divided by 10	-0.23	-0.03	-0.09	0.00	-0.17	-0.00
	(0.44)	(0.02)	(0.47)	(0.02)	(0.47)	(0.00)
Share of households who migrated for employment divided by 10	-0.01	-0.02	-0.00	-0.01	-0.00	-0.02
	(0.01)	(0.01)**	(0.00)	(0.01)	(0.01)	(0.00)***
Wage growth times share of households who migrated for employment divided by 100	0.26	0.02	0.10	0.01	0.15	0.01
	(0.20)	(0.01)**	(0.18)	(0.01)	(0.21)	(0.00)***
N	6,216	3,643	6,216	3,643	6,216	3,643

Notes: Baseline household sampling weights applied. Enumeration area clustered standard errors in parentheses. *** $p<0.01$, ** $p<0.05$, * $p<0.1$.

Table A.6: Matching estimate for Works on Farm Outcome, Using Pooled Samples and Omitting Observations in Households Having a or Head/Spouse or International Migrant

	(1) Has migrant child	(2) Has migrant son	(3) Has migrant daughter	(4) Has rural-urban migrant
Ethiopia: Drops observations in households having a head/spouse migrant	0.02	0.08	-0.03	0.05
	(0.02)	(0.02)***	(0.02)	(0.02)*
N	6,107	6,107	6,107	6,107
Malawi: Drops observations in households having a head/spouse migrant	0.05	0.00	0.11	0.16
	(0.03)**	(0.04)	(0.03)***	(0.04)***
N	3,561	3,561	3,561	3,561
Ethiopia: Drops observations in households having an international migrant	0.02	0.07	-0.02	0.04
	(0.02)	(0.02)***	(0.03)	(0.03)
N	6,032	6,032	6,032	6,032
Malawi: Drops observations in households having an international migrant	0.04	-0.02	0.11	0.15
	(0.03)*	(0.04)	(0.03)***	(0.04)***
N	3,580	3,580	3,580	3,580

Table A.7: Impacts of Youth Migration, Matching Estimates with Trimmed Sample for Ethiopia

	(1) Works on farm	(2) Hours planting	(3) Hours harvesting	(4) Works in enterprise	(5) Works wage labor	(6) Hours on wage labor
Pooled (N=6,090)						
Migrant son	0.07 (0.03)**	12.47 (19.85)	10.82 (10.30)	-0.01 (0.02)	0.02 (0.01)*	4.51 (9.51)
Migrant daughter	-0.05 (0.02)**	-17.56 (20.22)	-25.70 (10.60)**	-0.03 (0.02)	-0.01 (0.01)	19.33 (13.51)
Rural-urban migrant	0.05 (0.03)*	1.97 (22.98)	9.49 (10.10)	-0.02 (0.03)	0.02 (0.01)*	8.43 (10.94)
Sons (N=890)						
Migrant son	0.12 (0.06)**	-0.13 (48.46)	80.70 (17.49)***	-0.05 (0.03)	-0.01 (0.03)	-6.94 (28.02)
Migrant daughter	0.08 (0.06)	94.94 (43.59)**	74.05 (20.82)***	-0.08 (0.04)*	0.02 (0.01)	52.13 (17.88)***
Rural-urban migrant	0.14 (0.05)***	51.23 (55.77)	97.10 (19.44)***	0.06 (0.04)	0.08 (0.04)**	92.16 (41.39)**
Daughters (N=464)						
Migrant son	0.25 (0.12)*	-5.90 (28.53)	34.56 (32.59)	0.29 (0.09)***	0.02 (0.010)**	14.88 (7.72)*
Migrant daughter	0.03 (0.09)	23.97 (32.94)	19.60 (29.73)	0.07 (0.04)*	-0.01 (0.01)	0.62 (6.32)
Rural-urban migrant	0.06 (0.14)	-36.48 (51.76)	29.75 (44.34)	0.29 (0.11)***	0.02 (0.02)	20.87 (10.77)*
Male Heads/Spouses (N=2,031)						
Migrant son	0.01 (0.03)	-25.58 (46.26)	-28.34 (20.34)	-0.06 (0.04)	0.06 (0.02)**	67.86 (22.14)***
Migrant daughter	-0.07 (0.03)***	-148.49 (44.99)***	-23.74 (18.71)	-0.10 (0.03)***	-0.05 (0.02)**	36.29 (28.76)
Rural-urban migrant	0.01 (0.04)	-74.85 (45.02)*	-16.22 (23.11)	-0.09 (0.03)***	0.02 (0.03)	39.67 (29.92)
Female Heads/Spouses (N=2,705)						
Migrant son	0.07 (0.04)**	4.89 (25.65)	16.57 (13.82)	-0.01 (0.03)	0.00 (0.00)*	4.19 (15.46)
Migrant daughter	-0.04 (0.03)	40.13 (22.86)*	-11.18 (17.22)	-0.03 (0.03)	-0.01 (0.00)*	-7.29 (10.07)
Rural-urban migrant	0.03 (0.03)	-1.16 (26.29)	12.80 (15.78)	-0.03 (0.03)	0.00 (0.00)	12.51 (7.26)*

Notes: *** $p<0.01$, ** $p<0.05$, * $p<0.1$.

Table A.8: Impacts of Youth Migration, Matching Estimates with Trimmed Sample for Malawi

	(1) Works on farm	(2) Hours planting	(3) Hours harvesting	(4) Works in enterprise	(5) Works wage labor	(6) Hours on wage labor
Pooled (N=3,570)						
Migrant son	0.05 (0.04)	25.00 (7.53)***	19.99 (5.24)***	0.05 (0.04)	0.03 (0.01)**	45.05 (21.57)**
Migrant daughter	0.08 (0.02)***	-5.01 (7.02)	11.77 (4.42)***	0.00 (0.03)	-0.03 (0.01)	-46.69 (27.500)*
Rural-urban migrant	0.17 (0.05)***	41.63 (12.48)***	14.79 (5.46)***	-0.10 (0.05)*	-0.04 (0.02)*	62.53 (22.63)***
Sons (N=539)						
Migrant son	0.46 (0.10)***	62.40 (18.72)***	30.01 (17.14)*	0.12 (0.06)*	0.02 (0.02)	11.07 (45.25)
Migrant daughter	0.18 (0.06)***	-10.11 (16.18)	0.33 (9.24)	-0.01 (0.04)	0.04 (0.04)	-19.04 (55.48)
Rural-urban migrant	0.23 (0.12)*	-39.25 (24.35)	-17.05 (17.56)	-0.05 (0.07)	-0.12 (0.06)**	-27.64 (12.68)**
Daughters (N=384)						
Migrant son	0.12 (0.16)	-8.73 (19.60)	42.64 (17.94)**	0.00 (0.05)	0.03 (0.02)	1.13 (0.80)
Migrant daughter	0.22 (0.09)**	32.54 (17.93)*	-29.70 (15.75)*	-0.08 (0.06)	NA	NA
Rural-urban migrant	-0.27 (0.19)	94.99 (18.15)***	-49.22 (17.99)***	-0.33 (0.07)***	NA	NA
Male Heads/Spouses (N=1,140)						
Migrant son	-0.13 (0.04)***	14.92 (16.68)	20.42 (16.51)	0.09 (0.07)	0.08 (0.05)*	70.30 (59.46)
Migrant daughter	0.08 (0.03)***	3.30 (18.94)	21.12 (16.41)	0.12 (0.05)**	-0.10 (0.04)**	-129.79 (46.61)***
Rural-urban migrant	0.09 (0.06)	26.67 (32.50)	13.24 (23.05)	-0.02 (0.11)	0.01 (0.07)	156.80 (74.66)**
Female Heads/Spouses (N=1,507)						
Migrant son	0.02 (0.03)	-18.01 (17.37)	6.08 (11.99)	0.08 (0.04)**	-0.01 (0.01)*	23.66 (9.08)***
Migrant daughter	-0.02 (0.02)	-11.08 (14.93)	13.56 (10.02)	-0.01 (0.04)	-0.02 (0.02)	2.36 (26.36)
Rural-urban migrant	0.03 (0.02)	-16.17 (25.40)	-2.86 (16.46)	-0.07 (0.06)	-0.08 (0.04)*	77.69 (45.25)*

Notes: *** $p<0.01$, ** $p<0.05$, * $p<0.1$.

The Quiet Rise of Large-Scale Trading Firms in East and Southern Africa

NICHOLAS J. SITKO, WILLIAM J. BURKE & T. S. JAYNE

ABSTRACT   The share of smallholder-produced maize sold to large-scale traders (LSTs) has increased from virtually nil 10 years ago to 12 per cent and 37 per cent in Zambia and Kenya, respectively. We examine the causes and consequences of this transformation. LST investment has responded to growing market demand as well as to changes in farm structure and has been especially prominent in areas where medium-scale farms are concentrated. After controlling for distances travelled and other factors, farmers selling to LSTs receive prices that are 4.9 per cent and 3.6 per cent higher than those offered by small-scale traders, and are more likely to access input credit, private extension services, and price information.

1. Introduction

Sub-Saharan Africa (SSA) is experiencing rapid agrifood system transformation. Growing evidence points to transformations at the production, processing and retail segments of the food systems.[1] However, the so-called 'middle' segments of food systems – trading and wholesaling – have received surprisingly little attention, particularly for the staple cereals that account for over half of the total area under cultivation in SSA.[2] This dearth of attention is an important blind spot in our knowledge of recent transformations in African food systems. Yet the exceptional pace of transformation in the region's food systems at production and retail level suggests that the evidence generated about grain market performance just five to 10 years ago may be increasingly outdated for guiding investments and policies today.

For decades, grain marketing policies and development interventions in SSA have presupposed a dysfunctional grain marketing structure, dominated by small, poorly capitalised, and often geographically isolated market actors, which impedes supply chain coordination and risk management, thus imposing major transaction costs on market participants (Barrett, 2008; Fafchamps, 2004; Poulton, Kydd, & Dorward, 2006). While this image of an incoherent commodity aggregation market still holds in some areas, recent survey data suggest major changes are underway that warrant a fundamental reassessment of development policy and programmatic options.

Using data from Zambia and Kenya, this article explores the causes and consequences of the recent rise of large-scale grain trading firms in smallholder grain markets. Nationally representative rural household survey data shows that in Zambia between 2012 and 2015 smallholder maize sales to large-scale traders (LSTs) increased from 3 per cent to 12 per cent of total maize sales volume, or from approximately 40,000 mt to over 240,000 mt. In Kenya, there were virtually no direct sales by farmers to LSTs in 2004, but by 2007 LSTs directly purchased 21 per cent of farmers' total maize sales by volume, expanding further to 37 per cent in 2014.

The rise of LSTs in parts of Africa may portend important transformations occurring in the middle segment of the food system that challenges the dominant understanding of constraints and opportunities in these markets. This article elucidates these changes and their implications for development policy. Our objectives are threefold: to identify the functions and comparative advantages of large- and small-scale traders in grain markets; to identify factors driving the rapidly growing role of LSTs in Kenya and Zambia; and to assess what the rise of LSTs tells us about the on-going process of food system transformation in SSA and the implications for the future of small-scale farming.

The article is organised as follows. Section 2 develops a conceptual framework for understanding the rise of LSTs. Section 3 describes the data sources used in the analysis. Section 4 uses trader survey data to examine the evolution of LSTs in the region and how they engage in smallholder grain markets. Section 5 draws on nationwide household survey from Zambia and Kenya to document changes in the market share of LSTs in maize markets and to explore important drivers of the rise of LSTs. Section 6 uses survey data to determine how the rise of LST has affected grain prices received by farmers and access to farm credit and services. Section 7 offers concluding remarks and policy recommendations.

2. How and why markets evolve: a conceptual framework

Our thinking on the cause and consequences of the rise of large-scale traders in SSA is informed by two interrelated strands of literature: the economic structural transformation literature and the literature on food system transformation and modernisation. The structural transformation literature highlights several stylised facts about how economies shift from being predominately agrarian to more industrial and service-oriented (Johnston & Kilby, 1975; Johnston & Mellor, 1961; Mellor, 1976). In countries where the primary source of employment is agriculture, agricultural productivity growth typically initiates the process of transformation. Farms selling the greatest surpluses lead this process, and their earnings generated from the expansion of production creates demand for goods and services in the local rural economy. This, in turn, generates employment opportunities in the non-farm economy, thereby inducing rural-to-urban migration, a transition of the labour force from farm to non-farm, gradual farm consolidation by those that remain in agriculture, and ultimately a declining agricultural share of GDP. Indeed, recent cross-country analysis of 11 African countries indicates that farm productivity growth strongly influences the subsequent pace of job expansion and labour productivity in the off-farm sectors of the economy (Yeboah & Jayne, 2017). An important outcome of this process is that labour productivity increases through a combination of inter-sector gains – that is, the movement of labour from semi-subsistence farming with very low labour productivity to manufacturing and services – and within-sector agricultural productivity growth achieved through technology adoption, scale economies, shifts in the mix of agricultural products, and improved market access (Haggblade, Hazell, & Reardon, 2010; Jayne et al., 2016).

Market arrangements play a crucial role in the initial stages of sustained agricultural productivity growth among a broad segment of the rural population. In particular, market arrangements that lower transactions costs, increase farm gate prices relative to input costs, and overcome the idiosyncratic market risks support greater participation of small farms in agricultural supply chains and contribute to broad-based agricultural productivity growth (Barrett, 2008; Poulton et al., 2006; Reardon & Timmer, 2012).

Aspects of traditional marketing arrangements in SSA are ill-equipped to drive broad-based productivity growth. Myriad small firms (often only one person) with limited capital and asset bases, typically dominate traditional grain markets in SSA (Fafchamps, 2004). In this context, farm products often undergo numerous discreet, small-volume, spot market transactions before reaching consumers (Poulton et al., 2006). Consequently, while these markets may be reasonably competitive, they impose high costs and risks on participants due to a lack of scale economies and the accumulation of transactions costs (Poulton et al., 2006; Sitko & Jayne, 2014). Moreover, prices in these markets are typically volatile, due to market segmentation (Barrett, 2008; Gabre-Madhin, Barrett, & Dorosch, 2002), and limited financial capacity to store grain and withstand production fluctuations (Poulton et al., 2006). Finally, due to a high risk of contract default, transactions are often on a cash and carry basis, with limited capacity for supply chain coordination through forward contracts (Fafchamps, 2001). These market attributes tend to inflate marketing margins, and consequently push down producer prices, which undermines incentives for intensification.

Transformation of traditional market arrangements is therefore an important element in the process of economic transformation. The literature on food system transformation suggests that as traditional market arrangements give way to more modern forms, four changes typically occur in their structure and conduct. First, there is consolidation of food system functions at both the farm level and beyond (Reardon, Barrett, Berdegué, & Swinnen, 2009). Second, global agri-business firms enter into some segments of the food system (Reardon & Barrett, 2000). Third, exchange shifts away from spot market transactions toward greater vertical and horizontal integration in supply chains facilitated through supply chain contracts (Porter, 1985; Reardon & Timmer, 2012). Finally, private grades and standards become commonplace in governing supply chain relationships (Reardon, Codron, Busch, Bingen, & Harris, 1999). Virtually none of these shifts have been documented or commonly observed in staple food supply chains involving African smallholders.

These elements of food system transformations produce several potentially important effects that are relevant to our analysis. Farm and first-buyer consolidation enables scale economies in production, transport, and market information, and can lead to lower transactions costs and, often, greater capacity to absorb investment risks (Poulton et al., 2006). Multi-nationalisation brings with it global and regional supply chain expertise, experience in a range of risk management strategies, and considerable financial capabilities.

Consolidated agri-business firms gain footholds in traditional markets by driving down costs and passing these cost savings along. Porter (1985) argued that to drive down costs, firms typically deploy supply chain governance strategies, including vertical coordination mechanisms such as contracts. Vertical coordination and contracting serve two important functions. On the production side, resource supply contracts, such as input credit, help to address the idiosyncratic market failures that typically inhibit smallholder technology adoption (Morris, Kelly, Kopicki, & Byerlee, 2007). Further down the supply chain, contracts enable supply chain actors to coordinate activities and investments. In some cases, contracts can be collateralised, thus leading to improved liquidity conditions within supply chains. These contracts typically emerge in conjuncture with standards, which can lower the costs associated with ensuring production consistency, and can lay the foundation for the emergence of more sophisticated forward contracting arrangements (Coulter & Onumah, 2002).

The literature identifies three fundamental factors that drive food system transformation: 1) policy measures that remove barriers to trade – these barriers were huge in many African countries up to the 1990s and the sectoral policy reforms associated with structural adjustment made it possible for subsequent major investment in food systems by millions of small traders and processors since then (Jayne, Govereh, Mwanaumo, Nyoro, & Chapoto, 2002; Jayne et al., 2010; Sitko & Jayne, 2014); (2) demand pull, caused by population growth, urbanisation, rising incomes, and dietary changes (Tschirley, Reardon, Dolislager, & Snyder, 2015), and; (3) supply side pushes caused by foreign direct investment (FDI) and investments from domestic food system actors aimed at achieving economies of scale, scope, and specialisation (Reardon & Barrett, 2000). In the context of grain markets in SSA two factors are likely of particular importance. First, rapid population growth in the region drives aggregate food supply demand and puts upward pressure on food prices. Second, rapid changes in production systems, namely the growth of medium-scale farms in SSA, creates a segment of the rural population that is better capitalised and can produce on considerably higher scale than most African farms (Jayne et al., 2016).

Food system transformation can affect broader processes of income differentiation, productivity growth, and economic transformation in several ways. At a production level, Reardon and Timmer (2012) find that there is convergence in the literature that the impact of participation by farmers in modern versus traditional supply chains on incomes is moderately to substantially beneficial. This is achieved through some combination of lower transactions costs within modern supply chains, as well as contract premiums. A priori, we anticipate the rise of LSTs to positively affect farmers that sell to them, through some combination of access to contracts and supply chain services (for example input credit, market information, and so forth) and higher farm-gate prices. The possibility exists, however, that the rise of LSTs will squeeze out local supply chain actors – a process referred to as 'disin-termediation' – leading to less competitive market conditions and opportunities for LSTs to push down farm-gate prices due to their market power (Fafchamps, 2004).

This framework leads us to a four-step analysis. First, we use nationwide survey data to document changes in the importance of LSTs in staple maize markets in Kenya and Zambia. Second, we use LST trader survey data to examine the role of the rise of LSTs in transforming and modernising grain markets. Third, we examine why LSTs are expanding in smallholder markets, focusing on changing supply and demand conditions. Fourth, we use survey data and, controlling for a range of household-level and market access variables, to examine the effects of selling to LSTs on access to input credit and services, and farm gate prices.

3. Data sources

The data in this paper comes from two primary sources: structured surveys with LSTs in Kenya and Zambia and nationwide farm household survey data at different points in time.

LST trader surveys were carried out in September and October of 2016. In Kenya, LSTs were identified using the membership roster of the East African Grain Council (EAGC). EAGC is a membership organisation of grain traders. Its membership roster is considered representative of grain market actors in the region. In total, 26 firms registered with EAGC from Kenya list 'trader' as their primary business. Of these, trader surveys were carried out with 18, including all the multi-national traders involved in domestic grain sourcing in Kenya. The remaining eight firms were either not available or refused to be interviewed for this study. Thus, while not a full census of LSTs in Kenya, our survey captures data from the majority of large-scale firms involved in grain trading.

In Zambia, LSTs were identified through Grain Traders Association of Zambia (GTAZ), the primary lobby organisation for grain traders in Zambia. In total, interviews were conducted with 24 managing directors or owners of LST firms in Zambia. This included all domestic and multinational firms categorised as 'large-scale' in the GTAZ membership roster. Because membership in GTAZ is required to access a trading license in Zambia, we consider this membership roster to include all LSTs in Zambia.

Household survey data from Kenya comes from panel data collected by the Tegemeo Institute of Agricultural Development and Policy of Egerton University, in partnership with Michigan State University (MSU). The sampling frame was drawn from all non-urban divisions in the country, and these were allocated to Agro-Ecological Zones (AEZ). Divisions were selected from each AEZ proportional to the size of population. Beginning in 2004 questions on marketing channel were added to the survey instrument to allow us to distinguish between small- and large-scale traders. Since 2004 three waves of the survey have been conducted (2004, 2007, 2010), consisting of a balanced panel of 1200 maize-growing farm families living in 120 villages across 24 countries and eight AEZ.

Household survey data in Zambia comes from the Rural Agricultural Livelihoods Survey (RALS) carried out by the Indaba Agricultural Policy Research Institute (IAPRI) in partnership with MSU and the Central Statistical Office. This is a nationally representative longitudinal survey of smallholder households in Zambia carried out in 2012 and 2015. In total, 7254 households in 442 standard enumeration areas were interviewed in both panel waves.

An important challenge in collecting smallholder market channel data is ensuring that the distinction between large and small-scale trader is consistent across households in both countries. To address this challenge, enumerators in both countries asked three clarifying questions when respondents indicated that they sold grain to a trader. First, to their knowledge, does the trader purchase more grain than the average trader in the area? Second, how does the trader typically buy grain? Do they personally come to villages to buy or do they operate buying points and hire agents to buy on their behalf? Typically, even domestically owned LSTs will not personally enter villages to acquire grain. Instead, they use recognised agents and established buying points. Third, does the trader have a company name or is the trader buying grain as an individual? This question allows us to distinguish designated agents buying on behalf of LSTs from traders buying on their own account. If the respondent answers yes to the first question and yes to either question two or three, the market channel was classified as 'large-scale trader'.

4. The rise of large-scale trading and shifting market arrangements in Zambia and Kenya

Table 1 documents how smallholder marketing behaviour has changed over recent time in Kenya and Zambia, based on nationwide panel farm household survey data from Kenya and nationally-representative household survey data in Zambia. Two important observations come out of this table. First, of market channels captured in survey data, LST is the fastest growing in terms of the share of total maize sales in both countries. Second, the rise of LST appears to coincide with a decline in the share of total maize surplus purchased by national marketing boards, the Food Reserve Agency (FRA) in Zambia and the National Cereals and Produce Board (NCPB) in Kenya. The direction of causality in this relationship is unclear. LSTs may have gained market share by out-competing marketing boards or by filling a market niche created by a contraction of marketing board activities. The interaction between marketing board policy and the rise of LSTs is an important area for future research. But what can be safely concluded here is that LSTs share of maize sales by farmers has risen, especially in Kenya.

4.1. Market entry and structure

As shown in Table 2, the establishment of large-scale grain trading firms in Kenya and Zambia has mostly occurred since the turn of the century. On average respondents indicate that their firms began buying grain in Kenya in 2002, while in Zambia the average start date is 2008. In Zambia, the rise of large-scale grain trading coincides with the global food price spike of 2007/08, which gave rise to a range of food system investments across Africa, most notably in commercial farm land acquisitions (Deininger et al., 2011; German, Schoneveld, & Mwangi, 2013).

Between the two countries, we see variations in the relative role of multinational versus domestic ownership. In Kenya, only two major multinational firms are involved in grain trading, Cargill and Export Trading Group (ETG). By contrast, Zambia has seven multinational firms involved in grain trading. These include ETG and Cargill, as well as NWK Agri-Services, AFGRI, DomZam, Inter-Africa Grain, and Quality Commodities.

The higher concentration of multinational firms in Zambia relative to Kenya reflects several important underlying differences in the structure of the two markets. According to interviews, including one respondent who at different times managed grain-buying activities in both countries, the higher level of multinational activity in Zambia is due to three primary factors. First, grain-trading profit margins in Kenya are narrower and come mostly from spatial rather than temporal arbitrage due

Table 1. Share in total smallholder maize sales by volume, Kenya and Zambia various years

		Small-scale trader	Large-scale trader	NCPB/ FRA	Processor/ miller	Retailer/ consumer	Other	Total
				% of total volume sold to….				
Kenya	2007	38	21	29	5	7	0	100
	2014	39	37	8	4	9	3	100
Zambia	2012	10	3	81	3	2	1	100
	2015	17	12	60	8	2	1	100

Source: RALS 2012, 2015; Tegemeo HH survey 2004, 2007, and 2014.

Table 2. Summary statistics of large-scale trader survey

Variable	Kenya (n = 18)	Zambia (n = 24)
Mean year firms began buying grain	2002	2008
Median year firms began buying grain	2005	2008
Share of firms that are multinational	11.1	29.2
Domestic *Maize* Purchases 2015/16 marketing season (MT)		
Mean	9,103	21,603
Sum	163,850	518,461
Domestic *All Grain* Purchases 2015/16 marketing season (MT)		
Mean	20,334	38,215
Sum	366,020	917,171
Purchase channels (% of MT purchased) 2015/16		
Small-scale farms (<5 ha)	3.06	34.0
Medium-scale farms (5–20 ha)	22.22	40.83
Commercial farms (>20 ha)	3.33	3.67
Other traders	52.5	21.5
Imports	18.89	0
Sales channel (% of MT sold) 2015/16		
Large-scale mills	56.94	41.71
Small-scale mills	8.61	4.58
Animal Feed Processor	5.83	9.58
Oilseed crusher	1.67	2.71
Other trader	16.67	14.17
Export market	2.22	13.54
NGOs	8.06	13.71
Contract Utilization (% yes)		
w/small-scale traders	61	54
from processors/retailers	78	54
forward delivery contracts with farmers	17	58
Financing		
% that borrow to fund grain trade	89	46
Source of trade finance (% of those that acquired)		
Domestic commercial bank	75	8
Overseas commercial bank	6	13
Internal borrowing within firm/family	13	67
Informal credit	6	4
Other	0	8

to the two-season nature of production in the country and a staggered surplus production season with neighbouring Uganda and Tanzania. This favours nimble local traders that can leverage local market knowledge and social capital in order to link seasonally varying production zones to consumption markets.

Moreover, given relatively lower margins, firms have to handle significantly larger volumes of grain to remain profitable than they would in Zambia. Relatively low and spatially varying domestic surplus production, coupled with a lack of bulk handling facilities place limits on the total available surplus and the pace that grain is off-loaded to the market, and thus limit the attractiveness of the Kenyan market to multinational firms.

Second, domestic commercial lending rates in Kenya are lower than in Zambia and banks are more willing to lend to local grain traders. In Zambia, benchmark interest rates set by the Bank of Zambia held at 15.5 per cent throughout 2016, compared to rates between 8.5 per cent and 11.5 per cent in Kenya. As shown in Table 2, amongst financed traders, 75 per cent of the respondents in Kenya indicated that domestic commercial lending was their primary source of grain trade financing, compared to just 8 per cent in Zambia. Moreover, a larger share of trading firms in Kenya borrowed money (89%) than in Zambia (46%). So, amongst all traders interviewed, two out of three in Kenya were financed domestically, compared to less than one in 20 in Zambia. Finally, Zambia's position as a consistent grain surplus producer, and associated export opportunities to the region's deficit countries is considered an important driver of the multi-nationalisation of grain trading in Zambia.

4.2. Scale and supply chain structure

As shown in Table 2, in Kenya our sample of large traders accounted for over 163,000 mt of domestic maize purchases (excluding imports) in 2015/16. On average, respondents purchased over 9,000 mt of maize in that year from domestic suppliers. In Zambia, large-traders accounted for well over 500,000 mt of domestic maize purchases. This amounts to 37 per cent of the total forecasted maize sales by farmers in the country for 2016,[3] with the parastatal maize marketing board, the Food Reserve Agency also accounting for a similarly large proportion of total maize sold by farmers. Respondent LSTs purchased, on average, over 21,000 mt each in 2015/16. LSTs in Zambia therefore exercise significant market power and have significantly larger capital outlays than in Kenya.

While maize is the most widely traded crop for large-scale traders in both countries, LSTs typically buy and sell a range of other grains and export crops. In Kenya, traders purchase a wide range of pulses, such as green gram, pigeon pea, and groundnuts, for both domestic retail markets and export. Wheat is also an important commodity for some traders. In Zambia, traders also purchase wheat and soybeans in addition to maize, but are increasingly adding groundnuts, pigeon peas, and to a lesser extent sunflower to their crop portfolio. When the full range of grains are included, respondents purchased a total of 366,000 mt and 917,000 mt of grains in Kenya and Zambia respectively in 2015/16. This amounts to an average annual purchase volume of over 20,000 mt of grain per firm in Kenya and over 38,000 mt in Zambia.

The ways in which LSTs purchase maize in Zambia and Kenya vary. When we disaggregate the share of total purchases, including imports, by supply channel we find that large-scale traders in Kenya acquire stocks primarily through intermediaries and imports, while those in Zambia purchase the majority of their grain directly from small and medium-scale farms. In both cases, commercial farms play only a minor role in total grain purchases.

As mentioned earlier, because of the staggered seasonal nature of maize production in Kenya, large traders rely on smaller trader with local market knowledge and social capital to acquire grain. Large-traders in Kenya only maintain established grain buying points in a handful of locations in the breadbasket regions of the Rift Valley.

By contrast, Zambia produces grain according to a uni-modal rainfall pattern. Consequently, large-traders in Zambia frequently have established buying points in major production regions, which they operate during the main marketing season. These established buying points allow Zambian traders to buy a larger share of their total grain purchases directly from small and medium-scale farmers.

These purchasing patterns of LSTs suggest that processes of disintermediation that are common markers of food system transformation are more pronounced in Zambia than Kenya. As a result, we anticipate that the pace of decline in the prominence of traditional market channels in Zambia is likely to be faster than in Kenya. An important area for future research is to understand the implication of this on the competitiveness of the assembly markets on which most very small producers currently depend (Sitko & Jayne, 2014).

In both Zambia and Kenya, direct purchases from farmers are concentrated in the medium-scale farm sector. This is a farm sector that has exhibited significant dynamism in recent years, particularly in Zambia (Jayne et al., 2016; Sitko & Jayne, 2014). We will return to the role of land size dynamics in driving large-scale trader growth below.

Grain sales patterns by large-scale traders are similar between countries. In both countries, large-scale mills that process maize meal and wheat flour are the primary markets for traders. Export markets are particularly important for Zambia traders, who export to deficit countries in the region. In both countries, NGOs, particularly the World Food Programme's Purchase for Progress program, accounts for a non-trivial share of total sales. Edible oil crushers and animal feed processors are particularly important market channels in Zambia, where local soybean production is well established.

4.3. Supply chain contracts and coordination

The shift from predominantly spot market transactions to more coordinated contractual relationships along supply chains is an important element of supply chain transformation (Reardon & Timmer, 2012). Large-scale trader surveys show that downstream and upstream market relationships are increasingly characterised by formal and informal contracts.

Table 2 shows that the majority of large-scale traders in Kenya and Zambia utilise contracts with other, often smaller scale traders to purchase grain on their behalf. Due to a lack of formal contract enforcement mechanisms, these contracts are typically carried out with local traders that have an established business record with the firm. At a minimum, the contracts specify the price, quantity, and delivery point. In some cases quality requirements, particularly moisture content and colour, are included in the contracts. These contracts are used to enhance supply chain predictability, increase total traded volumes and to defray supply and price risk.

These contracts often include financing for the smaller-scale trader. Of the respondents that contract traders to buy grain on their behalf, 60 per cent in Kenya and 71 per cent in Zambia provide financing to the traders. In addition, supply contracts from large traders to small traders in Kenya are used to access short-term commercial bank loans. This is important, as it helps to address typical capital constraints that impede small-scale trader activities in SSA.

Downstream contracts are also an important feature of large-scale traders' business models. Like trader contracts, these processor contracts specify quantity, quality, price, and delivery location. As shown in Table 2, 78 per cent of all LST respondents in Kenya indicated that they receive processor contracts, compared to 54 per cent in Zambia. These contracts serve two important supply chain functions. First, they help to defray some price risk for traders. This is important, given the high level of price variability in the two countries. Prices in these markets frequently move dramatically as a result of policy changes, such as tariff waivers, export bans, or marketing board activities, limited supply and demand information, and global price movements (Jayne et al., 2010; Kirimi et al., 2011). Second, in some cases processors provide traders with financing to purchase grain. Of the respondents that receive processor contracts, 22 per cent in Kenya and 46 per cent in Zambia are provided with financing as part of the contract. More often, traders use the processor contracts to borrow from local commercial banks. Again, this is more prevalent in Kenya than in Zambia.

Taken together, the rise of large-scale trading is helping to drive a fledgling transition from predominantly spot market transactions to more formal marketing arrangements. In the absence of market concentration and market power, these arrangements could improve the capacity of the food system to lower and spread risk along supply chains, enable greater transparency, and serve to address some of the traditional liquidity constraints that impede African grain market performance (Poulton et al., 2006). However, important questions arise about the effects that LST's rising market share will have on market competition.

5. Changing grain supply and demand conditions and the rise of LSTs

5.1. Evolving demand conditions

Large-scale traders say expanding demand in local and regional markets has been the fundamental growth engine for their businesses. This increased demand has come from a combination of structural, quantitative, and qualitative changes in grain markets. The key structural change has been the shifting of supply chain responsibilities from processors to traders, which opens space in the market for more trading and wholesaling activity. This transfer of responsibility has likely co-evolved with the growth of large-scale traders and medium-scale farmers producing relatively large surpluses. The growth of large-scale traders appears to be creating more differentiated supply chain responsibilities, which in turn creates greater opportunities for growth for large-scale traders.

The quantitative expansion of demand is largely due to rapid population growth and urban population growth. Within both Zambia and Kenya, total populations have doubled between 1990 and 2015. Regionally as well, large and growing populations create tremendous demand growth for regional trade in staple foods. As of 2014, the FAO estimates total net maize demand in eastern and southern Africa is approaching 40 million tons and growing rapidly. This creates opportunities for food processors and wholesalers. But the nature of the opportunity is somewhat different in the two countries. Nearly 14 per cent of Kenya's maize consumption over 2009–2013 was imported from world markets, while Zambia was an exporter over this same period. Kenya's increasing dependence on imported grains is raising opportunities to link demand in burgeoning cities with supplies from global markets. Processing is thriving regardless of the source of the raw maize. In Kenya, for example, large-sale processors have increased total grain processing capacity by over 30 per cent between 2005 and 2015 (Export Processing Zone Authority (EPZA), 2005; Global Agriculture Information Network, 2015). As domestic large-scale processing capacity increases, total formal market demand for grain increases, which creates considerable opportunities for large-scale traders from local, regional and global sources. In Zambia, by contrast, essentially all of the urban demand for maize since 2010 has been sourced from domestic production. This provides greater investment and employment growth in the development of local supply chains dedicated to pulling surplus production off the farm and into cities, from local aggregation, wholesaling, processing and retailing. In Kenya, LST investment is responding to opportunities from both local and import supply chains.

In many countries, demand growth is outpacing domestic supply growth, pushing prices toward import parity (ReNAPRI, 2015). Figure 1 presents national annual nominal maize prices (in dots) against regional price averages and US gulf maize prices. It shows that prices in the region have trended upward since 1990, yet with significant inter-annual fluctuation at a country level and high levels of price heterogeneity between countries. This creates both regional arbitrage opportunities in grain trading and investment opportunities for processors and traders.

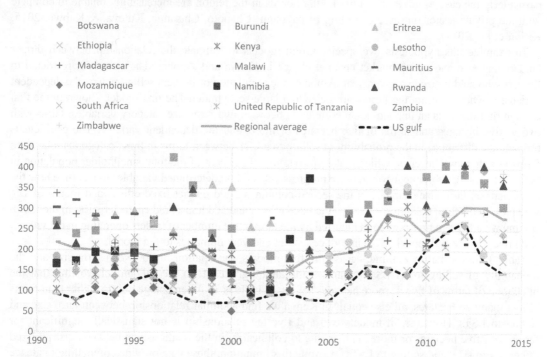

Figure 1. Average annual maize producers' prices for countries in eastern and southern Africa, regional averages, and US gulf prices 1990–2014.
Source: FAOSTAT (http://www.fao.org/faostat/en/).

Finally, urbanisation and income growth are creating qualitative changes in demand, particularly increased consumption of oils and animal proteins (Byerlee, García, Giertz, Palmade, & Gurcanlar, 2013; Masters et al., 2013; Tschirley et al., 2015). This drives demand for primary products, including both oilseeds and maize. In Zambia, for example, animal feed processing capacity has increased from less than 10,000 mt per year in 2000 to over 320,000 mt in 2015 (AgriProFocus Zambia, 2015).

The combination of these demand side factors create tremendous growth and profit opportunities for domestic and multinational firms willing to assume the risk of operating in these uncertain markets and capable of accessing the requisite capital to do so.

5.2. The co-evolution of medium-scale farms and large-scale traders

Alongside the demand growth in the region, and partially as a response to it, SSA is witnessing a rapid expansion of medium-scale farms (Jayne et al., 2016; Sitko & Jayne, 2014). Medium-scale farms (defined here as farms between five and 100 hectares) have increased over the last decade to control roughly 20 per cent of total farmland in Kenya, 32 per cent in Ghana, 39 per cent in Tanzania, and over 50 per cent in Zambia (Jayne et al., 2016). Investment in medium-scale farms in the region has been driven in large measure by increased interest in land by urban-based professionals and influential rural people. This investment followed many projections that the rise in world food prices represented a long-term structural change in global food conditions driven by US biofuels policy and rising long-term demand for grain in large middle-income countries (for example, see Von Braun, 2007). It remains to be seen whether domestic investment in medium-scale farms continues in the current period of moderate global food prices, but in any event the rapidly rising urban population and demand for food in Africa still presents strong incentives for local farm investment.

A priori we anticipate that the growth in larger, more capitalised farms, with larger surpluses to sell would provide incentives for new entry by relatively capitalised traders who could accommodate the larger volumes of these medium-scale farms better than traditional small-scale traders. This is particularly the case as government marketing boards in the region are increasingly unable to compete with the private sector on price or timing of payment (Chapoto, Chisanga, Kuteya, & Kabwe, 2015; Kirimi et al., 2011).

To examine this hypothesis, we specify probit models to estimate the relationship between farmer landholding size and maize market channel choice in Kenya and Zambia. The sample is restricted to farmers who sold maize in a given year. Amongst the population of farmers selling maize, the dependent variable is whether or not the farm sold maize to a large-scale trader. The first model, shown in the first column of Table 3, is an unconditional correlation between two farm size category variables, farms with two to five hectares and farms of five hectares or more, and the dependent variable. The coefficients estimate the difference in the probability of selling to a LST between farms in these categories relative to farms less than two hectares, which make up roughly 70 per cent of the total smallholder population in both countries. In subsequent columns we progressively add predetermined variables to examine how the coefficient on farm size changes. In the second column we add district fixed effects and month of sale variables. In the third column we remove the fixed effects and add household characteristics. In the fourth column we add grain transport costs incurred by the farmer, the number of traders operating in the village, and prices. In the full model, we reintroduce district and year dummies to the model.

Table 3 shows that in Zambia, across the five models, the relationship between farm size and the probability of selling to an LST remains stable and significant. In the full model we find that the likelihood of farms of five or more hectares selling to LSTs is 14.4 percentage points higher than farms of less than two hectares, all else equal. In Kenya we find a similar relationship between farm size and selling to LSTs. However, in models two and five the relationship is not statistically significant for farms with five hectares or more. This is due to collinearity in the relationships between district fixed effects, farm size, and selling to LSTs.[4] Despite this limitation, these data provide compelling evidence that the rise of LSTs, and the structural changes it creates in grain markets, is likely co-evolving with rapid growth in relatively larger producers.

Table 3. Factors associated with farmer choosing to sell maize to a large-scale trader (amongst those selling to traders) in Kenya and Zambia

Variables added in each column (left-to-right)

Explanatory variables	Simple 1 — Zambia	Simple 1 — Kenya	Month and district only 2 — Zambia	Month and district only 2 — Kenya	Household characteristics only 3 — Zambia	Household characteristics only 3 — Kenya	Price & TCs 4 — Zambia	Price & TCs 4 — Kenya	Full model 5 — Zambia	Full model 5 — Kenya
Farm is 2–5 hectares (cultivated and fallow land) (1 = yes)	0.082*** (0.02)	0.151*** (0.03)	0.077*** (0.02)	0.090*** (0.03)	0.093*** (0.02)	0.134*** (0.03)	0.095*** (0.02)	0.140*** (0.03)	0.092*** (0.02)	0.086*** (0.02)
Farm is 5 or more hectares (cultivated and fallow land) (1 = yes)	0.145*** (0.04)	0.188*** (0.05)	0.147*** (0.04)	0.042 (0.04)	0.136*** (0.04)	0.182*** (0.05)	0.134*** (0.04)	0.196*** (0.05)	0.144*** (0.04)	0.074 (0.05)
Adult equivalents					0.004 (0.00)	0.013*** (0.00)	0.005 (0.00)	0.011*** (0.00)	0.002 (0.00)	0.005* (0.00)
Level of education household head in years					-0.007*** (0.00)	0.002 (0.00)	-0.006** (0.00)	0.002 (0.00)	-0.005* (0.00)	0.005*** (0.00)
Female headed household					-0.034 (0.02)	0.024 (0.03)	-0.034 (0.02)	0.025 (0.03)	-0.024 (0.02)	0.064** (0.03)
Land is not formally owned (1 = yes)					-0.023 (0.03)	-0.001 (0.02)	-0.017 (0.03)	0.002 (0.02)	-0.036 (0.03)	0.022 (0.02)
All animal/equipment assets (local currency/hh)					0.001*** (0.00)	-0.000 (0.00)	0.001*** (0.00)	-0.000 (0.00)	0.000** (0.00)	-0.000 (0.00)
Quantity of fertiliser applied (kgs/maize ha)					0.025*** (0.00)	-0.000 (0.00)	0.025*** (0.00)	-0.000 (0.00)	0.019*** (0.00)	0.000* (0.00)
Price for commercial sale (Local currency/kg, rebased)							-0.002 (0.02)	0.003* (0.00)	0.035 (0.02)	0.004* (0.00)
Transportation cost for sale (local currency/kg, rebased)							0.050 (0.05)	-0.006** (0.00)	0.060 (0.04)	-0.007*** (0.00)
One or two commercial traders came to village (1 = yes)						-	-0.012 (0.03)	-	-0.005 (0.03)	
3 or more commercial traders came to village (1 = yes)	-	-				-	-0.010 (0.03)	-	0.017 (0.03)	
Year = 2015	-	-	0.023 (0.02)	0.109*** (0.02)		-	-0.010 (0.03)	-	0.003 (0.02)	0.060** (0.03)

(continued)

139

Table 3. (*Continued*)

Variables added in each column (left-to-right)

Explanatory variables	Simple 1		Month and district only 2		Household characteristics only 3		Price & TCs 4		Full model 5	
	Zambia	Kenya	Zambia	Kenya	Zambia	Kenya	Zambia	Kenya	Zambia	Kenya
Monthly dummy variables for time of sale	-	Yes	Yes	Yes			-		Yes	Yes
District dummy variables	-	Yes	Yes	Yes			-		Yes	Yes
Observations	2,794	1,411	2,555	1,373	2,794	1,411	2,720	1,410	2,496	1,372

Sources: Kenya: Tegemeo Institute survey data 2007, 2010. Zambia: IAPRI RALS survey data, 2012, 2015.

Notes: Kenya: 38 observations are in a district where no farmers sold to large scale traders (and thus present an incidental parameter problem if included in the district fixed-effect regression), so they are omitted from columns 2 and 5. One observation is missing month of sale data, and so is omitted from columns 4 and 5. Zambia: N changes because of missing data in column 4. In Columns 2 and 5 there are several districts where no farmer sold to large traders, so the observations from these districts are dropped.

6. Implications of the rise of LSTs on service provision to farmers and farm-gate price

The literature reviewed in the conceptual framework suggests that as traditional markets give way to more consolidated and integrated supply chains, the capacity to coordinate investments along the supply chain, including investments in input credit and other services, increases (Poulton et al., 2006). This is because larger firms can often better manage the sorts of risks, including default and price risk, which typically impede these investments in traditional market arrangements (ibid). Moreover, due to economies of scope and scale, coupled with other supply chain governance tools, such as price hedging and supply contracting, LSTs may be able to drive down transactions costs in ways that allow them to pay higher farm gate prices than traditional market actors (Reardon & Timmer, 2012). Evidence of these outcomes would suggest that the rise of LSTs is contributing in important ways to broader processes of economic transformation.

6.1. African farmers improving access to markets and services

According to interviews, input credit and extension services are provided by LSTs to farmers in order to increase available tradable surpluses and to help farmers meet quality standards, particularly for pulses and oilseeds. Table 4 shows that while more than half of LSTs in Zambia offer input credit to some farmers, only a quarter of LSTs in Kenya do. Zambia's large commercial farm sector is an important recipient of input credit. While the mean number of farmers provided with input credit for grain by LSTs is over 3400 in Zambia, the median is just 20. Many LSTs provide input credit to a small handful of large commercial farms, while a minority also extend credit to the smallholder sector. These are mostly firms that also have an investment in smallholder cash crop production, and have assumed many of the screening costs of providing input credit to smallholders through this side of their business (Sitko & Chisanga, 2016). Input credit is particularly important for driving productivity growth in Zambia, where domestic lending rates are higher than in Kenya and input markets are less dynamic (Ariga & Jayne, 2009).

The total value of input credit in Zambia is astounding. In 2015, LSTs estimate that they provided over 44,000 commercial and smallholder farmers with a combined $US 70 million in input credit for maize, soy, and wheat production. In Kenya, the scale of input credit provision is much more modest. Respondents estimate they granted US$144,000 in grain input credit to 1200 farmers.

Extension services area also an important element of LSTs business models. In Kenya, LSTs provide extension services, mostly for pulse production, to 8200 farmers. In Zambia, extension advice

Table 4. Input credit and extension service provision by LSTs

Input credit	Kenya	Zambia
% that provide to farmers	28	54
# of recipients		
mean	256	3,423
median	100	20
sum	1,281	44,504
total value (US$)		
mean	28,940	5,352,710
median	7,000	9,960
sum	144,700	69,585,224
Extension		
% that provide to farmers	33	42
# of recipients		
mean	1378	5675
median	125	200
sum	8271	51,076

Source: Large-scale trader survey (2016).

Table 5. Smallholder access to farm credit and information by market channel

Market channel for largest transaction	Zambia		Kenya	
	Did the HH receive price information from...? (% yes)	Did the HH receive seed on loan from...? (% yes)	Did the household receive cash credit for agriculture from ... (% Yes)	Did the household receive in-kind credit for agriculture from ... (% Yes)
Small trader	13.3	1.1	9.5	21.5
Large trader	17.7	5.5	14.2	12.8
FRA/NCPB	15.3	0.9	17.2	13.8
Miller	18.3	0.7	9.1	9.1
Other households	14.9	1.2	8.8	26.9

Source: Zambia: RALS 2015. Kenya: Tegemeo Institute survey data 2007 and 2010.

was provided to 51,000 farmers by LSTs. Extension services were provided for smallholder pulses, oilseeds, and maize, as well as for commercial wheat and soy production. One might ask what kind of extension services a trader is providing, or even qualified to provide. Multi-national firms are likely to provide specialists and host field days educating farmers on a range of topics including plant spacing, fertilisation, marketing and so on. Supplemental discussions with our respondents suggest that many domestic large-scale traders are farmers themselves and often trained by either government or other extension agents. The primary focus of the advice from these actors seems to be on encouraging fertiliser and improved seed use.

Table 5 uses household survey data to estimate the share of producers that receive input credit in Kenya and Zambia, and market information in Zambia, by market channel.[5] It shows that farmers that sell to large traders are statistically more likely to get price information (in Zambia) and more likely to receive seed credit (Zambia) and cash input credit (Kenya) than those selling to traditional small-scale traders. However, Kenyan farmers selling to small traders are more likely to receive in-kind loans than farmers selling to large traders. Because we do not observe the value or type of these in-kind loans, we cannot determine whether or not these loans are qualitatively different.

While the share of smallholder households receiving input credit from LSTs remains small relative to the total population, the fact that input credit for grain production is developing is encouraging. Given widespread capital constraints among smallholders, coupled with weather related production uncertainty, functional input credit systems are likely essential for achieving sustainable smallholder land productivity growth, particularly if these are linked to effective extensions services.

6.2. Price effect of selling to LSTs

To estimate the price effect of selling to LSTs relative to other commercial market channels (for example traditional small-scale traders and processors) we regress the log of the price the farmer reported receiving per kg of maize using OLS, on a dummy variable for whether or not the farm sold to a LST using transaction-level data from Zambia and Kenya. In Table 6 we then build on this model to control for an increasing number of factors. The first column shows the unconditional correlation between price and whether a farmer sold to a LST. We subsequently add transportation costs, farm size, year and month of sale 'fixed' effects, and finally district dummies. It is important to note that in these models we are not making any attempt to control for selection bias, since we're not really looking for a causal relationship. Instead, we are trying to develop a nuanced understanding of the factors associated with commercial prices received and the role of market channels.

We find that in all five specifications in Zambia and four out of five specifications in Kenya, selling to an LST is associated with receiving a statistically significantly higher price than other commercial market channels. Looking at column 5, we find that, once the full range of seasonal, household, and

Table 6. Factors associated with log maize price received by farmers in Zambia and Kenya

	Large trader 1		Transport cost 2		Farm size 3		Month and Year 4		District 5	
	Zambia	Kenya	Zambia	Kenya	Zambia	Kenya	Zambia	Kenya	Zambia	Kenya
Sold to large scale trader (1 = yes)	0.060***	0.069***	0.058***	0.070***	0.047***	0.082***	0.028***	-0.009	0.049***	0.036**
	(0.02)	(0.02)	(0.02)	(0.02)	(0.01)	(0.02)	(0.01)	(0.02)	(0.01)	(0.02)
Transport cost to point of sale (K/50kg/km, rebased)			0.006	0.002	0.006	0.004	0.008	0.004**	0.011**	0.005***
			(0.01)	(0.00)	(0.01)	(0.00)	(0.00)	(0.00)	(0.00)	(0.00)
Ln (Farm size: hectares cultivated and fallowed)					0.033***	-0.025**	0.002	0.008	0.017**	0.019**
					(0.01)	(0.01)	(0.01)	(0.01)	(0.01)	(0.01)
Year = 2015							0.240***	0.489***	0.242***	0.469***
							(0.01)	(0.01)	(0.01)	(0.01)
February							-0.089	-0.021	-0.075	-0.023
							(0.10)	(0.02)	(0.09)	(0.02)
March							-0.023	-0.022	0.019	-0.020
							(0.10)	(0.02)	(0.11)	(0.02)
April							-0.044	-0.016	-0.117	-0.011
							(0.08)	(0.02)	(0.10)	(0.02)
May							-0.208***	-0.067**	-0.240***	-0.066**
							(0.08)	(0.03)	(0.06)	(0.03)
June							-0.228***	-0.043	-0.219***	-0.009
							(0.07)	(0.03)	(0.05)	(0.03)
July							-0.195***	0.027	-0.193***	-0.022
							(0.07)	(0.05)	(0.05)	(0.04)
August							-0.158**	0.042	-0.145***	-0.023
							(0.06)	(0.03)	(0.05)	(0.03)
September							-0.133**	0.073***	-0.139***	0.024
							(0.07)	(0.02)	(0.05)	(0.02)
October							-0.131*	0.050*	-0.148***	-0.001
							(0.07)	(0.03)	(0.05)	(0.03)
November							-0.062	-0.010	-0.094*	-0.041
							(0.07)	(0.03)	(0.06)	(0.03)
December							-0.054	-0.001	-0.072	-0.013
							(0.07)	(0.02)	(0.06)	(0.02)
District fixed effects	-	-	-	-	-	-	-	-	yes	yes

(continued)

Table 6. (*Continued*)

	Large trader 1		Transport cost 2		Farm size 3		Dependent variable: ln(farmer maize price received) Month and Year 4		District 5	
	Zambia	Kenya	Zambia	Kenya	Zambia	Kenya	Zambia	Kenya	Zambia	Kenya
Constant	-0.0439***	2.710***	-0.0457***	2.707***	-0.0510***	2.713***	0.0069	2.504***	-0.0438	2.666***
	(0.008)	(0.01)	(0.008)	(0.01)	(0.008)	(0.01)	(0.034)	(0.02)	(0.042)	(0.05)
Observations	2,438	1,411	2,438	1,410	2,438	1,410	2,429	1,410	2,429	1,410
R-squared	0.01	0.006	0.01	0.006	0.01	0.010	0.24	0.561	0.35	0.627

Sources: Zambia RALS 2012 and 2015, Kenya Tegemeo Institute survey data 2007, 2010.

geographic variables are included, selling to a LST is associated with a 4.9 per cent higher price per kg of maize than other commercial market channels (compared to a 6% unconditional price difference) in Zambia and 3.6 per cent higher price per kg in Kenya (compared to a 6.9% unconditional price difference).[6]

Thus, even after controlling for factors that typically influence farm-gate price, farmers selling to LSTs still receive ahigher price on average than farmers selling through other commercial channels. This suggests that the supply chain attributes of LSTs described in Section 4 enable LSTs to drive down marketing costs in ways that allow them to provide farmers with higher farm gate prices than can be obtained in other commercial market channels.

7. Conclusion

This study presents evidence of rapid transformation occurring in the grain trading markets of Kenya and Zambia. The prevailing image of grain markets in sub-Saharan Africa being dominated by small-scale, poorly capitalised actors with limited capacity to manage risks or coordinate supply chain investments appears to have become outdated, at least in the two countries analysed here, Kenya and Zambia. In these two countries, large-scale trading firms (LSTs) are expanding their footprint in grain markets, with important implications for market conduct and performance.[7]

We have shown that these LSTs are co-evolving with other important transformations occurring in the demand and production segments of regional agrifood systems, namely the rapid growth in medium-scale farms and sustained regional grain demand caused by rapid population growth, income growth, and urbanisation. As these processes continue to unfold, we anticipate continued dynamism in grain trading and wholesaling.

However, it is important to note that the rise of LSTs is not solely determined by changes in the farm sector or in demand conditions. The underlying policy environment for agricultural commodity marketing and institutional infrastructure for private investment will influence the evolutionary trajectory of LSTs. Future research on the role of policies and institutions in shaping LST investment decisions in African smallholder grain markets will provide valuable insights into this important transformation.

We have shown that the growth of LSTs in smallholder grain markets has important implications for producers. The rise of LSTs creates slightly higher farm gate prices – 3 to 5 per cent higher than assembly traders after controlling for transport costs borne by the farmer. LSTs also create new opportunities for grain intensification through the provision of input credit, extension services. On balance, this transformation has the potential to bring significant social welfare benefits with it, but the process also carries societal risks. For example, the strong relationship between farm size and whether or not a farm sells to an LST suggests that, on the production end, the rise of LSTs is generating benefits that are disproportionately accruing to larger and more capitalised farmers. While 95 per cent of Kenyan farms and 75 per cent of Zambian farms cultivate less than five hectares, our results indicate that these farms are significantly less likely to sell to LSTs than medium and large-scale farms. So, while the rise of LSTs may bring beneficial spillover effects for small farms and small farmers, such as improved competition in local markets and higher prices in areas where LSTs operate, it may simultaneously contribute to agricultural growth without necessarily reducing rural poverty and with uncertain effects on rural wealth inequality. Understanding the potential spillover effects of the rise of LSTs on smaller farmers is an important area for future research.

Important emerging challenges for African governments include how to leverage the benefits of growing LST investment in grain markets, manage the downside risks associated with market concentration and power, and how to improve access to markets by poorer, more marginal segments of the rural population. Broader welfare benefits from the rise of LSTs will depend on how they influence consumer prices. This will hinge on a range of factors, including the degree of concentration in markets brought about by the rise of LST and levels of competitiveness in grain processing. Understanding the effects of the rise of LSTs on consumer prices and marketing margins is an important area for future research.

Policy tools and investments that might be considered to help strike this difficult balance include: 1) promoting competition from domestic traders through competitively priced and accessible commercial credit markets, where the ability to leverage grain stocks through warehouse receipts or moveable collateral legislation may be particularly important; 2) support horizontal aggregation structures to help small farms with limited surpluses to cost-effectively link to LST market channels; 3) implement policies to improve access to grain price information and predictability, including clearly defined policies for triggering government action in cross border trade and marketing board activities; and 4) develop innovative financial tools to help defray risk and costs to LSTs of providing input credit and other services to smallholders in order to help expand the scope and scale of these activities to marginal regions, communities, and producers.

Acknowledgements

The authors acknowledge support for this study from the Gates Foundation-funded Guiding Investments in Sustainable Agricultural Intensification in Africa (GISAIA) Project and from the USAID-funded Feed the Future Innovation Lab for Food Security Policy (FSP) to Michigan State University. The authors have appreciated discussions of earlier versions of this study with Jean Balie, Brian Chisanga, Antony Chapoto, Milu Muyanga, and David Tschirley.

Funding

This work was supported by the Bill and Melinda Gates Foundation [GISIAIA]; and United States Agency for International Development [Innovation Lab for Food Security Policy].

Disclosure statement

No potential conflict of interest was reported by the authors.

Notes

1. This includes evidence of rapid land accumulation by medium-scale farms in many countries and changing farm size distributions (Jayne et al., 2016; Sitko & Jayne, 2014) and growth in food processing and retail market formalisation in response to changes in urban food preferences (Tschirley et al., 2015).
2. While a few studies have examined horticulture and dairy (for example, Neven, Odera, Reardon, & Wang, 2009), virtually no attention has been given to potential structural change at the aggregation and wholesaling stages of the main staple commodities in Africa.
3. Kenya does not collect comparable data on forecasted maize sales.
4. In the Kenya data more than half (54%) of the farmers selling to large traders, and 40 per cent of the farms over five hectares are in just two districts – Uasin Gishu and Kakamega.
5. In Kenya, information on price information is not collected, however input credit information is more thorough and disaggregates by cash and in-kind while in Zambia only data on seed credit is available.
6. It is worth noting that seasonal price variation is substantial and statistically significant with up to 25 per cent higher prices during the lower-volume trading months. Also, the positive correlation between farm size and price diminishes after seasonal variation is modelled. Together, this suggests part of the reason larger farms get higher prices is that they are better positioned to wait for higher market prices (which is also when larger traders are more likely to remain active than small traders).
7. Very recent analysis from Tanzania points to highly similar findings (see Sitko, Jayne, & Muyanga, 2017).

References

AgriProFocus (2015). *Market study-poultry: Investment opportunities in the Zambian poultry sector (and the Katanga region of the DR Congo).* Commissioned by the Kingdom of The Netherlands in Zimbabwe in Conjunction with AgriProFocus Zambia and Poultry Association of Zambia. Retrieved from: http://agriprofocus.com/upload/Final_Market_Study_of_Poultry_Sector_in_Zambia_(for_publication)1445864268.pdf

Ariga, J., & Jayne, T. (2009). *Private sector responses to public investments and policy reforms: The case of fertilizer and maize market development in Kenya* (No. 921). International Food Policy Research Institute (IFPRI). Retrieved from: https://www.cabdirect.org/cabdirect/abstract/20103063377

Barrett, C. B. (2008). Smallholder market participation: Concepts and evidence from eastern and southern Africa. *Food Policy, 33*, 299–317. doi:10.1016/j.foodpol.2007.10.005

Byerlee, D., García, A., Giertz, A., Palmade, V., & Gurcanlar, T. (2013). Growing Africa: Unlocking the potential of agribusiness. *World Bank, Washington. DC.* Retrieved from: http://documents.worldbank.org/curated/en/327811467990084951/Main-report

Chapoto, A., Chisanga, B., Kuteya, A. N., & Kabwe, S. (2015). *Bumper harvests a curse or a blessing for Zambia: Lessons from the 2014/15 maize marketing season.* (Working Paper Number 93), Indaba Agricultural Policy Research Institute, Zambia. Retrieved from: http://pdf.usaid.gov/pdf_docs/PA00KF5B.pdf

Coulter, J., & Onumah, G. (2002). The role of warehouse receipt systems in enhanced commodity marketing and rural livelihoods in Africa. *Food Policy, 27*, 319–337. doi:10.1016/S0306-9192(02)00018-0

Deininger, K., Byerlee, D., Lindsay, J., Norton, A., Selod, H., & Stickler, M. (2011). Rising global interest in farmland: Can it yield sustainable and equitable benefits? *World Bank Publications.* Retrieved from: https://openknowledge.worldbank.org/bitstream/handle/10986/2263/594630PUB0ID1810Box358282B01PUBLIC1.pdf?sequence=1

Export Processing Zone Authority (EPZA) (2005) *Grain Production in Kenya 2005 report.* Retrieved from: http://www.epzakenya.com/UserFiles/files/GrainReport.pdf

Fafchamps, M. (2001). Networks, communities and markets in Sub-Saharan Africa: Implications for firm growth and investment. *Journal of African Economies, 10*(suppl_2), 109–142. doi:10.1093/jae/10.Suppl2.109

Fafchamps, M. (2004). *Market institutions in sub-Saharan Africa: Theory and evidence.* Cambridge, MA: MIT Press Books.

Gabre-Madhin, E., Barrett, C. B., & Dorosch, P. (2002). *Technological change and price effects in agriculture: Conceptual and comparative perspectives.* Washington, DC: International Food Policy research Institute (IFPRI). Retrieved from https://papers.ssrn.com/sol3/papers.cfm?abstract_id=601277

German, L., Schoneveld, G., & Mwangi, E. (2013). Contemporary processes of large-scale land acquisition in Sub-Saharan Africa: Legal deficiency or elite capture of the rule of law? *World Development, 48*, 1–18. doi:10.1016/j.worlddev.2013.03.006

Global Agriculture Information Network. (2015). *Kenya Grain and Feed Annual Report 2014.* USDA, Washington, DC. Found online at: https://gain.fas.usda.gov/Recent%20GAIN%20Publications/Grain%20and%20Feed%20Annual_Nairobi_Kenya_4-8-2014.pdf

Haggblade, S., Hazell, P., & Reardon, T. (2010). The rural non-farm economy: Prospects for growth and poverty reduction. *World Development, 38*, 1429–1441. doi:10.1016/j.worlddev.2009.06.008

Jayne, T. S., Chamberlin, J., Traub, L., Sitko, N., Muyanga, M., Yeboah, F. K., ... Kachule, R. (2016). Africa's changing farm size distribution patterns: The rise of medium-scale farms. *Agricultural Economics, 47*(S1), 197–214. doi:10.1111/agec.2016.47.issue-S1

Jayne, T. S., Govereh, J., Mwanaumo, A., Nyoro, J. K., & Chapoto, A. (2002). False promise or false premise? The experience of food and input market reform in Eastern and Southern Africa. *World Development, 30*, 1967–1985. doi:10.1016/S0305-750X(02)00115-8

Jayne, T. S., Mason, N., Myers, R., Ferris, J., Mather, D., Sitko, N., ... Boughton, D. (2010). *Patterns and Trends in Food Staples Markets in Eastern and Southern Africa: Toward the Identification of Priority Investments and Strategies for Developing Markets and Promoting Smallholder Productivity Growth* (No. 104). Michigan State University, Department of Agricultural, Food, and Resource Economics. Retrieved from: http://fsg.afre.msu.edu/idwp104.pdf

Johnston, B. F., & Kilby, P. (1975). *Agriculture and structural transformation; economic strategies in late-developing countries. Agriculture and structural transformation; economic strategies in late-developing countries.* New York, NY: Oxford University Press.

Johnston, B. F., & Mellor, J. W. (1961). The role of agriculture in economic development. *The American Economic Review, 51*, 566–593.

Kirimi, L., Sitko, N., Jayne, T. S., Karin, F., Muyanga, M., Sheahan, M., ... Bor, G., 2011. *A farm gate-to-consumer value chain analysis of Kenya's maize marketing System.* (*Working Paper, 44*) Tegemeo Institute of Agricultural Policy and Development. Retrieved from: http://ageconsearch.umn.edu/bitstream/202597/2/WP44-A-Farm-Gate-to-Consumer-Value-Chain-Analysis-of-Kenya-M.pdf

Masters, W. A., Djurfeldt, A. A., De Haan, C., Hazell, P., Jayne, T., Jirström, M., & Reardon, T. (2013). Urbanization and farm size in Asia and Africa: Implications for food security and agricultural research. *Global Food Security, 2*(3), 156–165. doi:10.1016/j.gfs.2013.07.002

Mellor, J. W. (1976). *New economics of growth.* Ithaca, NY: Cornell University Press.

Morris, M., Kelly, V., Kopicki, R., & Byerlee, D. (2007). *Fertilizer use in African agriculture: Lessons learned and good practice guidelines.* Washington, DC: World Bank.

Neven, D., Odera, M. M., Reardon, T., & Wang, H. (2009). Kenyan supermarkets, emerging middle-class horticultural farmers, and employment impacts on the rural poor. *World Development, 37*, 1802–1811. doi:10.1016/j.worlddev.2008.08.026

Porter, M. E. (1985). *Competitive strategy: Techniques for analyzing industries and competitors.* New York, NY: The Free Press.

Poulton, C., Kydd, J., & Dorward, A. (2006). Overcoming market constraints on pro-poor agricultural growth in Sub-Saharan Africa. *Development Policy Review, 24*, 243–277. doi:10.1111/dpr.2006.24.issue-3

Reardon, T., & Barrett, C. B. (2000). Agroindustrialization, globalization, and international development: An overview of issues, patterns, and determinants. *Agricultural Economics, 23*(3), 195–205.

Reardon, T., Barrett, C. B., Berdegué, J. A., & Swinnen, J. F. (2009). Agrifood industry transformation and small farmers in developing countries. *World Development, 37*, 1717–1727. doi:10.1016/j.worlddev.2008.08.023

Reardon, T., Codron, J. M., Busch, L., Bingen, J., & Harris, C. (1999). Strategic roles of food and agricultural standards for agrifood industries. In *estratto di presentazione al IAMA, World Food and Agribusiness Forum, Firenze, Italia*. Retrieved from: https://s3. amazonaws.com/academia.edu.documents/43610674/1999_IAMA_CODRON-Agricultural-standards.PDF?AWSAccessKeyId= AKIAIWOWYYGZ2Y53UL3A&Expires=1503495918&Signature=UGzbMiGOeUbIL3r92CCpso4x5kY%3D&response-con tent-disposition=inline%3B%20filename%3DStrategic_Roles_of_Food_and_Agricultural.pdf

Reardon, T., & Timmer, C. P. (2012). The economics of the food system revolution. *Annual Review of Resource Economics., 4*, 225–264. doi:10.1146/annurev.resource.050708.144147

ReNAPRI. (2015). *Anticipating the Future of Agriculture in the Region: Outlook for Maize, Wheat, Sugar, and Rice*. Lusaka, Zambia: Author. Retrieved from: http://www.bfap.co.za/documents/baselines/Renapri%20outlook%20FINAL% 20LOWRES_2015.pdf

Sitko, N. J., & Chisanga, B. (2016). *How Is Multinational Investment in Grain and Oilseed Trading Reshaping the Smallholder Markets in Zambia?* (No. 234948). Michigan State University, Department of Agricultural, Food, and Resource Economics.

Sitko, N. J., & Jayne, T. S. (2014). Structural transformation or elite land capture? The growth of "emergent" farmers in Zambia. *Food Policy, 48*, 194–202. doi:10.1016/j.foodpol.2014.05.006

Sitko, N. J., Jayne, T. S., & Muyanga, M. 2017. Food system transformation and market evolutions: An analysis of the rise of large-scale grain trading in Sub-Saharan Africa. International Development Working Paper 153, Michigan State University, East Lansing.

Tschirley, D., Reardon, T., Dolislager, M., & Snyder, J. (2015). The rise of a middle class in East and Southern Africa: Implications for food system transformation. *Journal of International Development, 27*, 628–646. doi:10.1002/jid.3107

Von Braun, J. (2007). The world food situation: New driving forces and required actions. *Trade and Industry Monitor, pp.* 85–103. Retrieved from: http://www.tips.org.za/files/von_Braun_J._2008_The_World_Food_Situation-new_driving_forces_ and_required_actions.pdf

Yeboah, F. K., & Jayne, T. S. (2017). Africa's evolving employment trends: Implications for economic transformation. *Africa Growth Agenda, 14*(1), 18–22.

Micro-Level Welfare Impacts of Agricultural Productivity: Evidence from Rural Malawi

FRANCIS ADDEAH DARKO, AMPARO PALACIOS-LOPEZ, TALIP KILIC &
JACOB RICKER-GILBERT

ABSTRACT *This article analyses the micro-level welfare impacts of agricultural productivity using a two-wave nationally representative, panel data from rural Malawi. Welfare is measured by various dimensions of poverty and food insecurity; and agricultural productivity is measured by maize yield and value of crop output per hectare. The poverty measures included per capita consumption expenditure, relative deprivation in terms of per capita consumption expenditure, poverty gap and severity of poverty; and the measures of food insecurity included caloric intake and relative deprivation in terms of caloric intake. Depending on the measure of welfare, the impact of agricultural productivity was estimated with a household fixed effects estimator, a two-part estimator or a correlated-random effect ordered probit estimator. The results indicate that growth in agricultural productivity has the expected welfare-improving effect. In terms of economic magnitude, however, both the direct effect and economy-wide spillover effect (in the non-farm sector) of a percentage increase in agricultural productivity on the poverty and food security measures are small. Efforts to effectively improve the welfare of rural agricultural households should therefore go beyond merely increasing agricultural (land) productivity.*

1. Introduction

Most of the world's poor people earn their living from agriculture, so if we knew the economics of agriculture, we would know much of the economics of being poor. (Schultz, 1980, p. 639)

Despite the significant progress over the past three decades, poverty and food insecurity remain major developmental challenges in sub-Sahara Africa (SSA). Current estimates indicate that the region has the highest rates of poverty and undernourishment in the world – about 46.8 per cent of the population of SSA live on less than $1.25 a day; 78 per cent live on less than $2.50 a day; and about 23.2 per cent (220 million people in absolute terms) are undernourished (FAO, IFAD, & WFP, 2015; World Bank, 2011). Although the Millennium Development Goal (MDG) of halving extreme poverty by the end of 2015 has been achieved in the world as a whole, it is yet to be achieved in SSA where the extreme poverty rate has only been reduced by a quarter (FAO, IFAD, & WFP, 2015; World Bank, 2011). The MDG of reducing hunger by half and the World Food Summit (WFS) target of reducing the number of undernourished people by half are also yet to be achieved in SSA (FAO, IFAD, & WFP, 2015). Many development projects implemented by governments of SSA countries and their development partners have therefore prioritised poverty reduction and food insecurity, particularly in rural areas where the majority of the poor and food insecure are located.

Supplementary Materials are available for this article which can be accessed via the online version of this journal available at https://doi.org/10.1080/00220388.2018.1430771

By virtue of the fact that the majority of the poor (75%) and food insecure in SSA live in rural areas and mainly depend either directly or indirectly on agriculture for livelihood, it is widely recognised that agriculture is a major channel through which poverty and food insecurity can be reduced in the sub-region (Ehui & Pender, 2005; IFAD, 2010). This notion is perhaps also based on the historical evidence that agriculture played an integral role in the marked success achieved in poverty reduction in Asia, and the evidence that growth in agriculture tends to be more beneficial to the poor than growth in other sectors of developing economies (DFID, 2004). There have therefore been major debates on the role that agriculture can potentially play in reducing poverty in SSA; but the empirical evidence backing such debates are limited.

With these considerations in mind, the present article informs the discussion by estimating the degree to which growth in agricultural productivity can affect the welfare of rural agricultural households using nationally representative panel data from Malawi. Specifically, the article examines the impact that increases in agricultural productivity can potentially have on the various dimensions – level, relative, depth and severity – of poverty and food insecurity of rural agricultural households. We focus on rural agricultural households because they represent the section of the SSA population that matter most for agriculture-led, welfare-improving initiatives.

This study adds to the development economics literature by providing a SSA, micro-level context to the existing literature on the welfare impacts of growth in agricultural productivity. Most of the empirical evidence on the subject are either at the macro-level (Breisinger, Diao, Thurlow, & Al Hassan, 2009; De Janvry & Sadoulet, 2010; Diao, Hazell, & Thurlow, 2010; Ravallion, 1990) or meso-level (Datt & Ravallion, 1998; Foster & Rosenzweig, 2004; Ravallion & Datt, 2002). To the best of our knowledge, Dzanku (2015) and Sarris, Savastano, and Christiaensen (2006) are the only studies that have addressed the micro-level welfare impacts of agricultural productivity in SSA. We improve upon and extend these studies in a number of ways. First, and perhaps most importantly, we extend the measures of household welfare beyond the *'incidence measures'* – measures (monetary or non-monetary) such as per capita consumption expenditure, whether or not a household is poor and so forth – used by Dzanku (2015) and Sarris et al. (2006). In addition to knowing the effect of agricultural productivity on the level of household welfare, it is important to also understand the extent to which growth in agricultural productivity affects household welfare relative to a pre-determined level of welfare (usually the poverty line) or the welfare of other households. Measuring poverty and food security in the relative, depth and severity dimensions provides such understanding.

Second, we conduct a simulation analysis to estimate how incremental changes in agricultural productivity affect poverty and ultra-poverty rates as well as the number of people that can potentially be lifted out of poverty and ultra-poverty. Third, the study controls for farm-wage income and income from off-farm economic activities. Because a significant proportion of rural agricultural households engage in off-farm income generating activities and most of them are net suppliers of labour in the agricultural labour market, failure to control for income from such activities in the welfare models of agricultural households could potentially result in omitted variable bias, thereby rendering the estimates inconsistent. Fourth, this study uses the approach developed by Oster (2015) and the control function approach to test and control for potential endogeneity of agricultural productivity in a household welfare equation due to omitted time-varying factors.

Lastly, this study uses a nationally representative panel data for the analyses. Although the data used by Dzanku (2015) is a panel of three years, it is not nationally representative – it covered eight villages in two (Eastern and Upper East) of the 10 regions of Ghana. Sarris et al. (2006) was based on cross-sectional data from two (Kilimanjaro and Ruvuma) of the 30 regions of Tanzania. The use of nationally representative, panel data in this paper allows us to: 1) control for unobserved (time variant and time-invariant) heterogeneity; 2) generalise the estimates for the whole of Malawi; and 3) use official national poverty lines.

Results from this study indicate that growth in agricultural productivity has the expected significantly positive effect on the welfare of rural agricultural households. However, both the *direct effects* and the economy-wide *spillover effect* (in the non-farm sector) of a percentage increase in agricultural productivity are small in terms of economic magnitude. The elasticity of per capita consumption expenditure with respect to maize yield and value of crop per hectare are 0.132 and 0.096 respectively; and the corresponding elasticity for per capita caloric intake are 0.06 and 0.054 respectively. The economy-wide *spillover effect* in the non-farm sector is estimated to be US$ 878,449.66 overall, and US$ 7.73 in per capita (of the rural agricultural population) terms. Efforts to effectively improve the welfare of rural agricultural households should go beyond the confines of merely increasing agricultural (land) productivity.

2. Background: agriculture, poverty and food insecurity in Malawi

Despite development in other sectors of the economy, like many other countries in SSA, agriculture continues to be the most important sector of Malawi's economy and an essential part of its social fabric. The sector accounts for approximately 30 per cent of gross domestic product (GDP), employs over 85 per cent of households, and serves as the main foreign exchange earner (60% for tobacco alone in 2014). With about 74 per cent of all rural income accounted for by crop production, agriculture is also the main source of livelihood for poor and rural households (Chirwa, Kumwenda, Jumbe, Chilonda, & Minde, 2008). The low share of agriculture in GDP relative to the large population and labour force employed in the sector proves that most people remain locked in low-productivity, subsistence agriculture. In other words, progress in transitioning smallholders from subsistence to commercial production, or out of agriculture altogether, has been limited.

Poverty in Malawi remains widespread. Estimates from the Third Integrated Household Survey (IHS3) indicate that 50.7 per cent of the population is poor and 24.5 per cent is ultra-poor; and the poverty and ultra-poverty gaps are 18.9 per cent and 7 per cent respectively. Using the international poverty lines based on purchasing power parities of $1.25 and $1.90 a day, the poverty rate for Malawi was 61.6 per cent and 70.9 per cent respectively in 2010 (World Bank, 2011). These figures classify Malawi, along with countries such as Burundi and Madagascar, among the poorest countries in SSA and the world as a whole. Malawi's headcount poverty barely dropped between 2004 and 2011, but countries such as Rwanda and Tanzania that had high poverty rates like Malawi in 2004 have recorded considerable reductions in poverty since then. In addition, countries such as Ghana, Ethiopia and Uganda had lower poverty rates than Malawi in 2004, but have also experienced declines in poverty rates since that time.

As in many other developing countries, poverty in Malawi is disproportionally a rural phenomenon. Between 2004/2005 and 2010/2011, although national poverty rates were high and decreased only slightly, poverty and ultra-poverty in urban areas fell significantly from 24.5 per cent to 17.3 per cent and from 7.5 per cent to 4.3 per cent respectively (World Bank, 2017). The poverty gap and severity of poverty in the urban areas also fell significantly from 7.1 to 4.8 percentage points and from 2.8 to 2.0 percentage points respectively between 2004 and 2011 (World Bank, 2017). In rural Malawi, however, poverty stagnated at about 56 per cent between 2004/2005 and 2010/2011, and the ultra-poverty rate increased significantly from 24.2 per cent to 28.1 per cent over the same period (World Bank, 2017). The poverty gap, severity of poverty and ultra-poverty also worsened in rural Malawi between 2004 and 2011.

Like poverty, food insecurity is prevalent and a rural phenomenon in Malawi. Nationally, the caloric intake of over 50 per cent of the population falls short of the minimum daily caloric requirement of 2100 calories per day between 2004 and 2013 (World Bank, 2017). In fact, the proportion of the undernourished population increased slightly from 50 per cent in 2004 to 51 per cent in 2013. Child malnutrition is also high in Malawi. Using the Demographic Health Survey (DHS), World Bank (2017) reports that the rate of stunting was 47.8 per cent in 2013, about a five percentage point decrease from the 2004 value. The percentage of underweight children dropped from 18.6 per cent to 14.1 per cent between 2004 and 2010 while the prevalence of wasting fell from 6.2 to 4.1 over the same period. Unsurprisingly, like poverty, undernourishment is disproportionally higher in rural areas than it is in the urban parts of the country. In 2013 for instance, undernourishment in rural Malawi was 53 per cent, about 11 percentage points higher than the corresponding value in urban areas (World Bank, 2017).

As in many agrarian developing countries, poverty reduction and improvement in other measures of welfare in Malawi have been identified to be closely linked to the performance of the agricultural sector. Chirwa and Muhome-Matita (2013) indicates that between 1990 and 2005, the agricultural sector grew by only 6.8 per cent per annum, and poverty fell by 0.2 per cent per annum. Because of this seemingly close relationship between the performance of the agricultural sector and poverty and the fact that poverty is predominantly rural and most of the rural households are farmers, most of the pro-poor development strategies in Malawi have focused on promoting growth in the agricultural sector. Notable among these development strategies is the large-scale Farm Input Subsidy Program (FISP) that the government is currently implementing. FISP has been the nation's main agricultural policy intervention in terms of government expenditure since its inception in the 2005/2006 agricultural year.

3. Conceptual framework

There are several pathways through which growth in agricultural productivity can potentially affect the welfare of agricultural households. First is through the *'food and income'* pathway. Increase in farm output per hectare can have the direct effect of increasing the availability of food and household income. De Janvry and Sadoulet (1996), Acharya and Sophal (2002) and Hazell, Ramasamy, and Aiyasamy (1991) provide evidence of the *'food and income'* pathway effect in Asia. De Janvry and Sadoulet (1996), for instance, observe that a percentage increase in total factor productivity would result in a 0.5 per cent increase in the income levels of smallholder farmers in Asia. Agriculture can also affect the welfare of households indirectly through the *'wage'* pathway. Agricultural expansion usually increases land under cultivation, intensity of cultivation and/or the frequency of cropping, which in turn increase the demand for hired farm labour (Hayami & Ruttan, 1985; Irz, Lin, Thirtle, & Wiggins, 2001; Lipton & Longhurst, 1989). The rising demand for hired farm labour drives up wages. Since hired farm labour is usually supplied by poor households, the increase in wages is likely to increase the income levels of poor households, and thus improve their welfare. Evidence of the 'wage' pathway is provided by Datt and Ravallion (1998) and Saxena and Farrington (2003). For instance, Saxena and Farrington (2003) reports that agricultural labour wages in India rose by 3 per cent per annum following increases in agricultural productivity between the 1970s and 1980s.

The *'food price'* pathway is yet another indirect channel through which improvement in agricultural productivity can affect the welfare of households. Increases in agricultural output supply can drive down food prices, and since most poor households in developing countries are net food buyers and spend a substantial part of their income on food, the reduced price of food will improve the poverty and food security status of households. A negative relationship between per capita food production and the price of staple foods has been observed in many SSA countries including Ghana, Ethiopia, Burkina Faso, Mali, and Sudan (Schneider & Gugerty, 2011); and in Asia (Biswanger and Quinzon, 1986; Otsuka, 2000). Improvement in agricultural productivity also indirectly affects the welfare of households through the *'non-farm sector'* pathway. Growth in agricultural productivity could provide raw material for the non-farm sector; and the increase in income that results from increases in agricultural productivity could increase the demand for goods and services produced in the non-farm sector. These will in turn stimulate employment in the non-farm sector through both forward and backward linkages and eventually increase off-farm income of households (Hanmer and Naschold, 2000; Mellor, 1999). The backward linkage involves farmers reinvesting the non-farm income in their agricultural activities. Results of several empirical evidence back the importance of the *'non-farm sector'* pathway (Delgado, Hopkins, & Kelly, 1998; Hazell & Hojjati, 1995; Bell, Hazell, & Slade, 1982; Timmer, 2003). Delgado et al. (1998), for instance, reports that a dollar increase in farm income results in a $0.96 and $1.88 increase in income elsewhere in the economies of Niger and Burkina Faso respectively.

Following Christiaensen and Demery (2006), in order to estimate the effect of agricultural productivity on the welfare of rural agricultural households, the indirect utility function of a rural agricultural households is defined as:

$$V(p, w, A) = \max_{q,L}[u(q, L)|\pi(p, w,, B) + wL = p.q]$$ (1)

where $U(q, L)$ is the utility of a rural agricultural household defined over the consumption of a vector of goods, q, and a vector of labour variables, L; $\pi(p, w, A, B)$ is the profit obtained from all (farm and off-farm) household enterprises, and depends on p (a vector of prices for goods q), w (vector of wage rates), A (agricultural productivity) and B (productivity of off-farm income-generating activities). The change in welfare resulting from a unit increase in agricultural productivity, A, is given by:

$$\alpha = \frac{dV}{\varphi dA} = [Q - q]\frac{dp}{dA} + \left[L - (L_f + L_{of})\right]\frac{dw}{dA} + p\frac{dQ}{dA}$$ (2)

where φ is the marginal utility of income; $[Q - q]$ is the difference between what the household produces and what it consumes; L_f and L_{of} are the optimal levels of farm and off-farm labour respectively; $\frac{dp}{dA}$ is the change in (food) prices resulting from a unit increase in agricultural productivity; $\frac{dw}{dA}$ is the change in agricultural wage resulting from the change in agricultural productivity; and $p\frac{dQ}{dA}$ is the monetary value resulting from a change in output caused by the change in agricultural productivity.

In this study, we estimate α. A breakdown of α into its individual components ($\frac{dQ}{dA}$, $\frac{dp}{dA}$ and $\frac{dw}{dA}$ in Equation (2)) is beyond the scope of this study. Because Equation (2) does not capture the effect of agricultural productivity on welfare that come by way of the 'non-farm sector' pathway, we call α the *direct effect*. In order to account for the effect that comes by way of the 'non-farm sector', we provide an estimate of the economy-wide *spillover effects* (independent of the estimation of the *direct effect*) of growth in agricultural productivity in the non-farm sector using the Benin, Thurlow, Diao, McCool, and Simtowe (2008) estimate of the multiplier between growth in the agricultural sector and the rest of the economy (1.11), the agricultural GDP of Malawi (US$ 962.16 million in constant 2010 prices), and the share of crop production in the agricultural GDP of Malawi (83%). The multiplier between the agricultural sector of Malawi and the rest of the economy of 1.11, means that a dollar increase in agricultural GDP results in an additional 0.11 dollar increase in the GDP of the non-agricultural sector (Benin et al., 2008).

4. Estimation strategy

In order to estimate the extent to which agricultural productivity affects the welfare of rural agricultural households, the empirical model is specified as:

$$W_{it} = \alpha A_{it} + X_{it}\,\beta + H_{it}\gamma + P_{it}\delta + G_{it}\tau + \varepsilon_{ij}$$ (3a)

$$\varepsilon_{ij} = c_i + \mu_{it}$$ (3b)

where i and t indexes household and year respectively; W represents our various measures of household welfare; A is household-level agricultural productivity; X is a vector of variables measuring other sources of household income such as agricultural wage income, and non-farm income; H is a vector of household characteristics, such as household size, landholding in hectares, and highest education achieved by a member of the household; P is a vector of prices including commercial price of urea fertiliser, and a spatial food commodity price index; G is a vector of household geo-variables such as distance to road, and agro-ecological zone; and ε is the stochastic error term. The variables making up each of the vectors are defined in Table 1. α, β, γ, δ, *and* τ are parameters, with α being the parameter of interest – the effect of agricultural productivity on household welfare. The error term, ε_{ij}, is made of two components – unobserved time-invariant factors c_i (also called unobserved heterogeneity); and unobserved time-varying factors μ_{it}, that affect the welfare of households. The

Table 1. Definition of variables in the welfare model

Variables	Definition
Dependent Variables (measures of welfare)	
Poverty measures	
Per capita consumption expenditure	Expenditure on food, non-food, durables goods and housing per capita ('000 MKW)
Relative deprivation in terms of consumption expenditure	Stark and Taylor's (1989) index ('000 MKW)
Poverty gap	Foster-Greer-Thorbecke (1984) index [0,1]
Severity of Poverty	Foster-Greer-Thorbecke (1984) index [0,1]
Food security measures	
Per capita caloric intake	Caloric intake from all sources of food (home-cooked and those purchased from outside) ('000)
Relative deprivation in terms of caloric intake	Stark and Taylor's (1989) index ('000 MKW)
Poverty and food security measure	
Composite welfare	1 = Poor and food insecure; 2 = Non-poor but food insecure or poor but food secured; 3 = Non-poor and food secured
Covariates	
Agricultural Productivity	
Value of crops per hectare	Value of annual crops per hectare ('000 MKW per hectare)
Maize yield	Quantity of maize produced per hectare ('000 Kg/ha)
Other sources of income	
Number of livestock	Number of livestock owned by the household
Net income from tree/permanent crop production	Net income from tree/permanent crop production ('000 MKW)
Net income from non-farm enterprise	Net income from -farm enterprise ('000 MKW)
Agricultural wage	Total agricultural wage earned ('000 MKW)
Other sources of income	= 1 if household has other sources of income such as ag and non-ag wage, remittances etc
Household characteristics	
Household size	Number of people in the household
Dependency ratio (%)	Percentage of dependents in the household
Male-headed	= 1 if household is headed by a male
Age of HH head	Age of household head (years)
Age of household head squared	Squared of the age of household head
Education of the most educated HH member	Number of years of education of the most educated household member
Landholding (Ha)	Hectares of land that household has the right to cultivate
Owns crop storage house	= 1 if household owns a crop storage house
Accessed credit	= 1 if household had access to credit of any sort
Extension for crop production	= 1 if household had access to extension service for crop production
Prices	
Commercial price of urea	Median price of urea in the enumeration (MKW/kg)
Laspeyres spatial price index	Laspeyres spatial price index (base = national price in March)
Household geo-variables	
Distance to nearest road	Distance from house to the nearest road (Km)
Distance to tobacco auction floor (Km)	Distance from house to nearest tobacco auction floor (Km)
Distance to boma (Km)	Distance from house to main district market (boma) in district in where household lives (Km)
Distance to weekly market (Km)	Distance from house to the nearest weekly market (Km)
Northern region	= 1 if household lives in the Northern region
Central region	= 1 if household lives in the Central region
Tropical-warm/subhumid	= 1 if household is located in the tropical-warm/subhumid agro-ecological zone
Tropical-cool/semiarid	= 1 if household is located in the tropical-cool/semiarid agro-ecological zone
Tropical-cool/subhumid	= 1 if household is located in the tropical-cool/subhumid agro-ecological zone

unobserved time-invariant factors include such factors as household's risk aversion and management ability, and the time-varying factors include such variables as household's health status, political turmoil and so forth.

4.1. Measures of agricultural productivity and welfare

Agricultural productivity is measured by maize yield and value of crop output per hectare. Maize yield is an important productivity measure because maize is the staple and the most widely cultivated crop in Malawi – it is cultivated by about 90 per cent of farmers on 70 per cent of their farm plots (NSO, 2012). In addition to maize, most households produce other food crops such as groundnut, pigeon pea and so forth, and cash crops such as tobacco. In order to account for the production of these other food and cash crops in the analyses, the study also measures agricultural productivity of a household as the monetary value of all crops produced by the household per hectare of land cultivated by the household. For a given household, the value of crops produced per hectare of land cultivated is estimated as follows: 1) multiplying the output harvested of each cultivated crop by the community-level median price of the cultivated crop; 2) summing the values of all the crops cultivated; and 3) dividing by the total hectares of land cultivated.

We measure welfare in terms of both poverty and food insecurity. The poverty measures of welfare include per capita annual consumption expenditure, relative deprivation in terms of per capita consumption expenditure, poverty gap and severity of poverty. The annual consumption expenditure variable is an aggregate expenditure variable made up of expenditures on food and non-food products. A more elaborate description of the construction of the consumption expenditure variable can be found in World Bank (2013).

Relative deprivation in terms of consumption expenditure was measured with Stark and Taylor's (1989) index. The greater the index is for a given household, the more deprived the household is relative to other households in terms of per capita consumption expenditure. Poverty gap and severity of poverty are measured by the Foster-Greer-Thorbecke index (Foster, Greer, & Thorbecke, 1984), where the latter is the square of the former. The Foster-Greer-Thorbecke index is typically a summary statistic but, following Mason and Smale (2013), it is made amenable for use in a regression model by constructing a household specific version of the index. Both poverty gap and severity of poverty take values of zero for non-poor households and a fraction for poor households.

The food security measures consist of per capita caloric intake and relative deprivation based on per capita caloric intake. Caloric intake is the total amount of calories contained in all the food items consumed by the household at home and away-from-home within the past week. The study further generated a measure of welfare called *composite welfare* that combines households' poverty and food security status. *Composite welfare* is an ordered categorical variable defined as one for poor and food insecure households; two for non-poor but food insecure or poor but food secured households; and three for non-poor and food secured households.

4.2. Choice of estimators

Depending on the measure of welfare, the effect of agricultural expenditure on welfare is estimated with a household Fixed Effects (FE) estimator, a two-part estimator, or ordered probit estimator with Mundlak-Chamberlain (MC) device (Mundlak, 1978). The household FE estimator is used when welfare is measured by per capita annual consumption expenditure, relative deprivation in terms of per capita consumption expenditure, per capita caloric intake or relative deprivation in terms of per capita caloric intake because these models are linear. The two-part estimator is used when the measure of welfare is either poverty gap or poverty severity; and the ordered probit estimator is used when welfare is measured by the composite measure.[1] The first part of the two-part estimator estimates the probability of being poor using a logit estimator while the second part estimates the extent of poverty conditional on being poor, using the fractional logit estimator (Belotti, Deb, Manning, & Norton, 2015). The two-part estimator is used instead of a simple fractional estimator because poverty and severity of poverty are corner solution outcomes – the dependent variables take on values of zero for non-poor households and continuous (fraction) for poor households (Wooldridge, 2010). Thus the two-part estimator accounts for the fact that there may be differences in how agricultural productivity affect the probability of being poor and how it affects the extent of poverty (Belotti et al., 2015; Wooldridge, 2010). The use of the two-part estimator also allows us to account for the fact that the continuous part of poverty gap and food insecurity are only observed for poor households.

4.3. Potential endogeneity of agricultural productivity in the welfare models

In order to obtain consistent estimates of the effect of agricultural productivity on the welfare of households, the correlation between the observed covariates in Equation (3a) and the unobserved time-invariant and time-varying factors must be controlled for. Because the data used in the analyses is panel, household fixed effects (FE) and the MC device are used to control for unobserved hetero-geneity in the models depending on the welfare measure. FE is used when the model is linear, that is when welfare is measured by per capita consumption expenditure, relative deprivation in terms of consumption expenditure, per capita caloric intake or relative deprivation in terms of caloric intake; and MC device is used when the model is non-linear, that is when welfare is measured by poverty gap or severity of poverty. The MC device is relevant in non-linear models; and it is analogous to fixed effects in linear models.

Even after controlling for unobserved heterogeneity using either household FE or MC device, the estimate of agricultural productivity on welfare will still be inconsistent if A_{it} is correlated with μ_{it}, unobserved time-varying factors. The correlation between A_{it} and μ_{it} could potentially come from three sources: errors in the measurement of agricultural productivity, reverse causality between agricultural productivity and welfare, and omitted variable bias. Plots size in our dataset is measured using GPS estimates, so we are confident that agricultural productivity is measured with minimal errors. Reverse causality is avoided by ensuring that the survey instrument was administered after harvesting of agricultural products was completed, as discussed earlier in the discussion of our dataset. Hence the direction of the effect will be agricultural productivity on welfare rather than vice versa.

Omitted variable bias, however, could be a problem since welfare and agricultural productivity are both potentially affected by unobserved institutional and location factors that may change over time (Dzanku, 2015; Keswell, Burns, & Thornton, 2012). We use two formal approaches to assess the robustness of our results to omitted variable bias resulting from unobserved time-varying factors. The first is an approach developed by Oster (2015) that is based on the assumption that observables and unobservables have the same explanatory power in explaining the dependent variable. Oster (2015) demonstrates that the 'controlled estimate' (the coefficient on the variable of interest from the model with the full set of observable controls) and the 'bias-adjusted estimate' (the coefficient on the variable of interest after controlling for both observables and unobservables) provide a useful range that can be used to examine the robustness of the 'controlled estimate' to omitted variable bias. The 'controlled estimate' is robust to omitted variable bias if the range does not contain zero and is within the confidence interval of the 'controlled estimate'. The Oster (2015) approach considers not only coefficient movements but also movements in R-squared values when including additional indepen-dent variables. The 'bias-adjusted estimate' is calculated as:

$$\beta^* = \beta^c - (\beta^{uc} - \beta^c) * \frac{R_{max} - R^c}{R^c - R^{uc}} \tag{4}$$

where β^c and R^c are the 'controlled estimate' and the R^2 of the regression from which the 'controlled estimate' was obtained respectively; and β^{uc} and R^{uc} are respectively the coefficient estimate and R^2 of the uncontrolled regression, the regression in which the variable of interest is the only independent variable. R_{max} is the R^2 of a hypothetical regression in which both observables and unobservables are controlled for, which is clearly unknown. Oster (2015) suggests that $R_{max} = \min\{2.2R^c, 1\}$. The R^c from our models are such that $2.2R^c>1$, suggesting that we choose $R_{max} = 1$ based on Oster (2015).

Meanwhile González and Miguel (2015) argues that R_{max} of 1 or close to 1 is likely to be too high for poverty analyses in developing countries where consumption and income levels are measured with a considerable level of error. Based on relatively high quality US data, González and Miguel (2015) suggested that R_{max} should not be greater than 0.9. An R_{max} of 0.89 was therefore chosen for our analyses.

Second, we use the control function approach to formally test for the potential endogeneity of agricultural productivity in the welfare models. This is done in order to consider the possibility of the underlying assumption of Oster (2015) not holding, and also to consider other potential sources of endogeneity. The control function approach requires the inclusion of instrumental variables(s) (IV) in the reduced form model of agricultural productivity (Wooldridge, 2010). We use the duration (days) of the photosynthetic period over the growing season as our IV. We expect this variable to be a strong instrument because it measures duration of the process by which green plants use sunlight to synthesise foods from carbon dioxide and water, and thus should be positively correlated with agricultural productivity. Many experiments in the agronomic literature provide a very strong indication of the positive relationship between photosynthesis and yield (Ainsworth et al., 2002; Bender, Hertstein, & Black, 1999; Long, Zhu, Naidu, & Ort, 2006; Mitchell et al., 1999). For instance, Bender et al. (1999) and Mitchell et al. (1999) indicate that a 50 per cent increase in photosynthesis is associated with a 35 per cent increase in grain yield. Apart from crop yield, the duration of the photosynthetic period is unlikely to directly affect welfare of rural agricultural households through any other channels. This is especially true when we control for other geo-spatial variables such as agro-ecological zone, distance to market, along with prices and household demographics, and using household-level FE and MC device to deal with remaining unobserved heterogeneity.

4.4. Data

Data used in this article come from the Malawi Integrated Household Panel Survey (IHPS). IHPS is a two-wave panel dataset collected by the National Statistical Office of Malawi (NSO) with support from the World Bank Living Standards Measurement Study – Integrated Surveys on Agriculture (LSMS-ISA) programme. The survey for the first wave of the data covered 3247 households (hereafter baseline households) in the 2009/2010 agricultural year. The sampling was representative at the national, regional and urban/rural levels. The survey for the second wave of the data was conducted in the 2012/2013 agricultural year and attempted to track and resample all the baseline households as well as individuals (projected to be at least 12 years) that split-off from the baseline households between 2010 and 2013 as long as they were neither guests nor servants and are still living in mainland Malawi. Once a split-off individual was located, the new household that he/she formed or joined was also brought into the second wave. In all, a total of 4000 households were traced back to 3104 baseline households. A majority, 76.80 per cent, of the 3104 baseline households did not split over time; 18.49 per cent split into two households; and the rest (4.70%) split into three to six households. Considering the 20 baseline households that died in their entirety between 2010 and 2013 and the fact that 4000 households could be traced back to 3104 baseline households, the data has an overall attrition rate of only 3.78 per cent at the household level.[2]

We drop all non-agricultural households (580 and 845 households in the first and second waves respectively), as well as urban agricultural households (370 and 438 households in the first and second waves respectively). The urban agricultural households were dropped because farming in Malawi is predominantly rural. In order to avoid reverse causality in our welfare models, we also dropped the households for which questions about their food and non-food consumption were asked before the harvesting of agricultural products. Households for which questions about food and non-food consumption were asked before harvesting and those for which the questions were asked after harvesting constituted different panels of the data, and the households in each of the panels were randomly selected (panels A and B in the Malawi LSMS parlance). Hence dropping the former households from the data used in this study does not pose any significant biases to our estimates and removes the potential for reverse causality in our estimates. In the end a panel of 2023 households, 946 households in the first wave and 1077 household in the second wave, was used for the analyses. Data for the instrumental variable, duration of the photosynthetic period, for the two growing seasons (2009/2010 and 2012/2013) was obtained from the MODIS Land Cover Group of Boston University (http://www. bu.edu/lcsc/data-documentation/) upon request, and matched onto the data for the other variables using GPS coordinates.

5. Results

5.1. Descriptive statistics

The descriptive statistics of the variables in the welfare models are presented in Table 2. The statistics indicate that agricultural productivity increased among rural agricultural households between 2010 and 2013: value of crops per hectare increased by 16.22 per cent (from MKW 44440 [US$123.5] to MKW 51650 [US$143.6]) and maize yield increased by 22.82 per cent (from 1340kg/ha to 1650kg/ha). The significant increase in agricultural productivity could have been due to increased use of inorganic fertiliser and other physical inputs, as well as to farmers getting better at combining inputs in crop production.

Table 2 also shows that, between 2010 and 2013, the poverty status of rural agricultural households in Malawi improved significantly in all dimensions (level, relativity, depth and severity) – per capita consumption expenditure increased by about 11.68 per cent; relative deprivation in terms of consumption expenditure decreased by about 4.15 per cent; and poverty gap and severity of poverty decreased by four and two percentage points respectively. The average per capita caloric intake was 2450 Kcal in the 2009/2010 agricultural year and 2360 Kcal in the 2012/2013 agricultural year. Compared to the minimum nutritional requirement of 2400 Kcal per day, the average rural household in Malawi is barely food secure in 2010 and food insecure in 2013.

5.2. Empirical results

Table 3 presents a summary of the results of the impact of agricultural productivity on the various measures of household welfare. The full model results are presented in the Supplementary Materials (Tables A1 to A6). The last column of Table 3 shows the range of the estimates based on the robustness check that follows Oster (2015). The range of estimates do not contain zero and the upper bounds are within the confidence interval of the 'controlled estimates', suggesting that our estimates are robust to omitted variable bias (Freier, Schumann, & Siedler, 2015; González & Miguel, 2015; Nghiem, Nguyen, Khanam, & Connelly, 2015; Oster, 2015). The formal test of endogeneity using the control function approach also rejects the hypothesis that agricultural productivity is endogenous in our welfare models after controlling for omitted variable bias with household FE (or MC device) and a full set of observable controls. Hence, overall, our estimates are robust not only to omitted variable bias but also to other potential sources of endogeneity. Results of the endogeneity test using the control function approach are presented in Tables A7 and A8 of the Supplementary Materials.

5.3. Direct effect of agricultural productivity on welfare

As indicated under the conceptual framework, the estimates from our models are the *direct effects* of agricultural productivity on the welfare of agricultural households. The model results indicate that growth in agricultural productivity has the expected, significant, inverse relationship with all measures of poverty (Table 3 as well as Tables A1 and A3 in the Supplementary Materials). All things being equal, a one percentage increase in maize yield and the value of crops per hectare will increase per capita consumption expenditure by 0.132 per cent and 0.096 per cent respectively; reduce relative deprivation in terms of consumption expenditure by 0.058 per cent and 0.042 per cent respectively;

Table 2. Descriptive statistics

Variables	Pooled Mean	2009/2010 agricultural year			2012/2013 agricultural year		
		Mean	Median	SD	Mean[a]	Median	SD
Dependent Variables (measures of welfare)							
Poverty measures							
Per capita consumption expenditure ('000)	129.16	121.62	95.83	97.81	135.83***	108.92	93.57
Relative deprivation in terms of consumption expenditure ('000)	150.15	153.53	164.70	31.69	147.15***	157.64	35.33
Poverty gap	0.11	0.13		0.20	0.09***		0.17
Severity of Poverty	0.05	0.06		0.11	0.04***		0.09
Food security measures							
Per capita caloric intake ('000)	2.4	2.45	2.13	1.28	2.36	2.09	1.20
Relative deprivation in terms of caloric intake ('000)	1.86	1.77	1.96	0.69	1.95***	2.13	0.67
Poverty and food security measure							
Composite Welfare	2.03	2.00	2.00	0.85	2.06	2.00	0.84
Independent variables							
Agricultural Productivity							
Value of crops per hectare ('000 MWK)	48.26	44.44	27.77	46.86	51.65 ***	35.45	60.27
Maize yield ('000 KG/HA)	1.51	1.34	1.01	1.14	1.65***	1.17	1.94
Other sources of income							
Number of livestock	0.30	0.28	0.05	0.84	0.33	0.05	1.02
Net income from tree/permanent crop production ('000 MWK)	2.31	1.49	0.00	4.00	3.03***	0.00	12.64
Net income from off-farm enterprise ('000 MWK)	22.32	11.17	0.00	50.97	32.20***	0.00	109.17
Agricultural wage (MWK/DAY)	25.82	19.52	0.00	42.45	31.39***	0.00	64.74
Other sources of income (MKW)	32.5	27.6	0.00	45	36.80***	0.00	49
Household characteristics							
Household size	5.08	4.9	5.00	2.26	5.23***	5.00	2.21
Dependency ratio (%)	122.56	124.54	100.00	86.40	120.8	100.00	87.58
Male-headed households	0.74	0.74	1.00	0.43	0.74	1.00	0.43
Age of HH head	43.49	43.77	40.00	16.48	43.24	40.00	15.41
Education of the most educated HH member	6.98	6.54	7.00	3.47	7.38***	8.00	3.10
Household landholding (Ha)	0.78	0.74	0.61	0.60	0.82	0.57	6.03
Owns crop storage house (%)	16	18	0.00	0.40	13***	0.00	0.34
Accessed credit (%)	17	10	0.00	0.30	23***	0.00	0.41
Extension for crop production (%)	53	0.4	0.00	0.49	66***	1.00	0.48
Prices							
Price of urea (MWK/KG)	222.63	223.2	232.02	22.87	222.12	240.00	47.32
Laspeyres spatial output price index	86.86	90.82	90.82	8.45	83.36***	82.06	7.26
Household geo-variables							
Distance to nearest road (KM)	9.81	9.47	5.33	9.65	10.11	6.00	9.95
Distance to tobacco auction floor (Km)	77.91	77.26	71.57	50.31	78.5	73.00	49.77
Distance to boma (Km)	38.21	47.7	46.42	26.94	29.81***	27.00	25.37
Distance to weekly market (Km)	4.38	4.57	4.00	5.71	4.21	3.00	6.37
Northern region	0.12	0.12	0.00	0.42	0.11	0.00	0.41
Central region	0.43	0.42	0.00	0.48	0.43	0.00	0.49
Tropical-warm/subhumid	0.27	0.27	0.00	0.45	0.28	0.00	0.45
Tropical-cool/semiarid	0.18	0.18	0.00	0.37	0.18	0.00	0.37
Tropical-cool/subhumid	0.03	0.03	0.00	0.24	0.02	0.00	0.23
Graded/Graveled	0.27	0.24	0.00	0.44	0.30***	0.00	0.44
Dirt road (maintained)	0.53	0.54	0.00	0.50	0.52	1.00	0.50
Dirt track	0.05	0.06	0.00	0.25	0.04	0.00	0.17

Notes: [a]Stars indicate significant difference in mean between 2009/2010 and 2012/2013 agricultural years; $*p < 0.1$; $**p < 0.05$; $***p < 0.01$.

Table 3. Elasticity of agricultural productivity on household welfare

Measure of Agricultural Productivity	Measure of household welfare	Estimates	Range of Estimates [based on Oster (2015)][a]
Log of maize yield	*Poverty measures*		
	Log of per capita consumption expenditure	0.132*** (0.020)	[0.132 0.173]
	Log of relative deprivation	−0.058*** (0.009)	[−0.058−0.076]
	Poverty gap	−0.034*** 0.006)	−
	Severity of poverty	−0.017*** (0.004)	−
	Food security measures		
	Log of calories consumed per capita	0.060** (0.023)	[0.060 0.107]
	Log of relative deprivation	−0.036 (0.024)	[−0.036−0.085]
	Composite welfare[b]		
	Probability of being poor and food insecure	−0.057*** (0.017)	−
	Probability of being non-poor and food secure	0.060*** (0.018)	−
Log of value of crop per ha	*Poverty measures*		
	Log of per capita consumption expenditure	0.096*** (0.017)	[0.096 0.130]
	Log of relative deprivation	−0.042*** (0.007)	−0.042−0.058]
	Poverty gap	−0.019*** (0.004)	−
	Severity of poverty	−0.008*** (0.002)	−
	Food security measures		
	Log of calories consumed per capita	0.054*** (0.019)	[0.054 0.094]
	Log of relative deprivation	−0.040* (0.020)	−0.040−0.081]
	Composite welfare[b]		
	Probability of being poor and food insecure	−0.043*** (0.010)	−
	Probability of being non-poor and food secure	0.046*** (0.011)	−

Notes: [a]Psacalc of Oster (2015) only applies to linear regression. [b]The estimates of composite welfare presented in this table are the marginal effects of the probability of being in the first (poor and food insecure) and third (non-poor and food secure) categories. See Tables A7 and A8 for the estimates in the full model that has estimates of all the three categories. *$p < 0.1$; **$p < 0.05$; ***$p < 0.01$.

reduce the poverty gap by 0.034 and 0.019 percentage points respectively; and reduce the severity of poverty by 0.017 and 0.008 percentage points respectively.

The inverse effect of agricultural productivity on poverty is also reflected in its effect on poverty rate and the number of people that can be lifted out of poverty (Table 4).[3] These estimates are based on only the *direct effect* estimates and should therefore be interpreted as lower bound estimates. The simulation results indicate that a 50 per cent increase in maize yield will reduce the poverty (ultra-poverty) rate among rural agricultural households by at least 6.77 (2.54) percentage points from 40.78 per cent (11%) to 34.01 per cent (8.46%).[4] The 50 per cent increase in maize yield will correspond-ingly lift at least 622,015 people out of poverty and 281,718 people out of ultra-poverty. It should be noted from the simulation results that the gains in poverty reduction accruing from incremental changes in agricultural productivity taper off around 55 per cent. This could be because beyond a 55 per cent increase in agricultural productivity the remaining poor households are so far below the poverty line, with very little land to cultivate, that further increases in agricultural productivity are unable to lift them above the poverty line.

The direction of the *direct effect* of agricultural productivity on the welfare measures support the widely-held notion that growth in agricultural productivity could be an effective channel for

Table 4. Effect of increases in agricultural productivity on the transition of households out of poverty

Increase in maize yield	% of poor households in 2013		% of Ultra-poor households in 2013		Number of people lifted out of poverty		Number of people lifted out of ultra-poverty	
	Maize yield	Value of crop	Maize yield	Value of crop	Maize yield	Value of crop	Maize yield	Value of crop
0%	40.78	40.78	11.00	11.00	–	–	–	–
5%	35.74	35.19	9.39	8.61	555,969.31	573,745.06	253,024.14	295,786.78
10%	35.45	35.19	9.26	8.39	555,969.31	573,745.06	260,351.78	295,786.78
15%	35.45	34.99	9.26	8.39	555,969.31	585,601.25	260,351.78	295,786.78
20%	35.19	34.99	9.11	8.39	567,825.50	585,601.25	260,351.78	295,786.78
25%	35.08	34.70	9.11	8.39	571,433.63	598,899.56	260,351.78	295,786.78
30%	34.99	34.67	9.11	8.27	576,370.13	598,899.56	260,351.78	302,815.31
35%	34.77	34.67	9.05	8.10	581,876.44	598,899.56	260,351.78	302,815.31
40%	34.62	34.67	8.65	8.10	588,786.94	598,899.56	270,491.66	302,815.31
45%	34.36	34.47	8.65	8.10	601,266.94	603,817.88	270,491.66	302,815.31
50%	34.01	34.38	8.46	7.97	622,015.25	603,817.88	281,718.41	310,142.97
55%	33.95	34.27	8.34	7.97	622,015.25	610,175.81	288,746.94	310,142.97
60%	33.86	34.16	8.00	7.94	626,781.38	616,297.88	308,266.31	311,868.25
65%	33.76	34.16	7.94	7.94	626,781.38	616,297.88	311,868.69	311,868.25
70%	33.76	34.16	7.79	7.81	626,781.38	616,297.88	320,494.97	311,868.25
75%	33.62	34.11	7.79	7.81	631,964.19	619,649.56	320,494.97	311,868.25
80%	33.17	34.11	7.64	7.81	657,617.88	619,649.56	320,494.97	311,868.25
85%	33.17	34.06	7.64	7.81	657,617.88	622,357.19	320,494.97	311,868.25
90%	33.08	34.01	7.64	7.81	662,993.94	625,088.63	320,494.97	311,868.25
95%	33.08	34.01	7.64	7.81	662,993.94	625,088.63	320,494.97	311,868.25
100%	33.03	34.01	7.56	7.81	662,993.94	625,088.63	325,017.94	311,868.25
Raising productivity of all households to:								
Quarter of district highest	32.16	31.17	6.60	6.52	728,040.63	763,563.25	327,458.78	374,495.47
Half of district highest	28.98	28.44	5.95	5.13	863,750.31	890,375.00	350,718.66	420,365.44
Three-quarters of district highest	27.29	27.34	5.23	4.76	909,683.69	934,795.81	377,188.38	424,577.97
District highest (full potential)	25.32	26.69	5.14	4.76	1,021,293.50	966,361.06	382,145.03	424,577.97

improvement in the welfare of rural agricultural households in Malawi. It should however be noted that the *direct effects* and the associated number of people lifted out of poverty are small in terms of economic magnitude, and the increase in poverty reduction through agricultural growth tapers off at around a 55 per cent increase. Similar significant but small *direct effects* of agricultural productivity on measures of poverty have been observed in other parts of SSA. Dzanku (2015) observed that a percentage increase in value of output per ha will increase per capita consumption expenditure by 0.207 per cent, all things being equal. In Tanzania, Sarris et al. (2006) estimated the elasticity of per capita consumption expenditure with respect to agricultural productivity (value of output per ha) to be 0.15 in rural households in the Kilimanjaro region.

Among other things, the economic magnitude of the *direct effect* observed in this study is small for two main reasons. First, and perhaps most importantly, because Malawi is at import parity, it could be that the increase in agricultural productivity does not have a big impact on food prices (Ricker-Gilbert, Mason, Darko, & Tembo, 2013). Meanwhile, Otsuka (2000) and Biswanger and Quinzon (1986) observe that much of the positive impact that the green revolution technology in Asia had on poverty and inequality resulted from lower food prices accruing from output expansion. Schuh (2000) also suggests that the greatest achievement of world agriculture in the fight against poverty came via the supply of affordable food to the masses; and Datt and Ravallion (1998) indicated that absolute poverty levels can be largely impacted by even smaller changes in food prices. The second reason why the economic magnitude of the direct effect is small could be the fact that the average smallholder farm is just 0.42 hectares, meaning very high productivity increases will be needed to have a meaningful *direct* impact on per capita household consumption for an average family of five members.

We also find that growth in agricultural productivity also has the expected, inverse *direct effect* on food insecurity and the composite measure of welfare (Table 3 as well as Tables A2, A4, A5 and A6 in the Supplementary Materials). A one percentage increase in maize yield and value of output per hectare will, all things being equal, increase caloric intake by 0.06 per cent and 0.054 per cent respectively. For the composite measure of welfare, the estimates indicate that a percentage increase in maize yield and value of crops per hectare will decrease the probability of being poor and food insecure by 0.057 per cent and 0.043 per cent respectively; and increase the probability of being non-poor and food secure 0.060 per cent and 0.046 per cent respectively.

5.4. Spillover effects of agricultural productivity on welfare

Though not directly calculated in our simulation, we use estimates from Benin et al. (2008) to estimate the growth multiplier between the agricultural sector and the rest of the Malawian economy. Benin et al. estimate the multiplier to be 1.11, so with the agricultural GDP of US$ 962.16 million (in constant 2010 prices), and the share of crop production in the agricultural GDP of Malawi (83%), we estimate the *spillover effects* of a percentage increase in agricultural productivity on the rest of the economy to be US$ 87,844,966 (that is [(0.83*962157345.64)*0.11]); where (0.83*962157345.64) is the additional increase in agricultural GDP resulting from a percentage increase in crop output, and 0.11 is the increase in the GDP of the non-agricultural sector that results from a dollar increase in the GDP of the agricultural sector. Although this spillover effects look big overall, on per capita (number of rural agricultural population, about 11.36 million) basis, it is just US$ 7.73. Moreover, the extent to which rural agricultural households benefit from the *spillover effects* depends on the level of their participation in the non-farm sector of the economy; the higher their participation, the higher the welfare benefits. The data used in this study suggests that only about 18 per cent of agricultural households in both 2010 and 2013 participated in the non-farm sector; and the average income that these households obtained from their non-farm income generating activities is only MKW 22,320 (US $ 62.03) in 2010 and MKW 32,200 (US$ 89.49) in 2013. Hence, like the *direct effects*, the *spillover effects* in the non-farm sector is small.

Ultimately, where do the findings of this study fit in the broader discourse of the potential role of agriculture in improving the welfare of households in Malawi and other countries in SSA; and how does it contribute to, or advance, the discourse? This study points to an important aspect of the welfare-improving role of agriculture that is worth attention. It reveals that it would be challenging for agriculture to bring about the needed improvement in the welfare of rural households if attention is given solely to increasing agricultural productivity through yield increases. In fact, a look at the success stories of agriculture-led poverty reduction in Asia (during the Green Revolution) and SSA reveals that the successes were realised mainly through means (such as extensification, commercialisation and/or crop diversification) other than mere increases in agricultural (land) productivity. Binswanger and Quizon (1986) and Otsuka (2000) demonstrates that the welfare-enhancing effects of the Green Revolution technology in Asian countries such as Thailand and Nepal came mainly from lowered food prices that resulted from the expansion of farmland. In Malawi, Mukherjee and Benson (2003) find that land and crop diversification significantly reduce poverty in rural areas; and that households that grow tobacco (a high-value crop) are significantly less likely to be poor. Households that moved out of poverty in Kenya between 1997 and 2007 more than doubled their landholdings and cultivated 70 per cent more land in 1997 than in 2007 (Muyanga, Jayne, & Burke, 2010). Kristjanson, Mango, Krishna, Radeny, and Johnson (2010) reports that 23 per cent of households that graduated out of poverty attributed their success to increased land cultivation; 49 per cent attributed it to crop diversification; and in areas of low potential for crop production, 50 per cent of the households attributed their success to diversification away from maize to crops of higher value. Cunguara (2008) reports that between 2002 and 2005, households that moved out of poverty in Mozambique increased the land cultivated by 10 per cent. In Zambia, households moving out of poverty increased their landholdings from 5ha to 23ha (Banda, Hamukwala, Haggblade, & Chapoto, 2011). It is also worth mentioning that, agricultural extensification is not likely to be realised in most parts of SSA because the average landholding and farm size is very small for most agricultural households (Harris & Orr, 2013). The current landholding in Malawi for instance is less than a hectare per household, and with increasing population pressure, landholdings are likely to get smaller in the future. Hence crop diversification from crops of low value to high-value crops appears to be the channel that can complement growth in agricultural (land) productivity to bring about the needed agricultural-led improvement in the living standards of rural agricultural households in SSA.

Given the significant but small effect that increases in agricultural productivity have on the welfare of rural agricultural households, and the fact that agricultural extensification is not likely to be realised, crop production ought to be supported by other policy moves. This study finds that other important determinants of the welfare of rural agricultural households include household size, landholdings, ownership of crop storage house, and prices of consumable goods.

6. Conclusions

This article estimates the extent to which agricultural productivity affects the welfare of agricultural households in Malawi using two waves of a nationally representative panel data from rural Malawi. Welfare was measured in terms of poverty and food insecurity, and agricultural productivity was measured by maize yield and value of crop output per hectare. The poverty measures considered included per capita consumption expenditure, relative deprivation in terms of consumption expenditure, poverty gap and severity of poverty; and the food security measures included caloric intake and relative deprivation in terms of caloric intake.

The results indicate that increasing agricultural productivity has a statistically significant and positive effect on the welfare of rural agricultural households in Malawi. However, the impact (both the *direct effects* and the economy-wide *spillover effects*) is small in terms of economic magnitude. Hence, overall, this study suggest that agricultural productivity will have to increase by a large amount in order to bring about the needed improvement in the welfare of rural agricultural households. Thus, rural household welfare-improving initiatives must go beyond the confines of increasing agricultural (land) productivity. Other findings of this study suggest that non-agricultural measures such as the promotion of off-farm income-generating activities, smaller household size, and ownership of a crop storage house and favourable prices of consumable goods should also be considered as possible welfare-improving initiatives.

It is important to note that the estimated impacts found in this article relate to the ability of rural households to increase agricultural productivity within a season. Maintaining these increases over time is an additional challenge. For example, if maize yields increase due to adoption of a new variety of maize in the current year, will this variety be able to maintain its productivity in the face of a climate that is becoming drier and hotter over time? Sustainably increasing crop productivity and having that translate into poverty reduction will require investment in research, extension, and market development.

Acknowledgements

Funding for this research was provided by the Bill and Melinda Gates Foundation under the Guiding Investments in Sustainable Agricultural Intensification in Africa (GISAIA) project. The authors are grateful to the two anonymous referees who reviewed the paper, as well as Thomas Jayne (guest editor) and Richard Palmer-Jones (managing editor) for their useful comments and suggestions. All remaining errors are our own. The data and stata codes used in the analyses are available upon request.

Disclosure statement

No potential conflict of interest was reported by the authors.

Notes

1. The two-part estimator is implemented using the *twopm* command in stata (Belotti et al., 2015). *Twopm* has a variety of estimators that can be used for the first and second parts depending on research interest. More importantly, marginal effects for the combined model can be easily recovered using the margins command.
2. Attrition bias in the data could not be tested for in our data because there are no regression-based tests for attrition when fixed effects or MC devise models are used with a panel of only two waves. A panel of more than two-waves are required for such tests (Mason & Smale, 2013; Wooldridge, 2010). That notwithstanding, the study is confident that attrition bias is not likely to be a concern because as indicated earlier, the attrition rate is only 3.78 per cent at the household level.
3. Estimates of yield gap reported by Global Yield Gap Atlas (www.yieldgap.org), indicate that maize yield (and yield of cereals in general) in countries such as Zambia, Tanzania, Uganda, Kenya and Ethiopia that are in the same geographical area as Malawi can be increased by over 300 per cent. Hence the range of the incremental changes in agricultural productivity (0–100%) used in the simulation analysis is reasonable.
4. The simulations assume that there are no general equilibrium effects in the sense that changes in the determinants do not affect the partial regression parameters or other exogenous variables. This assumption is (highly) likely to be valid because the simulated changes are incremental (0%, 5%, 15%, ..., 100%). The results should therefore be interpreted with this caveat in mind.

References

Acharya, S., & Sophal, C. (2002). Farm size, productivity and earnings. *Cambodian Development Review, 6*(4), 1–3.
Ainsworth, E. A., Davey, P. A., Bernacchi, C. J., Dermody, O. C., Heaton, E. A., Moore, D. J., ... Curtis, P. S. (2002). A meta-analysis of elevated [CO_2] effects on soybean (Glycine max) physiology, growth and yield. *Global Change Biology, 8*, 695–709. doi:10.1046/j.1365-2486.2002.00498.x
Banda, D. J., Hamukwala, P., Haggblade, S., & Chapoto, A. (2011). *Dynamic pathways into and out of poverty: A case of smallholder farmers in Zambia* (Working Paper No. 56). Zambia: Food Security Research Project.
Bell, C., Hazell, P., & Slade, R. (1982). *Project evaluation in regional perspective*. Baltimore, MD: Johns Hopkins University Press.
Belotti, F., Deb, P., Manning, W. G., & Norton, E. C. (2015). Twopm: Two-part models. *The Stata Journal, 15*(1), 3–20.
Bender, J., Hertstein, U., & Black, C. R. (1999). Growth and yield responses of spring wheat to increasing carbon dioxide, ozone and physiological stresses: A statistical analysis of 'ESPACE-wheat' results. *European Journal of Agronomy, 10*, 185–195. doi:10.1016/S1161-0301(99)00009-X

Benin, S., Thurlow, J., Diao, X., McCool, C., & Simtowe, F. (2008). *Agricultural growth and investment options for poverty reduction in Malawi* (IFPRI Discussion Paper 74). Washington, DC: International Food Policy Research Institute.

Binswanger, H. P., & Quizon, J. B. (1986). *What can agriculture do for the poorest rural groups?* (Report No. 57). Washington, DC: Agricultural and Rural Development Department, World Bank.

Breisinger, C., Diao, X., Thurlow, J., & Al Hassan, R. M. (2009, August 16-22). *Potential impacts of a green revolution in Africa – the case of Ghana.* A Paper presented at the 27th IAAE Conference, Beijing, China.

Chirwa, E. W., Kumwenda, I., Jumbe, C., Chilonda, P., & Minde, I. (2008). *Agricultural growth and poverty reduction in Malawi: Past performance and recent trends* (Working Paper No. 8). Regional Strategic Analysis and Knowledge Support System (ReSAKSS).

Chirwa, E. W., & Muhome-Matita, M. (2013, June 19-21). *Agricultural Growth and Poverty in Rural Malawi.* Paper presented at the GDN 14th Annual Global Development Conference on Inequality, Social Protection and Inclusive Growth, Manila, The Philippines.

Christiaensen, L., & Demery, L. (2006). *Down to earth: Agriculture and poverty reduction in Africa.* Washington, DC: World Bank.

Cunguara, B. A. (2008). *Pathways out of poverty in Rural Mozambique* (M.Sc. Thesis). Michigan State University.

Datt, G., & Ravallion, M. (1998). Farm productivity and rural poverty in India. *The Journal of Development Studies, 34*(4), 62–85. doi:10.1080/00220389808422529

De Janvry, A., & Sadoulet, E. (1996). *Growth, inequality and poverty in Latin America: A causal analysis, 1970–94* (Working Paper no. 784). California, USA: Department of Agricultural and Resource Economics, University of California at Berkeley.

De Janvry, A., & Sadoulet, E. (2010). Agricultural growth and poverty reduction: Additional evidence. *The World Bank Research Observer, 25*(1), 1–20. doi:10.1093/wbro/lkp015

Delgado, C., Hopkins, J., & Kelly, V. (1998). *Agricultural growth linkages in Sub-Saharan Africa* (IFPRI Research Report 107). Washington, DC: International Food Policy Research Institute.

Department for International Development, DFID. (2004). *Agriculture, growth and poverty reduction.* (A working paper). Oxford: Agriculture and Natural Resources, UK Department for International Development (DFID); and Thomson of Oxford Policy Management.

Diao, X., Hazell, P., & Thurlow, J. (2010). The role of agriculture in African development. *World Development, 38*(10), 1375–1383. doi:10.1016/j.worlddev.2009.06.011

Dzanku, F. M. (2015). Household welfare effects of agricultural productivity: A multidimensional perspective from Ghana. *The Journal of Development Studies, 51*(9), 1139–1154. doi:10.1080/00220388.2015.1010153

Ehui, S., & Pender, J. (2005). Resource degradation, low agricultural productivity, and poverty in sub-Saharan Africa: Pathways out of the spiral. *Agricultural Economics, 32,* 225–242. doi:10.1111/agec.2005.32.issue-s1

FAO, IFAD, & WFP. (2015). *The state of food insecurity in the world 2015.* Meeting the 2015 International Hunger Targets: Taking Stock of Uneven Progress, Rome, FAO.

Foster, A. D., & Rosenzweig, M. R. (2004). Agricultural productivity growth, rural economic diversity, and economic reforms: India, 1970–2000. *Economic Development and Cultural Change, 52*(3), 509–542. doi:10.1086/420968

Foster, J., Greer, J., & Thorbecke, E. (1984). A class of decomposable poverty measures. *Econometrica, 52,* 761–766. doi:10.2307/1913475

Freier, R., Schumann, M., & Siedler, T. (2015). The earnings returns to graduating with honors – Evidence from law graduates. *Labour Economics, 34,* 39–50. doi:10.1016/j.labeco.2015.03.001

González, F., & Miguel, E. (2015). War and local collective action in Sierra Leone: A comment on the use of coefficient stability approaches. *Journal of Public Economics, 128,* 30–33. doi:10.1016/j.jpubeco.2015.05.004

Hanmer, L., & Nashchold, F. (2000). *Attaining the international development targets: Will growth be enough?* (Working paper).

Harris, D., & Orr, A. (2013). Is rainfed agriculture really a pathway from poverty? *Agricultural Systems, 123,* 84–96.

Hayami, Y., & Ruttan, V. (1985). *Agricultural development: An international perspective.* Baltimore, MD: Johns Hopkins University Press.

Hazell, P., & Hojjati, B. (1995). Farm/Non-farm growth linkages in Zambia. *Journal of African Economies, 4*(3), 406–435. doi:10.1093/oxfordjournals.jae.a036840

Hazell, P., Ramasamy, C., & Aiyasamy, P. K. (1991). *The green revolution reconsidered: The impact of high-yielding rice varieties in South India.* Baltimore, MD: Johns Hopkins University Press for the International Food Policy Research Institute.

International Fund for Agricultural Development, IFAD. (2010). *Rural poverty report 2011: New realities, new challenges: new opportunities for tomorrow's generation".* Rome: IFAD.

Irz, X., Lin, L., Thirtle, C., & Wiggins, S. (2001). Agricultural productivity, growth and poverty alleviation. *Development Policy Review, 19*(4), 449–466. doi:10.1111/dpr.2001.19.issue-4

Keswell, M., Burns, J., & Thornton, R. (2012). Evaluating the impact of health programmes on productivity. *African Development Review, 24*(4), 302–315. doi:10.1111/afdr.2012.24.issue-4

Kristjanson, P., Mango, N., Krishna, A., Radeny, M., & Johnson, N. (2010). Understanding poverty dynamics in Kenya. *Journal of International Development, 22*(7), 978–996. doi:10.1002/jid.1598

Lipton, M., & Longhurst, R. (1989). *New seeds and poor people.* London, UK: Unwin Hyman.

Long, S. P., Zhu, X., Naidu, S. L., & Ort, D. R. (2006). Can improvement in photosynthesis increase crop yields? *Plant, Cell & Environment, 29*, 315–330. doi:10.1111/pce.2006.29.issue-3

Mason, N., & Smale, M. (2013). Impacts of subsidized hybrid seed on indicators of economic well-being among smallholder maize growers in Zambia. *Agricultural Economics, 44*, 659–670. doi:10.1111/agec.2013.44.issue-6

Mellor, J. W. (1999, November). *Pro-poor growth – The relationship between growth in agriculture and poverty reduction.* Paper prepared for USAID. United States Agency for International Development. Ministry of Agriculture and Food Security, MoAFS. 2012. Guide to Agriculture Production and Natural Resources Management in Malawi, Lilongwe, Malawi: MoAFS.

Mitchell, R. A. C., Black, C. R., Burkart, S., Burke, J. I., Donnelly, A., De Temmmerman, L., ... Van Oijen, M. (1999). Photosynthetic responses in spring wheat grown under elevated CO_2 concentrations and stress conditions in the European, multiple-site experiment 'ESPACE-wheat'. *European Journal of Agronomy, 10*, 205–214. doi:10.1016/S1161-0301(99)00010-6

Mukherjee, S., & Benson, T. (2003). "The determinants of poverty in Malawi", 1998. *World Development, 31*(2), 339–358. doi:10.1016/S0305-750X(02)00191-2

Mundlak, Y. (1978). On the pooling of time series and cross section data. *Econometrica, 46*(1), 69–85. doi:10.2307/1913646

Muyanga, M., Jayne, T. S., & Burke, W. J. (2010). *Pathways into and out of poverty: A study of rural household wealth dynamics in Kenya.* Nairobi: Tegemeo Institute.

National Statistical Office (NSO) of Malawi. (2012). *Malawi second integrated household survey (IHS3) 2010-2011.* Zomba, Malawi: Basic Information Document.

Nghiem, H. S., Nguyen, H. T., Khanam, R., & Connelly, L. B. (2015). Does school type affect cognitive and non-cognitive development in children? Evidence from Australian primary schools. *Labour Economics, 33*, 55–65. doi:10.1016/j.labeco.2015.02.009

Oster, E. 2015. *Unobservable selection and coefficient stability: Theory and evidence* (NBER Working Paper, No. 19054).

Otsuka, K. (2000). Role of agricultural research in poverty reduction: Lessons from the asian experience. *Food Policy, 25*, 447–462. doi:10.1016/S0306-9192(00)00017-8

Ravallion, M., & Datt, G. (2002). Why has economic growth been more pro-poor in some states of India than others? *Journal of Development Economics, 68*(2), 381–400. doi:10.1016/S0304-3878(02)00018-4

Ravallion, M. (1990). Rural welfare effects of food price changes under induced wage responses: Theory and evidence for Bangladesh. *Oxford Economic Papers, 42*(3), 574–585. doi:10.1093/oxfordjournals.oep.a041964

Ricker-Gilbert, J., Mason, N., Darko, F. A., & Tembo, S. (2013). What are the effects of input subsidy programs on maize prices? Evidence from Malawi and Zambia. *Agricultural Economics, 44*, 671–686. doi:10.1111/agec.2013.44.issue-6

Sarris, A., Savastano, S., & Christiaensen, L. (2006). *Agriculture and poverty in commodity-dependent African countries: A household perspective from rural Tanzania* (Commodities and Trade Technical Paper 9). Rome: Commodities and Trade Division, Food and Agriculture Organization.

Saxena, N., & Farrington, J. (2003). *Trends and prospects for poverty reduction in rural India: Context and options* (ODI Working Paper 198). London, UK: Overseas Development Institute.

Schneider, K., & Gugerty, M. K. (2011). Agricultural productivity and poverty reduction: Linkages and pathways. *The Evans School Review, 1*(1), 1. doi:10.7152/esr.v1i1.12249

Schuh, G. E. (2000). The household: The neglected link in research and programs for poverty alleviation. *Food Policy, 25*, 233–241. doi:10.1016/S0306-9192(00)00003-8

Schultz, T. W. (1980). Nobel lecture: The economics of being poor. *Journal of Political Economy, 88*, 639–651. doi:10.1086/260895

Stark, O., & Taylor, E. (1989). Relative deprivation and international migration. *Demography, 26*, 1–14. doi:10.2307/2061490

Timmer, P. (2003). *Agriculture and pro-poor growth.* In *Pro-Poor Economic Growth Research Studies. United States Agency for International Development.* Washington, DC: Development Alternatives Inc. and Boston Institute for Developing Economies.

Wooldridge, J. M. (2010). *Econometric analysis of cross section and panel data* (2nd ed.). Cambridge, MA: The MIT Press.

World Bank. (2011). Poverty & equity data. Retrieved September 30, 2015 from http://data.worldbank.org/topic/poverty

World Bank. (2013). *Methodology for poverty analysis in Malawi in 2010-2013.* Author.

World Bank. (2017). *Republic of Malawi poverty assessment.* Washington, DC: Author.

Table A1: Effect of Maize Yield (Kg/ha) on Poverty

Dependent variable: maize yield	Log consumption expenditure	Log relative deprivation	Poverty gap[a]	Poverty severity[a]
	HH fixed effects	HH fixed effects	logit & fractional logit with MC Device	logit & fractional logit with MC Device
	Coefficient	Coefficient	Unconditional APE	Unconditional APE
Log of maize yield (Kg/ha)	0.132***	-0.058***	-0.034***	-0.017***
	(0.020)	(0.009)	(0.006)	(0.004)
Log of value of other crops (MKW/ha)	0.002	-0.001	-0.001	-0.001
	(0.003)	(0.002)	(0.001)	(0.000)
Log net income from tree crops (MKW)	0.002	-0.000	-0.001	-0.000
	(0.003)	(0.001)	(0.001)	(0.001)
Number of livestock	0.043***	-0.020**	-0.009	-0.002
	(0.014)	(0.008)	(0.011)	(0.007)
Log of net income from off-farm activities	0.003	-0.002	-0.001	-0.000
	(0.002)	(0.002)	(0.001)	(0.000)
Log of agricultural wage	-0.002	0.001	-0.000	0.000
	(0.003)	(0.001)	(0.001)	(0.000)
Other income sources (1/0)	0.003	-0.011	0.001	0.000
	(0.028)	(0.014)	(0.009)	(0.006)
Household size	-0.148***	0.068***	0.031***	0.016***
	(0.009)	(0.006)	(0.003)	(0.002)
Dependency ratio (%)	-0.001***	0.000***	0.000	0.000
	(0.000)	(0.000)	(0.000)	(0.000)
Male-headed household (1/0)	0.018	-0.007	-0.011	-0.003
	(0.051)	(0.030)	(0.017)	(0.009)
Age of Household head (years)	0.009	-0.006	0.002	0.002**
	(0.007)	(0.004)	(0.001)	(0.001)
Age of household head squared	-0.000*	0.000*	-0.000	-0.000
	(0.000)	(0.000)	(0.000)	(0.000)
Education of most educated HH member (years)	0.008	-0.001	-0.005*	-0.004**
	(0.010)	(0.005)	(0.003)	(0.002)
Log of landholding (Ha)	0.129***	-0.048***	-0.047***	-0.024***
	(0.030)	(0.014)	(0.006)	(0.004)
Owns crop storage house (1/0)	0.109***	-0.048**	-0.030**	-0.015**
	(0.033)	(0.018)	(0.013)	(0.007)
Accessed credit (1/0)	0.049	-0.021	-0.011	-0.014**
	(0.031)	(0.019)	(0.011)	(0.006)
Accessed extension for production (1/0)	0.008	0.005	-0.018*	-0.012**
	(0.028)	(0.013)	(0.010)	(0.006)
Distance to road (Km)	-0.002	0.002	0.000	0.001
	(0.005)	(0.003)	(0.002)	(0.002)
Distance to tobacco auction (Km)	-0.001	0.001	0.001	0.001*
	(0.002)	(0.001)	(0.001)	(0.000)
Distance to boma (Km)	0.002**	-0.000	-0.001***	-0.000**
	(0.001)	(0.000)	(0.000)	(0.000)
Distance to weekly market (Km)	0.003	-0.001	-0.001	-0.000
	(0.003)	(0.001)	(0.001)	(0.000)
Log of price of Urea fertilizer (MKW/Kg)	0.127	-0.049	-0.076*	-0.036
	(0.143)	(0.062)	(0.045)	(0.028)
Laspeyre's spatial price index	-0.007***	0.002*	0.003***	0.002***
	(0.003)	(0.001)	(0.001)	(0.000)
Northern region	-0.196	0.141	-0.283*	-0.296***
	(0.230)	(0.115)	(0.157)	(0.099)
Southern region	-0.060	0.019	-0.129	-0.181**
	(0.177)	(0.102)	(0.127)	(0.081)
Graded/Graveled	-0.077	0.033	0.021	0.001
	(0.098)	(0.059)	(0.016)	(0.011)
Dirt road (maintained)	-0.015	0.017	-0.003	-0.016
	(0.105)	(0.061)	(0.020)	(0.012)
Dirt track	0.096	-0.020	-0.027	-0.028**
	(0.128)	(0.065)	(0.028)	(0.014)
Agro-ecological zone fixed effect	Yes	Yes	Yes	Yes
Year (1 = 2013)	0.135***	-0.051***	-0.024**	-0.010**
	(0.036)	(0.015)	(0.010)	(0.005)
Constant	11.641***	11.582***		
	(0.902)	(0.391)		
Time averages (CRE)	NA	NA	Yes	Yes
Observations	2,023	2,023	2,023	2,023
R-squared	0.825	0.804		

*** p<0.01, ** p<0.05, * p<0.1. Standard errors in parentheses. APE means average partial effect

[a] Estimation was based on a two-part model: first part, logit of probability of being poor; and second part, fractional model of extent of poverty.

Table A2: Effect of Maize Yield (Kg/ha) on Food Security

	Log caloric intake	Log relative deprivation
	HH fixed effects	HH fixed effects
	Coefficient	Coefficient
Log of maize yield (Kg/ha)	0.060**	-0.036
	(0.023)	(0.024)
Log of value of other crops (MKW/ha)	0.005	-0.002
	(0.004)	(0.004)
Log net income from tree crops (MKW)	0.002	0.001
	(0.003)	(0.004)
Number of livestock	0.024	0.000
	(0.025)	(0.027)
Log of net income from off-farm activities	-0.003	0.001
	(0.002)	(0.003)
Log of agricultural wage	-0.002	0.001
	(0.003)	(0.004)
Other income sources (1/0)	0.024	-0.008
	(0.030)	(0.037)
Household size	-0.104***	0.103***
	(0.011)	(0.015)
Dependency ratio (%)	-0.001***	0.001***
	(0.000)	(0.000)
Male-headed household (1/0)	-0.029	0.052
	(0.050)	(0.061)
Age of Household head (years)	0.012	-0.011
	(0.008)	(0.008)
Age of household head squared	-0.000*	0.000
	(0.000)	(0.000)
Education of most educated HH member (years)	-0.003	0.018
	(0.009)	(0.013)
Log of landholding (Ha)	0.054**	-0.041
	(0.026)	(0.033)
Owns crop storage house (1/0)	0.042	-0.023
	(0.034)	(0.037)
Accessed credit (1/0)	0.033	-0.008
	(0.033)	(0.046)
Accessed extension for production (1/0)	0.008	-0.014
	(0.026)	(0.034)
Distance to road (Km)	0.002	-0.004
	(0.004)	(0.008)
Distance to tobacco auction (Km)	-0.002	0.001
	(0.001)	(0.002)
Distance to boma (Km)	0.001	0.000
	(0.001)	(0.001)
Distance to weekly market (Km)	0.001	-0.001
	(0.003)	(0.003)
Log of price of Urea fertilizer (MKW/Kg)	0.256	-0.097
	(0.156)	(0.179)
Laspeyre's spatial price index	0.005*	-0.007**
	(0.003)	(0.003)
Northern region	0.071	-0.218
	(0.250)	(0.286)
Southern region	-0.008	-0.249
	(0.252)	(0.266)
Graded/Graveled	-0.050	0.115
	(0.088)	(0.081)
Dirt road (maintained)	0.031	-0.004
	(0.088)	(0.082)
Dirt track	0.157	-0.031
	(0.105)	(0.091)
Agro-ecological zone fixed effect	Yes	Yes
Year (1= 2013)	0.052	0.041
	(0.036)	(0.035)
Constant	5.555***	8.579***
	(0.893)	(1.137)
Time averages (CRE)	NA	NA
Observations	2,023	1,935
R-squared	0.703	0.691

*** p<0.01, ** p<0.05, * p<0.1. Standard errors in parentheses

Table A3: Effect of Value of Crops (MKW/ha) on Poverty

	Log consumption Expenditure	Log relative Deprivation	Poverty Gap[a]	Poverty Severity[a]
	HH fixed effects	HH fixed effects	logit & fractional logit with MC Device	logit & fractional logit with MC Device
	Coefficient	Coefficient	Unconditional APE	Unconditional APE
Log value of crops (MKW/ha)	0.096***	-0.042***	-0.019***	-0.008***
	(0.017)	(0.007)	(0.004)	(0.002)
Log net income from tree crops (MKW)	0.003	-0.001	-0.001	-0.000
	(0.003)	(0.001)	(0.001)	(0.001)
Number of livestock	0.040***	-0.019**	-0.009	-0.003
	(0.014)	(0.008)	(0.012)	(0.007)
Log of net income from off-farm activities	0.003	-0.002	-0.001	-0.000
	(0.002)	(0.002)	(0.001)	(0.000)
Log of agricultural wage	-0.001	0.001	-0.000	0.000
	(0.003)	(0.001)	(0.001)	(0.000)
Other income sources (1/0)	0.007	-0.012	0.002	0.001
	(0.027)	(0.013)	(0.009)	(0.006)
Household size	-0.151***	0.069***	0.032***	0.015***
	(0.009)	(0.006)	(0.003)	(0.002)
Dependency ratio (%)	-0.001***	0.000***	0.000	0.000
	(0.000)	(0.000)	(0.000)	(0.000)
Male-headed household (1/0)	0.031	-0.013	-0.013	-0.005
	(0.053)	(0.030)	(0.017)	(0.009)
Age of Household head (years)	0.010	-0.006	0.002	0.002*
	(0.007)	(0.004)	(0.001)	(0.001)
Age of household head squared	-0.000*	0.000*	-0.000	-0.000
	(0.000)	(0.000)	(0.000)	(0.000)
Education of most educated HH member (years)	0.007	-0.001	-0.004	-0.003*
	(0.010)	(0.005)	(0.003)	(0.002)
Log of landholding (Ha)	0.092***	-0.031**	-0.041***	-0.021***
	(0.026)	(0.013)	(0.006)	(0.003)
Owns crop storage house (1/0)	0.111***	-0.049**	-0.029**	-0.015**
	(0.033)	(0.020)	(0.013)	(0.008)
Accessed credit (1/0)	0.050	-0.021	-0.013	-0.015***
	(0.032)	(0.020)	(0.010)	(0.006)
Accessed extension for production (1/0)	0.004	0.007	-0.015	-0.010*
	(0.028)	(0.013)	(0.011)	(0.006)
Distance to road (Km)	-0.003	0.003	0.000	0.001
	(0.005)	(0.003)	(0.002)	(0.002)
Distance to tobacco auction (Km)	-0.002	0.001	0.001*	0.001**
	(0.002)	(0.001)	(0.000)	(0.000)
Distance to boma (Km)	0.002**	-0.000	-0.001***	-0.000*
	(0.001)	(0.000)	(0.000)	(0.000)
Distance to weekly market (Km)	0.003	-0.001	-0.001	-0.000
	(0.003)	(0.001)	(0.001)	(0.000)
Log of price of Urea fertilizer (MKW/Kg)	0.168	-0.070	-0.081*	-0.039
	(0.143)	(0.064)	(0.046)	(0.028)
Laspeyre's spatial price index	-0.009***	0.003**	0.004***	0.002***
	(0.003)	(0.001)	(0.001)	(0.000)
Northern region	-0.262	0.171	-0.268*	-0.291***
	(0.226)	(0.119)	(0.154)	(0.094)
Southern region	-0.044	0.013	-0.135	-0.187**
	(0.163)	(0.101)	(0.123)	(0.077)
Graded/Graveled	-0.076	0.034	0.020	-0.000
	(0.101)	(0.060)	(0.018)	(0.010)
Dirt road (maintained)	-0.042	0.030	0.001	-0.015
	(0.109)	(0.062)	(0.023)	(0.012)
Dirt track	0.046	0.004	-0.019	-0.024*
	(0.129)	(0.066)	(0.029)	(0.014)
Agro-ecological zone fixed effect	Yes	Yes	Yes	Yes
Year (1 = 2013)	0.133***	-0.050***	-0.025**	-0.011**
	(0.036)	(0.015)	(0.010)	(0.005)
Constant	11.532***	11.647***		
	(0.865)	(0.379)		
Time averages (CRE)	NA	NA	Yes	Yes
Observations	2,023	2,023	2,023	2,023
R-squared	0.822	0.802		

*** p<0.01, ** p<0.05, * p<0.1. Standard errors in parentheses

[a] Estimation was based on a two-part model: first part, CRE logit of probability of being poor; and second part, CRE fractional model of extent of poverty.

Table A4: Effect of Value of Crops (MKW/ha) on Food Security

	Log of Caloric intake	Log relative Deprivation
	HH fixed effects	HH fixed effects
	Coefficient	Coefficient
Log value of crops (MKW/ha)	0.054***	-0.040*
	(0.019)	(0.020)
Log net income from tree crops (MKW)	0.002	0.000
	(0.003)	(0.004)
Number of livestock	0.022	0.002
	(0.026)	(0.027)
Log of net income from off-farm activities	-0.003	0.000
	(0.002)	(0.003)
Log of agricultural wage	-0.001	0.001
	(0.003)	(0.004)
Other income sources (1/0)	0.025	-0.010
	(0.030)	(0.036)
Household size	-0.106***	0.104***
	(0.011)	(0.015)
Dependency ratio (%)	-0.001***	0.001***
	(0.000)	(0.000)
Male-headed household (1/0)	-0.029	0.050
	(0.051)	(0.061)
Age of Household head (years)	0.013	-0.011
	(0.008)	(0.008)
Age of household head squared	-0.000*	0.000
	(0.000)	(0.000)
Education of most educated HH member (years)	-0.004	0.018
	(0.009)	(0.013)
Log of landholding (Ha)	0.045*	-0.035
	(0.025)	(0.033)
Owns crop storage house (1/0)	0.041	-0.022
	(0.033)	(0.038)
Accessed credit (1/0)	0.036	-0.009
	(0.032)	(0.044)
Accessed extension for production (1/0)	0.006	-0.012
	(0.026)	(0.034)
Distance to road (Km)	0.001	-0.004
	(0.004)	(0.008)
Distance to tobacco auction (Km)	-0.002	0.001
	(0.001)	(0.002)
Distance to boma (Km)	0.001	0.000
	(0.001)	(0.001)
Distance to weekly market (Km)	0.001	-0.001
	(0.003)	(0.003)
Log of price of Urea fertilizer (MKW/Kg)	0.256	-0.107
	(0.162)	(0.184)
Laspeyres spatial price index	0.005	-0.007**
	(0.003)	(0.003)
Northern region	0.043	-0.183
	(0.250)	(0.281)
Southern region	0.000	-0.239
	(0.258)	(0.267)
Graded/Graveled	-0.045	0.119
	(0.087)	(0.079)
Dirt road (maintained)	0.025	0.007
	(0.090)	(0.080)
Dirt track	0.143	-0.014
	(0.104)	(0.088)
Agro-ecological zone fixed effect	Yes	Yes
Year (1= 2013)	0.054	0.041
	(0.036)	(0.036)
Constant	5.530***	8.716***
	(0.907)	(1.144)
Time averages (CRE)	NA	NA
Observations	2,023	1,935
R-squared	0.702	0.691

*** p<0.01, ** p<0.05, * p<0.1. Standard errors in parentheses

Table A5: Effect of Maize Yield (Kg/ha) on Composite Welfare

	Estimate	Average Marginal Effects		
		Category 1	Category 2	Category 3
Log of maize yield (Kg/ha)	0.204***	-0.057***	-0.003	0.060***
	(0.061)	(0.017)	(0.002)	(0.018)
Log of value of other crops (MKW/ha)	0.011	-0.003	-0.000	0.003
	(0.010)	(0.003)	(0.000)	(0.003)
Log net income from tree crops (MKW)	-0.002	0.001	0.000	-0.001
	(0.008)	(0.002)	(0.000)	(0.002)
Number of livestock	0.124	-0.035	-0.002	0.037
	(0.084)	(0.024)	(0.001)	(0.025)
Log of net income from off-farm activities	-0.003	0.001	0.000	-0.001
	(0.006)	(0.002)	(0.000)	(0.002)
Log of agricultural wage	-0.002	0.001	0.000	-0.001
	(0.008)	(0.002)	(0.000)	(0.002)
Other income sources (1/0)	0.018	-0.005	-0.000	0.005
	(0.086)	(0.024)	(0.001)	(0.025)
Household size	-0.297***	0.084***	0.004*	-0.088***
	(0.036)	(0.010)	(0.002)	(0.010)
Dependency ratio (%)	-0.002***	0.001***	0.000	-0.001***
	(0.001)	(0.000)	(0.000)	(0.000)
Male-headed household (1/0)	-0.035	0.010	0.000	-0.010
	(0.135)	(0.038)	(0.002)	(0.040)
Age of Household head (years)	0.005	-0.001	-0.000	0.002
	(0.012)	(0.003)	(0.000)	(0.004)
Age of household head squared	-0.000	0.000	0.000	-0.000
	(0.000)	(0.000)	(0.000)	(0.000)
Education of most educated HH member (years)	0.026	-0.007	-0.000	0.008
	(0.022)	(0.006)	(0.000)	(0.007)
Log of landholding (Ha)	0.291***	-0.082***	-0.004*	0.086***
	(0.055)	(0.015)	(0.002)	(0.016)
Owns crop storage house (1/0)	-0.006	0.002	0.000	-0.002
	(0.100)	(0.028)	(0.001)	(0.029)
Accessed credit (1/0)	0.040	-0.011	-0.001	0.012
	(0.101)	(0.028)	(0.001)	(0.030)
Accessed extension for production (1/0)	0.074	-0.021	-0.001	0.022
	(0.069)	(0.020)	(0.001)	(0.020)
Distance to road (Km)	0.010	-0.003	-0.000	0.003
	(0.014)	(0.004)	(0.000)	(0.004)
Distance to tobacco auction (Km)	0.005	-0.001	-0.000	0.001
	(0.004)	(0.001)	(0.000)	(0.001)
Distance to boma (Km)	0.004**	-0.001**	-0.000	0.001**
	(0.002)	(0.001)	(0.000)	(0.001)
Distance to weekly market (Km)	0.006	-0.002	-0.000	0.002
	(0.010)	(0.003)	(0.000)	(0.003)
Log of price of Urea fertilizer (MKW/Kg)	0.699*	-0.197*	-0.009	0.206*
	(0.368)	(0.104)	(0.008)	(0.109)
Laspeyre's spatial price index	0.001	-0.000	-0.000	0.000
	(0.007)	(0.002)	(0.000)	(0.002)
Northern region	0.671	-0.189	-0.009	0.198
	(0.654)	(0.184)	(0.011)	(0.194)
Southern region	0.363	-0.102	-0.005	0.107
	(0.697)	(0.196)	(0.010)	(0.206)
Graded/Graveled	-0.212	0.060	0.003	-0.063
	(0.353)	(0.100)	(0.005)	(0.104)
Dirt road (maintained)	-0.135	0.038	0.002	-0.040
	(0.363)	(0.102)	(0.005)	(0.107)
Dirt track	0.263	-0.074	-0.004	0.078
	(0.427)	(0.120)	(0.006)	(0.126)
Agro-ecological zone fixed effect	Yes	Yes	Yes	Yes
Year (1=2010)	-0.202**	0.057**	0.003	-0.060**
	(0.089)	(0.025)	(0.002)	(0.026)
Constant cut1	0.444			
	(2.417)			
Constant cut2	1.415			
	(2.411)			
Time averages (CRE)	Yes	Yes	Yes	Yes
Observations	2,023	2,023	2,023	2,023

*** p<0.01, ** p<0.05, * p<0.1. Standard errors in parentheses

Category 1 = Poor and food insecure; Category 2 = Non-poor but food insecure or poor but food secured; Category 3 = Non-poor and food secured

Table A6: Effect of Value of Crops (MKW/ha) on Composite Welfare

	Estimate	Average Partial Effects		
		Category 1	Category 2	Category 3
Log value of crops (MKW/ha)	0.154***	-0.043***	-0.002	0.046***
	(0.038)	(0.010)	(0.001)	(0.011)
Log net income from tree crops (MKW)	-0.001	0.000	0.000	-0.000
	(0.008)	(0.002)	(0.000)	(0.002)
Number of livestock	0.120	-0.034	-0.002	0.035
	(0.084)	(0.024)	(0.001)	(0.025)
Log of net income from farm off- activities	-0.002	0.001	0.000	-0.001
	(0.005)	(0.002)	(0.000)	(0.002)
Log of agricultural wage	-0.002	0.000	0.000	-0.000
	(0.008)	(0.002)	(0.000)	(0.002)
Other income sources (1/0)	0.018	-0.005	-0.000	0.005
	(0.086)	(0.024)	(0.001)	(0.026)
Household size	-0.301***	0.085***	0.004*	-0.089***
	(0.036)	(0.010)	(0.002)	(0.010)
Dependency ratio (%)	-0.002***	0.001***	0.000	-0.001***
	(0.001)	(0.000)	(0.000)	(0.000)
Male-headed household (1/0)	-0.029	0.008	0.000	-0.009
	(0.140)	(0.039)	(0.002)	(0.041)
Age of Household head (years)	0.006	-0.002	-0.000	0.002
	(0.012)	(0.003)	(0.000)	(0.003)
Age of household head squared	-0.000	0.000	0.000	-0.000
	(0.000)	(0.000)	(0.000)	(0.000)
Education of most educated HH member (years)	0.023	-0.006	-0.000	0.007
	(0.022)	(0.006)	(0.000)	(0.007)
Log of landholding (Ha)	0.252***	-0.071***	-0.003*	0.074***
	(0.052)	(0.015)	(0.002)	(0.015)
Owns crop storage house (1/0)	-0.004	0.001	0.000	-0.001
	(0.097)	(0.027)	(0.001)	(0.029)
Accessed credit (1/0)	0.054	-0.015	-0.001	0.016
	(0.102)	(0.029)	(0.001)	(0.030)
Accessed extension for production (1/0)	0.068	-0.019	-0.001	0.020
	(0.070)	(0.020)	(0.001)	(0.021)
Distance to road (Km)	0.009	-0.002	-0.000	0.003
	(0.014)	(0.004)	(0.000)	(0.004)
Distance to tobacco auction (Km)	0.004	-0.001	-0.000	0.001
	(0.004)	(0.001)	(0.000)	(0.001)
Distance to boma (Km)	0.004**	-0.001**	-0.000	0.001**
	(0.002)	(0.001)	(0.000)	(0.001)
Distance to weekly market (Km)	0.007	-0.002	-0.000	0.002
	(0.010)	(0.003)	(0.000)	(0.003)
Log of price of Urea fertilizer (MKW/Kg)	0.714*	-0.201*	-0.010	0.211*
	(0.383)	(0.108)	(0.008)	(0.114)
Laspeyre's spatial price index	-0.001	0.000	0.000	-0.000
	(0.007)	(0.002)	(0.000)	(0.002)
Northern region	0.583	-0.164	-0.008	0.172
	(0.642)	(0.181)	(0.010)	(0.190)
Southern region	0.380	-0.107	-0.005	0.112
	(0.688)	(0.194)	(0.010)	(0.203)
Graded/Graveled	-0.193	0.054	0.003	-0.057
	(0.353)	(0.099)	(0.005)	(0.104)
Dirt road (maintained)	-0.156	0.044	0.002	-0.046
	(0.367)	(0.103)	(0.005)	(0.108)
Dirt track	0.224	-0.063	-0.003	0.066
	(0.428)	(0.121)	(0.006)	(0.126)
Agro-ecological zone fixed effect	Yes	Yes	Yes	Yes
Year (1 = 2013)	0.207**	-0.058**	-0.003	0.061**
	(0.089)	(0.025)	(0.002)	(0.026)
Constant cut1	1.387			
	(2.446)			
Constant cut2	2.359			
	(2.440)			
Time averages (CRE)	Yes	Yes	Yes	Yes
Observations	2,023	2,023	2,023	2,023

*** p<0.01, ** p<0.05, * p<0.1. Standard errors in parentheses

Category 1 = Poor and food insecure; Category 2 = Non-poor but food insecure or poor but food secured; Category 3 = Non-poor and food secured

Table A7: Testing for Endogeneity of Agricultural Productivity Using Control Function Approach

	Dependent variable		
	Log of maize yield	Log Consumption expenditure	Log caloric intake
Log of maize yield (Kg/ha)		0.162	-0.036
		(0.106)	(0.180)
Log of duration of photosynthetic period (days)	-0.677**		
	(0.256)		
Residuals from auxiliary regression		-0.031	0.100
		(0.103)	(0.176)
Log of value of other crops (MKW/ha)	0.017***	0.002	0.007
	(0.006)	(0.004)	(0.004)
Log net income from tree crops (MKW)	0.019***	0.002	0.004
	(0.005)	(0.003)	(0.005)
Number of livestock	0.060	0.041***	0.029
	(0.040)	(0.015)	(0.028)
Log of net income from off-farm activities	-0.005	0.003	-0.003
	(0.004)	(0.002)	(0.002)
Log of agricultural wage	-0.006	-0.002	-0.002
	(0.006)	(0.003)	(0.003)
Other income sources (1/0)	-0.003	0.005	0.020
	(0.061)	(0.030)	(0.030)
Household size	0.009	-0.148***	-0.103***
	(0.024)	(0.009)	(0.011)
Dependency ratio (%)	-0.000	-0.001***	-0.001***
	(0.000)	(0.000)	(0.000)
Male-headed household (1/0)	0.138	0.014	-0.014
	(0.095)	(0.053)	(0.050)
Age of Household head (years)	0.027	0.008	0.015*
	(0.018)	(0.007)	(0.008)
Age of household head squared	-0.000	-0.000*	-0.000**
	(0.000)	(0.000)	(0.000)
Education of most educated HH member (years)	-0.003	0.008	-0.003
	(0.014)	(0.010)	(0.009)
Log of landholding (Ha)	-0.469***	0.144**	0.009
	(0.063)	(0.059)	(0.088)
Owns crop storage house (1/0)	0.051	0.107***	0.049
	(0.056)	(0.034)	(0.036)
Accessed credit (1/0)	0.029	0.047	0.038
	(0.074)	(0.031)	(0.033)
Accessed extension for production (1/0)	0.043	0.007	0.011
	(0.052)	(0.028)	(0.025)
Distance to road (Km)	0.008	-0.002	0.002
	(0.010)	(0.005)	(0.004)
Distance to tobacco auction (Km)	-0.003	-0.001	-0.002
	(0.003)	(0.002)	(0.002)
Distance to boma (Km)	-0.002	0.002**	0.001
	(0.001)	(0.001)	(0.001)
Distance to weekly market (Km)	0.001	0.002	0.001
	(0.009)	(0.003)	(0.004)
Log of price of Urea fertilizer (MKW/Kg)	0.448	0.114	0.299
	(0.328)	(0.148)	(0.186)
Laspeyre's spatial price index	-0.015**	-0.007*	0.003
	(0.007)	(0.003)	(0.005)
Northern region	-0.015	-0.199	0.078
	(0.836)	(0.230)	(0.249)
Southern region	0.592	-0.076	0.043
	(0.628)	(0.174)	(0.267)
Tropical-warm/sub humid	0.257	0.209	0.112
	(0.182)	(0.143)	(0.118)
Tropical-cool/semiarid	-0.260	0.006	0.056
	(0.227)	(0.096)	(0.150)
Tropical-cool/sub humid	0.147	-0.540**	0.250
	(0.349)	(0.209)	(0.242)
Graded/Graveled	0.344**	-0.086	-0.021
	(0.171)	(0.105)	(0.108)
Dirt road (maintained)	0.185	-0.019	0.045
	(0.197)	(0.106)	(0.095)
Dirt track	0.141	0.095	0.161
	(0.239)	(0.128)	(0.105)
Year (2013)	-0.051	0.136***	0.047
	(0.071)	(0.037)	(0.039)
Constant	7.617***	11.243***	6.568***
	(1.814)	(0.982)	(1.206)
Observations	2,023	2,023	2,023
R-squared	0.740	0.825	0.703

*** p<0.01, ** p<0.05, * p<0.1; Standard errors in parentheses

Table A8: Testing for Endogeneity of Agricultural Productivity Using Control Function Approach

VARIABLES	Dependent variable		
	Log of value of output per ha	Log consumption expenditure	Log caloric intake
Log of value of output per ha		0.195	-0.041
		(0.140)	(0.215)
Log of duration of photosynthetic period (days)	-0.568**		
	(0.233)		
Residuals from auxiliary regression		-0.100	0.097
		(0.141)	(0.213)
Log net income from tree crops (MKW)	0.015**	0.002	0.004
	(0.006)	(0.003)	(0.005)
Number of livestock	0.121***	0.028	0.034
	(0.039)	(0.022)	(0.037)
Log of net income from off-farm activities	-0.011**	0.004*	-0.004
	(0.005)	(0.003)	(0.003)
Log of agricultural wage	-0.014**	-0.000	-0.003
	(0.006)	(0.003)	(0.005)
Other income sources (1/0)	-0.080	0.018	0.014
	(0.090)	(0.034)	(0.036)
Household size	0.052*	-0.157***	-0.100***
	(0.027)	(0.013)	(0.017)
Dependency ratio (%)	-0.000	-0.001***	-0.001***
	(0.000)	(0.000)	(0.000)
Male-headed household (1/0)	0.007	0.029	-0.027
	(0.131)	(0.052)	(0.050)
Age of Household head (years)	0.024	0.008	0.015*
	(0.020)	(0.007)	(0.008)
Age of household head squared	-0.000	-0.000*	-0.000*
	(0.000)	(0.000)	(0.000)
Education of most educated HH member (years)	-0.007	0.008	-0.005
	(0.019)	(0.010)	(0.009)
Log of landholding (Ha)	-0.187***	0.110***	0.027
	(0.059)	(0.037)	(0.048)
Owns crop storage house (1/0)	0.054	0.103***	0.048
	(0.077)	(0.034)	(0.037)
Accessed credit (1/0)	0.083	0.040	0.046
	(0.100)	(0.034)	(0.036)
Accessed extension for production (1/0)	0.107*	-0.005	0.015
	(0.058)	(0.033)	(0.028)
Distance to road (Km)	0.027	-0.005	0.004
	(0.018)	(0.006)	(0.007)
Distance to tobacco auction (Km)	-0.001	-0.001	-0.002
	(0.005)	(0.002)	(0.001)
Distance to boma (Km)	-0.002	0.002***	0.001
	(0.001)	(0.001)	(0.001)
Distance to weekly market (Km)	0.005	0.002	0.002
	(0.007)	(0.003)	(0.004)
Log of price of Urea fertilizer (MKW/Kg)	-0.051	0.174	0.251
	(0.324)	(0.148)	(0.159)
Laspeyre's spatial price index	-0.009	-0.007**	0.003
	(0.007)	(0.003)	(0.004)
Northern region	0.851	-0.353	0.132
	(0.861)	(0.260)	(0.331)
Southern region	0.715	-0.110	0.064
	(0.733)	(0.176)	(0.295)
Tropical-warm/sub-humid	0.594	0.126	0.114
	(0.472)	(0.157)	(0.160)
Tropical-cool/semiarid	0.218	-0.068	0.088
	(0.437)	(0.096)	(0.146)
Tropical-cool/sub-humid	0.796	-0.674**	0.275
	(0.559)	(0.258)	(0.289)
Graded/Graveled	0.567***	-0.129	0.005
	(0.194)	(0.130)	(0.151)
Dirt road (maintained)	0.664***	-0.104	0.085
	(0.219)	(0.148)	(0.169)
Dirt track	0.867***	-0.032	0.218
	(0.280)	(0.178)	(0.203)
Year (2013)	-0.016	0.134***	0.053
	(0.082)	(0.037)	(0.037)
Constant	13.576***	10.042***	7.132***
	(1.807)	(1.935)	(2.597)
Observations	2,023	2,023	2,023
R-squared	0.752	0.822	0.703

*** p<0.01, ** p<0.05, * p<0.1; Standard errors in parentheses

Changing Patterns of Wealth Distribution: Evidence from Ghana

ABENA D. ODURO & CHERYL R. DOSS

ABSTRACT *A largely unexplored feature of structural transformation is the change in the composition of an economy's asset holdings. In most poor economies, assets are concentrated in land. In rich economies, physical and human capital are more important. This paper focuses on the changes in the composition of household wealth and the share of assets owned by women in Ghana over two decades of relatively rapid growth and significant structural changes. We find that land's share of household portfolios decreased and the share of financial assets increased. Women's share of land, savings and business assets rose over the period.*

1. Introduction

A largely unexplored feature of structural transformation is the shifting composition of assets, corresponding to the changing sectoral composition of output. As economies develop, there is a tendency for wealth to shift from land – normally the most important form of wealth in poor agrarian economies – to a wider range of assets, including housing, financial assets and business assets. This pattern was apparent in the United States and Britain in the late nineteenth century; during this period, financial assets became a larger component of wealth, and land became correspondingly less important (Keister, 2000; World Bank, 2011). The same pattern appears to hold broadly today in developing countries. According to one set of detailed estimates, natural capital (including agricultural land, forests, and mineral resources) accounted for 30 per cent of the total wealth of low-income countries in 2005. By contrast, natural capital accounted for only 25 per cent of the wealth of low-middle-income countries, 15 per cent of the wealth of upper-middle-income countries, and 2 per cent of the wealth of high-income countries (World Bank, 2011, Table 2.3, p. 30).

A related feature is that historically, as the composition of wealth changed, the share of assets owned by women has also increased. A simple explanation is that as sources of wealth beyond land become available, it is easier for a wider group of people, including women, to accumulate them. Inheritance patterns of financial assets tend to be more gender neutral than inheritance patterns for land (Deere & Doss, 2006). In many economies, it has been both easier and socially more acceptable for women to own non-farm businesses than to own agricultural land (Green & Owens, 2003; Rutterford & Maltby, 2006). In such contexts, economic growth may reduce some of the constraints on women's opportunities to accumulate assets.

Women's ownership of assets, particularly productive assets, and the accumulation of wealth is important for several reasons. First, as a normative matter, men and women should have equal opportunities to acquire and retain assets. In addition, wealth and control over productive assets are empowering for women and may increase their bargaining power within households and the community (Doss, 2013). Empirical evidence shows that women's ownership of assets is correlated with positive outcomes, including better health and nutrition outcomes for their children (Allendorf, 2007), reduced exposure to domestic violence (Panda & Agarwal, 2005; Friedemann-Sanchez and Lovatón, 2012; Oduro, Deere, & Catanzarite, 2015) and higher proportions of household expenditure on food and education (Doss, 2006).

The evidence on these associations between structural change and women's increased asset ownership comes primarily from developed country contexts where structural transformation has been observed over a relatively long time horizon. Much of the evidence is also drawn from macro sources and national aggregate statistics. This paper contributes to the literature by analysing whether the same patterns hold in micro data from Ghana, a country that is now in the early stages of structural transformation. Do we see similar shifts in the patterns of asset holdings? And to what extent do women benefit from these changes? Structural transformation is happening at a rapid pace in many countries. Because increased gender equity in asset holding is often a key policy goal, it is important to understand the extent to which this is occurring with structural transformation.

The two decades from 1990–2013 were a period of rapid economic growth for Ghana, with substantial movement of people out of the agricultural sector and rapid urbanisation. Although many aspects of Ghana's economic transformation have been analysed, there has been little documentation of the patterns of wealth accumulation over this period.

Ghana is a particularly interesting context in which to study the changing patterns of asset ownership, for two reasons. First, we have high-quality data from nationally representative household surveys, stretching back 20 years, on the composition of household asset holdings. This is an unusually rich data source for a developing country. A second reason for focusing on Ghana is the richness of the data in terms of sex disaggregation of asset holdings; the data identify individual, not just household, holdings of land, businesses, and savings. In addition, in Ghana, most assets are owned individually, rather than held jointly by couples or others (Doss, Deere, Oduro, & Swaminathan, 2014). This makes it easier to look specifically at women's ownership of assets and how it has changed over time.

This paper contributes to the literature by examining how the patterns of asset holdings have changed during two decades of economic growth in Ghana. The available data allow us to consider two questions: how the composition of household wealth has changed and how women's share of wealth has changed. We find that land is decreasing as a share of wealth over this period; the share of wealth held in housing and financial assets has increased, although the latter increase is smaller than would be expected. Overall, women's share of wealth in Ghana has increased over this period.

2. Structural transformation and the composition of household wealth

Structural transformation is defined as the 'reallocation of economic activity across the broad sectors agriculture, manufacturing, and services' (Herrendorf, Rogerson, & Valentinyi, 2014, p. 855). Historically, that has meant a shift from agriculture to manufacturing and then to services. The process of structural transformation may be triggered by an increase in labour productivity in agriculture, which makes possible the release of labour to industry and services without a decline in agricultural output (Gollin, Parente, & Rogerson, 2002). Structural transformation can also occur because of an expansion in manufacturing and the concomitant increase in the demand for labour. When the genesis of structural transformation is either or both of these processes, the movement of labour is from agriculture into manufacturing and eventually services. This is the path that was taken by present-day industrialised countries.

Africa's experience with structural transformation has not necessarily conformed to this pattern. Enache, Ghani, & O'Connell (2016) identify two paths of structural transformation in Africa. One is the movement from agriculture into a mixture of sectors. The second involves movement directly from agriculture into services – often non-tradable services. For example, a natural resource boom can lead to increased spending on imported manufactured goods, thus creating conditions for the emergence of a services sector (Gollin, Jedwab, & Vollrath, 2016). Policies biased towards the urban population such as excessive taxation of agriculture and food subsidies can pull labour out of agriculture and into the services sector (Osei & Jedwab, 2017).

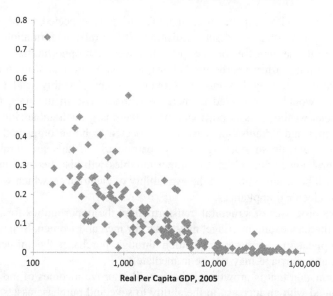

Figure 1. Value of crop/pasture land as a share of total wealth, 2005.
Source: Calculated using the World Bank wealth of nations data. http://data.worldbank.org/data-catalog/wealth-of-nations.

The shift out of agriculture is visible in cross country comparisons of the share of wealth held in agricultural land. The value of cropland and pasture land as a share of total wealth shows a strong negative relationship with real per capita GDP (see Figure 1). Richer countries have a much smaller proportion of their wealth in the form of land.

Moving from national aggregates to more detailed data from household surveys, we find similar patterns in three countries at varying levels of economic development and structural transformation, in data collected through the Gender Asset Gap Project (GAGP). Ownership data was collected on a full range of household assets in 2010 in Ghana, Ecuador, and the state of Karnataka, India. The GAGP data for Ghana will be analysed in the later part of this paper. Ecuador is a relatively urbanised country with a human development index (HDI) rank of 77 in 2010 and gross national income (GNI) per capita in purchasing power parity dollars of 7931 (UNDP, 2010). Most wealth (62%) is held in the form of the family's primary residence. This is followed by other real estate (10%), consumer durables (9%), non-agricultural businesses (8%), and agricultural lands (7%) (Deere & Díaz, 2011). The importance of consumer durables in Ecuador suggests that this may be an important form of assets as countries urbanise. Yet, they are not included as assets in most analyses. Although Ecuador has undergone some structural transformation, little of the wealth is in the form of financial assets.

India ranked 119 on the HDI scale in 2010 and has a per capita GNI in purchasing power parity dollars of 3337. For Karnataka, the analyses were done separately for rural areas, urban areas, and the urban centre Bengaluru (Swaminathan et al., 2011). In rural areas, land comprises 62 per cent of household wealth and the principal residence 25 per cent; thus, the remaining categories are all minimal. In urban areas, we see a shift away from land (20%) to the principal residence (53%) and other real estate (12%). In the capital, Bengaluru, the principal residence is 79 per cent of household wealth. As expected, we see very large differences in the composition of assets across locations within India and land is less important in household asset portfolios in Ecuador than it is in India. Overall, the historical and cross-country patterns suggest that the composition of asset holdings will change through the period of structural transformation.

3. Structural transformation, asset accumulation, and gender

The relationship between structural transformation and asset accumulation depends upon the factors driving the process of structural transformation. Structural transformation based on increased agricultural productivity and/or expansion in manufacturing is expected to be growth enhancing, therefore presenting opportunities for asset acquisition. Structural transformation that moves people out of agriculture into the services sector may provide fewer such opportunities.

Although theory does not offer specific predictions, we conjecture that structural transformation in the context of a rapidly growing low-income economy might plausibly lead to changes in asset composition. Savings would be expected to increase with the rise in incomes, thus increasing the importance of financial wealth in asset portfolios when there is growth enhancing structural transformation. Rising incomes and urbanisation would be expected to be accompanied by a rise in home ownership and improvements in housing quality, particularly if the structural transformation is accompanied by a growing middle class. Consumer durables will also become important. A critical determining factor will be urbanisation and the availability of electricity – which would be expected to increase demand for electrical appliances.

Within the various processes of structural transformation, the opportunities for asset accumulation, through purchase, inheritance, and marriage, may differ for men and women. Structural transformation will have direct implications for asset acquisition through purchase; the influence on acquisition through inheritance and marriage may not be immediate.

Structural transformation that is growth enhancing will improve incomes of individuals and households and be associated with an increase in the ability to save and purchase assets. However, because women and men have different employment rates and women tend to be concentrated in low wage employment, they may be disadvantaged in the market. In addition, the process of structural transformation may involve different rates of exit from agriculture for women and men and different rates of absorption into high productivity sectors.

Inheritance regimes inform who inherits property. The laws and social norms may be biased against wives and daughters. In addition, the marital regime prescribes the extent to which property within marriage is considered jointly owned or whether it remains the individual property of the husband or wife. Marital regimes that treat all property acquired while married as the joint property of both spouses tend to have higher levels of asset ownership by women (Deere, Oduro, Swaminathan, & Doss, 2013).

Institutional reforms, such as changes in the laws around women's property rights, may affect women's accumulation of assets. The Married Women's Property Acts in the United States increased women's rights to own property (Shammas, 1993) and similar Acts in the UK changed the composition of women's asset holdings (Combs, 2006). Recent changes in the Hindu Succession Act in India increased the likelihood of daughters inheriting joint family property, although sons continue to be favoured (Deininger, Goyal, & Nagarajan, 2013).

The shift in employment from agriculture may have no immediate bearing on laws, rules, norms and practices that shape the marital and inheritance regimes. However, urbanisation and rising incomes can impact aspirations and expectations, creating conditions for changes in these laws, rules, norms and practices over the long-term.

Much of the empirical work on women's wealth categorises households by the sex of the head (Paxton, 2009) or compares households headed by a single individual with those headed by a couple (for example, Rossi & Sierminska, 2015; Schmidt & Sevak, 2006). However, female-headed households tend to be different from male-headed households in many respects: they are generally smaller; have few, if any, adult men; and tend to be poorer. Thus, the comparison masks many of the differences between men and women more generally and ignores the majority of women who live in households that are defined as male headed.

Very few analyses have individual level asset data across a range of assets, either to consider the share of assets owned by women or whether the composition of assets held differs by sex. Using estate duty data from the United States, Shorrocks (1982) does not find differences in portfolio composition by sex, but he does not provide information on women's share of assets. In Karnataka, India, women only own 19 per cent of household gross physical asset wealth (Doss et al., 2014). In Ecuador, where there is no significant gender gap in the value of household gross physical asset wealth, the asset portfolios of men and women differ, with men's portfolios being much more diverse than women's (Deere & Díaz, 2011).

In general, increased access to financial assets and changes in legal frameworks have been two of the factors that have benefitted women. We expect to see women's share of asset ownership increasing with structural transformation. We recognise, however, that the pace of institutional reforms and change in attitudes towards women owning assets will be a moderating influence on the effect of structural transformation on women's asset ownership.

4. Ghana: context and background

Since the beginning of the 1990s Ghana has posted fairly robust growth rates. Growth rates in the 1990s followed a fluctuating pattern, beginning in 1990 with a growth rate of 3.3 per cent and ending in 1999 with a rate of 4.4 per cent. The period 2000 to 2006 was one of continuously increasing growth rates from 3.7 per cent to 5.9 per cent. Between 2007 and 2011, the cyclical pattern of growth rates returned, although the overall trend was upwards, peaking at 14 per cent in 2011 when oil production began. Growth rates declined after that to 7.3 per cent in 2013. Growth of output has exceeded that of population, translating into positive and generally rising per capita growth rates. On average, per capita income growth rates increased by about 0.53 per cent per annum during the period 1990–2014.

Revised gross domestic product figures, as a result of the rebasing of the economy in 2010, revealed that Ghana had attained lower middle-income status in 2007. Ghana's economy has undergone structural transformation, with movements out of agriculture primarily into services rather than manufacturing, following the second path prevalent in Africa described above. Agriculture's share of gross domestic product (GDP) declined from 45 per cent to 24 per cent between 1990 and 2012 (Table 1). The share of manufacturing in GDP remained fairly constant, averaging about 10 per cent between 1990 and 2006 and then decreasing to 6 per cent in 2012. Although manufacturing decreased, overall the industrial sector's share increased, driven largely by the production of oil and gas beginning in 2011 and the expanding construction sector. The services sector also expanded quite rapidly, with its share of GDP rising to 47 per cent in 2012 from 38 per cent in 1990 (Table 1).

The changes in the structure of production have been accompanied by shifts in employment. Agriculture's share of employment declined over the period (Table 1). The service sector's share of

Table 1. Structure of output and employment 1990–2013

Structure of Production	1990	2000	2012
Agriculture (%)	45.1	39.4	23.6
Industry (%)	16.9	28.4	28.9
Manufacturing (%)	9.8	10.1	6.0
Services (%)	38.1	32.2	47.5
Composition of Employment	1992	1999	2013
All			
Agriculture (%)	62	55	44.7
Industry (%)	10.1	14	14.4
Services (%)	27.9	31.1	40.9
Women			
Agriculture (%)	58.7	50.3	41.4
Industry (%)	9.8	14.5	11.3
Services (%)	31.9	35.6	47.3
Men			
Agriculture (%)	66.2	59.8	48.2
Industry (%)	10.4	13.5	17.8
Services (%)	23.1	26.5	34.0

Source: World Bank, World Development Indicators.

employment increased by 15.4 percentage points compared to an increase of 1.5 percentage points for industry.

Ghana is also experiencing rapid urbanisation.[1] The urban population has increased steadily from 32 per cent of the total in 1984 to about 44 per cent in 2000 and about 51 per cent in 2010.

In the midst of these changes, women's labour force participation has been fairly stable at about 75 per cent in the last two decades. Over the 40-year period beginning in 1970, the share of employed women who work in agriculture has tended to be lower than that for men while the share of employed women working in the services sector, particularly wholesale and retail trade, has tended to be higher than that for men (Ghana Statistical Service, 2005).[2] The share of both men and women employed in agriculture dropped 17–18 percentage points between 1992 and 2013 (Table 1). By 2013, 47 per cent of working women and 34 per cent of working men were employed in the services sector.

Labour productivity in the agriculture sector in Ghana has historically been lower than in the other sectors (de Vries, timmer, & de Vries, 2015; Osei & Jedwab, 2017). Structural transformation has involved reduction in the share of employment in the sector with the lowest labour productivity. Labour, however, is not concentrated in the sector with the highest labour productivity, which is industry. It is concentrated in the services sector which has high, but declining productivity (de Vries et al., 2015). The movement out of agriculture, particularly by women, could provide opportunities to earn higher incomes, however, women are employed predominantly in the wholesale and retail sector. Labour productivity in this sector has been lower than the average for the services sector and has been on the decline (de Vries et al., 2015). Employment in this sector is composed largely of own-account workers with unstable incomes. Thus, even though women are moving out of agriculture, they are not necessarily earning higher wages and increasing their ability to purchase assets.

Changes have also occurred in women's access to assets through inheritance in Ghana. Ghana has a pluralistic legal system comprising formal legal laws and customary laws and practices. The Wills Act of 1971 provides guidelines on how wills are to be prepared and administered but is silent on the distribution of assets by sex of surviving children. The Intestate Succession Act of 1985 provides for children and surviving spouses to inherit a portion of the self-acquired property of someone who dies intestate.

However, customary law and practices, which vary across ethnic groups, usually determine the distribution of property. Ghana has two major systems of inheritance. In patrilineal systems, children inherit from their fathers, whilst in matrilineal systems they inherit from their maternal uncles. In neither system do spouses inherit from one another. Among many patrilineal groups, sons tend to be favoured in the distribution of fathers' assets whilst mothers' property is equally shared. Among some patrilineal groups, women cannot inherit land (Oduro, Baah-Boateng, & Boakye-Yiadom, 2010). Inheritance practices are changing over time and the Intestate Succession Act of 1985 has played a role in supporting some of these changes (Oduro et al., 2010; Quisumbing, Payongayong, Aidoo, & Otsuka, 2001).

The marital regime under customary law is that of separation of property. Marriage does not confer rights to the spouse's property. The Matrimonial Causes Act of 1971 does not provide explicit guidelines on how properties are to be distributed on divorce, leaving this to the determination of judges. Until recently, on divorce, women who made claims to property acquired during the sub- sistence of the marriage had to prove that they had made substantial financial contribution to its acquisition. The lacunae in the formal legal regime are addressed by Article 22 of the 1992 Constitution of the Republic of Ghana that requires parliament to enact legislation regulating the property rights of spouses. Although this legislation has not yet been enacted, a Property Rights of Spouses Bill has been placed before Parliament. In the meantime, judgments in the courts have begun to recognise the contribution of women's unpaid work in the home to the acquisition of their spouses' property (Deere et al., 2013). These changes in the legal institutions and the social norms over this period have opened some new opportunities for women to acquire assets.

Economic transformation in Ghana provides mixed opportunities for women to acquire assets. Despite the economic growth of the last two decades, women's continued concentration in vulnerable employment, particularly as own account workers and unpaid family workers, limits their ability to purchase assets. Traditional inheritance norms still restrict women's ability to inherit assets such as land and livestock despite the legal changes. However, the rapid urbanisation coupled with the expansion of the financial sector, particularly in urban locations means that new opportunities may become available.

5. Data and methods

We rely on two sources of data for this analysis. The Ghana Living Standards Surveys (GLSS) are nationally representative household surveys collected regularly by the Ghana Statistical Service. We use four rounds of data, from 1991/1992 to 2012/2013. The surveys collected data from 4523 households (1991/1992), 5998 households (1998/1999), 8687 (2005/2006) and 16,772 households (2012/2013). Although there are some slight changes in the surveys over this period, the wording on the questions about assets is consistent.[3]

These surveys have detailed data on asset holdings at the household level including information on the value of land, housing, other real estate, consumer durables, business assets, livestock, savings, financial shares, and agricultural equipment. In addition, the surveys identify the individual holder of the land and the owner of all businesses and financial assets. Thus, the values of these assets can be disaggregated by gender. The GLSS surveys are not a panel and do not follow the same households over time. Thus, we analyse the overall patterns of asset holding, in terms of the composition of assets, over time.

The second source of data is the Gender Asset Gap Project (GAGP) Ghana survey. The project conducted a nationally representative individual level asset survey in 2010, composed of 2170 households. This is the first nationally representative survey in Africa with such detail. The sampling frame is based on that of the GLSS. In this analysis, we use the household asset inventory which detailed all assets owned by anyone in the household, the identity of the owner (with provision for recording of joint ownership) and the asset value. The only assets not detailed in the household inventory are financial assets. Questions about financial assets were asked to two household members who provided information only about their own. The GAGP household inventory collected data on the same categories of assets as the GLSS.

Most assets in Ghana are individually owned, including about 93 per cent of privately owned agricultural land and 96 per cent of businesses (Oduro, Baah-Boateng, & Boakye-Yiadom, 2011). It is straightforward to allocate the value of the asset to its owner when it is individually owned. In the instances of joint ownership of an asset, we have assumed that each owner has equal claim to the asset and distribute the value equally among them.

There are a few key differences between the GLSS surveys and the GAGP survey. For agricultural land, the GLSS asks about the value of all land held by households. This includes both privately owned land and family land. The latter is land under customary tenure where a household has some claims but not full ownership rights. In the GAGP survey, the value of land is only asked for privately owned land. And while one household member in the GLSS provides information on everyone's financial assets, in the GAGP, we have information only for the two respondents who each detail their own.

In the analysis that follows, we report gross wealth values rather than net values. Neither the GLSS nor the GAGP surveys collected comprehensive data on indebtedness.[4] However, indebtedness among households in Ghana is relatively low (Grown et al., 2015). A very small fraction of land and buildings that are purchased or buildings that are constructed by their owners are financed using debt (Grown et al., 2015).

We calculate the per cent of total household wealth held in each asset category for each survey round. Thus, we focus on the proportions of household wealth held in different forms, rather than the total wealth levels. Women's share of asset ownership is calculated as the sum of the value of the asset owned by all women divided by the sum of the value of the asset across all owners in all households.

Because we consider the percentage of asset wealth held in different forms at particular moments in time, we do not have to worry about deflating. The patterns we present here incorporate both the impacts of the changes in the composition of the physical and financial assets as well as changes in their relative value over time.

We begin by presenting evidence on the composition of household asset wealth over time. We then present evidence on women's share of land, business and financial wealth over time using data from the four GLSS surveys. This is followed by a discussion on the composition of asset wealth of women and men using the GAGP data.

Data on asset values from household surveys are noisy measures.[5] All of these surveys use values as reported by the respondent. Particularly in times of rapid economic change, people may not know the current value of their assets. In addition, the shares of any one asset category may be affected by reporting discrepancies in any other. Thus, we focus on the general patterns of change over the period.

6. Distribution of household asset holdings over time

The overall patterns observed in the Ghanaian data are generally consistent with the expectations of what we would see through structural transformation. The importance of land in households' wealth portfolios has declined steadily over this period, from 35 per cent in 1991/1992 to 23 per cent in 2012/2013. The decline was most rapid between 1991/1992 and 1998/1999 (see Table 2). However, financial assets remain a relatively small proportion of household wealth. Financial savings comprise just over 5 per cent of households' wealth portfolios in the most recent period, although there has been an increase in their share over time. Shares in companies have remained a minuscule proportion of household wealth at 0.2 per cent. (In this section, we collapse savings and shares into a single category of financial assets; however, only the savings data is disaggregated by sex.)

The share of wealth held as housing (the primary residence) increased over the period from about 32 per cent to about 39 per cent, although there was a drop in 1998/1999. The share held in consumer durables went consistently up, rising by four percentage points to 13 per cent in 2012/2013.

The 1998/1999 survey was a bit of an anomaly. The share of wealth held in the form of housing was below the overall trend and the shares of business assets and livestock was above.

6.1. Household asset holdings by location

Comparisons of rural and urban areas provide some insights into the patterns of structural transformation and asset holdings. Generally, the patterns are as we would expect. Land, other real estate and livestock feature much more prominently in rural wealth portfolios than they do those of urban households (Table 3). Housing and consumer durables consistently comprise the largest share of assets in the urban portfolio. Wealth held in the form of livestock comprises a larger share of rural portfolios whilst the share of business assets is larger in urban portfolios. Business opportunities with higher returns and financial institutions tend to be located in urban areas and we see this reflected in the larger shares held in financial assets in urban areas than in

Table 2. Composition of household asset wealth over time (%)

	1991/1992	1998/1999	2005/2006	2012/2013
Land	35.3	28.5	25.6	22.9
Housing	31.7	24.0	35.4	38.8
Other real estate	13.7	16.3	15.4	9.6
Consumer durables	9.0	9.2	11.8	13.0
Business assets	4.0	6.5	3.5	3.3
Livestock	3.8	10.7	3.7	5.4
Ag. equipment	0.6	2.7	1.2	1.7
Savings	1.7	1.8	3.3	5.2
Shares	0.2	0.2	0.1	0.2
Total	100.0	100.0	100.0	100.0

Source: Calculated by authors from GLSS data.

Table 3. Composition of household wealth over time, by location (%)

	1991/ 1992	1998/ 1999	2005/ 2006	2012/ 2013	1991/ 1992	1998/ 1999	2005/ 2006	2012/ 2013
	Urban				Rural			
Land	10.0	7.4	7.2	9.6	50.0	38.8	40.9	43.7
Housing	53.7	40.8	57.7	49.9	19.1	15.9	20.3	21.4
Other real estate	7.6	11.4	7.7	9.2	17.1	18.6	21.8	10.2
Business assets	5.9	13.3	6.5	4.4	2.9	3.2	1.0	1.5
Livestock	1.3	5.5	1.1	2.0	5.2	13.2	5.8	10.9
Agricultural equipment	0.5	1.8	0.5	1.3	0.6	3.5	1.8	2.3
Financial assets	3.4	3.2	3.5	7.9	1.1	1.5	3.2	2.9
Consumer durables	17.6	17.2	19.7	16.7	4.0	5.3	5.3	7.1
Total	100.0	100.0	100.0	100.0	100.0	100.0	100.0	100.0

Source: Calculated by authors from GLSS.

rural areas. The within location changes in the patterns of wealth held over time are less dramatic than the differences between the two areas. The overall trends in composition of household wealth are consistent with a story of people moving from rural to urban areas and shifting to an urban bundle of assets.

6.2. Explaining the trends

Looking at the shifting composition of household assets over time, the importance of land in the wealth portfolio has declined as anticipated. This is largely because of the increased opportunities to earn incomes outside of agriculture and to hold wealth in different forms.

Land and housing make up the largest share of households' wealth portfolios. Purchase is becoming of increasing importance in the acquisition of land, particularly urban land (Oduro et al., 2011). Unfortunately, the GLSS data does not have information on modes of acquisition which makes it impossible to disentangle the effect of rising incomes on the share of land in household asset portfolios. Most assets are owned outright since credit is not an important source of financing asset acquisition.

The increasing share of housing wealth in households' asset portfolios is a reflection of both increased incidence of home ownership and rising housing values. The incidence of owner occupancy has increased from 37 per cent in 1991/1992 to about 46 per cent in 2012/2013.

Rising incomes and urbanisation can explain the increasing share of consumer durables in households' asset portfolios. The proportion of households that own consumer durables has risen since 1991/1992 from 77 per cent to 96 per cent in 2012/2013. Growth and development have been accompanied by the acquisition of increasingly more valuable and sophisticated consumer durables such as televisions, refrigerators, cookers, cars and DVDs. For example, the incidence of ownership of refrigerators and freezers and televisions increased five-fold between 1991/1992 and 2012/2013. By 2012/2013 about 60 per cent of households owned televisions and 42 per cent owned refrigerators or freezers. Consumer durables are not only consumption goods; they may be used to supplement an income and they can be sold during times of crisis to smooth consumption (Doss et al., 2017). Rising incomes and the spread of electricity can explain the rise of consumer durables in wealth portfolios, particularly in urban areas.

The share of financial savings in households' asset portfolios has increased but from a very low base and remains low. Yet, more households are holding savings. Overall, between 1991/1992 and 2012/ 2013 the per cent of urban households with savings increased by 18 percentage points and the share of rural households by 12 percentage points.

Developments in the supply side of the financial sector can explain this increase. The number of financial institutions increased during the period and this is reflected in the financial and insurance sector's share of GDP increasing from 2.7 per cent of GDP in 2006 to 6.5 per cent in 2013 (Ghana Statistical Service, 2015). Yet, the coverage of commercial banks is low at 5.4 per 100,000 adults (Demirguc-Kunt, Klapper, Singer, & Oudheusden, 2015). This is higher than the average of 3.5 for sub-Saharan African countries but lower than the average of 7.2 for lower-middle-income countries overall. The stock exchange was established in 1989 and by December 2015 had 42 companies listed.

The requirements to open a savings account exclude large segments of the population from the formal financial sector. For example, a national identity card or a utility bill is required to open an account and some institutions require a guarantor who is a client. Considering that Ghana does not have universal coverage of electricity and water, and most people do not have a passport or driver's licence, these requirements can exclude a large proportion of potential customers.

In addition, the rates of return on financial assets in Ghana tend to be low. Savings deposits with commercial banks may even yield a negative return. Although savings rates have ranged between 2 per cent and 18 per cent, they were lower than the inflation rates of 18.1 per cent in 2008, 16 per cent in 2009 and 8.6 per cent in 2010 (Bank of Ghana, 2012). Rates on Treasury bills issued by the Government of Ghana are typically higher than savings deposit rates and inflation rates; for example the 91-day Treasury bill rates were 24.7 per cent, 23.7 per cent and 12.3 per cent in December 2008, 2009 and 2010 respectively (Bank of Ghana, 2012). However, returns on assets such as housing tend to be higher. For six of the 12 years from 1999 and 2010, the rate of increase in housing prices was higher than 91-day Treasury bill rates.[6] Thus, while the opportunities for holding financial assets are expanding, they are still relatively limited and many people choose to invest elsewhere.

There is not a clear story for why the livestock shares of wealth have fluctuated. The number of livestock held have increased steadily over the period (Ministry of Food and Agriculture, 2011). Livestock prices fluctuate both seasonally and over time, which may influence the values reported.

The slight decline in the share of business wealth has occurred at the same time as the incidence of business ownership among households has risen. The majority of businesses either have no workers or employ less than five workers. The industrial census of firms conducted in 2003 found that about 54.5 per cent of firms in the mining and quarrying, manufacturing and utilities sectors employed less than five people. Thus, business wealth may be declining in importance because despite the shift out of agriculture, business ventures in the non-agriculture sector tend to be small.

7. Women's share of asset wealth

The historical pattern suggests that structural transformation of the economy presents new opportunities for women to increase their asset ownership. Yet, as noted above, there are still many constraints facing women in their accumulation of assets in Ghana. Thus, it is useful to look at the data on the share of each type of asset held by women. The discussion of the trends over time focuses on land, business assets, and savings, since these are the three assets that can be disaggregated by sex in the GLSS.

Table 4 presents the share of land, savings, business and total wealth that is held by women over time. Women consistently own a lower share of wealth held in the form of each of these assets compared to men. However, women's share of wealth from each of these assets is substantially higher in 2012/2013 than in 1991/1992. In the earliest period, women owned 14.2 per cent of the wealth held in these asset categories, while men owned the remaining 85.8 per cent. By 2012/2013, women's share had increased to 23.9 per cent of the wealth. Of the three assets for which individual data is available over time, women's share of household asset wealth is highest for savings (31.6%). Yet, as we saw earlier, a relatively small amount of total wealth is held in the form of savings.

Table 4. Share of asset wealth held by women over time and by location (%)

Form of wealth	1991/1992	1998/1999	2005/2006	2012/2013
Ghana				
Land	12.9	20.5	15.9	22.0
Savings	22.3	27.7	26.9	31.6
Business	22.4	23.3	22.3	25.2
Total	14.2	21.3	17.4	23.9
Urban				
Land	9.1	24.5	30.3	33.4
Savings	29.1	26.0	32.4	32.3
Business	30.0	15.8	21.6	23.4
Total	18.8	19.7	27.4	30.9
Rural				
Land	13.2	20.1	13.7	18.2
Savings	10.1	29.3	17.3	28.4
Business	13.2	38.3	26.8	32.7
Total	13.2	21.7	14.1	19.2

Source: Calculated by authors from GLSS.

7.1. Women's share of asset wealth by location

We saw above that the change in the composition of assets within locations over time was relatively small. Instead, the larger story is due to migration from rural to urban areas. Yet, in both locations, we see an overall increase in the share of wealth held by women.

Women's share of land wealth among urban households has increased steadily over time – more than tripling over the period. This contrasts with women's share of land wealth among rural households which has increased at a slower rate, rising by five percentage points. Women's share of financial savings among urban households increased from 29 per cent in 1991/1992 to 32 per cent in 2005/2006 and 2012/2013 despite the dip in 1998/1999. Women's share of financial savings among rural households followed a more uneven pattern but is substantially higher in 2012/2013 (28%) than in 1991/1992 (10%). For urban households, women's share of business wealth has declined over the period. This is driven primarily by a small number of men in urban areas who have accumulated relatively large business enterprises.

7.2. Women's share of all assets owned in 2010

We now turn to a discussion of women's share of asset wealth using the GAGP data that includes individual asset ownership information on all assets owned by anyone in the household. The advantage of the GAGP data set is that it allows analysis by sex over a broader range of assets, however it is only available for 2010. Thus, it allows us to consider whether land, business assets, and savings are typical of the patterns across a wider range of assets.

Women own a smaller share of asset wealth than men across all asset types (Figure 2), not just land, businesses and savings. Overall, women own 30.2 per cent of household gross physical wealth. The numbers for land, savings and business assets are roughly comparable with those from the GLSS analysis for 2012/2013.

The assets for which women own a relatively higher share of household wealth are housing, businesses, consumer durables, and savings. These are also assets whose share of household wealth overall is increasing over time. This suggests that if we do not include analysis of these assets, we will miss key components of the unfolding story on the gendered pattern of asset ownership.

The fact that women own a relatively small proportion of agricultural land, agricultural equipment, and livestock is consistent with the concerns articulated in the literature on agricultural productivity, which suggests that women have less access to key agricultural inputs (Doss, Kovarik, Peterman,

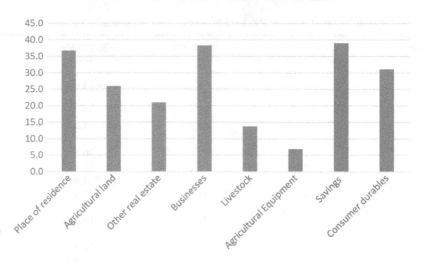

Figure 2. Women's share of gross household asset wealth, 2010 (%).
Source: Authors' calculations from GAGP data.

Quisumbing & Van Den Bold, 2015; Kieran, Sproule, Doss, Quisumbing, & Kim, 2015; Peterman, Behrman, & Quisumbing, 2014). While women could potentially access land for farming without owning it, these data suggest that the value of the agricultural land that women own is much less than that owned by men.

With this data that includes a wider range of assets, we can also consider the extent to which poor women are disproportionately disadvantaged in their asset ownership. For each asset category, Figure 3 presents women's share of the value of those assets by welfare quintile.[7]

Women's share of housing wealth and livestock wealth increases by quintile. While women in the lowest quintile own 29 per cent of the housing in value terms, in the richest households, women own a higher fraction of the housing wealth, at 42 per cent.

For the other assets, the pattern is less clear. Women's share of business wealth, consumer durables and agricultural equipment is lower in the fourth and fifth quintiles than it is in the other quintiles. This is because men in the fourth and fifth quintiles own much larger businesses than women, even though the incidence of business ownership is higher for women. Similarly, women's share of the ownership

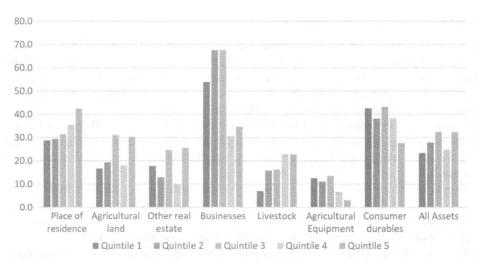

Figure 3. Women's share of gross household asset wealth by asset and welfare quintile, 2010 (%).
Source: Authors' calculations from GAGP data.

of consumer durables and agricultural equipment declines by quintile because men in the fourth and fifth quintiles are more likely to own the more expensive consumer durables and large equipment. No clear patterns by quintile emerge for women's share of agricultural land wealth and their share of other real estate wealth, although women's share of these assets is higher in the fifth quintile than in the lowest quintile. Among the poorest three quintiles, women's share of wealth is highest for businesses and consumer durables. In the fourth quintile, consumer durables and the place of residence have the highest shares of women's wealth, whilst in the fifth quintile it is the place of residence and businesses.

7.3. Explaining the gender patterns

Of the three assets for which information on women's share is available over time, their share of asset wealth has risen. Yet women still own a relatively low share of total wealth.

One way that people acquire assets is through the market. Yet women continue to be disadvantaged in their earnings. Many women continue to work unpaid on farms or enterprises owned by family members and this share is higher in 2010 (14.4%) than in 2000 (7.8%) (Ghana Statistical Service, 2013). In the paid labour sectors, women's wages still lag behind men's and the situation is getting worse, not better. In 1991/1992 the ratio of women's to men's basic hourly wage was 0.87 (Ghana Statistical Service, 1995). It declined to 0.69 in 1998/1999 (Ghana Statistical Service, 2000) and to 0.66 in 2012/2013 (Ghana Statistical Service, 2014). This evidence suggests that women's capacity to purchase assets has lagged behind that of men's.

The geographical spread of cities has contributed to the emergence of land markets.[8] These markets provide women the opportunity to purchase land if they have the means. It may be easier for women, particularly urban women who will have higher incomes than rural women, to acquire land through purchase than through inheritance.

There is evidence that in some parts of the country inheritance practice is becoming more inclusive and women do inherit these assets (Oduro et al., 2010, 2011). Fathers and spouses in matrilineal communities may get around the traditional barriers placed on the inheritance of a man's property by his wife and children by gifting these assets to them (Amanor, 2001; Quisumbing et al., 2001). We find that women owners are more likely than men owners to have acquired agricultural land, the place of residence and other real estate as gifts (Oduro et al., 2011).

Both the GLSS and GAGP data sets reveal that women's share of asset wealth is highest for financial savings. Cultural constraints on women's ownership of these assets are less severe. A major constraint for women would be their ability to earn incomes large enough to build up their financial savings. Yet, this is a hopeful sign that women may benefit through structural transformation.

8. Conclusions

The composition of assets held by households has changed over this recent period of rapid economic growth in Ghana. Consistent with the changes that happened over a much longer period of structural transformation in Europe and the United States, the share of land has decreased in household portfolios and the share of housing has increased.

Increases in incomes and urbanisation have happened relatively quickly. Unlike in the historical periods in the industrialised countries, the availability of consumer goods in Ghana has expanded fast. Thus, we see a fairly rapid increase in the value of consumer durables held by households. Yet, some of the other changes have been slower to materialise. While the share of financial assets is growing, it is still relatively small.

Women's share of asset ownership relative to men's has increased as the historical pattern would have suggested. Although social norms can transform rapidly, it is not surprising that women have not benefited as much from the new opportunities as might have been possible. Changes in inheritance practices, in particular, may happen more slowly than other economic changes. We see women's share of assets growing particularly among those assets that are becoming a relatively larger proportion of the household wealth portfolio. This suggests that policies should work to ensure that as these opportunities for asset ownership increase, women are well placed to take advantage of them.

Finally, it is worth noting that data on the value of assets collected in household surveys tends to be noisy. We might expect that this is especially true during rapid economic changes, where the values of assets may change quickly. We have shown that the incidence of ownership of some assets, particularly housing, financial assets, and consumer durables have increased. With data at four time periods, we do see the overall trends that we would expect, but it is not necessarily linear trends between any two years. There are some anomalies in the patterns for a particular asset in a particular year. This suggests that one should be cautious about interpreting trends based on only two data points.

Acknowledgements

The authors wish to thank Carmen Diana Deere and Douglas Gollin for their comments on this paper and Jana Bischler for excellent research assistance.

Notes

1. Note that urbanisation is not necessarily the same as a change in the structures of production; in principle, it is possible for movements out of agriculture to take the form of rural non-farm activities.
2. In 1970, 54 per cent of employed women and 59 per cent of employed men worked in the agriculture sector. The share of employed women and men employed in the wholesale and retail trade was 26.1 per cent and 3.9 per cent respectively.
3. We do not use the first two rounds of the GLSS survey because the questions are different enough to make the data less comparable across time.
4. The GAGP has detailed information on indebtedness for a maximum of two adult members of the household.
5. We tried several methods to deal with outliers, including winsorizing the data, but the patterns did not substantially change.
6. The housing price index produced by the Ghana Statistical Service, which includes utility prices increased by 42 per cent, 27 per cent and 64.3 per cent in 2001, 2002 and 2003 respectively compared to 91-day Treasury bill rates of 29 per cent, 26 per cent and 20 per cent.
7. Welfare is measured as real household consumption expenditure per adult equivalent based on consumption data collected through the GAGP.
8. Between 1986 and 1987, the capital city, Accra, expanded by 171.9 square miles (Yeboah, 2003).

Disclosure statement

No potential conflict of interest was reported by the authors.

References

Allendorf, K. (2007). Do women's land rights promote empowerment and child health in Nepal? *World Development, 35*, 1975–1988.
Amanor, K. S. (2001). *Land, labour and the family in Southern Ghana: A critique of land policy under neo-liberalisation.* (Research Report no.116). Uppasala: Nordiska Afrikainstitutet.
Bank of Ghana. (2012, March). *Statistical bulletin.* Accra.
Combs, M. B. (2006). Cui Bono? The 1870 British married women's property act, bargaining power and the distribution of resources within marriage. *Feminist Economics, 12*(1–2), 51–83.
de Vries, G., Timmer, M., & de Vries, K. (2015). Structural transformation in Africa: Static gains, dynamic losses. *The Journal of Development Studies, 51*, 674–688.
Deere, C. D., & Díaz, J. (2011). *Acumulación de Activos: Una apuesta por la equidad.* [Asset Accumulation: The challenge for equity]. Quito, Ecuador: FLACSO.
Deere, C. D., & Doss, C. R. (2006). The gender asset gap: What do we know and why does it matter? *Feminist Economics, 12*(1–2), 1–50.
Deere, C. D., Oduro, A. D., Swaminathan, H., & Doss, C. (2013). Property rights and the gender distribution of wealth in ecuador, Ghana and India. *Journal of Economic Inequality, 11*(2), 249–265. doi:10.1007/s10888-013-9241-z.
Deininger, K., Goyal, A., & Nagarajan, H. (2013). Women's inheritance rights and intergenerational transmission of resources in India. *Journal of Human Resources, 48*(1), 114–141.

Demirguc-Kunt, A., Klapper, L., Singer, P., & Oudheusden, P. (2015). *The global findex database 2014: Measuring financial inclusion around the world*. (Policy Research Working Paper 7255). Washington, DC: World Bank.

Doss, C. (2006). The effects of intrahousehold property ownership on expenditure patterns in Ghana. *Journal of African Economies, 15*(1), 149–180.

Doss, C. (2013). Intrahousehold bargaining and resource allocation in developing countries. *World Bank Research Observer, 28* (1), 52–78.

Doss, C., Kovarik, C., Peterman, A. A. Q., & Van Den Bold, M. (2015). Gender inequalities in ownership and control of land in Africa: Myth and reality. *Agricultural Economics, 46*(3), 403–434.

Doss, C., Oduro, A. D., Deere, C. D., Swaminathan, H., Baah-Boateng, W., & J. Y., Suchitra (2017). Assets and shocks: A gendered analysis of Ecuador, Ghana and Karnataka, India. *Canadian Journal of Development Studies/Revue Canadienne D'études Du Développement*, 1–18. doi:10.1080/02255189.2017.1316244

Doss, C. R., Deere, C. D., Oduro, A. D., & Swaminathan, H. (2014). The gender asset and wealth gaps. *Development, 57*, 400–409.

Enache, M., Ghani, E., & O'Connell, S. (2016). *Structural transformation in Africa. A historical view* (Policy Research Working Paper WPS7743). Washington, DC: World Bank.

Friedemann-Sánchez, G., & Lovatón, R. (2012). Intimate partner violence in Columbia: Who is at risk? *Social Forces, 91*, 663–688.

Ghana Statistical Service. (1995). *Ghana living standards survey. Report on the third round (GLSS3)*. Accra.

Ghana Statistical Service. (2000). *Ghana living standards survey. Report on the fourth round (GLSS4)*. Accra.

Ghana Statistical Service. (2005). *Population data analysis reports. Volume 1. Socio-economic and demographic trend analysis*. Accra.

Ghana Statistical Service. (2013). *Population and housing census. National Analytical Report*. Accra.

Ghana Statistical Service. (2014). *Ghana living standards survey. Round six (GLSS6). Main Report*. Accra.

Ghana Statistical Service. (2015). *Revised 2014 annual gross domestic product*. Accra. Retrieved May 21, 2016, from http://www.statsghana.gov.gh/docfiles/GDP/GDP2015/Annual_2014_GDP_Rev2_June_2015%20edition.pdf

Gollin, D., Jedwab, R., & Vollrath, D. (2016). Urbanization with and without industrialization. *Journal of Economic Growth, 21* (1), 35–70.

Gollin, D., Parente, S. L., & Rogerson, R. (2002). The role of agricultural development. *American Economic Review, 92*(2), 160–164.

Green, D. R., & Owens, A. (2003). Gentlewomanly capitalism? Spinsters, widows and wealth holding in England and Wales, c. 1800–1860. *The Economic History Review, 56*, 510–536.

Grown, C., Deere, C. D., Catanzarite, Z., Oduro, A. D., Suchitra, J. Y., Swaminathan, H., & Boakye-Yiadom, L. (2015). Who borrows? An analysis of gender, debt and assets in Ghana, Ecuador and Karnataka, India. Retrieved from http://www.unwomen.org/en/digital-library/publications/2015/6/who-borrows-an-analysis-of-gender-debt-and-assets.

Herrendorf, B., Rogerson, R., & Valentinyi, Á. (2014). Growth and structural transformation. *Handbook of Economic Growth, 2*, 855–941.

Keister, L. (2000). *Wealth in America: Trends in wealth inequality*. Cambridge, MA: Cambridge University Press.

Kieran, C., Sproule, K., Doss, C., Quisumbing, A., & Kim, S. M. (2015). Examining gender inequalities in land rights indicators in Asia. *Agricultural Economics, 46*(S1), 119–138.

Ministry of Food and Agriculture. (2011). *Agriculture in Ghana - Facts and figures, 2010*. Accra, Ghana: MOFA, Statistics, Research and Information Directorate.

Oduro, A. D., Baah-Boateng, W., & Boakye-Yiadom, L. (2010). *Asset accumulation by women in Ghana. Understanding the process* (Working Paper No. 4). Bangalore: Gender Asset Gap Project. Retrieved from https://sites.google.com/view/genderassetgap/working-papers?authuser=0

Oduro, A. D., Baah-Boateng, W., & Boakye-Yiadom, L. (2011). *Measuring the gender asset gap in Ghana*. Accra: University of Ghana and Woeli Publishing Services.

Oduro, A. D., Deere, C. D., & Catanzarite, Z. (2015). Women's wealth and intimate partner violence: Insights from Ecuador and Ghana. *Feminist Economics, 21*(2), 1–29.

Osei, R. D., & Jedwab, R. (2017). Structural change in a poor African country: New historical evidence from Ghana. In M. S. McMillan, D. Rodrick, & C. Sepúlveda (Eds.), *Structural change, fundamentals and growth: A framework and case studies* (pp. 161–196). Washington, DC: International Food Policy Research Institute.

Panda, P., & Agarwal, B. (2005). Marital violence, human development and women's property status in India. *World Development, 33*, 823–850.

Paxton, J. (2009). Subsistence saving strategies of male- and female-headed households: Evidence from Mexico. *Eastern Economic Journal, 35*(2), 209–231.

Peterman, A., Behrman, J. A., & Quisumbing, A. R. (2014). A review of empirical evidence on gender differences in nonland agricultural inputs, technology and services in developing countries. In A. R. Quisumbing, R. Meinzen-Dick, T. L. Raney, A. Croppenstedt, J. A. Behrman, & A. Peterman (eds), *Gender in agriculture: Closing the knowledge gap* (pp. 145–186). New York, NY: Springer.

Quisumbing, A. R., Payongayong, E., Aidoo, J. B., & Otsuka, K. (2001). Women's land rights in the transition to individualized ownership: Implications for tree-resource management in western Ghana. *Economic Development and Cultural Change, 50* (1), 157–181.

Rossi, M., & Sierminska, E. (2015). *Housing decisions, family types and gender. A look across LIS countries* (LIS Working Paper Series No. 654).

Rutterford, J., & Maltby, J. (2006). "The widow, the clergyman and the reckless": Women investors in England, 1830–1914. *Feminist Economics*, *12*(1–2), 111–138.

Schmidt, L., & Sevak, P. (2006). Gender, marriage and asset accumulation in the United States. *Feminist Economics*, *12*(1–2), 139–166.

Shammas, C. (1993). A new look at the long-term trends in wealth inequality in the United States. *The Ameican Historical Review*, *98*, 412–431.

Shorrocks, A. (1982). The portfolio compostion of asset holdings in the United Kingdom. *The Economic Journal*, *92*(366), 268–284.

Swaminathan, H., Suchitra, J. Y., & Lahoti, R. (2011). *KHAS: Measuring the gender asset gap*. Bangalore: Indian Institute of Management.

UNDP. (2010). Human development report 2010. *The real wealth of nations: Pathways to human development*. New York: Palgrave Macmillan.

World Bank. (2011). *The changing wealth of nations: Measuring sustainable development in the new millenium*. Washington, DC: Author.

Yeboah, I. (2003). Demographic and housing aspects of structural adjustment and emerging urban Accra, Ghana. *Africa Today*, *50*(1), 107–119.

Index

Note: Page numbers in italics refer to figures and in bold refer to tables. Page numbers followed by 'n' with number refer to endnotes.

working-age population: economic activity status of 34, **35**, **55–6**; and employment categories 29; employment structure among 31–3, 39–41; in rural *versus* urban areas **32**; sectoral employment shifts among 34–9; urbanisation and demographic shifts among 30–1

World Bank 85

World Bank Enterprise Survey 77n3

World Food Programme's Purchase for Progress program 135

World Food Summit (WFS) 149

Zambia, large-scale traders (LSTs) in: farmers selling maize to **139–40**; grain supply and demand conditions 136–8; input credit and extension services **141**, 141–2; market entry and structure 133–5; and medium-scale farms 138; price effect of selling to 142, **143–4**, 145; scale and supply chain structure 135–6; smallholder maize sales **133**; statistics of large-scale trader survey **134**; supply chain contracts and coordination 136; survey data 132